KENTUCKIANS
IN
MISSOURI

KENTUCKIANS
IN
MISSOURI

Including Many Who Migrated by
Way of Ohio, Indiana, or Illinois

BY STUART SEELY SPRAGUE

Professor of History
Morehead State University

GENEALOGICAL PUBLISHING CO., INC.
Baltimore, Maryland 1984

FOREWORD

Kentuckians in Missouri is intended to aid those genealogists looking for Missourians of Kentucky descent. It may also be helpful to genealogists seeking ancestors of Kentuckians who never left the Commonwealth—siblings, for example—or whom tradition says left for Ohio, Indiana, or Illinois.

The biographical sketches contained in Missouri county histories, biographical compilations, and similar works usually include the date and the county and state of birth of the biographee. Similar information about his parents frequently appears as well. From the multitude of biographical and genealogical sketches found in such works I have compiled this record of over 4,000 persons who were born in Kentucky but who later migrated to Missouri, some by way of Ohio, Indiana, or Illinois.

Arranged in tabular form under county of origin, the entries include some or all of the following information: the name of the Kentucky migrant, his birthdate, the names of his parents and their dates and places of birth (if known), the name of the Missouri county in which the migrant first settled—if different from his "current" county of residence—and the earliest known date of his residence in Missouri. Source citations with specific page references are also included.

The following abbreviations are used throughout the work:

( ) maiden name

[ ] married surname (used only in the index)

** born in the same Kentucky county as the biographee

/ divides information pertaining to the father from the mother

- - no information

c circa, as in c1845 (about 1845)

STUART SEELY SPRAGUE
Center for Historical Studies
Clearfield, Kentucky

S O U R C E S   A N D   A B B R E V I A T I O N S

ADAI Eugene Morrow Violette
      History of Adair County...Together with Reminiscences and
      Biographical Sketches, Edited by C.N. Tolman; Photos by
      W.M. Denslow.
      Kirksville, Missouri: The Denslow Company, 1911.

ANDE History of Andrew and DeKalb Counties.
      St. Louis: The Goodspeed Publishing Company, 1888.

ANPL Annals of Platte County, Missouri, from its Exploration Down to
      June 1, 1897; with Genealogies of its Noted Families, and
      Sketches...By William McClung Paxton...
      Kansas City, Missouri: Hudson-Kimberly Publishing Co., 1897.

ASPS History of Adair, Sullivan, Putnam and Schuyler Counties.
      Chicago: The Goodspeed Publishing Company, 1888.

AUDR History of Audrain County, Missouri, Written and Compiled from
      the Most Authentic Official and Private Sources, Including
      a History of its Townships, Towns and Villages. Together
      with...Biographical Sketches of Prominent Citizens...
      Saint Louis: National Historical Company, 1884.

BATC Biographical History of Atchison County, Missouri. Illustrated
      with Farm Scenes, Views of Residences and Pictures of Peo-
      ple, Live Stock, etc. Issued by the Atchison County Mail.
      Rock Port, Missouri: Atchison County Mail, 1905.

BATE S. L. Tathwell
      The Old Settlers' History of Bates County, Missouri. From
      its First Settlement to the First Day of January, 1900.
      Amsterdam, Missouri: Tathwell and Maxey, 1900.

BENC William Van Ness
      Reminiscences of Bench and Bar.
      Saint Louis: S.H. & Thomas & Company, 1878.

BJAS Malcolm G. McGregor
      The Biographical Record of Jasper County, Missouri...
      Chicago: The Lewis Publishing Company, 1901.

BOON History of Boone County, Missouri, Written and Compiled from the
      Most Authentic Official and Private Sources; Including a
      History of its Townships, Towns, and Villages...Biographical
      Sketches and Portraits of Prominent Citizens...
      Saint Louis: Western Historical Company, 1882

BUCH   The History of Buchanan County, Missouri, Containing a History
        of the County, its Cities, Towns, etc., Biographical
        Sketches of its Citizens, Buchanan County in the Late War,
        General and Local Statistics, Portraits of Early Settlers
        and Prominent Men,...Illustrated.
        Saint Joseph, Missouri: Union Historical Company, 1881.

CALI   History of Caldwell and Livingston Counties, Missouri...In-
        cluding a History of Their Townships, Towns, and Villages,
        Together with a Condensed History of Missouri...Biographi-
        cal Sketches of Prominent Citizens...
        Saint Louis: National Historical Company, 1886.

CALL   History of Callaway County, Missouri, Written and Compiled
        from...Official and Private Sources, Including a History
        of its Townships, Towns, and Villages...Biographical
        Sketches of Prominent Citizens...
        Saint Louis: National Historical Company, 1884.

CAUD   Herschel Schooley
        Centennial History of Audrain County.
        Mexico, Missouri: The McIntyre Publishing Company, 1937.

CHHO   T. Berry Smith and Pearl Sims Gehrig
        History of Chariton and Howard Counties, Missouri.
        Topeka: Historical Publishing Company, 1923.

CLCA   W.H.S. McGlumphy and Carrie Polk Johnston
        History of Clinton and Caldwell Counties, Missouri.
        Topeka: Historical Publishing Company, 1923.

CLPL   History of Clay and Platte Counties, Missouri; Written and Com-
        piled from the Most Authentic Official and Private Sources,
        Including a History of Their Townships, Towns, and Villages,
        etc...Biographical Sketches of Prominent Citizens...
        Saint Louis: National Historical Company, 1885.

CMMB   History of Cole, Moniteau, Morgan, Benton, Miller, Maries
        and Osage Counties, Missouri. From the Earliest Time
        to the Present, Including a Department Devoted to the
        Preservation of Sundry Personal, Business, Profession-
        al and Private Records...
        Chicago: The Goodspeed Publishing Company, 1889.

CSBA   The History of Cass and Bates Counties, Missouri, Containing
        a History of These Counties, Their Cities, Towns, etc.,
        Biographical Sketches of Their Citizens, General and Lo-
        cal Statistics, History of Missouri...
        Saint Joseph, Missouri: National Historical Company, 1883.

-4-

DAGE   John C.Leopard, Buel Leopard, R.M.McCammon and Mary McCammon Hillman
            History of Daviess and Gentry Counties, Missouri.
            Topeka: Historical Publishing Company, 1922.

DAVI   The History of Daviess County, Missouri. Kansas City,
            Missouri: Birdsall & Dean, 1882.

DUNK   Mary F. Smyth-Davis
            History of Dunklin County, Missouri, 1845-1895. Embracing an
            Historical Account of the Towns and Post-Villages of Clarkton,
            Cotton Plant, Cardwell, Caruth...(etc.)...With an Album of its
            People and Homes, Profusely Illustrated.
            Saint Louis: Nixon-Jones Printing Company, 1896.

FJWC   History of Franklin, Jefferson, Washington, Crawford, and Gascon-
            ade Counties, Missouri. From the Earliest Time to the Present;
            Together with Sundry Personal, Business and Professional
            Sketches and Numerous Family Records.
            Chicago: The Goodspeed Publishing Company, 1888.

FGRU   James Everett Ford
            A History of Grundy County. Treating of its Transformation
            from the Heart of the Wilderness of Yesterday to the Heart
            of the Mighty Nation of Today...
            Trenton, Missouri: The News Publishing Company, 1908.

GREE   See GREH

GREF   Jonathan Fairbanks and Clyde Edwin Tuck
            Past and Present of Greene County, Missouri; Early and Recent
            History and Genealogical Records of Many of the Representa-
            tive Citizens.
            Indianapolis: A. W. Bowen, 1915.

GREH   History of Greene County, Missouri...Including a History of its
            Townships, Towns, and Villages, Together with a Condensed
            History of Missouri...Biographical Sketches and Portraits
            of Prominent Citizens...
            Saint Louis: Western Historical Company, 1883.

HAME   History of Harrison and Mercer Counties, Missouri. From the Earliest
            Time to the Present...
            Saint Louis: The Goodspeed Publishing Company, 1888.

HOAT   The History of Holt and Atchison Counties, Missouri, Containing
            a History of These Counties, Their Cities, Towns, etc., Bio-
            graphical Sketches of Their Cities, General and Local Sta-
            tistics...History of Missouri...
            Saint Joseph, Missouri: National Historical Company, 1882.

HOCH   History of Howard and Chariton Counties, Missouri.
             Saint Louis: National Historical Company, 1883.

HOCO   History of Howard and Cooper Counties, Missouri, Written
             and Compiled From the Most Authentic Official and
             Private Sources, Including a History of its Townships,
             Towns and Villages. Together with a Condensed History
             of Missouri...
             Saint Louis: National Historical Company, 1883.

HPCD   History of Hickory, Polk, Cedar, Dade and Barton Coun-
             ties, Missouri...
             Chicago: The Goodspeed Publishing Company, 1889.

HSTC   The History of Henry and St. Clair Counties, Missouri, Con-
             taining a History of These Counties, Their Cities,
             Towns, etc., Biographical Sketches of Their Citizens,
             General and Local Statistics, History of Missouri...
             Saint Joseph, Missouri: National Historical Company, 1883.

IMCD   J. A. Sturges
             Illustrated History of McDonald County, Missouri, from
             the Earliest Settlement to the Present Time.
             Pineville, Missouri, 1897.

JACK   The History of Jackson County, Missouri, Containing a History
             of the County, its Cities, Towns, etc., Biographical
             Sketches of its Citizens, Jackson County in the Late
             War... History of Missouri, Map of Jackson County...
             Kansas City, Missouri: Union Historical Company, 1881.

JASP   History of Jasper County. Des Moines: Mills, 1883.

JOHN   Ewing Cockrill
             History of Johnson County.
             Topeka: Historical Publishing Company, 1918.

KC&   A Memorial and Biographical Record of Kansas City and Jackson
             County, Missouri.
             Chicago: The Lewis Publishing Company, 1896.

LAFA   History of Lafayette County, Missouri, Carefully Written and
             Compiled From the Most Authentic Official and Private
             Sources, Including a History of its Townships, Cities,
             Towns and Villages, Together with a Condensed History
             of Missouri...Biographical Sketches of Prominent Men...
             Saint Louis: Missouri Historical Company, 1881.

LCDW   History of Laclede, Camden, Dallas, Webster, Wright, Texas,
             Pulaski, Phelps, and Dent Counties, Missouri...
             Chicago: The Goodspeed Publishing Company, 1889.

LCKS   History of Lewis, Clark, Knox, and Scotland Counties, Missouri,
         From the Earliest Time to the Present; Together with Sundry
         Personal, Business and Professional Sketches and Numerous
         Family Records...
         Saint Louis: The Goodspeed Publishing Company, 1887.

LINC   History of Lincoln County, Missouri, From the Earliest Time to
         the Present...
         Chicago: The Goodspeed Publishing Company, 1888.

LINN   The History of Linn County, Missouri. An Encyclopedia of Useful
         Information, and a Compendium of Actual Facts...
         Kansas City, Missouri: Birdsall & Dean, 1882.

MARI   History of Marion County, Missouri, Written and Compiled from the
         Most Authentic, Official and Private Sources. Including a
         History of its Townships, Towns and Villages, Together with
         a Condensed History of Missouri; the City of Saint Louis; a
         Reliable and Detailed History of Marion County...
         Saint Louis: E.F. Perkins, 1884.

MONI   James Everett Ford
         A History of Moniteau County, Missouri...
         California, Missouri: H. Crawford, 1936.

MOSH   History of Monroe and Shelby Counties, Missouri, Written and Com-
         piled from the Most Authentic Official and Private Sources,
         Including a History of Their Townships, Towns and Villages,
         Together with a Condensed History of Missouri...Biographical
         Sketches of Prominent Citizens...
         Saint Louis: National Historical Company, 1884.

NLBM   Mary Louise Palmer
         History of Newton, Lawrence, Barry and McDonald Counties,
         Missouri, From the Earliest Times to the Present....
         Chicago: The Goodspeed Publishing Company, 1888.

NODA   The History of Nodaway County, Missouri, Containing a History of
         the County, its Cities, Towns, etc., Biographical Sketches
         of its Citizens, Nodaway County in the Late War...History
         of Missouri, Map of Nodaway County, etc.
         Saint Joseph, Missouri: National Historical Company, 1882.

NW   Walter Williams
         A History of Northwest Missouri...
         Chicago: The Lewis Publishing Company, 1915.

PETT   The History of Pettis County, Missouri, Including an Authentic
         History of Sedalia, Other Towns and Townships, Together with
         Cuts of Elegant Residences, Portraits of Prominent Citizens...
         N. pl: n. p., 1882.

PIKE   The History of Pike County, Missouri. An Encyclopedia of Useful
Information, and a Compendium of Actual Facts...
Des Moines, Iowa: Mills and Company, 1882.

PJAC   Political History of Jackson County. Biographical Sketches of
Men Who Have Helped to Make It.
Kansas City, Missouri: Marshall & Morrison, 1902.

PLAS   Portrait and Biographical Record of Lafayette and Saline Counties, Missouri, Containing Biographical Sketches of Prominent and Representative Citizens, Together with Biographies...
Chicago: Chapman Brothers, 1893.

RAMA   History of Randolph and Macon Counties, Missouri, Written and
Compiled from the Most Authentic Official and Private
Sources, Including a History of Their Townships, Towns
and Villages...
Saint Louis: National Historical Company, 1884.

RAY   History of Ray County, Missouri, Carefully Written and Compiled
from the Most Authentic Official and Private Sources, Including a History of Its Townships, Cities, Towns and Villages...
Saint Louis: Missouri Historical Company, 1881.

SALI   History of Saline County, Missouri, Carefully Written and Com-
piled From the Most Authentic Official and Private Sources,
Including a History of Its Townships, Cities, Towns and
Villages, with a Condensed History of Missouri...Biographi-
cal Sketches of Prominent Men and Citizens Identified with
Interests of the County.
Saint Louis: Missouri Historical Company, 1881.

SCMW   History of Saint Charles, Montgomery, and Warren Counties, Mis-
souri, Written and Compiled From the Most Authentic Official
and Private Sources, Including a History of Their Townships,
Towns and Villages, Together with a Condensed History of
Missouri...
Saint Louis: National Historical Company, 1881.

SEGO   History of Southeast Missouri, Embracing an Historical Account
of the Counties of Ste. Genevieve, Saint Francois, Perry,
Cape Giradeau, Bollinger, Madison, New Madrid, Pemiscot,
Dunklin, Mississippi, Stoddard, Butler, Wayne, and Iron...
Chicago: The Goodspeed Publishing Company, 1888.

SERD   Robert Sidney Douglass
History of Southeast Missouri; a Narrative Account of Its
Historical Progress, Its People and Its Principal Interests...
Chicago and New York: The Lewis Publishing Company, 1912.

STLO   John Thomas Scharf
            History of Saint Louis City and County from the Earli-
            est Period to the Present Day, Including **Biographical**
            Sketches...
            Philadelphia: H. Everts & Company, 1883.

USBI   The United States Biographical Dictionary and Portrait Gal-
            lery of Eminent Self-Made Men, Missouri Volume.

VADA   See ADAI

VERN   History of Vernon County, Missouri.
            Saint Louis: Brown and Company, 1887.

A D A I R   C O U N T Y

BIRTHDATE	NAME OF BIOGRAPHEE	PARENTS/BIRTHPLACE/BIRTHDATE	SOURCE/PAGE		FIRST MO.CO.	DATE
06 Jul 1817	James Anderson		JACK	736	Andrew	1865
00 000 1813	Jacob F. Antle		NLBM	1011	Daviess	1851
00 000 1820	John Botts		RAY	562	Macon	c1857
14 Oct 1844	Shelby Brockman	Carey & Rebecca(Perkins) Ky/Ky	VERN	792	Johnson	----
00 000 1848	W.T. Browning	William D & C.A(Atkinson)	JOHN	955		1852
00 000 1812	John J.G. Burton	Hutchins & Elizabeth(Stepp)Va/Va	SALI	640	Howard	1819
00 Mar 1831	William Z. Burton		CMMB	755		1849
15 Jul 1835	William F. Busby	William & Sarah SC/SC	JASP	958		1850
29 Jul 1846	Berry M. Chambers		JASP	843		1878
00 000 0000	William Canaday		ASPS	952		1835
24 Nov 1819	Elijah J. Christeson	Elisha & Agnes(Drake) Md/--	LCDW	774	Pulaski	1829
00 000 1823	Robert L. Christeson	Elisha	LCDW	776	Pulaski	1829
01 Nov 1826	Kinsey Coates	Charles & Nancy(Royce) Va/--	CSBA	1178		1865
18 Jan 1853	John W. Deaton	John P & Nancy W(Pollard)Va08/Va15	GREF	856		1874
09 Feb 1839	William Edrington	Benjamin & Emily Ky/Ky	CALI	946		1843
00 000 1844	Hubert Elliott	William & Susan	JOHN	747	Moniteau	1849
15 Nov 1829	Joseph H. Grady	Lincefield & Louisa(Simpson)**/La	RAMA	1017		1855
12 Mar 1868	R.L. Guy		SERD	1188	Scotland	1875
00 000 1824	Clayton Harmon	William & Sarah(Pendleton) Va/Va	ASPS	816		1855
27 Dec 1827	Judge Vandiver Hill	George & Melinda(Christison)Va/--	USBI	425	Pulaski	1835
00 000 0000	Burgess Hurt		HPCD	744		1842
18 Jan 1841	Columbus G. Ingram		SALI	812		1876
24 Nov 1819	Mitchell M. Lampton	Louis	PETT	687		1856
07 Oct 1806	Randolph McDonald		RAY	669		1835
00 000 1853	Asa H. McGinnis	Anderson & Nancy	DAGE	900		1881
07 Sep 1844	Richard H. McWhorter		RAY	640		1871
00 000 1849	James W. Nunn	John M & Jane C(Breeding)**21/Ky25	LCKS	808		1857
02 Dec 1829	B.F. Paxton		JASP	774		1850

BIRTHDATE	NAME OF BIOGRAPHEE	PARENTS/BIRTHPLACE/BIRTHDATE	SOURCE/PAGE	FIRST MO.CO.	DATE
00 000 0000	John E. Price	James & Margaret Va/Va	QWMB 1081		1848
26 Jan 1809	Capt. David Prowell	James & Margaret(Fletcher) NC/WV	BOON 1093		----
15 Mar 1827	Capt. James Prowell	James & Margaret Va/Va.	HPCD 770	Boone	1851
10 Dec 1813	Robert Prowell		BOON 1095		----
20 Sep 1833	Benjamin C. Ridge	William & Sophia(Dillingham)Md/Ky	PLAF 511		1836
00 000 0000	Benjamin C. Ridge	William	LAFA 565		1834
09 Jul 1825	Isaac M. Ridge	-- & (Bailey)	KC& 19		1834
03 Mar 1816	Jacob Smith	Va/Va	BENC 489	Linn	1846
30 Dec 1819	William M. Steele	Robert & Cynthia(Vaughan) Va/Va.	RAMA 663	Howard	1826
24 Feb 1839	John A. Stults		JASP 857		1875
06 Mar 1837	A.M. Turk	Noah G & Ann B(Carter) Ky07/Ky	NLBM 993	Jasper	1854
00 000 0000	B.K. Turk	Noah G & Ann B(Carter) Ky07/Ky	NLBM 994	Jasper	1854
24 Aug 1843	William S. White	Albert & Polly(Stotts)	NLBM 999		1850
15 Dec 1815	J.S. Wright	Isaac & Elizabeth(Ownby) Va/Va	JASP 1064	Clark	1838

A L L E N   C O U N T Y

BIRTHDATE	NAME OF BIOGRAPHEE	PARENTS/BIRTHPLACE/BIRTHDATE	SOURCE/PAGE	FIRST MO.CO.	DATE
00 000 1850	Milliard F. Allen	Lee & Elizabeth(Russell) Ky25/Ky	HSTC 1166		1856
10 Dec 1843	Euphrates Boucher	Harrison & Zerilda(Woolsey)**14/Ky	NLBM 1010	DeKalb	1866
22 Jan 1809	John G. Boucher		NLBM 1015		1844
09 Dec 1813	William Boucher	Gabriel & Mary(Smith) **/Ky	NLBM 902	Neosho	1840
16 Jun 1827	Manuel B. Bright	George & Nancy(Burton) **/**	NLBM 904		1841
03 Aug 1829	George Colbert	William & Orpha(Sultzer) Ky/Ky	NLBM 911	Jasper	1852
25 Aug 1833	John Colbert	William & Orpha(Sultzer) Ky/Ky	NLBM 911		1851
00 000 0000	Addison Dearing		FJWC 981		1824
14 Feb 181	Emory F. Duncan		JASP 994	Howard	1823
00 000 1827	William H. Ferguson	Obadiah & Lucinda(Collins)Va00/**06	FJWC 1035		----
18 Aug 1815	Elizabeth Hagans		NLBM 1015		----
16 Feb 1824	Oliver Hatler	Michael & Sarah E(Bracken) SC/Ky	RAMA 1051		1841

A L L E N   C O U N T Y   (C O N T.)

BIRTHDATE	NAME OF BIOGRAPHEE	PARENTS/BIRTHPLACE/BIRTHDATE	SOURCE/PAGE		FIRST MO.CO.	DATE
07 Oct 1841	Judge J.M. Hickman	Anthony G & Mary(Dearing) Hickman/--	BJAS	241	Moniteau	1849
07 Oct 1841	James M. Hickman		JASP	782	Moniteau	----
04 Dec 1825	W.S. Holland		SALI	724		1840
00 000 1853	Thomas C. Legrand	Abram B & Letitia(Griffin)Tn10/**	NLBM	853		1857
13 May 1820	John Lightfoot	Henry J & Barbara(Lambert)Va95/SC99	HPCD	671		1853
07 Sep 1834	Dr. James E. Loafman	William F & Ellen(Pulliam) Ky/Ky	HPCD	672		1860
02 Aug 1837	I. McAdams	William	BUCH	817		1851
00 000 1830	Rev. George W. Mitchell	Richard & Rebecca(Brown)Va/NC	SEGO	1154	Cape Giradeau	----
04 Mar 1843	Thomas Mottley		JASP	738		1849
20 Jul 1843	Nathan K. Pope	John C & Sarah(Lightfoot)**22/Simpson	HPCD	609		1853
00 000 1830	Emily Pruitt	Moses	NLBM	984		1847
25 Apr 1835	Richard T. Read	Richard & Frances(Duncan) Va/Va	NLBM	974	Jasper	1854
28 May 1856	J.E. Rickman	Thomas & Eliza J(Weaver) Ky00/--	NLBM	975		1857
10 Aug 1828	Thompson Roten	John & Anna(McReynolds)	KC&	596	Platte	1843
13 Dec 1822	Judge R.A. Short	Lannon & Elizabeth(Carpenter)NC/Ky	VERN	688	Cole	1830
06 Jan 1836	Joseph A. Simmons	Samuel & Amanda(Williams) Ky/Ky	NLBM	980		1868
21 Apr 1827	John J. Spilman	John & Mary(Boucher)	NLBM	985		1847
00 000 0000	Judge Nathan C. Spilman		NLBM	984		1847
00 000 0000	J.E. Wagoner		LAFA	489		1849
09 Feb 1834	J.J. Warden	John & Martha(Kelly) Ky01/Ky01	PLAF	456		----
18 Jan 1834	Judge John Willoughby	William Ky/--	BJAS	72		1851
18 Jan 1834	Hon. J.T. Willoughby		JASP	755		1851

BIRTHDATE	NAME OF BIOGRAPHEE	PARENTS/BIRTHPLACE/BIRTHDATE	SOURCE/PAGE	FIRST MO.CO.	DATE
22 Mar 1823	William M. Baxter	Emblen & Elizabeth(Kennedy)Ky/Ky	MARI 644	Shannon	1854
08 Jan 1832	Hon. John S. Blackwell	John & Rachel(Lawrence) Va/Ky	PLAF 576		----
23 Feb 1805	Henry Boggess		RAY 799		1833
07 Mar 1850	Champ Clark		PIKE 782		1875
01 May 1832	John H. Davis	James & Tebitha(Jewell) Ky/Ky	CSBA 642	Clay	1857
00 000 1824	Thomas W. Freeman		BENC 341		1851
22 Jun 1841	Thomas D. George	David & Arreneous(Walker) Ky/Ky	CALI 377		1853
10 Mar 1819	Susan Griffin		NW 934		----
00 000 1829	John Guy		RAY 759		1839
12 Feb 1840	John M. Hughes	William & Mary(Sweasey)Nicholas/Nelson	NODA 782		1861
00 000 0000	Henry W. Hunt		NW 1262		1829
26 Sep 1827	Thomas McGinnis		RAY 617	Montgomery	c1847
22 Jan 1843	Samuel O. McGuire		RAY 785		1861
08 May 1854	Wiley Mountjoy	LeRoy J & Louisiana(Cardwell)--/Ky	CLPL 1027		1869
29 May 1813	David Parker		NW 934		1839
07 Aug 1849	Richard S. Paxton	Richard H & Mildred(Burrus)Va/Ky	VERN 680		1881
06 Apr 1799	Rev. Eli Penney		NW 1852		1841
00 000 1850	Judge John T. Perry	Berry & Polly(Searcy)	MOSH 1129	Clay	1852
11 Mar 1812	Lucy T. Phillips	Richard D & Mary J(Terrell)Va/Va	LCKS 861		1834
08 May 1819	Fountain Poindexter	Robert Va/--	BUCH 860		1857
18 Feb 1840	James S. Raines	Adam B & Melinda	VERN 512	Moniteau	1849
06 Jul 1826	Judge S.A. Richardson	Colonel John C Va/--	NW 1684	Ray	1831
26 Jul 1826	Judge Samuel A. Richardson	Col. John C Va/--	DAVI 554	Ray	1831
16 Jan 1840	Thomas C. Saffell	Jacob Ky/--	PIKE 796	Ralls	1844
04 Dec 1842	William Saffell	Jacob & Julia A	PIKE 982	Ralls	1844
00 Apr 1842	Jacob E. Thomas	Richard & Nancy Mercer/**	CSBA 1412		----
26 Jul 1830	Kedar Wall		RAY 764		1833
00 000 0000	Dr. M.E. White	John B & Jane(Clark) Va/Va	PETT 752		1882

BIRTHDATE	NAME OF BIOGRAPHEE	PARENTS/BIRTHPLACE/BIRTHDATE	SOURCE/PAGE	FIRST MO.CO.	DATE
00 Mar 1823	Alexander Bryan	Moses A & Eliza(Weaver) --/Ky	LCDW 772	Pulaski	1858
24 Jun 1831	Dr. James H. Dodson	Dr. Jesse & Elisabeth R(Harden)Va/--	SEGO 1026		1846
08 Sep 1852	Jehoidia H. Held	Peter & Lurana(Sams) Switzerland/--	SEGO 761		1856
28 Oct 1844	William H. Reeves	Curtis & Eliza(Bryant) Ky/Ky	SEGO 994		1844
16 Nov 1800	Lewis N. Sanders		LAFA 508		1856

BIRTHDATE	NAME OF BIOGRAPHEE	PARENTS/BIRTHPLACE/BIRTHDATE	SOURCE/PAGE	FIRST MO.CO.	DATE
04 Aug 1808	Joel Allen		FJWC 709	Miller	----
01 Oct 1816	Judge Aden C. Atteberry	William & Mary(Miller)SC85/SC95	RAMA 1041	Howard	1817
14 Jun 1817	Zephemiah E. Atteberry	Thomas & Susanna(Clemons)Va/Va	RAMA 939	Monroe	1840
13 Aug 1833	Joseph P. Bailey	William & Elizabeth(Foster)Va/Va	CSBA 551		1865
25 Aug 1825	James Barbour		JASP 864		1843
10 Jul 1810	Thomas J. Bates		NW 1143		1839
19 Dec 1817	John A. Beauchamp	Robinson P & Dolly(Winn)	CLPL 299	Ray	1838
20 Nov 1810	William D. Bell	Isaac & Elizabeth(Dills) --/SC	NODA 725		1867
03 Feb 1822	Judge John W. Bradley	Richard & Mary(Ratcliff)	RAMA 579		1828
00 000 1809	Dr. E.B. Bush	William T & Sarah(Mathews)Va/Va	HAME 502		1860
00 000 1800	Maston Cape	John	FJWC 872	Washington	1819
27 May 1837	Dr. Joel D. Cook	George B & Nancy(Howel) Va/Ky	CSBA 723		c1855
11 Oct 1836	Andrew S. Cox	Lewis A & Carolina P(Baird) Ky/Ky	RAMA 1022		1842
22 Jun 1816	Francis M. Cox	Moses & Hannah(Baird) NC/NC	RAMA 1022		1842
12 Jan 1841	S.M. Cox	Lewis A & Caroline(Baird) Ky/Ky	HOCH 1172	Marion	1842
22 May 1843	J.T. Crawley	William & Mary(Stallsworth)Tn/Ky	HAME 512		1855
22 Jun 1820	Rev. W.T. Crenshaw	Col. Thompson & Martha(Wagner)	CSBA 682		c1854

Date	Name	Parents	Birth	Code	No.	Place	Year
15 Oct 1847	W.H. Crews			BUCH	1044		1864
15 Oct 1847	W.H. Crews			CSBA	551		1865
04 Aug 1840	Isaac N. Denham	Joseph M & Mary A(Parks)	Ky/Ky	HSTC	747		1844
00 000 1829	Dr. Hezekiah E. Depp	John & Mary(Ellis)	Ky/Ky	PETT	640		1836
26 Jan 1816	James F. Duncan			CLPL	939	Clay	1832
16 Dec 1817	Robert T. Ellis	Eleazer & Jane	Va/Va	VERN	417	Macon	1840
04 Sep 1851	Henry Eubank	Reuben B & Martha(Thompson)**/Hart		SALI	598		1854
27 Apr 1833	James Eubank			SALI	684		1855
09 Feb 1824	Reuben B. Eubank	Henry & Maria(Garnett) Va95/**07		PLAF	131		---
09 Feb 1824	Reuben B. Eubank			SALI	682		1855
05 Dec 1806	Mrs. Francisca Ferguson			BUCH	1046		---
19 Oct 1806	Rev. William Ferguson	Thomas & Hannah		PETT	952		1841
00 000 1845	Adolphus P. Fishback	John M & Elizabeth(Button)	Va/--	LCKS	744		1865
29 Jan 1845	Dr. Samuel M. Forest	John M & Martha(Malone)		RAMA	553		1857
30 Oct 1826	Samuel Forrester	John & Mary(Willis)		CALI	870		1856
27 May 1815	John L. Gardner	John & Letty(Woods)		GREE	753		---
24 Dec 1860	James M. Garnett	James F & Josephine	Ky/Ky	JASP	683		1878
03 Jun 1828	Dr. R.W. Garnett	William I & Emily(Willis)		HSTC	1146		1855
23 Oct 1811	John Hall	William & Mary(McDonald)		CALL	565		1819
00 000 1826	D.W. Handy	Robert A & Rosana		DAVI	848	Boone	1865
00 000 1820	Hon. Samuel T. Harrison	Feuben & Elizabeth(Hill)Va/Va		CMMB	772	Saint Louis	1826
23 Oct 1830	John M. Hogan	Johr & Mary(Dunn)	Ky/Ky	CSBA	1196	Clay	1857
20 May 1828	William Kelley	David & Rachel(Harris)	Va/Va	ASPS	1079	Scotland	1857
00 000 0000	Amanda J. Kinslow	Ezekiel & Elizabeth(Anderson)**/**		SEGO	660		c1830
16 Mar 1847	Marquis M. Laurence	Thomas G & Candanza(Fitzgerald)Eng/Ky		SEGO	938		1875
28 Aug 1822	Elizabeth V. Linn			COOP	896		1850
19 Mar 1830	John G. Linn	John & Nancy(DePoyster)	NC/SC	VERN	779		1848
09 Feb 1850	Joseph R. Lowe	Caleb & Mary P(Crabtree)	Ky/Ky	JASP	633		1875
06 Dec 1832	Dr. James M. McAdams	James & Dicy(Carter)		VERN	663		1871
00 Mar 1815	James Mayfield			COOP	896		1850
00 000 1836	Hon. John O. Morrison	Joseph F & Martha(Faulkner)Va00/Va06		LCDW	797	Barry	1867
18 Feb 1826	George A. Murrell	George		SALI	573		1850

B A R R E N   C O U N T Y   (C O N T.)

BIRTHDATE	NAME OF BIOGRAPHEE	PARENTS/BIRTHPLACE/BIRTHDATE	SOURCE/PAGE	FIRST MO.CO.	DATE
16 Jun 1820	Jesse Nelson	John H & Mary(Houser) Ky/Ky	CSBA 744		1868
00 000 1849	H.E. Neville		CMMB 802		1851
26 Aug 1851	Americus B. Newell	Carroll & Eliza(Edwards)	CSBA 745		1868
00 Jan 1816	J.W. Newland	Va/Va	SALI 741	Pettis	1856
29 Apr 1825	E.J. Nichols		BOON 1050		1829
00 000 1835	G.W. Parker		LAFA 490		1853
24 Feb 1842	James A. Pedigo		NODA 814		1864
26 Dec 1830	Dr. Richard T. Pendery	James & Rebecca(Crane)Va/Boyle10	LCKS 1104	Marion	1844
00 000 1838	Alpheus Pitchford	Fleming & Susan(Russell)	CMMB 804		1855
00 000 0000	Capt.John P. Quesenberry		RAY 572		1840
00 000 1828	Dr. John Ray		NLBM 1045		1852
19 Jan 1804	Strother Renick	William & Betsy(Renick) Md62/Md	PLAS 539		1820
19 Jan 1804	Strother Renick		LAFA 483		1821
20 Apr 1828	Joseph Roark	Josiah & Ruth(Campbell) Ky/Ky	VERN 870		1836
01 Apr 1852	R.G. Robertson		CALL 698	Montgomery	1858
27 Jan 1831	J.M. Rock		GRUN 633		1842
05 Sep 1829	John W. Rock	Joshua & Mary(Farhis) Va/--	HOCO 467		1841
29 Sep 1790	Robert Scott		JOHN 764		1817
00 000 1846	Bedford Shobe	Abel & Martha(Anderson)	PETT 727		1848
25 Apr 1842	E.T. Smith	Daniel	CLIN 57		1857
30 Jun 1818	George W. Sturgeon		NODA 634		1856
08 Jan 1823	William P. Tanner	Frederick & Elizabeth Ky/Ky	NLBM 885	Lawrence	1870
28 May 1843	Elliot W. Thompson	David & Mary(Waller)	CALI 1156		1866
00 000 1814	Evans Tracy		GREF 1869		1840
23 Jul 1849	George T. Waggoner	Martin & Jane(Davis) Va/Va	HOAT 477		1853
24 Sep 1831	Judge B.D. Wedin	Caleb & Eliza S(Moore)	LAFA 634		1855
00 000 1831	Judge B.D. Wedin	Caleb & Eliza S(Moore) SC/Ky	PLAF 202		----
02 Nov 1837	Thomas J. Wells	Ahasuerus & Nancy(Fisher)Ky97/Ky00	HSTC 602	Carroll	1843

05 Aug 1847   Robert H. Wren   Isaac N & Amelia(Depp)   Ky/Ky   HAME   654   1854
08 May 1812   S.R. Young   Edward & Keziah(Rennick)   Va/--   HOAT   187   1854

B A T H   C O U N T Y

BIRTHDATE	NAME OF BIOGRAPHEE	PARENTS/BIRTHPLACE/BIRTHDATE	SOURCE/PAGE		FIRST MO.CO.	DATE
19 Jul 1864	J.W. Adams	Hiram & Elizabeth(Markland)Ky/Ky	JOHN	636	Cooper	1868
00 000 1802	James M. Atkins		CALL	813		1827
01 Jan 1827	Marion C. Barnes	Noble & Mary(Boyd) Va/Ky	AUDR	684	Ralls	1853
24 May 1849	Dr. Benjamin F. Berry		CSBA	435		1872
26 Oct 1844	Milford H. Berry		CSBA	434	Cooper	1870
22 May 1811	Alexander Brown, Sr.		BUCH	1021	Daviess	1835
00 000 1853	T.C. Bryam	A.W. & Emily(Robinson) Ky/Ky	JOHN	751	Cass	1869
01 Oct 1833	William C. Busby	Lewis & Eliza Ky/Ky	MARI	911		1835
00 000 1815	Capt.John P. Caldwell	Walter & Mary(Breckinridge)Va77/Va78	LCKS	725		1818
10 Dec 1821	Lewis P. Collins		SALI	610		1844
24 Nov 1875	Charles L. Ficklin	Thomas & Mary(Young) Mercer51/**49	NW	1184		----
21 Mar 1815	Mrs. Rachel Gooch		LINN	804		1848
13 Nov 1861	Alfred N. Gossett		PJAC	125		----
11 Apr 1857	Martin R. Gossett		PJAC	179		1867
00 000 0000	Samuel Hackett	Rev. J.D	HOAT	837		1865
05 Jan 1824	Thomas A. Hale	David D & Maudalina(Hicks)	SEGO	1030		1881
30 Oct 1851	Ashby Hamilton	Matthew & Mahala(Ledford)Va94/**04	CSBA	1264		1873
01 Apr 1847	W.T. Hardin	George & Ellen --/Madison	NODA	959		1873
00 000 1820	Felix Hawkins	Gregory F & Sarah(Cannon) Ky/Ky	LCKS	760		1830
00 000 1829	Lewis Hawkins	Jordan & Dorcas(Fletcher)	LCKS	761		1870
19 Jul 1818	Dr. Madison C. Hawkins	Gregory & Sarah	LCKS	758		1830
17 Dec 1842	Dr. W.L. Hedges	James F & Ruth J(Brown)Bourbon22/Nich	JOHN	491		1872
00 000 0000	Elbert B. Hensley		MONI	418		----
14 Feb 1842	Isaac Hon	J.C & Elizabeth L(Hawkins) Ky/Ky	CSBA	627		1855
02 Jun 1847	J.V. Hon	John & Elizabeth(Hawkins)	CSBA	497		1855

B A T H   C O U N T Y   (C O N T.)

BIRTHDATE	NAME OF BIOGRAPHEE	PARENTS/BIRTHPLACE/BIRTHDATE	SOURCE/PAGE		FIRST MO.CO.	DATE
27 Oct 1819	John C. Hon	Rev.Peter & Elizabeth(Clark)Ky/Ky	CSBA	538		1855
22 Apr 1823	Hon. N.O. Hopkins	Joseph & Margaret(Murphy)	HOAT	860	Jackson	1836
16 Nov 1833	C.B. Hulen	John C & Sallie(Bruton)Madison/Montgo	BOON	591		1843
11 Jan 1819	A.C. Hyde		BUCH	782		1840
03 Sep 1825	John D. Jones	James F & Elizabeth(Stephens)Flem/**	HOAT	773	Andrew	1868
00 000 0000	Sallie King		CALL	813		1827
18 Sep 1838	George W. M'Clain		GRUN	686	Mercer	1854
08 Jun 1830	John T. Maxey		JASP	818		1881
15 Jan 1822	Rev. A.K. Miller		NODA	970		1873
20 Nov 1822	William P. Miller	William & Cassandra(Ross)	GRUN	590	Gentry	1841
00 000 1810	Judge James W. Morrow		HOCO	251		----
00 000 1810	James W. Morrow		CHHO	196		----
10 Jan 1810	James W. Morrow	Robert & --(Trimble)	BENC	387		c1835
26 Oct 1818	Hon. Lewis Myers	Jacob & Lucy(Corbin) Pa92/Va	GRUN	698		1855
11 Oct 1829	Francis M. Naylor	Ignatius & Susan(Kerns) Ky/Ky	DAVI	761	Platte	1849
00 000 1804	Ignatius Naylor		ANPL	227		----
07 Aug 1837	Northcut Naylor	George T & Mary Ann(Jones) --/**	CLPL	861		1849
25 Dec 1829	Joel L. Pierce	Peter & Philadelphia(Ledford)	AUDR	613	Ralls	1831
00 Nov 1852	William L. Prater	Isaac & Margaret(Baird)	CSBA	543		1853
05 Apr 1812	Philip Purvis		LCKS	1202	Ralls	1821
18 Apr 1833	A.J. Reed		NODA	628		1879
21 Jun 1860	Dr. Granville A. Richart	Dr. D.M & Mary J(Allen)Bour32/**	PLAF	219		----
19 Oct 1812	Mrs. Elizabeth Shepherd		PIKE	443		1829
14 Jan 1817	Thomas Smith		PIKE	728	Lincoln	1817
00 000 0000	George W. Spencer	Jack & Mary(Leach)	GREF	940		1884
15 Jul 1820	Elizabeth Sudduth	Francis & Sarah(Musick)	MARI	789	Ralls	1828
19 Apr 1819	Benjamin F. Tomlinson	Archibald & Elizabeth(Briggs)Va/NC	AUDR	854	Ralls	1858
02 Nov 1845	Hon.Marcus L. Tribble	Orson & Nancy(Pazado) Clark95/--	NLEM	886		1878

BIRTHDATE	NAME OF BIOGRAPHEE	PARENTS/BIRTHPLACE/BIRTHDATE	SOURCE/PAGE	FIRST MO.CO.	DATE
24 Oct 1845	Jacob A. Trumbo	Adam A & Hannah Ky/Ky	CLPL 369		1877
05 Nov 1828	Margaret M. Trumbo	Manasset & Hanna(Taylor)	GRUN 700		1854
23 Mar 1840	N.B. Vanlandingham	Manly B & Sarah(Grey) Ky/Ky	HOAT 936		1874
27 Feb 1830	Chapman W. Wade	Greenberry B & Mary(Kelso)	LCDW 1153	Franklin	1839
01 Nov 1803	Greenberry Wade		SERD 969		c1831
18 Jun 1815	Littleberry Wade	James & Nancy(Bay)	MOSH 438	Marion	1835
29 Mar 1849	Crit Whaley	Charles C & Amanda B(Hill) Va/Ky	CSBA 525		1871
09 Mar 1847	William G. Wilson	M & Mary(Whalen) **/**	NODA 983	Cass	1868
00 000 1843	Waller Young		BUCH 965		1853

B E L L   C O U N T Y   (N O N E)

B O O N E   C O U N T Y

BIRTHDATE	NAME OF BIOGRAPHEE	PARENTS/BIRTHPLACE/BIRTHDATE	SOURCE/PAGE	FIRST MO.CO.	DATE
18 Feb 1829	Thomas V. Anderson	William & Martha(Hines) Va/Ky	LCKS 992		1865
00 000 1857	W.B. Anderson	Thomas V & Mary A(Roberts)**32/**32	LCKS 703		1854
14 Oct 1846	Julius A. Baker	George W & Rebecca J	MOSH 954		1852
27 Jul 1876	Richard I. Bruce	Silas & Lucy N(Ryle) Va/Va	NW 1125	Clinton	1881
28 Mar 1837	J.P. Burris	Seth C & Rebecca(Pulley) Ky/Ky	HOCH 1138		1851
03 Dec 1819	Charles S. Carter		CLIN 127		1876
25 Dec 1830	M.P. Cloudas	Pitman Va/--	CLIN 12		----
23 Dec 1863	John N. Denham		CSBA 449		c1865
00 000 1833	J.W. Duncan	Hon. John Ky/--	LCKS 736		----
00 000 0000	Sarah Earls		HOLT 349		----
02 Mar 1834	William G. Fowler	John B & Mary **/Mason	SALI 596	Scotland	1859
00 000 1834	William G. Fowler	J.B & Mary(Stillwell) Ky00/Mason	PLAS 505		----

BIRTHDATE	NAME OF BIOGRAPHEE	PARENTS/BIRTHPLACE/BIRTHDATE	SOURCE/PAGE	FIRST MO.CO.	DATE
12 Feb 1832	Benjamin W. Gaines	Henry & Susan(Skinner)	SALI 683	Howard	1880
07 Nov 1837	William I. Garnett		SALI 683		----
12 Nov 1847	W.T. Gibson	James & Margaret(Current) **/**	JOHN 684	Saline	1853
15 Dec 1835	Thomas J. Grant	Thomas G & Lucy M(Allen)	RAMA 558	Monroe	1841
00 000 1830	I.N. Graves	Reuben	SALI 684		1849
10 Apr 1833	Oscar K. Graves		SALI 799		1855
18 May 1810	William W. Graves	Reuben	SALI 798	Ky/--	1843
22 Mar 1814	Thomas E. Gregory	Peter	PETT 870	Va/--	1848
28 Jan 1831	James D. Haydon	Jarvis	CSBA 449	Va/--	----
20 Dec 1844	Thomas A. Hogan	David & Virginia(Watts)	PLAS 243	Ky/Ky	----
18 Jun 1837	J.R. Hutchison		JACK 990	Ray	1868
02 Feb 1844	Capt.James B.S. Kirtley	William & Elizabeth(Shelby)	LAFA 568		1844
10 Jul 1846	Samuel L. Kirtley	Elijah & Mary(Sanfords) Ky/Ky	HSTC 750	Boone	1856
28 Oct 1812	William Kirtley		LAFA 677		1844
00 000 1836	George W. Latimer	Randall	SALI 677		1844
07 Sep 1820	Dr. Alexander W. McPherson	Mark & Jane(Boggs)	GREE 786	St. Louis	1843
00 000 1813	Hon. William M. McPherson		STLO 1490		1841
21 Jul 1849	Charles E. Marshall		SALI 843	Carroll	c1859
11 Jul 1826	William G. Mirrick	John T & Elizabeth(Youell)NY00/**08	HOCO 536	Boone	c1852
20 Apr 1804	William Moore		MOSH 938	Marion	1833
02 Oct 1866	James R. Piatt	John J & Orphelia W(Riddell)**46/**	CHHO 591		1888
01 Aug 1820	Joseph A. Piner	Presley	BUCH 858		----
18 Nov 1837	J.L. Riddle	Fountain & Eliza E(Herndon)	HOCH 1214		1859
14 Feb 1835	E.W. Robinson	F.F & Emily(Waller) Va/Va	LCKS 1110		c1845
16 Sep 1828	Erastus M. Ross	John W & Nancy(Graves) Va/Va	RAMA 975		1871
17 Nov 1828	P.S. Ryle		CSBA 456		1857
10 Jan 1832	William Salle	William & May(Myers) Va/Ky	CSBA 1174	Polk	1860
00 000 1822	J.C. Simpson		MARI 670	Monroe	1855

BIRTHDATE	NAME OF BIOGRAPHEE	PARENTS/BIRTHPLACE/BIRTHDATE	SOURCE/PAGE	FIRST MO.CO.	DATE
27 Apr 1814	Simon W. Souther		JOHN	804		1855
30 Sep 1837	John L.L. Stephens	Hiram & Harriett(Brady) Va76/-- **/**	CSBA	717		1844
12 Nov 1810	Matilda Stice		LCKS	1202		----
06 Jan 1842	Benjamin N. Tanner	S.H & Rebecca(Gatten) Ky/--	CHHO	435		----
25 Dec 1827	George M. Utz	Jonathan & Catherine(Yager)Va/Va	DAVI	639		c1854
18 Jan 1832	Mark Whitaker	John & Frances(Connors)**81/Ky00	PLAS	602		----

B O U R B O N   C O U N T Y

BIRTHDATE	NAME OF BIOGRAPHEE	PARENTS/BIRTHPLACE/BIRTHDATE	SOURCE/PAGE	FIRST MO.CO.	DATE
08 May 1806	Amos Allen		JACK	885		1838
17 May 1820	William W. Allen	Asa & Sally(Duly) Va/Clark	SALI	579		1867
00 000 1813	Coleman R. Ammerman	Joseph & Rebecca(Reed) **/Va	LCKS	703		1836
15 Oct 1797	Moredecai Amos		PIKE	604		1817
13 Mar 1805	Dr. Matthew R. Arnold	Lewis & Margaret(Throckmorton)	BOON	746		----
18 Mar 1835	Harmon D. Ayres	Harmon & Charlotte(Lutton)**10/--	SALI	550		1878
13 Mar 1835	Harmon D. Ayres	Harmon & Charlotte A(Lutton)**10/***15	CALI	647	Saline	1878
31 May 1861	Will T. Ayres	Harmon D & Sallie(Turner) **/Ky	CALI	1067		1878
25 Oct 1825	J.F. Baker	Thomas & Sarah(Delay) Ky/Ky	BJAS	489		----
12 Feb 1810	Martin Baker	Martin	SALI	815	Lewis	1834
27 Sep 1832	Thomas J. Barker	Judge Thomas & Frances(Dawson)Ky/Va	MOSH	431		1839
16 Sep 1801	Mrs. Jane Mulherrin Barton		PIKE	445		1817
00 000 0000	Elijah Baxter		MARI	785		c1820
31 May 1812	Hon. George K. Biggs	William & Elizabeth(McCune)Ky87/Ky90	LCKS	865		1817
25 Apr 1825	Col. Hiram M. Bledsoe	Hiram M & Susan T(Hughes)Cumber/**	CSBA	532		1839
08 Dec 1832	Christopher C. Booth	Stephen	SALI	813	Lafayette	1866
00 000 1832	Christopher C. Booth	Stephen & Mary(Congleton)Va86/--	PLAS	646		----
03 Apr 1800	Benjamin P. Bowles	David & Elizabeth(Martin) Ky/Ky	MARI	730		----
20 Nov 1834	John Bowling	Robert & Jane C(Neal) --/Ky	MOSH	1154		1837

-21-

BOURBON COUNTY (CONT.)

BIRTHDATE	NAME OF BIOGRAPHEE	PARENTS/BIRTHPLACE/BIRTHDATE	SOURCE/PAGE	FIRST MO.CO.	DATE
00 000 1815	Judge John J. Bradley	Layton & Nancy(Delany) Va79/Va82	LINC	510	Pike	1830
25 Dec 1829	A. Breckenridge		CLIN	169	Clay	1852
00 000 1837	Adam A. Breckenridge		CLIN	9		1874
00 000 0000	J.D. Breckenridge	Adam A & Rebecca(Wilmot)**37/Ky	CLCA	768		1874
18 Mar 1837	Judge Adam A. Breckinridge John		NW	823	Clinton	1878
07 Oct 1807	James D. Brown	John & Nancy A(Davis)	PIKE	1008		1818
22 May 1830	Eli Browning	John M.S & Octavia(Kennedy)Ky/Ky	CSBA	1234	Saline	1854
29 Nov 1816	George Buchanan	Va/--	CLIN	170	Platte	1836
00 000 1830	James R. Caldwell Thomas		CMMB	702	Callaway	1840
00 Dec 1826	Spencer M. Carter		MARI	913		1856
00 000 1798	Elizabeth Cave	Richard & Sarah	AUDR	899	Boonw	1819
14 Nov 1819	J.M.B. Chamberlain	William & Mary(Branstetter)	PIKE	925		1828
04 Nov 1841	Hon. William H. Chiles	Col. Henry C & Maria(Wilson)	USBI	658	Lafayette	1858
19 Mar 1843	George W.R. Chinn	L.F & Lucy H(Jackson)	CLPL	994	Knox	----
28 Mar 1825	Richard M. Chinn	Ky/Ky	LAFA	484		1866
00 000 1812	James Clark	-- & Mary(Becket) Md/Md	LCKS	1017		1855
30 May 1807	Dr. Elijah S. Clarkson Maj. William & Mary(Smith)Va/--	SALI	734	Saint Louis	1857
25 Dec 1824	Charles V. Clay	Charles & Polly(Hatheman)	MOSH	460		1828
11 Feb 1839	Col. Green Clay		CAUD	290		1873
05 Dec 1830	J.C. Carrington		BUCH	1068		1867
18 Oct 1824	James M. Clay	George W & Rebecca(Winn)	CLIN	11	Clay	1839
27 Oct 1820	L.B Clay	George & A(Bainbridge) Ky/Ky	LCKS	728	Warren	1821
24 Oct 1817	George W. Clinkenbeard Jonathan	Tn/--	HAME	508		1839
06 Mar 1841	James G. Collier		RAY	783	Saline	1855
31 May 1837	Dr. Robert W. CollinsWilliam & Rachel	CSBA	465		1855
11 Aug 1824	John H. Croswhite	James & Frances(Hughes)	BOON	582		1826
00 000 1804	Joseph Culbertson		CALL	561		1832
29 Oct 1829	William D. Cummins		PIKE	607		1853

Date	Name	Parents	Code	No.	Place	Year
14 Apr 1834	Elder W.R. Cunningham		LAFA	498		----
21 Dec 1843	Henry Curtright	Hezekiah M & Cynthia A(Stipp)Ky/Ky	MOSH	442		1844
02 Jul 1825	William H. Curtright	Henry & Elizabeth Ky/Md	BOON	647		1852
23 Jan 1851	Garrett M. Davis	Garrett & Rebecca(Trible) Ky/--	SALI	739		1879
28 Jan 1814	William Davis	Thomas & Sarah(Ruddell) Va/Va	HSTC	733	Pike	1825
07 Oct 1833	G.W. Dawson		CLIN	163	Clay	1865
16 Oct 1848	Moses R. DeGroff	Abram P	NLBM	1064	Monroe	1859
16 Oct 1848	Moses R. DeGroff	Abram P & Margaret E(Robnett)	GREF	840	Monroe	1850
00 000 1826	John Delaney		JOHN	818		1869
03 Mar 1799	George Dickson	Josiah & Isabell(Reed) Scot/Scotland	SALI	553	Cooper	1819
00 000 1808	Thomas Diggs	David M & Susan	LINC	525	Saint Louis	1815
19 Jan 1828	Benjamin F. Dimitt		BOON	1025		1847
26 Apr 1817	William T. Dimitt	Richard Md/--	BOON	1087		1861
17 Jul 1818	J.G. Dorman	Matthew & Atlanta(Barnes) Md/Va	HSTC	510		1855
09 Apr 1807	John Duncan		CALL	561		1832
00 000 0000	Stephen Duncan		NW	1287		----
00 000 1830	W.H. Eades	Horatio & Margaret(Mosterman)**/**	HAME	520		1854
13 Oct 1832	Benjamin N. Eales	George & Margaret C(Northcutt)Ky/Ky	MARI	921		1839
10 Jun 1810	John H. Edwards	John & Polly(Garrard)	MOSH	548		1857
20 Jun 1835	John M. Edwards	-- & Margaret(Killer)	MOSH	548		1856
24 Sep 1829	W.R. Elliott	Joseph & Eliza C Ky/Ky	CSBA	1274		1879
28 May 1813	Judge Edward L. Ellis	Elder Samuel & Jane(Todd) Va/Ky	HAME	521		1857
08 Jan 1836	Robert H. Ellis	Dr. R.B	RAY	755		1837
00 000 1818	Robert T. Elsberry	William N & Lydia P(Owen)Md92/Ky00	LINC	535		1837
14 Aug 1815	Abel G. Estes	Robert & Elizabeth(Griffith)	PIKE	608		1827
01 Oct 1822	John Ewalt	Henry Ky/Ky	LCKS	1034	Lewis	1845
00 000 1805	Jacob W. File		SEGO	634	Boone	1821
07 Jan 1827	Robert H. Finch		RAY	684		1849
06 Jul 1801	Maxemelia Fisher	Solomon & Mary A(Fetty) Va/Va	PIKE	1016		1818
03 Feb 1847	H.C Fitzgerald		LAFA	510		1852
21 Aug 1825	Major Luther T. Forman	Joseph & Margaret(Barbee)	LINN	440	Marion	c1831
18 Oct 1818	Hon. John W. Forman	William & Nancy(Rice) **/**	LCKS	742		1836

B O U R B O N   C O U N T Y   (C O N T.)

BIRTHDATE	NAME OF BIOGRAPHEE	PARENTS/BIRTHPLACE/BIRTHDATE	SOURCE/PAGE	FIRST MO.CO.	DATE
00 000 0000	Benjamin Franklin		KC& 429		1831
06 Sep 1806	John Garner	William & Susan(Canada) Tn/Ky	MARI 816		1825
14 Aug 1818	Milvin Godman	William & --(Drummonds) Va/**	SALI 744	Marion	----
27 Jun 1845	William C. Godman		SALI 744		1868
00 000 1871	J.W. Golden	Morris	NW 839		----
15 Feb 1818	Daniel Grant	Daniel & Susan(Anderson)	LINN 723		1821
05 Jun 1858	N.S. Griffith		JACK 888	Boone	1880
21 May 1821	Washington H. Griffith		NODA 699		1829
00 000 0000	Wilber Griffith		PIKE 690		1819
00 000 1826	John M. Grimes		CLIN 210	Clay	1829
09 May 1813	Col. Charles A. Haden	Joel H & Martha(Smith) Va/Ky	GREH 694	Howard	1824
00 000 1820	G.W. Hall	James & Frankie(Rice) Ky/Ky	ASPS 1165	Scotland	----
16 Apr 1843	James F. Hall	Jesse & Sarah E(Gardner)	AUDR 486		1858
03 Oct 1827	William J. Hannah	Joseph & Mary(Sparks) **/Harrison	LCKS 1047		1830
01 Aug 1824	Daniel S. Hardin		KC& 586	Lafayette	1854
20 Dec 1830	Edward H. Harris	Richard & Frances(Wilson) Ky/--	COOP 824		1840
20 Dec 1830	E.H. Harris	Richard & Frances T(Wilson)Va/Ky	HOCO 1095		1843
00 Oct 1803	James Harrison	John	STLO 1264	Howard	1822
08 Feb 1796	Peyton R. Hayden		BENC 57	Cape Giradeau	1817
08 Feb 1796	Peyton R. Hayden		HOCO 775		1818
17 Apr 1832	T.J. Hayden	Benjamin & Martha A(Griffith)	MARI 697		----
28 May 1819	John S. Hedges		JACK 889		1857
03 Oct 1829	T.S. Hedges		LCKS 1050		1857
26 Jul 1812	Joseph W. Henderson		JOHN 926		1839
04 Aug 1830	Frank G. Henry		LAFA 556	Carroll	1858
14 Feb 1828	Thaddeus Hickman	William & Mary(Tureman) **/Mason	BOON 658		----
09 Oct 1830	William W. Hillix		NW 2016		1854

-24-

Date	Name	Parents/Spouse	Birthplaces	Code	No.	County	Year
09 Aug 1817	William H. Holliday	-- & Nancy(McCune)	Ky92/Ky	PLAS	418		----
00 000 1851	Josephine Honey	William & Margaret P(Stephens)	Ky/--	JOHN	577		----
00 000 0000	Henry T. Howerton			LCKS	1055		c1825
09 Feb 1797	Andrew S. Hughes			BENC	141	Clay	1827
00 000 0000	Charles J. Hughes	William & Lucy(Neal)	Va/Va	USBI	644	Boone	----
27 Jun 1822	Margaret Hughes	Charles J		NW	1093		1867
08 Jul 1825	Benjamin B. Hume	Charles & Lucy	Va/Va	CSBA	468		1825
06 May 1808	John Humphreys	John & Susanna(Whitledge)	**/**	PIKE	930		1819
09 Jun 1798	John H. Hutchinson	William & Margaret	Md/Ky	HOCH	890	Howard	1829
24 Nov 1820	Rev. D.V. Inlow	Henry & Saloam	Va/Va	MARI	735	Pike	1873
17 Oct 1825	Rev. E.D. Isbell	James & Fanny		BOON	659		1829
00 000 1811	Samuel B. Jacoby			PIKE	611		1839
04 Jan 1826	William H. Johnson	Abel & Mary(Hibler)	Ky/Ky	MOSH	567		1844
15 Jun 1825	Isaac M. Jump	John & Jane(Moore)		PIKE	613		1840
20 Dec 1806	Dr. William Keith			BOON	592		1829
17 Sep 1828	Dr. D. Kemper	Peter & Rebecca	Ky/Ky	BOON	1125		1864
21 Feb 1815	Benjamin L. Kendrick			HOCH	747		1857
22 Nov 1821	W. Kennedy			JACK	937		----
00 000 1819	Francis J. Kern			NW	1117		----
00 000 0000	W.J. Kines			CLCA	365		c1835
01 Mar 1830	George T. Langston	Jacob & Cornelia(Northcutt)		BOON	774		1844
16 Jul 1837	J.M. Larimore	W.L		STLO	1230		1844
29 Aug 1835	N.G. Larimore			STLO	1229		1820
00 000 1818	O.H.P. Lear	Thomas M	Va/--	MARI	650		1870
15 Dec 1850	Edwin T. Letton	Lemuel P & Catherine(Couchman)		VERN	556	Johnson	1840
25 Dec 1829	Eli J. Link	Israel & Elizabeth C(Hufford)Scott/Sc		CLPL	878	Clay	1832
28 Sep 1828	A.W. Lydick	Johr. & Anna W(Biddle)		MARI	792		1836
18 Dec 1800	William S. McClanahan	Thomas & Nancy(Green)		LINN	451		1819
05 Jun 1798	Isaac McCoskrie	Andrew & Nancy(McDougal)	Ky/Va	CALI	c990	Boone	1829
00 000 0000	William McCray			NW	1924		1829
28 Oct 1819	William McCray			CLCA	658		1828
28 Oct 1819	William McCray	Edward & Sarah(Townsend)	De/Md	CALI	538	Callaway	

BIRTHDATE	NAME OF BIOGRAPHEE	PARENTS/BIRTHPLACE/BIRTHDATE	SOURCE/PAGE	FIRST MO.CO.	DATE
18 Oct 1849	Thomas G. McCrosky	James D & Flora(Canterbury)Va/Ky	CLIN 227	Daviess	1857
16 Oct 1811	Harvey T. McCune	John & Polly(Shannon) Ky/Ky	NLBM 951	Pike	1816
27 Apr 1850	David W. M'Intyre	Robert & Rachel(Haley)	JASP 355		1883
13 Mar 1836	Dr. Joseph M. McKim	S.H & Hettie A(Miller) Ky07/Ky17	LCKS 1078		c1858
08 Dec 1811	James S. McLoed	William & Mary(Stark) 89/--	PIKE 620		1820
08 Feb 1833	Henly J. Maddox	James & Mahala	MARI 793		1834
07 Jul 1834	William T. Maddux	Basil & Frances Va/Va	MARI 793		1834
10 Mar 1862	John Martin	R. Newton & Sallie(Bedford)Ky/Ky	VERN 667		1877
30 Oct 1816	Dr. John W. Martin		BUCH 1034		1854
30 Jan 1825	Frank S. Menefee	Dr. Jonas & Jane Q(Allen)	HOCO 1129	Knox	1860
06 Apr 1837	Capt. Timothy Middaugh		CLIN 106	Caldwell	1838
19 Oct 1829	James M. Miller	James & Nancy W(Baker) Ky91/Ky93	LCKS 800		1838
10 Sep 1810	Capt. Benjamin P. Moore		ANPL 80		--
27 Jul 1836	Elisha Moore		JACK 923		1841
15 Aug 1857	John T. Moreland	Thomas R & Catherine(Hedges)**/--	SALI 720		1858
21 Nov 1808	Major Jesse Morin	John & Sarah(Fishback) Va/Va	USBI 844	Howard	1816
07 Nov 1820	Benjamin F. Morison	John & Betsey E(Richardson)**/Ky	LCKS 1090		1851
05 Aug 1834	Charles T. Murdock	John T & Nancy(Chinn) Va04/Harrison04CLPL 1003			1847
29 Mar 1852	John T. Neal	John B & Lucy(Collins) **/**	CSBA 508		--
19 Jan 1822	Judge T.B. Nesbit	John & Jane Ky/Ky	CALL 685		1824
20 Jun 1831	J.W. Nichols	James & Margaret(Wallace) Ky/Ky	HOCH 1037		1866
16 May 1818	William H. Nichols	William & Mary(McCoy) Ky/Ky	LCKS 1095		1866
04 Mar 1796	Daniel Nolley	John & Nancy(Dance) Va/Va	CALL 692		1829
16 Jan 1831	Kinzea H. Norris	William J & Sarah(Stevens) Ky/Ky	PIKE 584		--
17 Oct 1835	George E. Northcutt	Eli & Eleanor(Ellis) --/**	CALL 568	Boone	1868
00 000 1823	Rev. J.K. Northcutt	Eli & Eleanor(Ellis) Va99/--	NLBM 1042	Boone	1836
07 Apr 1842	J.M. Northcutt	Benjamin	NODA 809		1844
10 Jul 1812	Alfred Oden	Ky/--	PIKE 857		1828

Date	Name	Parents	Origin	Ref	No.	County	Year
03 May 1846	J.M. Offitt			PIKE	975	Platte	1849
08 Dec 1816	Amsley Owen	Stephen & Nancy(Layson)	NY86/**92	MARI	703		1853
00 Oct 1823	John Owens	Elijah & Mary	**/**	NODA	1022		1852
17 Jun 1811	Canada Ownbey	Joseph & Hannah		VADA	765		1820
00 000 0000	Judge George F. Palmer	Thomas & S(Glendenning)		MOSH	1072		----
06 Jan 1827	W.H. Parker	William & Fannie(Collins)	Md/Va	CSBA	509	Jackson	1841
18 Jul 1805	William Parker			JACK	894		1838
20 Sep 1818	Dr. J.C. Parrish	Callaway & Nancy(Shropshire)	Va/Va	RAMA	622	Monroe	1843
23 Jul 1830	Joseph Patten			HSTC	618		1858
00 Feb 1800	Mrs. Jane M. Patterson			PIKE	442		c1817
14 Oct 1803	Thomas D. Patton			PIKE	623		1824
03 Jun 1813	Jonathan Pierce	Mordecai & Sarah(Barnard)	Ky/Ky	MARI	970		1837
07 Jan 1797	Dr. J.W. Points	Arthur & Ellen		BOON	1127		1836
08 Sep 1811	Alfred Pond			MARI	623		1852
00 Aug 1818	Robert T. Prewett			HOCO	251		1824
01 Aug 1818	Robert T. Prewett	Rev. Joel		BENC	533		1824
02 Jan 1840	William H. Prewett	James M & Mattie(Bedford)	--/SC	VERN	511	Saline	1852
02 Jan 1840	William W. Prewett	Joel	Ky/--	VERN	683	Howard	1823
10 Nov 1809	Judge William S. Price	James & Sarah A(Smoot)	Va/**	CALL	570		1828
25 Jun 1803	George S. Priest			PETT	852		----
09 Oct 1792	William Reading			PIKE	978		1820
24 Feb 1830	Dr. Hardin B. Redmond	William & Elizabeth		SALI	564	Cooper	1845
17 May 1797	William Reed	John S & Jane		PIKE	1035		1817
06 Jun 1814	Abram Renick			JACK	895		1843
22 Sep 1844	Prof. John J. Rice			CALL	757		1869
18 Jun 1817	Dr. W.C. Riley	Samuel	Pa/--	PETT	795	Callaway	1826
16 Dec 1844	David T. Robertson			HOCO	538		----
19 Feb 1838	Rev. William H. Robertson	Solomon & Eliza(Nelson)	In/Ky	HOCO	744		----
15 Mar 1806	Hezekiah Robey	Hezekiah	Md/--	MARI	528		1857
06 Feb 1837	A.W. Robinson	Maxwell & Elizabeth(Fidler)	Ky/Ky	AUDR			1821
08 Jan 1821	Alexander C. Robinson	John M & Lucian(Butler)	SC00/--	BOON	787	Howard	
03 Jun 1808	William Rowe			LAFA	595		1843

BIRTHDATE	NAME OF BIOGRAPHEE	PARENTS/BIRTHPLACE/BIRTHDATE	SOURCE	PAGE	FIRST MO.CO.	DATE
07 Dec 1816	Dr. John T. Russell	Joseph & Elizabeth(Penn) Va/--	CSBA	513		1866
00 000 1830	Robert T. Russell		LAFA	675	Callaway	1836
24 Mar 1830	Robert T. Russell	Dr. Robert S & Sallie C(Ware)Ky07/Ky	PLAS	489		----
26 Jul 1838	John W. Scott	Washington & Ruth Ann(Duncan)**12/--	CLCA	517		1839
18 Dec 1812	Washington Scott	William & --(Smith)	ANPL	232		1837
00 000 1831	Benjamin F. Settles	John T & Mary(Shrader)	PETT	726		1865
15 Aug 1825	Custer C. Sharp	Abraham & Margaret(Custer) **/**	LCKS	1119		1839
00 000 1829	Charles R. Shawhan		LAFA	498	Jackson	1865
27 Sep 1847	John T. Shawhan	Daniel & Minerva Bourbon01/Harris07	JACK	942		1868
00 000 0000	John Sites		MARI	766		----
09 Apr 1809	William Sites	John Pa/--	MARI	821		1824
00 000 0000	Charles Smith		MOSH	1025	St. Charles	1818
25 Nov 1820	John D. Smith		PIKE	906	Clay	1855
07 May 1821	Robert H. Smith	William & Elizabeth(Cress)	BOON	953	Callaway	1826
00 000 0000	Robert T. Smith	-- & --(Sidener)	LCKS	960	Monroe	1835
00 000 1801	Thomas B. Smith	Daniel & Nancy(Barker)	HOCO	1080		c1812
06 Sep 1835	William E. Smith	Benjamin F & Polly A(Wilson)	BOON	609		1857
24 Nov 1824	William H. Smith		PIKE	873		1832
00 000 0000	William L. Smith		LAFA	684		----
20 Oct 1845	H.D. Smithson		JOHN	766		1866
26 Oct 1856	James G. Sparks	W.B & Fannie(Breckinridge)	CSBA	518		1878
00 000 0000	John Spurgeon		LINN	623		----
00 000 0000	James Stark		PIKE	593		----
00 000 0000	G.D. Steele		PIKE	938		1826
07 Jan 1831	John W. Stockman	Francis & Sallie A(Kelly) Eng88/--	HAME	750	St. Joseph	1837
00 000 0000	J.N. Stone		NW	1058	Platte	----
01 Jan 1821	Thomas F. Stone	Elijah & Elizabeth(Foster)	NW	1986		1846
10 Mar 1794	Mrs. Elizabeth S. Sutton		PIKE	438	Boone	1837
24 Sep 1814	John W. Tate	George W & Nancy	JACK	944		1838

Date	Name	Parents/Spouse	Origin	Code	No.	County	Year
28 Dec 1832	Dr. M.B. Taylor	Matthew & Mary(Baker)		HSTC	754		1870
08 Jul 1814	W.L. Taylor	Simon & Rebecca		MARI	655		1837
00 000 1815	Edward D. Terrell			JOHN	628		1860
12 Aug 1836	Thomas Terry	George S	Ky12/Ky16	PETT	903	Callaway	1836
29 Aug 1822	John M. Thatcher	Eleven & Sabrina(Hornback)		CLPL	969	Clay	1825
00 000 1839	Robert H. Thomas	Robert B & Mary Ann(Ewalt)	--/**	BUCH	914	Jackson	1844
04 Jul 1826	Samuel Thomas	Joseph & Sally(Oden)	Ky/Va	PIKE	862		1827
09 Oct 1809	C.T. Thornton	Charles & Ann W(Buckner)	Va/Va	CSBA	522		1857
00 000 1837	William G. Throckmorton	Thomas & Lucinda E(McKim)	Ky/Ky	LCKS	1135		1841
00 000 1814	Jason Tillitt	Jiles & Mary(Wigenton)	Ky/--	PIKE	629	Boone	1818
01 Nov 1828	Simeon H. Treadway	Peter D & Margaret(Evans)	Ky/Ky	MARI	999		1864
15 Nov 1825	A.J. Triplett	Hon. James C & Nancy(Lydick)	Va/Ky	ASPS	921	Monroe	1832
18 Dec 1821	Capt. John P. Turner	Joseph & Susan(Parks)	Va/--	HSTC	782		1844
11 Nov 1850	John T. Vanhook	John W & Margaret	Ky/Ky	SALI	745	Cass	1879
00 000 0000	Nancy Vernon			CALL	151		1834
02 Feb 1824	George W. Varlandingham Merritt			MOSH	605		1826
29 Jan 1827	A.J.V. Waddell		Va/Md	JOHN	738	Lafayette	1854
19 Nov 1805	Judge Anthony S. Walker			HOCO	964		1826
23 Jul 1829	William H. Warren	William & Charlotte(Herndon)		MOSH	1036		1835
00 000 0000	Jane Watt			PIKE	593		1816
26 Oct 1863	James Watson	Dr. J.M & Elizabeth(Taylor)		NW	2009		1867
17 May 1820	William Washington	Asa & Sally(Duly)	Va/Clark	SALI	578		---
04 Feb 1809	Washington Wheat			JACK	945		1878
06 Jan 1834	Calvin Wigginston	James		PIKE	874		1835
22 Apr 1794	John Wigginton			JACK	973	Howard	1813
03 Mar 1826	James Williams	James & Elizabeth(Wright)	Ky/Ky98	CLPL	446	Platte	1851
00 000 0000	Caleb Wood	Malcum & Angelica		MOSH	430		1830
00 000 0000	Fielder Wood	Malcum & Angelica		MOSH	430		1830
00 000 0000	John Wood	Malcum & Angelica		MOSH	430		1831
00 000 0000	Thomas Wood	Malcum & Angelica		MOSH	430		1833
04 Apr 1858	James T. Ware			PJAC	89		---
21 Jan 1806	James B. Young	Nathan & Mary(Griffeth)		MARI	712		1835

BIRTHDATE	NAME OF BIOGRAPHEE	PARENTS/BIRTHPLACE/BIRTHDATE	SOURCE/PAGE		FIRST MO.CO.	DATE
29 Jul 1853	H.B. McIntyre	Alexander & Mary J(Jones) Scotland/--	CLCA	578		1874
23 Aug 1835	Judge Jacob M. Poage	Hugh Allen & Eliza.(Murphy) Va/Pa	NW	1444	Daviess	1867

BIRTHDATE	NAME OF BIOGRAPHEE	PARENTS/BIRTHPLACE/BIRTHDATE	SOURCE/PAGE		FIRST MO.CO.	DATE
17 Sep 1839	Evan S. Anderson	Addison A & Catherine(McDowell)Tn09/--	MOSH	399		----
00 000 1835	O.P.W. Bailey	Ky/Ky	JACK	737		1852
22 Mar 1831	Thomas D. Bailey	Ky/Ky	RAMA	539	Boone	1839
18 Aug 1852	Beverly D. Bolling	Alfred & Cyrena(Baker)	LINN	757	Johnson	1858
06 Oct 1824	Bryant Brinton	James P & Lucinda(Kenley)	BUCH	1057		1837
14 Jun 1842	John P. Bryan	James P & Eliza 05/01	BUCH	1043		1845
00 000 1824	Benjamin Cambron		SEGO	691		----
00 000 0000	Col. James Chiles		KC&	661		1826
18 Aug 1794	Adam Christison		JACK	913	Howard	1817
29 Oct 1791	James Clemens	Jeremiah	USBI	562	Saint Louis	1816
07 Oct 1827	James Crane	Tarlton L & Polly	MARI	731		1833
11 May 1819	Henry Deer	Lewis & Nancy	SALI	620	Buchanan	1847
12 Nov 1832	Thomas J. Doke	John L & Nancy(Yeager)	CLPL	899	Ralls	1854
12 Nov 1819	Gen. Joseph B. Douglass William	Md/--	BOON	853		1827
27 Nov 1812	Frederick R. Fields	James & Sarah(Ripperdam)	KC&	364		1846
00 000 1845	C.G. Ford	John R & Caroline	LAFA	508	Pettis	1858
12 Apr 1843	C.Y. Ford	John R & Carries(Foster) **01/Ms14	PLAS	275		----
08 May 1801	John R. Ford	Charles & Elizabeth Va/Va	LAFA	641	Pettis	1858
18 Dec 1844	J.W. Greenwood	Armstead & Elizabeth(Bolling)Ky07/Ky92	JOHN	634		----
00 000 0000	Joseph W. Hall		SALI	653		----

Date	Name	Parents / Notes	Code	No.	County	Year
15 Jul 1844	Charles G. Hamilton		KC&	75		1849
00 000 1833	Isaac Hamilton		SALI	711	Howard	c1839
24 Jul 1826	Jerry Harlan	Henry & Bertha(Bryant) **98/03	HOCO	1037		1855
18 Jun 1826	Frank M. Harrison	Frank & Frances(Crutcher)	MOSH	993	Monroe	c1831
20 Oct 1839	Gabriel C. Jones	Laban & Rachel(Walker) Va/Ky	NLBM	940		1872
03 Oct 1820	William S. Jones	Joshua Va/--	JACK	967		1854
05 Jan 1826	John Kenley	Hiram & Patsey(Gray)	ASPS	831		1845
30 Jun 1841	Dr. E.M. Kerr		CALL	673		1869
03 Jul 1832	John A. Lobb		JACK	805		1852
27 May 1854	Charles H. Lucas	William C & Hannah F	HSTC	1090		1870
06 Feb 1852	John H. Lucas		PJAC	203		----
00 000 1831	Charles McBride		JACK	808		----
00 000 1832	William B. Miller	Gen. William & Elizabeth(Gaines)Ky/Va	PLAS	337		1837
07 Apr 1827	William B. Miller	Gen. William & Elizabeth	SALI	654		1837
00 000 1810	Rev. John Montgomery		PETT	851		1857
09 Aug 1812	Dr. Thomas J. Montgomery		PETT	703		1857
29 Feb 1836	T.L. Montgomery		---	---		1836
02 Jun 1837	William G. Oldham	James & Lucy(Graves)	LCKS	808		----
00 000 1840	James R. Parr	John & Elizabeth(Compton)Va08/Ky11	FJWC	801	Jackson	1852
30 Aug 1861	Sherwood T. Peter		SERD	802		1867
15 Jul 1838	Squire Jeremiah W. Phillips	Allen & Elizabeth M(Doswell)	RAMA	660		----
20 Oct 1815	Allen Pipes	George & --(Jackman)	HOCO	557	Boone	1877
31 Mar 1811	Judge David Pipes		BOON	1051		1817
00 000 1835	Abraham Pope		RAY	729		1857
15 Nov 1843	Isham Powell	Golston & Mary(Coulter) **/**	RAMA	680		1857
13 Jul 1860	L.W. Preston	Francis A & Mary(Sedore) Ky32/Ky34	GREF	1659		----
28 Sep 1845	Milton T. Roberson		JOHN	772		1869
15 Jan 1832	Dr. J.H.C. Robinson		BUCH	1051		1849
05 Aug 1845	Samuel Russell	Richard & Elizabeth(Williams)Merl8/**	CALI	668	Jackson	1849
00 000 0000	Dr. John H. Sampson		NW	689	Buchanan	1837
08 Jul 1829	Mrs. Elizabeth Smith		BUCH	995	Jackson	1840
03 Apr 1836	Jeremiah B.P. Smith	Ephraim & Elizabeth(Pope)Garrard95/**	MOSH	595		1850

BIRTHDATE	NAME OF BIOGRAPHEE	PARENTS/BIRTHPLACE/BIRTHDATE	SOURCE/PAGE		FIRST MO.CO.	DATE
26 Feb 1853	Robert C. Sneed	John M	PETT	734		----
00 000 0000	J.W. Sutton	William	JOHN	558		----
20 Oct 1831	William H. Taylor	Jesse & Elizabeth(Anson)	VERN	873		----
15 Aug 1833	B. Vanarsdale		LAFA	668		1856
25 Jun 1837	Elder William W. Warren	Dr. Wm & Maris S(Speed)Ky08/Ky	HSTC	1100	Howard	1843
19 May 1808	R.C. Williams	John G & Ann(Todd) Eng/Scotland	CSBA	526	Lafayette	1878
18 Mar 1847	John G. Williamson	R.C & Sarah(Graham) Ky/Ky	CSBA	573		1859
15 Feb 1851	John T. Wilson		JACK	864		1852
28 Apr 1828	F.F Yager		JACK	884		1850
01 Oct 1812	Judge Jacob Yankee		PETT	1096		1835

B R A C K E N   C O U N T Y

BIRTHDATE	NAME OF BIOGRAPHEE	PARENTS/BIRTHPLACE/BIRTHDATE	SOURCE/PAGE		FIRST MO.CO.	DATE
28 Jul 1830	H.B. Baker	Isaac	CLIN	168		1847
10 Nov 1832	John N. Browning	Caleb & Penelope	SALI	613	Scotland	1856
13 Apr 1823	Judge John S. Chick	Capt. William & Mildred C(Harding)	MOSH	1157		1840
19 Sep 1844	James K.P. Dawson	William & Priscilla(Patterson)**11/**	LCKS	1166		1845
02 Apr 1838	Thomas S. Dougherty	Thomas & Dianna(Tolman) Ky/Ky	AUDR	463	Scott	1845
06 Oct 1840	Dr. Henry R. Field	Ambrose & Elizabeth(Reeder)Va/Va	CSBA	1345		1867
04 Oct 1843	William Jackson	William & Lettie(Ellis) Ky/Ky	HPCD	910		1880
10 Feb 1820	George J. M'Cready	George W Md/Va	GRUN	332		1839
10 Sep 1851	James McDowell	Arthur & Elizabeth	QMMB	975		1869
07 Mar 1822	Ephraim Minor		BOON	723		1873
15 May 1830	Abraham P. Patterson	Abraham & Jane C(Chisholm)De83/Md	LCKS	1196	Marion	1839
06 Jan 1834	Benjamin F. Records	Laban S & Martha(Stites) Ky07/Ky	KC&	66		----

BIRTHDATE	NAME OF BIOGRAPHEE	PARENTS/BIRTHPLACE/BIRTHDATE	SOURCE/PAGE	FIRST MO.CO.	DATE
00 000 1796	Thomas Reynolds		CHHO 196		----
12 Mar 1796	Thomas Reynolds		BENC 345	Howard	1829
22 Sep 1796	William Sallee	Abraham & Lucy(Haden) Va/Va	MARI 763		----
17 Nov 1844	R.C. Smarr	John H Ky/--	CLIN 56		1869
06 Mar 1811	Eliza Stoube	Jacob & Mary(Wiley)	MARI 789		----
14 Sep 1821	Judge John Taylor	Joseph & Elizabeth(Heaverin)Md/Ky	HOCH 998		1850
29 Aug 1838	J.F. West		BUCH 937	Mercer	1855
20 Dec 1818	George H. Wood	William & Elizabeth(Huston)Pa/Md	NODA 859		1853

B R E A T H I T T   C O U N T Y   (N O N E)

B R E C K - N R I D G E   C O U N T Y

BIRTHDATE	NAME OF BIOGRAPHEE	PARENTS/BIRTHPLACE/BIRTHDATE	SOURCE/PAGE	FIRST MO.CO.	DATE
00 000 0000	W.C. Adkisson	Samuel & Lucy(Parks) **/**	DAGE 663		1879
10 May 1826	J.R. Avitt		LAFA 551		1853
10 May 1826	James R. Avitt	Andrew & Jane(Helm) Ky/Ky	PLAS 639		----
28 Apr 1842	Alexander Barger		DAGE 921	Harrison	----
22 Apr 1834	N.R. Barr	Elias & Sally(Beauchamp)**/Washington	CSBA 1326		1873
00 000 1841	Thomas A. Barr	Jerry B & Eliza Ann(Dowell)**/**	LCKS 710		1852
20 Mar 1828	Alexander M. Bedford	Johr & Elizabeth(Howard)Nelson98/**04	ANDE 488		----
20 Jul 1836	Arthur Brown	William B.C & Matilda J	LAFA 685		1844
15 Oct 1834	John L. Eidson	William A & Martha(Clarkson)Va/Va	HOCH 1052		1854
11 Sep 1824	Judge James H. Howard	William & Rhoda(Atkinson) Ky/Ky	SEGO 896		1845
00 000 0000	William D. Huff	Benjamin Germany/--	SEGO 981		1843
27 Sep 0000	James P. Jolly	Samuel & Malinda(Robertson)**/**	DAGE 552		1852
08 Jun 1838	Singleton L. Kasey	Singleton L & --(Boatright)Va96/Va	RAMA 1087		1866
00 000 1819	General Benj. F. Loan		BUCH 246	Platte	1838
11 Feb 1835	Judge Bedford B. Lockard	Boyle D & Rhoda B(Trent)Va08/**12	SEGO 1042		1860
14 Sep 1840	Richard B. Lowry	Thomas & Mildred(Clarkson) Va/Va	HOCH 973		1857

BIRTHDATE	NAME OF BIOGRAPHEE	PARENTS/BIRTHPLACE/BIRTHDATE	SOURCE/PAGE	FIRST MO.CO.	DATE
07 Jul 1826	Robert E. McGavock	Robert & Ann(Hickman) WV/Ky	HOCO 578		1847
20 May 1843	Martha E. Maddox		SEGO 1042		----
05 Apr 1831	John W. Reed	Peter & Nancy(Gray)	LCKS 1204		1851
23 Jan 1841	William Robertson		GRUN 593		1850
24 Mar 1852	Clinton B. Sebastian	Alexander H & Tabitha A(Jacobs)	BOON 952		1854
00 Nov 1817	Martin Shelman	Adam & Mary(Hays) Va/Va	NODA 679		1856

B U L L I T T   C O U N T Y

BIRTHDATE	NAME OF BIOGRAPHEE	PARENTS/BIRTHPLACE/BIRTHDATE	SOURCE/PAGE	FIRST MO.CO.	DATE
15 Jan 1837	A.C. Bogard	Clifton & Eliza(Webb) **/**	SEGO 957		1870
00 000 1799	Joshua Cole		FJWC 875	Washington	1818
15 Mar 1830	Joseph Crenshaw	Richard & May J(Moore) Ky04/Md03	SEGO 965		1832
07 Nov 1848	John T. Dawson	Thomas & Elizabeth(Cook) Ky07/Ky10	SEGO 969		1880
08 Oct 1823	George W. Drake	Charles & Mary(Swearingen) Va/Md	HOCO 544		1833
31 Aug 1812	Susan Froman	Isaac **/---	SEGO 968		1845
00 000 1831	C.C. Hare		JACK 786		1868
26 Oct 1836	John L. Howlett	Luke & Eliza(Lee) Va/Ky15	SEGO 980		1858
11 Nov 1811	Jeremiah F. Jenkins	William N & Priscilla B(Hoskins)Md/Md	LCKS 1180		1861
31 Mar 1839	James A. Lee	William T & Dorothy **/**	SEGO 985		1848
15 Aug 1833	John S. Lemon		BUCH 807		1850
00 000 1821	Thomas Lithacumb		HAME 567	Harrison	1855
00 Sep 1833	John Middleton	Thomas & Elizabeth(Wright)	PIKE 584		1837
12 Jun 1836	Joseph H. Moore		SEGO 943		----
00 000 0000	Alfred Simmons		HOCO 1110		----
00 000 1806	Jane Turley		FJWC 875	Washington	1818
00 000 0000	Upton Wilson		LAFA 634	Johnson	1837

BUTLER COUNTY

BIRTHDATE	NAME OF BIOGRAPHEE	PARENTS/BIRTHPLACE/BIRTHDATE	SOURCE/PAGE	FIRST MO.CO.	DATE
11 Jan 1847	Dr. John L. Burke		LINN 602	Livingston	1865
19 Mar 1831	James W. Hill	William & Martha(Wade) Ky/NC	CSBA 729		1876
15 Jul 1848	J.G.W. Hunt	J.D & Rebecca R(Williams)Montg08/--	JASP 632		1866
00 000 1812	Isaac N. Lewis	James A & Margaret(Tygot)NC83/Va83	LCKS 917		----
08 Nov 1825	Lycurgus Lindsey	Amos & Mary(Madison) SC87/Ky	HPCD 598		1836
08 Mar 1835	Benjamin K. McReynolds	Benjamin S & Elizabeth(Askew)	CSBA 1228	Johnson	1867
01 Feb 1833	William A. McReynolds	Benjamin S & Elizabeth(Askew)Ky06/09HSTC 713			1882
16 Sep 1829	P.W. Moore	James I Va/--	HSTC 670		1855
27 Apr 1829	Dr. A.E. Simpson	Isaac & Rachel B(Tygart) Ky/Ky	SEGO 1000		1858
13 Dec 1821	Lycurgus Wilson	John & Mary	LAFA 696	Saint Louis	1828
00 000 1843	John A. Young		SE 1227		----

CALDWELL COUNTY

BIRTHDATE	NAME OF BIOGRAPHEE	PARENTS/BIRTHPLACE/BIRTHDATE	SOURCE/PAGE	FIRST MO.CO.	DATE
01 Aug 1836	Dr. James E. Caldwell	William D Fayette01/Franklin09	HAME 676		1875
07 Apr 1833	Thomas J. Caldwell	Elder William P.C	JOHN 828		1845
24 Oct 1825	Dr. Joseph Cartwright	James A Clay/--	PETT 865	Saint Louis	1854
00 000 0000	John W. Cash		LAFA 507		1857
17 Nov 1826	Jeremiah W. Champion	Drury C	BOON 1019		1828
09 Jun 1829	Hon. George W. Colley	Cyrus SC00/--	LCDW 778		1832
11 Feb 1831	James A. Dobbins		SALI 801	Saint Louis	1848
06 Dec 1821	John G. Fowler	Joseph & Anne(Johnson) 91/**00	PETT 1020		1840
00 000 1852	James W. Harper	Henry H & Cynthia A(Castleburry)Ky/KySEGO 978			1860
26 Feb 1809	Col. William G. Hawkins	Harrison & Jane(Robinson)NC/NC	PIKE 808		1827
17 Jul 1831	Capt. Irwin W. Jenkins	William & Susan(Gateley)	GREH 901		1836

-35-

BIRTHDATE	NAME OF BIOGRAPHEE	PARENTS/BIRTHPLACE/BIRTHDATE	SOURCE/PAGE	FIRST MO.CO.	DATE
25 Dec 1823	George H. Jones	Robert & Eleanor S(Hays) Ky91/Md	MARI 959	Montgomery	1827
00 000 1812	Robert R. Laughlin		CMMB 1154		1833
27 Apr 1821	W.F. Lewis		JACK 953		1858
29 Nov 1853	Kate Lillicrap		SERD 1059		----
23 Dec 1828	Daniel O. Lowery		JASP 736		1866
00 000 0000	James Maxwell		NW 756	Saint Joseph	1838
05 Jan 1827	James F. Mitchell		PETT 1057	Hickory	1850
05 Mar 1810	George M. Pemberton	Jesse B & Tabitha(Brooks) Va70/--	PETT 977		1836
23 Apr 1812	Thomas B. Pemberton	Jesse B & Tabitha(Brooks) Va70/--	PETT 977		1836
07 Nov 1835	J.M. Pickerell	James & Nancy(Ballard) Tn/Callaway	BJAS 486		----
00 000 0000	Thomas W. Rackerby	John H & Georgiana(Dudley) Va/--	NLBM 971	Saint Louis	1865
00 000 0000	W.C. Rackerby	J. H & Georgiana(Dudley) Va/Va	BJAS 357		----
30 Mar 1846	Rev. Clark Smith	Spencer R & Sarah(Clayton)	NLBM 981		1856
14 Apr 1815	Robert J. Smith	Robert & Lucy(Gordon)	LAFA 639		1831
00 000 0000	George H. Traylor		SERD 1033		1898
20 Jun 1817	John J.C. Woolf	Alfred **84/Ky86	HSTC 1171		1837

C A L L O W A Y   C O U N T Y

BIRTHDATE	NAME OF BIOGRAPHEE	PARENTS/BIRTHPLACE/BIRTHDATE	SOURCE/PAGE	FIRST MO.CO.	DATE
20 Feb 1852	Milton Belise	Ira & Lucinda(Smith) NC15/Tn	CSBA 1327	Saint Clair	1859
00 000 0000	George M. Shelly	Col. James M & Louisa(Stubblefield)NC	USBI 748	Kansas City	1870
06 Dec 1824	W.W. Woodford		GREH 720		1843
13 Sep 1819	Jacob Woodward	Edward Va95/--	GREF 1836		1837

C A M P B E L L   C O U N T Y

BIRTHDATE	NAME OF BIOGRAPHEE	PARENTS/BIRTHPLACE/BIRTHDATE	SOURCE/PAGE	FIRST	MO.CO. DATE
00 000 1813	William H. Anderson	John H Va/--	JOHN 464		1833
17 Mar 1833	James J. Franklin	Fayette & Mary A(Tyree) Va06/--	CSBA 1402		----
19 Oct 1820	A.E. Ginn	John & Abigail(Brackin) Va/Ky	ANDE 560		----
08 May 1850	Jasper Gosney	Robert H & America(Yelton) 17/21	CALL 771	Warren	1879
15 Nov 1843	John T. Hopkins	Gennethen & Nancy(Armstrong)	MOSH 995		1869
23 Nov 1816	Samuel E. Jayne	Ebenezer & Debora(Egleston)NY86/NY91	LCKS 1179		1850
08 Jan 1837	Edward L. Libbee	Silas & Mary(Boyd)	MARI 737		1871
16 May 1863	Elisha B. Madcox	Charles & Barbara(Vaughn) Ky33/Ky40	GREF 1780		1901
06 Feb 1814	John Maphet	John & Patience(Harris) Oh/Bullitt	ASPS 853		1853
08 Apr 1842	Charles Morehead	W.C	BUCH 835		1865
16 Apr 1816	Dr. E.B. Smith	Dr. A.B & Rebecca(Linseg)	HOCH 1163		1837
08 Feb 1818	Walter J. Van Horn		PIKE 733		1848
05 Jun 1841	Thomas J. Walker	Ellis & Margaret(Fleak)	ADAI 546		1869
10 Dec 1816	Archibald S. Yontsey Adam	Md/--	DAVI 451		1838

C A R L I S L E   C O U N T Y   (N O N E)

C A R R O L L   C O U N T Y

BIRTHDATE	NAME OF BIOGRAPHEE	PARENTS/BIRTHPLACE/BIRTHDATE	SOURCE/PAGE	FIRST	MO.CO. DATE
19 Jan 1835	William T. Baird	Barzilla A & Mary M(Scanland)Ky03/--	ADAI 609		----
19 Jan 1835	William T. Baird	Barzilla A & Mary(Scanland)Bourb03/--	ASPS 939		1857
25 Jan 1848	Antoine G. Craig		CLIN 13		1855
26 Jun 1850	J.T. Craig	Lewis E & Letitia(Tandy) Ky/Ky	KC& 605	Cooper	1860
21 Mar 1846	John S. Craig		CSBA 1371	Cooper	1862

CARROLL COUNTY (CONT.)

BIRTHDATE	NAME OF BIOGRAPHEE	PARENTS/BIRTHPLACE/BIRTHDATE	SOURCE/PAGE	FIRST MO.CO.	DATE
22 Dec 1842	Louis N. Craig		NODA	744	Pettis	1871
26 Jan 1850	L.W. Craig	Walton & Laurinda(Peak) **03/Scott09	ANDE	498		1874
00 000 1803	Walton Craig		NW	1777	Andrew	1856
00 000 1839	John R. Dawkins	James & Mary H(Lewis) Henry/Ky	ASPS	1146		1856
23 Jun 1826	E.D. Gullion	George P & Leah(Scott) Ky/Ky	MARI	760		1853
03 Aug 1839	John H. Hayden		AUDR	773		----
29 Sep 1827	Major David H.Lindsay	Richard C & Julia H(Bond)Scott/Scott	CLIN	38		1851
03 Sep 1848	William A. M'Cracken	John A & Catherine(Barbee)	GRUN	700	Putnam	----
03 Sep 1848	Judge W.A. McCracken	John A & Catherine	FGRU	314	Putnam	----
15 Jan 1831	Lemuel B. Mitchell	James & Sophia Ky/Ky	ASPS	999		1858
13 Nov 1847	R. O'Neal		NODA	898		1871
10 Apr 1851	Dr. James W. Smith	J.L & Mary E(Davis) **/**	CSBA	518		1860
15 Jul 1833	Dr. I.S. Talbot	Ky/Ky	BUCH	963		----
21 Mar 1838	Hon. John F. Tandy	J.P & Elizabeth(Parnell) Ky/Ky	IMCD	305	Lewis	1850
16 Dec 1816	John V. Turner		BENC	417	Cooper	1842

CARTER COUNTY

BIRTHDATE	NAME OF BIOGRAPHEE	PARENTS/BIRTHPLACE/BIRTHDATE	SOURCE/PAGE	FIRST MO.CO.	DATE
08 Jun 1838	Jasper N. Bailey	Jessee & Margaret(Webb)	DAVI	628		1846
04 Nov 1830	John T. Carver	Morgan & Harriet(Pierce) Va55/--	HSTC	1167		----
11 Aug 1826	Henry G. Deering	John NCO1/Va	DAVI	702		1848
17 Nov 1842	John D. Savage	Nicholas & Mary(McCrosky) WV/Va	HAME	616		1875
27 Jun 1839	Landon C. Thompson		BUCH	982	Platte	1852

-38-

C A S E Y   C O U N T Y

BIRTHDATE	NAME OF BIOGRAPHEE	PARENTS/BIRTHPLACE/BIRTHDATE	SOURCE/PAGE	FIRST MO.CO.	DATE
11 Feb 1834	John Allen	James & --(Bromson)	CLPL	510		----
29 Sep 1834	James M. Ashley	John & Elizabeth(Montgomery)Ky/Va	PLAS	383		----
27 Sep 1829	Elijah B. Bailey	Samuel & Rebecca	RAY	638		1853
00 000 0000	William G. Bowman	William & Elizabeth A(Wilkerson)	HOCH	1136		1857
13 Mar 1851	F. Chilton	James M & Rachel D **/**	DAGE	671		----
04 Feb 1807	Osborn N. Coffey	Jesse & Elizabeth(Riffe) Ky/Ky	LINC	521		1831
31 May 1848	George T. Cooley	Thomas H & Letitia(Anderson)Ky/Ky	BJAS	410		----
11 Feb 1824	Clayton T. Davenport	Ephraim	PETT	990		1878
01 Jun 1808	Benjamin Dawson		NW	931		1851
16 Nov 1825	B.E. Edwards	Judge Wm B & Mariah(Bledsoe)Ky/Ky	HSTC	747	Johnson	1843
10 Mar 1837	D.N. Edwards	William & Mariah(Bledsoe) Ky/Ky	HSTC	1181	Johnson	1843
15 Oct 1837	Charles M. Hutchinson	Thomas	DAVI	599		----
11 Apr 1834	Dr. George Hutchinson	Judge Thomas & Polly Ann(Tate)Va/Ky	DAVI	599	Livingston	1845
07 Feb 1836	Jeremiah Hutchinson		CALI	1012		----
04 Jul 1833	John P. Hutchinson	Jeremiah & Emily Ky/Ky	CALI	1011		1851
30 Aug 1834	Sandy E. Jones	John S	JOHN	874		1836
27 Feb 1853	R.P. Martin	Jesse & Eliza Ky/Ky	JASP	699	Camden	1858
02 Apr 1834	William R. Mayfield	James & Mary(Johnson) Tn/Ky	LCDW	734		----
00 000 0000	Henry Minton		NW	1478	Holt	1847
13 Jan 1845	Robert Murphy	William & Melianda(Henson)	DAGE	493		1855
05 Nov 1843	Clark W. Noel	Willis B & Eliza(Mann) Mercer18/--	NLBM	1080		1846
27 Aug 1846	W.H. Noel	B.S & Nancy	IMCD	234		1846
16 Jan 1836	William D. Oliver	Isaac & Mary(Downey) NC/NC	BOON	601		1838
00 000 0000	Lewis Pigg		NW	2033	Ray	1839
16 Nov 1831	Harrison P. Polson	Rev. Benjamin & Sarah(Wall)Va82/NC95	RAMA	693		1837
00 000 1807	Peter B. Riffe	Christopher & Elizabeth(Casey)Md/Va	PETT	719		1880
00 000 1824	Levi N. Rigney		DAGE	484	Johnson	----
17 May 1831	Franklin J. Ross		RAY	635		1843

BIRTHDATE	NAME OF BIOGRAPHEE	PARENTS/BIRTHPLACE/BIRTHDATE	SOURCE/PAGE	FIRST MO.CO.	DATE
17 Jan 1834	Mathias W. Speed	Judge Jas & Dorinda(Weatherford)Ky/Ky	MOSH 599		1834
16 Sep 1835	James R. Taylor	Louellen & Elizabeth Ky/Ky	JASP 647		1841
05 Dec 1826	Dr. F.J.C. Walker	Hon. James T & --(Carter) SC95/Va00	PLAS 605		----
00 000 1829	James W. Walker	James T & --(Carter) NC/Va	PETT 750		1843
24 Apr 1836	L.H. Warinner	Willis & Clemency(Mason) Ky10/--	USBI 768	Ray	1836
27 Sep 1816	Joel M. Weatherford	Joel & Margaret(Day) Va/Ky	PIKE 986		1829
06 Sep 1825	George W. Williams	Thomas & Jane(Jones)	---- ---	Cooper	1836

C H R I S T I A N   C O U N T Y

BIRTHDATE	NAME OF BIOGRAPHEE	PARENTS/BIRTHPLACE/BIRTHDATE	SOURCE/PAGE	FIRST MO.CO.	DATE
00 000 1816	Samuel J. Blakely	John & Hannah(Hardin) Ga/Ky	LINC 508	Howard	1818
08 Sep 1820	E. Clark Bouldin	Va/--	PETT 934		1850
27 Aug 1835	T.J. Boyd	NC/NC	JASP 675	Newton	1837
29 Jul 1839	Milton J. Bozarth	Josiah & Jane	VADA 741		1860
06 May 1850	Dr. J.P. Brasher	Dr. Alfred M & Minerva Ky10/Tnl4	HPCD 722		1856
00 000 1827	Morgan W. Bryant	I.S & R,E(Petty)	SEGO 960		1873
16 Feb 1819	J.M.C. Bullock	Lawrence & Mary J(Morris)Va79/Va	CSBS 641		1840
15 Sep 1853	Prof. Andrew S.Caldwell	J.S Esquire	PETT 627		1879
00 000 0000	Robert S. Cash	Isaac & Eva(Stiles) Ky/Ky	CALI 362		1869
00 000 1813	Joseph Chick	Alburn W & Eliza A(Robinson)Va14/**	MOSH 894	Callaway	1830
28 Feb 1843	J.C. Clark	Hardin & Nancy(Scates)	BATE 44	Cooper	c1863
04 Sep 1820	Dr. Logan Clark	Dr. J.H	PETT 630	Callaway	1824
22 Jun 1834	Judge T.B. Clark	John & Betsey(Chick) NC/Ky	QMMB 1041		1863
17 Jan 1848	Isaac N. Cooper	James C & Hannah(Henderson)SC91/Ky96 Albert J & Eliza J(McDonald)**08/20	JOHN 885		1834

Date	Name	Parents	Birth	Code	No.	County	Year
21 Jan 1863	William J. Crattree	Emsley & Elizabeth(Pyle)	NC/--	CSBA	1243	Polk	1857
20 Jan 1859	Fairfield B. Croft			VERN	417		1873
00 Jan 1804	Hon. Joe Davis			HOCO	251		1818
14 Jan 1804	Joe Davis			BENC	183		1818
28 Mar 1814	James R. Devaul			GRUN	432	Chariton	1820
29 Jan 1830	William Draper	John		JOHN	885		1834
22 Feb 1839	Dr. N.M. Edwards			SALI	752		1881
00 000 1820	William U. Forbis	John & Elizabeth(McLean)	NC/Va	NLBM	1025		1844
00 000 0000	Mears P. Fort			SERD	567		1880
28 Nov 1833	Edward P. French	Pinkrey & Deborah(Clark)		AUDR	647		1838
00 000 1833	Edward P. French	Pinckney	1797/--	CAUD	296	Callaway	1838
09 Dec 1808	David Galbreath	Tokle & Catherine(Graham)		AUDR	601	Callaway	1830
14 Oct 1812	Major Henry M. Gorin	John D & Martha(Thomas)	Va/SC	LCKS	1173		1841
06 Jan 1813	Alexander W. Graham			SCMW	790	Montgomery	1816
18 Apr 1806	Daniel Gray	Robert & Mary		GREH	755		1831
16 Oct 1815	William A. Gray	Joseph & Matilda(Scriggs)	Va77/Va82	HSTC	813		1836
00 000 1834	Abner Greer	Jonathan & Mary(Hopson)	SC04/Va11	SEGO	929		1866
13 Jan 1821	Thomas A. Gunnell	John T & Elizabeth(Major)	Va/Va	SALI	659		1844
10 Jan 1829	W.B. Halyard	George & Sarah(Chesis)		JASP	539	Nicholas	1842
00 Dec 1818	Job Harned			PETT	957		1841
08 Jul 1808	John G. Hayden			JACK	787	Marion	1826
00 000 0000	William B. Jones	Henry & Nancy(Flint)		ASPS	1077	Cooper	1835
00 000 1824	James A. Lander	John S & Elizabeth(Haggard)	)Ky92/Ky91	CMMB	972		1846
20 Feb 1831	Dr. Davis J. Lindley	Jonathan & Margaret(Armstrong)	)**06/**HPCD	HPCD	752		1859
00 000 1814	Rev.Jacob Lindley	Jahu & Parenia(Gibson)	NC82/NC82	HPCD	750		1832
00 000 1813	William Lindsey	Johr & Margaret(Carr)	NC/Ky	LINC	565	Pike	1818
00 000 1795	Arthur McFarland	Johr.	Va/--	SEGO	875		1816
17 May 1821	John Mason			SERD	1002	Callaway	c1848
01 Dec 1812	Joseph Means	Robert & Sarah(McDonald)	)NC78/Ky92	HSTC	585	Howard	1818
18 Jan 1809	William Means			BUCH	1061	Howard	1820
23 Jan 1812	Robertson Moore	Joseph & Rebecca(Robertson)	NC/Tn	HOCO	458	Chariton	1817
00 000 1838	George F. Moseley	William C & Louisa H(Shelton)		JOHN	694		1860

BIRTHDATE	NAME OF BIOGRAPHEE	PARENTS/BIRTHPLACE/BIRTHDATE	SOURCE/PAGE	FIRST MO.CO.	DATE
21 Jan 1840	J.E. Payne	Edward & Mary Ann(Callaway)Ky/Ky	JACK	877		1857
21 Jan 1841	James E. Payne	Edward & Mary Ann(Callaway)	PLAS	188		----
29 Oct 1829	M.J. Payne		USBI	73	Saint Louis	1849
02 Jan 1822	Alexander Read	William & Polly(Chick) Ky/Ky	AUDR	662		----
24 Aug 1821	Fedilio C. Sharp	Absalom M	BENC	375		1843
20 Mar 1832	Milton A. Shaw		CSBA	605		1867
21 Feb 1820	Dr. Turner R.H. Shaw	Rev. Thomas & --(Burdett)Va/Garrard	CALL	716	Boone	1840
31 Jul 1807	J. Bradley Thompson	Samuel & Matilda S(Bradley)NC84/Va85	RAMA	1055		1876
00 000 0000	Dr. G.T. Thomson	James & Catherine Va/Va	HPCD	951		----
20 Feb 1835	A.J. Tisdale	William T & Lydia	SALI	871	Ray	1836
00 000 1837	Dr. Alfred W. Titterington	Adam & Sarah(Smith)Eng84/Va94	LCDW	813	Le Clede	1858
11 Jul 1842	George W. Tribble	George W & Patsey(Embry) Ky04/--	GREH	892		1879
00 000 1834	Col. A.T. Watson		SALI	736		1866
28 Nov 1838	James M. Williams	Lemuel B & Attry **/**	SALI	713	Pettis	1841
00 000 0000	John L. Williams		SALI	717	Cooper	1841
16 Jan 1826	Dr. E.A. Wills	Rev. Marquis P & Sarah(Smith)	JASP	601	Boone	c1827
03 Nov 1818	Drewery M. Wooldridge	Edward & Margaret(Brasher)NC79/--	USBI	709	Cedar	1870
22 Dec 1832	Dr. Madison B. Wooldridge	Edward & Margaret(Brasher)Va/Tn	HPCD	790		1858
22 Dec 1832	Madison B. Wooldridge	Edward	GREF	1140		----

C L A R K   C O U N T Y

BIRTHDATE	NAME OF BIOGRAPHEE	PARENTS/BIRTHPLACE/BIRTHDATE	SOURCE/PAGE	FIRST MO.CO.	DATE
00 000 1827	W. Spencer Adams	Elcanah & Margerie(Tredway)Va06/**04	LCDW	766	Ray	c1825
15 Mar 1815	George W. Baker	George & Martha A Va/Va	SALI	629	Cooper	1839
31 May 1822	R.M. Barnes	Alfred & Henry(Lackland) Md/Md	CALL	814		----

Date	Name	Parents	Notation	Code	No.	Place	Year
05 Mar 1841	Charles Berkley	John W & Sallie A(Lisle)	Ky13/Ky24	HOCO	360		1861
24 Aug 1824	David Bishop			CMMB	911		1830
24 Aug 1824	David Bishop	Levin & Judith(Booth)	Md89/--	MONI	523		----
04 Oct 1809	John W. Boyle	James & Jane(Forman)	Va76/--	CALI	1006		----
25 Sep 1790	James Brasfield			ANPL	28	Clinton	1824
05 Apr 1825	John S. Brasfield	James & Jane(Lafferty)	**90/**	USBI	584	Clinton	1834
22 Apr 1814	James G. Bright			BUCH	688		1842
08 Dec 1856	Albert C. Brockman	Jacob & Narcissa(Quisenbury)		AUDR	915		1877
00 000 0000	Asa Brockman			RAY	609		1826
29 Mar 1807	Jacob E. Brockman			HOCH	785		1822
14 Feb 1858	James W. Brockman	Asa T & Susan A(Hugiely)	Ky/Ky	AUDR	870	Boone	1877
27 May 1854	John H. Brockman	Asa T & Susan A(Hugiely)	Ky/Ky	AUDR	870	Boone	1877
04 Jun 1844	James Browning	Francis C & Nancy(Johnson)	**98/**06	HOAT	150	Platte	1846
00 000 0000	Napoleon B. Browning	Francis C & Nancy(Johnson)	**98/**06	HOAT	150	Platte	1846
00 000 0000	Stephen Bruner			CALL	880		1818
10 Mar 1826	Dr. John B. Burbridge	Thomas & Elizabeth(Ferguson)	Va/Ky	PLAS	553		1860
10 Mar 1826	John B. Burbridge			LAFA	538		1850
02 Nov 1837	J. Porter Bush	Jereniah & Nancy H(Gentry)		MOSH	314		1860
04 Mar 1843	Owen M. Bush	Philip W & Jane(Monroe)**12/Jessam23		HSTC	706	Scotland	1841
31 Mar 1831	R.N. Bush	Nelson & Nancy(Neal)	Va/Ky	CSBA	483		c1865
28 Dec 1810	Alfred Bybee			CSBA	439		1840
07 May 1841	Dr. Paul E. Calmes	John W & Ann(Evans)	Woodford/**	HSTC	1104		1857
00 000 1831	C.C. Chiles			JACK	870		1831
27 Jun 1832	S.J. Chiles			JACK	900		1832
18 Jan 1837	James W. Clark	James & Eliza(Burris)		MOSH	531	Ralls	1852
00 000 0000	Robert P. Clark			HOCO	866		1817
27 May 1850	D.B. Clawson			NOSA	930		1866
25 Dec 1813	W.H. Chaney		Ky/Ky	PETT	842		----
00 000 0000	James M. Chorn			HOCO	366		----
00 000 1840	Andrew L. Clinkinbeard	Jchn & Sally(Strode)	**93/Ky	HSTC	564		1874
00 000 1816	Benjamin F. Combs	Fielding & Mary(Foreman)		RAMA	1118	Ralls	1819
00 000 1849	John W. Conner	Moses S & Margaret F(Conkwright)**/**		PETT	632		----
00 000 1825	S. Conner	James	Ky/--	PETT	631		----

BIRTHDATE	NAME OF BIOGRAPHEE	PARENTS/BIRTHPLACE/BIRTHDATE	SOURCE/PAGE		FIRST MO.CO.	DATE
10 Nov 1821	Richard Cornelius	Isaiah & Elizabeth(Haynie)Eng/Ky	LCKS	1024	Monroe	1857
00 000 1827	Judge Enoch Crim	John R & Mildred(Sears) **06/**08	ASPS	1143	Monroe	1836
00 000 1826	Robert Croswhite	William & Mary(Hagerty) --/Va	AUDR	875		1839
20 Jul 1829	J.S. Davenport	Stephen & Susanna(Simmons)**/Estill	KC&	264		1833
19 May 1809	Rev. James C. Davis		MOSH	461		1872
14 Feb 1837	Squire Samuel Dooky		CLPL	517		c1866
11 Aug 1800	Isaac Dunaway	William Pa/--	HSTC	666	Lafayette	1819
25 Apr 1836	J.W. Edwards	Thomas W & Nancy(Combs)	HOCO	1056	Pettis	1838
19 Sep 1833	John M. Embree	Tarleton & Martha(Vivian)	CSBA	1235	Johnson	1858
18 Dec 1816	William L. Embree		PETT	952		1832
08 Mar 1837	Charles L. Eubank	Stephen & Nancy(Berkley)**90/Ky19	HOCO	376		1859
12 Mar 1870	John W. Everman	Daniel B & Josephine(Crow) 44/44	NW	1123	Daviess	1886
08 Oct 1812	Martilus Ferrill	James Ky/SC	CSBA	740	Cooper	1823
09 Sep 0000	Prof.Joseph Ficklin	Joseph Mercerill/--	BOON	861	Grundy	1851
30 Jul 1832	Hiram B. Foster		RAMA	1025		1852
00 000 1828	John D. Foster	Peyton & Mary(Daniel) Bourbon/--	SEGO	926	Adair	1851
00 000 0000	Chris. T. Garner	Jesse W & Dorcia(Trigg)	RAY	538		1819
21 Jan 1811	John C. Garner	Col. Jesse W	RAY	780		1855
30 Aug 1815	Stephen T. Garner		HOCO	576		1817
00 000 1826	Hon. William L. Gatewood	Joseph & Lucy C(Winn) Va/--	SCMW	852		----
11 Dec 1834	Robert B. Gay	John & Rebecca Ky/Ky	BOON	1121		1837
20 Apr 1816	John L. Gosney	Richard & Jane(Leckey) Va??/--	CLPL	943		1856
13 Jan 1815	Thomas M. Gosney	Richard & Jane(Lackey) Va/Va	CLPL	467		1845
01 May 1817	John Groom	William & Mary Ky/Ky	NODA	869	Boone	1820
03 Nov 1842	P.J. Haggard		PETT	894		1869
00 000 1824	Dinwiddie Halley	Henry & Polly(Patton) Eng/--	ASPS	1063	Macon	----
29 Jul 1810	David Hampton	George & Kittie(Routt) Ky/Va	HOCH	1145	Boone	1833
01 Oct 1835	D.T. Hampton	George W & Nancy(Jones) Ky/Ky	HSTC	667	Boone	1839

Date	Name	Parents/Spouse	Origin	Code	No.	County	Year
00 Sep 1812	George W. Hampton	David & Mary(Bryant)	NC/NC	HSTC	668		1839
11 Jan 1832	W.M. Hawkins		Va91/--	CLIN	164	Buchanan	----
17 Jul 1828	John Hazelrigg	Dillard & Sallie(Renick)		BOON	591		----
03 Feb 1815	Cuthbert H. Hickman	Richard & Susan		SALI	807		1841
25 Oct 1810	Charles R. HieronymusJohn			PETT	873	Howard	1822
04 Oct 1830	R.J. Hukel	William L & Narcissa(Schooler)Ky/Ky		CSBA	1266	Boone	1835
16 Nov 1842	Dr. R.F. Hulett	Silas & Pauline	Ky/Ky	CSBA	1380		1858
26 Nov 1800	Mrs. Harriet M'Creery Jackson Elijah			PIKE	430		1831
00 000 1811	Benjamin F. Jeans			PIKE	612		1828
23 Oct 1804	Snelling Johnson	Philip & Margaret		MONI	324		1819
30 Dec 1851	Clay W. Judy	John & Elizabeth(Richart)		MOSH	379	Audrain	1864
23 Jan 1820	John A. Judy	John & Susan(Burroughs) **87/**		AUDR	608		1864
19 Mar 1809	Reason S. Judy	John J & Catherine(Sullivan)Va/Va		CSBA	538	Jackson	1819
25 Apr 1841	W.H. Lane	William H & Polly Ann(Emerson)		CSBA	698		1873
12 Oct 1831	Dr. A.J. Lawrence			CLIN	139	Clay	1867
05 Apr 1856	Dr. James M. LawrenceDr. Andrew J & Elizabeth(Lott)			CALI	438	Clay	1867
14 Sep 1819	Dr. J.M. Lawrence	John B & Elizabeth(Eve)	Va/Va	BUCH	1034	Platte	1855
09 Nov 1841	Robert M. Lawrence	Robert & Lucy(Ecton)	Ky/Ky	RAMA	593		1865
00 000 0000	Judge William W. Lott		Va/Va	NW	1059		----
01 Aug 1816	Judge W.H. Lott			CLIN	174	Caldwell	1839
00 000 1810	Obadiah Lowe	Daniel & Delita(Barber)	Ky/Ky	ASPS	992		1861
23 Jul 1828	Ira H. McCarty	George & Sallie(Miller)	Va/Va.	LCKS	933		1851
10 May 1826	M.C. McChristy	John & Elizabeth(Lowery)	Bourbon/SC	MARI	740		1828
09 Oct 1821	David B. McClure	Samuel	**/Barren	AUDR	803	Boone	1831
04 Apr 1830	Francis McDonald			AUDR	890	Callaway	1857
31 Oct 1815	William McGhee	Benjamin & Martha(Wiley)		CALL	568		1833
25 Oct 1821	D.C. McIntire	Hugh		HSTC	706		1841
25 Dec 1828	Julia A. McPherson			BUCH	1030		----
09 Mar 1816	James March	Absalom & Elizabeth(Brandenburg)Ky/**		**LCKS	1071	Boone	1828
07 Sep 1829	Martillus Margason	John & Elizabeth(Griggs)	NY/**	NLBM	955		1872
09 Nov 1806	Caleb Martin	John & Nancy(Delaney)	Va/--	HOCH	1035		1819
30 May 1841	G. Thomas Martin	Samuel & Ann J		SALI	652		1850

CLARK COUNTY (CONT.)

BIRTHDATE	NAME OF BIOGRAPHEE	PARENTS/BIRTHPLACE/BIRTHDATE	SOURCE/PAGE	FIRST MO.CO.	DATE
29 Feb 1812	James T. Martin	Robert B & Susan(Pearson)	MOSH 426		1824
00 000 0000	Samuel T. Martin	Dr. Samuel D & Elizabeth(Taylor)	SALI 651		---
04 Oct 1847	Dr. Zachary T. Martin		CLIN 248		1880
12 May 1844	David C. Morrison	Archibald & Catherine	SALI 628		1854
00 Oct 1850	Raleigh Morgan	R.S & Amanda(Trimble) Va/Ky	NW 808		---
29 Nov 1828	John S. Muir	John & Lavina(Evans) Ky/Ky	KC& 655		---
00 000 1820	Moses G. Mullins	Anthony	JOHN 828	Howard	1826
09 Aug 1838	Levi Noland	John & Belle(Garner)	JOHN 965		1879
24 Oct 1818	Henry B. Oliver	John & Cynthia A(Lawrence)	RAMA 664	Howard	1828
24 Oct 1818	Henry B. Oliver	John & Cynthia A	RAMA 598		1836
00 000 1810	John W. Oliver		SCMW 881		1826
00 000 0000	Crayton Owen		CSBA 1184		1853
22 Jun 1809	Henry Palmer	James & Elizabeth Ky/Ky	BOON 1126		---
00 000 1811	Joel Palmer	James & Elizabeth(Foster)	BOON 602		1833
05 Feb 1834	Thomas L. Peddicord	Nathan & Nancy(Dawson) Md34/Va	CALI 335	Pettis	1854
22 Apr 1807	Harvey W. Pemberton	John & Lucy(Vivion)	BOON 780		1826
23 Dec 1819	David H. Pigg	William & Polly(Hampton)	HSTC 652		1843
00 000 0000	Sanford J. Preston		VERN 511		c1830
15 Jul 1830	Elkanah Quisenberry	Colby B	GREH 890		1875
05 Dec 1835	Philip Quisenberry	William	MOSH 383	Monroe	1866
17 Mar 1812	Capt. W.K. Ramey	James Ky/--	PETT 942	Howard	1820
15 May 1833	Dr. Preston Ramsey	Maj. William H & May(Garden)Ky/Ky	BUCH 1036		1867
20 Jan 1837	Jesse A. Ramsey		HOCO 976		1872
00 000 0000	John Rawlins		CALI 1251	Howard	1825
26 May 1812	Capt. Allen G. Reed	Capt. Joseph	CLPL 358		c1832
13 Aug 1853	William L. Reed	Joseph S & Mary(Bush)	HOCO 403		1865
00 Apr 1810	Benjamin B. Reynolds	Michael & Sallie(Blackwell)Ire/Ky	PIKE 815		1832
11 Jun 1826	Dr. Stephen J. Reynolds	Dr. Michael & Lucy A(Winn)Ire/Ky	PIKE 416		1832

-46-

Date	Name	Parents / Spouse	Origin	Place	No.	County	Year
22 Apr 1813	Zachariah W. Rowland	William & Nancy		SALI	642	Randolph	1830
29 Mar 1818	Dr. J.A. Rogers	Dr. Henry & Betsy(Reed)	Ky/Ky	HSTC	539		1842
02 Aug 1824	Henry O. Ryan	James & Wealthy(Rockwell)	**/**	ASPS	1016		1858
00 000 0000	Joseph Scholl	Joseph & Lavinia(Boone)		CALL	931		1821
23 May 1815	Nelson Scholl	Septimus & Sallie		CSBA	652	Jackson	1843
09 Jul 1831	Thomas Shepherd	William & Elizabeth		SALI	617	Audrain	1839
02 Jan 1849	J.M. Sphar	Willis F & Mary E	**/**	SALI	743		1869
18 May 1827	John Stevinson			RAY	623	Jackson	1855
19 May 1817	William Stewart	Roy & Elizabeth(Williams)		AUDR	848		1857
04 May 1829	William T. Summers	William & Sallie	Ky/Ky	BOON	1132		1851
09 Jul 1821	George T. Swetnam	John & Sarah(Goff)		RAMA	524	Howard	1828
11 Jan 1820	Elder Jonas G. Swetnam	Judge John & Sarah(Goff)		RAMA	664	Howard	1828
00 000 1821	Ben I. Taul			NW	1306		----
08 Oct 1821	Capt. Sam F. Taylor			LAFA	668		1849
08 Feb 1820	James S. Thomas	George & Susan(Strode) Bourbon99/--	Ky/--	SALI	560		1870
20 Jan 1845	B.F. Trimble	William		CLIN	64	Clay	1867
14 May 1842	James A. Trimble			CLIN	64		1873
01 May 1829	John H. Trimble	William & Margaret(Fry)	Ky/Ky	CLPL	416		1856
24 Mar 1821	George W. Vivion			LAFA	532		1833
11 Oct 1848	William H. Wallace	Rev. J.W		PJAC	199		1857
11 Oct 1848	William H. Wallace			JACK	859		----
21 Apr 1826	William Warren	Thomas	Ky/--	PETT	1077		1856
00 000 0000	Benjamin Watts			HOCO	419		1835
00 Aug 1838	F.L. Wayman			PLAS	601		----
06 Jan 1822	James Williams	Joseph & Sarah(Crin)	Ky/Va	MOSH	394		1826
00 May 1805	William Wills	David & Polly(Raker)	NC/NC	SALI	599	Howard	1838
11 Sep 1816	Edward C. Wilson	William & Polly(Ballard)		AUDR	620	Monroe	1844
12 Oct 1822	John B. Wormall	-- & Mary(Mullins)	Va/Ky	USBI	865	Jackson	----
00 000 1794	Anthony Wyatt	Richard		SQMW	1057		----
00 000 0000	James E. Young	Frank		CLCA	551		1835

BIRTHDATE	NAME OF BIOGRAPHEE	PARENTS/BIRTHPLACE/BIRTHDATE	SOURCE/PAGE	FIRST MO.CO.	DATE
00 000 1809	Lucretius Baker	Va/Va	PETT 841		1855
00 000 1826	Lt. Samuel Baker		ASPS 760	Chariton	1828
07 Feb 1827	Dr. A.D. Clark		RAY 781		1831
04 Oct 1806	William Cornett	Robert & Charlotte(Calliham)Va/Va	AUDR 453	Boone	1828
13 Nov 1828	Thomas J. Gibson		BUCH 755	Grundy	1839
07 Jul 1830	John Hutson	Joseph & Margaret(Bowlin)**08/**10	NODA 535		1839
31 Mar 1836	John Lewis	Samuel & Lydia(Baker) **/**	CLCA 481		----
18 May 1820	William Lewis	Samuel Ky/Ky	DAVI 806		1857
04 Jan 1811	William M'Cammon		GRUN 586		----
00 000 1835	Perry McCollum	Daniel & Lydia(Johnson) Ky06/Ky08	ASPS 842	Linn	1855
05 Oct 1813	Judge Jefferson Morrow	William & Sarah(Jay) Ire/NC	RAMA 1195	Howard	1818
09 Apr 1833	John Oxford	Jonathan & Elizabeth(Spurlock)NC/Ky	DAVI 762		----
00 000 1841	T.G. Rogers	NC/--	HAME 614		----
02 Oct 1826	Jesse Spencer		JASP 891	Polk	1839
29 Dec 1842	Elijah Spurlock	William & Sally(Hurd)	CALI 669		1865
00 000 1842	John T. Summers	Mason	NW 844		----

BIRTHDATE	NAME OF BIOGRAPHEE	PARENTS/BIRTHPLACE/BIRTHDATE	SOURCE/PAGE	FIRST MO.CO.	DATE
16 Oct 1845	L.P. Davis	C.J Va/--	ASPA 1055		1856
27 Jun 1869	John H. Dunmire	George T & Viana M(Phillips)Pa37/--	DUNK 190		1878
17 Mar 1846	Alvin Farris	Ky/Ky	PETT 1090	Cedar	1856
25 Apr 1841	Ambrose B. Hopkins	George W & Sarah(Looney) Ky95/Ky05	HSTC 520		1851
12 Feb 1843	John R. Hopkins		HSTC 1113		1850
00 000 1837	Dr. Thomas H. Jeffries	William & Clara(Lawson)Tn12/Tn13	NLBM 1032		1863
20 Apr 1823	Hon. James W. Jones		LCDW 1117	Chariton	1843

BIRTHDATE	NAME OF BIOGRAPHEE	PARENTS/BIRTHPLACE/BIRTHDATE	SOURCE/PAGE	FIRST MO.CO.	DATE
00 000 1838	David C. Pierce	Louis & Rachel(Cowan) Ky12/--	NLBM 866		1869
15 Apr 1832	Col. William A. Shelton	Ezekiah & Elizabeth(Mason)**08/Va	USBI 188	Putnam	1845
15 Apr 1831	Col. William A. Shelton	Ezekiah H & Elizabeth(Mason)**/Ky	ASPS 1105		1845
31 Dec 1851	Joseph H. Sturgess	John	SALI 699	Henry	1858
09 Mar 1845	William E. Sturgess		SALI 706		1867
28 Feb 1847	A.M. Woodson		JACK 993		1869
15 Jun 1844	William S. Young	Andrew & Edith(Smith) Ky/NC	HAME 657		----

C R I T T E N D E N   C O U N T Y

BIRTHDATE	NAME OF BIOGRAPHEE	PARENTS/BIRTHPLACE/BIRTHDATE	SOURCE/PAGE	FIRST MO.CO.	DATE
11 Sep 1829	George W. Cruce	James & Nancy(Harrison)	HSTC c1732		1854
13 Oct 1830	Lafayette Cruce	Richard	JOHN 842	Hickory	1841
12 Apr 1866	John T. Gee		SERD 1260		1902
00 000 1854	C.M. Reese	G.C & Mary(Mansfield)	CSBA 1411	Pettis	----
00 000 0000	H.C. Reese	G.C & Mary(Mansfield) Tn/--	CSBA 1288	Johnson	1856
06 Aug 1858	David A. Robertson	William & Narcissa(Asher) Ky/Ky	LCDW 1142	Butler	1880

C U M B E R L A N D   C O U N T Y

BIRTHDATE	NAME OF BIOGRAPHEE	PARENTS/BIRTHPLACE/BIRTHDATE	SOURCE/PAGE	FIRST MO.CO.	DATE
18 Jun 1856	George W. Alexander	Milton & Martha A	LINN 789		1860
27 Dec 1853	Albert M. Allen	L.C & Fannie(Pace) **31/Mo31	HSTC 675	Linn	1858
18 Mar 1831	Lewis C. Allen	George & Parmelia(Crissman)Va87/**98	HSTC 675	Linn	1858
00 000 1826	E.C. Arnold	Louis M	LCKS 912		----
09 May 1817	Judge Edmund Bartlett	Edmund & Sally Va/Va	BATE 143	Morgan	1837
09 May 1817	Judge Edmund Bartlett	Edmund & Sally(Packwood) Va/Va	CSBA 1286	Morgan	1837
27 Oct 1804	William T. Beaty	Alexander & Catherine(Travis)Va/Md	HSTC 794	Saline	1830

CUMBERLAND COUNTY (CONT.)

BIRTHDATE	NAME OF BIOGRAPHEE	PARENTS/BIRTHPLACE/BIRTHDATE	SOURCE/PAGE	FIRST MO.CO.	DATE
00 000 1798	Rev. Hiram M. Bledsoe		LAFA	636		1832
19 Jul 1811	William Bridges		NLBM	904		1836
00 000 1803	Benjamin Campbell	Benjamin & Chloe(Farris) Va/Va	CMMB	1041		1836
08 Mar 1795	Hon. George Crawford		HOCO	943	Saint Charles	1819
05 Mar 1816	John Crawford	George Ky/--	COOP	971		----
24 Sep 1802	Col. John E. Crawford	John & Martha(Robinson) Pa/Pa	PETT	1087		1837
03 Jun 1838	Jesse B. Ellington	Samuel D & Mary A(Perkinson)	HOCO	1076		1839
00 000 1849	Thomas A. Emerson	Samuel R & Elizabeth(Bledsoe)Green/**HSTC	1080	Pettis	1851
00 000 1806	James Farrell		SEGO	1127		1831
13 Aug 1807	Frederick Hisaw		NLBM	1028		1836
31 Oct 1828	Josephine Hunter		BUCH	880		----
25 Aug 1820	John L. Jones	Claven & Elizabeth(Giles) Va/NC	CSBA	732	Linn	1838
06 Nov 1857	William B. Jones	Robert E & Sarah Ann(Morris)	LINN	612		----
00 000 1817	Rev. John P. Maxey		HOCO	1023		----
00 000 1807	William Mobley	James M & Peggy(Rawlen) SC/SC	CMMB	1074		1833
06 Aug 1828	John D. Mobley	Hezekiah Va/--	JOHN	643	Randolph	1840
16 Dec 1847	J.T. Pendleton	George L & Martha A(Cole) Ky/Va	LCDW	959	Hickory	----
00 Jan 1854	A.F. Snow	Frank G & Martha J(Ryan) Ky/Ky	CMMB	1008		1871
00 000 1825	Hon. James Tittington		LCDW	812	Miller	1850
12 Feb 1826	Dr. John Q.Tittington	Adam & Sarah(Smith) Ire/Va	LCDW	756		1850
15 Feb 1816	J.H. Trice	Tandy	CLIN	65		1846
00 000 1834	Thomas B. Turk		GREF	1030	Lawrence	1865
09 Apr 1820	John A. Wells	Joel & Martha(Allen) Ky/NC	HSTC	697		1851
23 Jan 1833	Cornelius P. Wright		RAY	685		1854

DAVIESS COUNTY

BIRTHDATE	NAME OF BIOGRAPHEE	PARENTS/BIRTHPLACE/BIRTHDATE	SOURCE/PAGE	FIRST MO.CO.	DATE
13 Sep 1853	Joseph R. Allgood	A.S & Matilda(Waltrip) Ky/Ky	SEGO 1152		1877
15 Jan 1831	J.B. Cabness	Milford & Louisa(Roland) Tn/--	CSBA 483	Jackson	1831
22 Aug 1838	James Clarkson	Jabez & Cynthia A(Small)Mercer/**	SEGO 963		1833
11 Nov 1837	Philip B. Coppage		SERD 932		----
12 Nov 1809	Dr. Pleasant M. Cox	Meredith & Margaret(McFarland)Va/Va	HSTC 1189	Lincoln	1818
14 Jul 1820	John Crow	James & Rhoda(Stemmons)Boyle88/Boyle	PIKE 846		1827
27 Aug 1855	Allen Daley	Dr. Frank & Narcissa(Haynes) Ky/Ky	VERN 635		1874
11 Nov 1876	Harry Henderson	John T Ky/--	SERD 1045		1882
01 Jul 1824	John H. Johnson	Jack & Lucy(Huston) NC/NC	GREF 836	LeClede	1877
15 Sep 1863	Dr. Samuel A. Johnson	John H & Anna M(Singleton)**24/32	GREF 1622	LeClede	1878
15 Mar 1828	G.B. Lancaster		CLIN 36	Buchanan	1844
21 Dec 1818	Louis Martin	John & Elizabeth(Atkins) Va/Va	SEGO 941		1828
00 000 0000	Mastin V. Owen	Martin B & Jane(Haggard)	CSBA 1184		----
28 Oct 1812	John J. Smith		PIKE 746		1817
13 Aug 1833	Sarah A. Thompson	Thomas & Lucinda(Marks) --/Va	BJAS 525		----
29 Dec 1816	Stephen T. Vititow	Daniel & Sarah V(Jones)	JASP 714		1837
17 Mar 1845	Isom A. Waltrip	Maston & Martha(Idson?) Ky/Ky	SEGO 1179		1859
28 Dec 1837	Judge James W. Waltrip	James & Martha(Biven) Ky/Ky	DUNK 271		1856
28 Dec 1837	Judge James W. Waltrip	John & Martha(Biven) Ky/Ky	SEGO 1179	Dunklin	1856
08 Mar 1844	Thomas Waltrip	John & Elizabeth(Downs) Ky/Ky	DUNK 273		1873

EDMONDSON COUNTY

BIRTHDATE	NAME OF BIOGRAPHEE	PARENTS/BIRTHPLACE/BIRTHDATE	SOURCE/PAGE	FIRST MO.CO.	DATE
19 Apr 1833	Henry R. Johnson	Henry & Elizabeth	SALI 713	Cooper	1846
14 Jan 1831	William Johnson	Henry & Elizabeth	SALI 713	Cooper	1846

EDMONDSON COUNTY (CONT.)

BIRTHDATE	NAME OF BIOGRAPHEE	PARENTS/BIRTHPLACE/BIRTHDATE	SOURCE/PAGE	FIRST MO.CO.	DATE
17 Jun 1827	Michael C. Jones	Felix W & Onor(Jones)	LCDW 1117		----
10 Mar 1844	Willis Merideth		RAY 610	Lafayette	1857
26 Oct 1832	J.D. Pace		PETT 898		1853
20 Jan 1841	J.M. Short		JACK 954	Saline	1847
04 Oct 1852	D.A. Smith		JASP 373		1869
00 000 1852	John Souders	Isaac & Avan(Amos)	SEGO 1089		1881
02 Oct 1841	Capt. J.H. Studivant	J.A & Adaline(Shackleford) Ky28/Ky30	HOCO 525	Benton	1867
20 Aug 1812	Lucinda Thompson		BUCH 1037		----
29 Dec 1825	Drury L. Woodson	Shadrack & Betsey(Haines) Va/Va	MOSH 502	Marion	1826

ELLIOTT COUNTY (NONE)

ESTILL COUNTY

BIRTHDATE	NAME OF BIOGRAPHEE	PARENTS/BIRTHPLACE/BIRTHDATE	SOURCE/PAGE	FIRST MO.CO.	DATE
28 Jan 1825	Stephen W. Barker	Elias & Elizabeth(Warner) Ky/Ky	PLAS 493		----
26 May 1842	D.R. Clark	William & Marion(McKiney) Va/Va	HSTC 678		1868
22 Feb 1805	James A. Clark	Bennett & Martha(Bullock) Va/Va	LINN 430	Howard	1817
26 Oct 1826	Ancel Collins	Michael & Rebecca(Noland) Va/Ky	KC& 83		1834
14 Mar 1826	Henry R. Davis	Martin W & Nancy(Ricketts)	HPCD 880	Clay	1839
00 000 1797	Samuel H. Green		SALI 545		----
01 Mar 1807	J.C. Harris	John & Fannie(Hill) Va/Va	CLPL 1098	Jackson	1838
30 Apr 1845	John M. Herndon		CLPL 1099	Buchanan	1871
26 Jul 1845	T.W. Holman	George W & Eliza J(Harris)	LCKS 1176		1857

Date	Name	Parents	Code	No.	Place	Year
01 May 1773	Jones Hoy	Philip & Margaret	ANPL	66	Howard	1815
23 Oct 1804	Snelling Johnson		CMMB	966		1819
08 Sep 1862	Isaac B. Kimbrell	Marion B & Catherine(Griffith) Ky/Ky	NLEM	942	Callaway	1872
18 Jul 1804	Dr. Elijah McLean	David & Leanora(Oldham) NO65/Ky71	FJWC	781	Howard	1810
29 Jul 1852	William H. McMonigle	Aaron B & Sarah J(Allison)Ky33/Ky34	CLPL	953		1853
27 Feb 1818	Sidney S. Meadows		NW	1559	Holt	1865
00 000 1816	John Noland		CLPL	864	Lafayette	1831
01 Feb 1807	Dr. W.W. Noland		JACK	991	Clay	1825
25 Apr 1813	Simpson Park		CLPL	960		1842
00 000 0000	William G. Price	Morton M & Fannie(Crosthwait)Harri/KyKC&		549		1885
08 Jan 1862	William J. Quinn	Sidney R	NW	862		----
24 Jan 1854	Annie C. Railsback		NW	1856		
02 Jul 1854	Daniel Railsback	David & Martha E(Tuggle) 08/--	DAGE	924	Daviess	1857
16 Sep 1869	William A. Railsback	James T & Mary Ann(Reed)Clark27/**36	CLCA	590	Platte	1871
18 Nov 1833	Dudley Roach		BUCH	994		1843
20 Jun 1847	J.M. Roberts	George & Polly E(Gum) Ky/Ky	ANDE	581		1856
02 Nov 1842	D.M. Scrivner	Martin D & Pamelia(Clements)Mad06/07	KC&	541	Clay	1855
04 Jul 1841	V.H. Scrivner	John & Hulda(Tudor) **/--	DAGE	438	Clay	----
00 000 0000	Susanna Simmons		KC&	264		1832
00 000 1856	J.T. Wagers	Simpson & Martha(Gentry) Ky/Ky	DAGE	617		----
00 000 1826	Riley Walker		NW	827		----
10 Apr 1827	Mitchell Warford	Jewell & Nancy(Servner) **/**	CSBA	1253		1867
00 000 0000	G.K. White		CLPL	883		1834
00 000 0000	R.C. White	Joel & Elizabeth	JACK	864	Platte	1843
23 Feb 1818	Elizabeth Willis		ANPL	154		1837
21 Jul 1828	Eli W. Wilson	Eli B & Nancy(Webber) Va/Va	LCDW	1157	Lafayette	1832

F A Y E T T E   C O U N T Y

BIRTHPLACE	NAME OF BIOGRAPHEE	PARENTS/BIRTHPLACE/BIRTHDATE	SOURCE/PAGE	FIRST MO.CO.	DATE
23 Jul 1846	Rev. Frank W. Allen		CALL 610		1858
02 Jul 1830	William M. Allen	James H & Sarah(McDowell)**01/--	HOCO 1089		1830
11 Aug 1807	Gen.David R. Atchison	William & Catherine(Allen)Pa/Ga	CLIN 179	Clay	1830
00 Aug 1807	Gen.David R. Atchison		BUCH 234		----
09 Aug 1840	David R. Atchison		NW 2055		----
08 Mar 1823	Alonzo C. Ball		NW 1425	Boone	1854
10 Oct 1826	Bright C. Barrow	David D & Jane(Gillstrap) Ky/Ky	RAMA 1144		1834
20 Jul 1860	Noah Beard	Andrew & Mary(Hughes) Ky/Ky	JOHN 706	Benton	1892
09 Sep 1809	Anthony Benning		LAFA 537		----
00 000 0000	Richard H. Benton		LAFA 500		1853
28 Sep 1841	R.H. Benton	Levi T & Harriet H(Chinn)Scott97/Harr	PLAS 500		1853
16 Sep 1854	Robert B. Berrie	Thomas & Christina(Brown)	PLAS 438		c1860
19 Feb 1821	Francis P. Blair	Francis Preston Va91/--	BENC 394		1842
10 May 1815	A.D. Blythe	Samuel & Jemima(Lay) Ky/Ky	CLPL 1092	Howard	----
00 000 0000	Thomas J. Boggs		HOCO 778		1821
00 000 1839	Elijah Boothe	Elijah & Sarah(Woods)	BOON 643		1840
00 000 1838	Parker T. Bowman	Robert T & Elizabeth E(Dickerson)	CMMB 751		1851
01 Sep 1824	Gabriel Boyce		FJWC 862		----
06 Feb 1838	Henry Boyer		SALI 834		1860
01 Sep 1824	James Bradley	Terry	BOON 1082		1824
06 Feb 1838	B. Gratz Brown	Mason	STLO 633		1849
05 Feb 1828	Col. William Brown	Samuel S & Anna(Harrison)	PLAS 622		----
00 Mar 1789	Durrett Bruce		BOON 549		1834
13 Feb 1800	Joseph T. Bryan	Enoch & Jane(Turner)	CALL 630		1830
09 Nov 1826	John W. Bush	Daniel & Frances(Sears) Ky/Ky	AUDR 874	Randolph	1866
17 Feb 1816	G.F. Campbell		MARI 667		1831
00 000 1804	Alfred W. Carr		BENC 320	Lincoln	1828

Date	Name	Parents	Origin	Place	County	No.	Year
03 Mar 1834	David Castleman	David & Virginia(Harrison)	Va/Va	HOCO		979	1855
00 Oct 1832	Capt.Lewis Castleman	Col.David & Virginia(Harrison)Wood/--HOCO		--HOCO	Saint Louis	1049	1879
28 Mar 1810	Taylor Chandler	Henry & Ragan(Coonrod)	Va/Pa	MARI		814	1832
17 Jan 1804	Joseph Charless	Joseph & Sarah(Jordan)	Ire72/De71	STLO		1390	1808
31 Jul 1873	Charles C. Chavose	John Franklin		GREF		1901	----
16 Jun 1834	Dr. George E. Chinn			HOCO	Johnson	498	1855
03 Oct 1825	Judge John Chrisman	Joseph & Eleanor H(Soper)	Va/Ky	CLPL		306	1851
23 Nov 1822	William Chrisman	Joseph & Eleanor(Soper)	Va00/Md	KC&		584	1848
00 000 1831	John W. Christian			PETT	Boone	1046	1840
19 Sep 1827	Charles C. Clayton			PIKE	Montgomery	606	1852
10 Apr 1810	Clinton Cockrill	Joseph & Nancy(Lucas)	Md/Md	ANPL		115	1842
10 Apr 1810	Clinton Cockrill	Joseph & Nancy(Lucas)	Md/Md	CLPL		996	1819
27 Dec 1811	Felix G. Cockrill	Joseph & Nancy(Lucas)	Md/--	ANPL		117	1842
10 Apr 1804	Fielding Cockrill	Joseph & Nancy(Lucas)	Md/--	ANPL		114	----
17 Feb 1822	John M. Collins	James & Mary(Christian)	Ky/Va	RAMA	Howard	671	1834
31 Mar 1821	James W. Cook			JACK		756	1856
23 Sep 1829	Dr. J.N. Coons	Joseph & Elizabeth(Nelson)Va91/**06		MARI		857	1857
20 Jan 1828	Moranda Cornett	Major William C	Mason97/--	BUCH		871	1839
06 Apr 1814	David P. Cox	Daniel & Lydia(Hurst)	Scott/Scott	AUDR	Boone	927	1836
09 Jul 1824	James N. Cox	Daniel & Lydia(Hurst)	--/Ky	RAMA	Boone	550	1836
12 Jun 1826	J.W. Crim	Martin & Margaret	Ky/Ky	MARI	Knox	694	1840
17 Oct 1836	Samuel M. Crim	Martin & Margaret	Ky/Ky	MARI	Knox	694	1840
16 May 1826	Henry Crumbaugh	John & Mary(Snyder)		BOON		850	1838
19 Sep 1823	Lawrence Daly	Loren	**/--	VERN	Boone	634	1874
00 000 0000	C.M. Dawson			JOHN		744	1846
18 Dec 1807	Thomas D. Dougherty	Robert & Sarah	Va/Va	JASP		930	1869
03 May 1849	Alfred O. Downing	Samuel & Amanda(Offatt)	--/Ky	LAFA		563	1857
12 Aug 1842	Samuel Downing	Samuel & Amanda		LAFA		563	1857
20 Jun 1808	A.R. Downing			MOSH	Knox	974	1830
25 Dec 1824	James R. Dudley	Robert & Sarah(Rogers)		MARI		646	1827
12 Jun 1807	Rev. James W. Dudley	General James	Va/--	AUDR	Boone	733	1857
01 Mar 1823	William Dudley	Robert G & Sarah(Rogers)		MARI		859	----

BIRTHPLACE	NAME OF BIOGRAPHEE	PARENTS/BIRTHPLACE/BIRTHDATE	SOURCE/PAGE	FIRST MO.CO.	DATE
26 Oct 1800	Nicholas Dysart	James & Martha (Cowden) Ky77/--	RAMA	673		1818
14 Nov 1806	John Ellis	Hezekiah & Nancy (Duvall)	MARI	647		1830
26 Jul 1825	Walter T. Featherston	Burwell & Sarah (Wymore)	MOSH	401	Randolph	1841
09 Sep 1826	W.L. Ferguson	John B Ky/--	CLIN	21		1853
14 Feb 1822	Charles H. Fink	John & Matilda (Hammond)	HPCD	889		1869
16 Jun 1811	Edmund W. Forbis	George & Mary (Perrigan) Ky/Ky	BOON	655		1837
28 Dec 1799	George B. Forbis		BOON	1028		1836
18 Jan 1835	William C. Foster	Anthony & Permelia (Carey) Clark/Clark	RAMA	554		1848
30 Oct 1802	James C. Fox		MOSH	552		1819
02 Mar 1793	Elder Franklin	Lewis	JACK	769		1829
00 Dec 1836	James P. Gaugh		JACK	773		1856
30 000 1802	Caleb W. Gay		MOSH	1137		1836
10 Feb 1837	W.W. Gray	William & Maria (Lamme)	HOCO	507		1867
22 Jan 1823	Edwin T. Guerin	Gen.Bertrand A & Frances (Hickey) Fr/Ky	PLAS	462		----
03 Feb 1837	John T. Haley	Ambrose & Malinda (Snyder) Bourbonll/Pa	RAMA	607		1870
11 Mar 1856	Robert B. Haligan		RAY	627		----
03 Oct 1816	Dr. Robert R. Hall	Andrew W & Sarah (Clifford) Va/Tn	RAMA	607		1850
02 Aug 1833	Elijah Happy		RAY	625		1850
05 Mar 1831	Harvey Happy	James	RAY	618		1852
22 Jul 1829	Elizabeth Hart		BUCH	1034		----
18 May 1810	Elder D.P. Henderson	James & Margaret (White)	LCKS	764	Boone	1849
16 Jun 1838	Charles C. Hersman	Joseph & Margaret (Scott)	CALL	749	Monroe	c1853
26 May 1839	Col. John J. Hickman	Hon. James L	BOON	881		----
19 Sep 1812	Harvey J. Higgins		LAFA	533		1840
13 Mar 1850	Daniel B. Holmes	John & Sally A (Gilbert) Va/Md	KC&	445		1872
19 Sep 1812	Harvey Higgins	Azariah & Elizabeth K NJ/Ky	PLAS	404		----
24 Jul 1834	John Hollyman	Thomas & Jane (Langdon)	MARI	956		1836
00 000 1811	Robert P. Huston	Robert	PETT	1051	Boone	1823

Birth Date	Name	Parents/Spouse	Code	No.	County	Death
03 Sep 1828	W.T. Hutchinson		PETT	957		1845
00 Aug 1814	Derrick A. January		STLO	1351		1836
31 May 1809	Thomas T. January	Thomas & Mary B(Thruston) Va68/Va	USBI	371	Saint Louis	1840
00 000 1827	Tilford Jenkins	Willis	CLPL	402		----
22 Mar 1820	James Johnson	Travers	HAME	555		----
11 Aug 1803	Sallie Keller		ANPL	159		1840
22 Oct 1841	Frank M. Kidd		SALI	740		1878
01 Feb 1854	Lewis P. Knoble	David & Charlotte(Myers) Ger/Oh	PLAS	356		----
00 000 1810	Warren Lewis		SEGO	875		----
15 Apr 1792	George Lincoln	Thomas	USBI	328	Clay	1822
28 Dec 1821	John K. Lincoln	George	NW	1064	Marion	c1840
28 Mar 1832	Capt. Charles B. McAfee	Robert & Martha(Cavanaugh)Ky/Va	USBI	796	Macon	c1834
28 Mar 1829	Judge Charles B. McAfee	Robert & Martha(Kavanaugh)Ky/Va	GREF	922		1829
31 Mar 1858	J.O. McBride	W.H & Mattie J(Randall) Ky/Ky	CSBA	1348		1860
02 Aug 1822	Robert D. McCann	Robert D & Susan(Dawson) Clark/Bourbo	MOSH	573		1839
19 Aug 1839	William D. McClanahan	Elijah & Harriet(Dunlap)	CSBA	568	Jackson	1851
00 Sep 1795	Robert McConnell		PIKE	617		1800
06 Feb 1834	Dr. John McDowell	Joseph N & Amanda V(Drake) --/Ky	USBI	125	Saint Louis	1840
00 000 1788	Robert Masterson	James Va/--	MARI	651	Saint Louis	1816
04 Dec 1826	Preston H. Minor	Daniel & Elizabeth(Vance) Va97/Va93	CALI	1184		1852
07 Feb 1816	Butler Moore	Butler & Courtney(Webster) Va/Va	PLAS	132		----
00 May 1808	John B. Moore	Wharton R & Mary(Browning) Va/Va	CALL	796		1819
01 Jul 1817	Wilburn K. Nation	SC/--	DAVI	677	Callaway	1833
00 000 1809	George B. Nelson	James & Elizabeth(Boone) Va69/Va76	LCKS	806	Marion	1829
00 000 1783	Robert Nichols		CALL	594	Boone	1828
20 Nov 1811	J.W. Noe	George & Catherine(Smith) Ky/Va	BOON	601		----
05 Oct 1845	Alfred W. Offutt		CALL	938		----
11 Apr 1835	Otho Offutt	Samuel R & Eliza(Hayes) Va/Va	CLPL	864		1843
01 May 1825	Dr. John C. Oliver	Dr. Presley T & Jane(Christian)Ky/Ky	RAMA	499	Washington	1850
01 Jun 1824	Joseph S. Oots	Sampson & Mary Va/Pa	SALI	595		1855
05 Jun 1828	Col. George O'Rear	Jeremiah & Lydia(Westbrook)Va78/Va83	JASP	565		c1851
05 Sep 1853	Hon. Howard S. Parker	Warren O & Rebecca E(McConnell)Ky/Ky	LINC	361	Saint Louis	1874

BIRTHDATE	NAME OF BIOGRAPHEE	PARENTS/BIRTHPLACE/BIRTHDATE	SOURCE/PAGE	FIRST MO.CO.	DATE
12 Oct 1829	Hezekiah E. Patrick	Robert & Dorcus(Owen) Va/Ky	RAMA 680		1830
04 Sep 1844	Edward C. Pew	John & Mary(Longmore) Va/Va	RAMA 503	Saint Louis	1860
27 Apr 1821	Dr. Robert C. Prewitt	Robert C & Elizabeth M(Elgin)Va/Md	LINC 605		1835
29 Oct 1808	William C. Prewitt	Vaul A & Mildred(Ellis)	PIKE 588		1829
01 Apr 1825	Alexander Proctor	Rowland T & Diana(Chapman)**/Cumberl	KC& 18	Randolph	1836
00 000 0000	Capt. William A. Redd	Waller & Rebecca	LAFA 654		----
06 Aug 1816	Adam K. Reyburn		RAY 578	Boone	c.1817
00 000 1845	Dr. T.F. Risk	John C & Mary Ann(Hues) NY/Va	LCKS 1206		1877
00 000 1823	J.V. Robinson	John & Fannie(Berry) Va93/Va03	CSBA 595		----
19 Nov 1828	Joseph K. Rogers	William & Frances	BOON 929	Marion	1830
21 Apr 1805	William H. Russell		BENC 402	Fulton	1834
21 Apr 1805	William H. Russell		CALL 268		1834
15 Dec 1825	John Sacry	George	RAY 611		1854
30 Apr 1819	John J. Sanders	Joel	HOCH 1107		1828
25 Jun 1799	Henry Schooler	Benjamin & Martha(Foster) Va/Va	PIKE 625		1828
26 Jul 1798	Henry Schooler		PIKE 726		1828
23 Mar 1819	Capt. Robert Scott	John & Sallie(McDaniel) Ky/Ky	CSBA 514		1866
08 May 1834	J.R. Schrest	John & Lydia(Vaughn) **11/Ky08	KC& 473		1854
00 000 0000	Lafayette Sexton		SERD 644	Bollinger	1840
29 Oct 1843	Reuben N. Shanks	William B & Lucy(Harris)	MOSH 1081		1845
00 000 1820	G.B. Sharp	James & Jane(Calahan) Kenton97/NC93	LCKS 833		1868
15 Oct 1839	William Shepherd	William & Phoebe	SALI 619	Monroe	1841
00 000 0000	Dr. R.W. Shipley		JACK 842		1865
08 Oct 1800	David H. Shock		BOON 788	Howard	1820
26 Nov 1834	Samuel Shryock	Daniel	BOON 729		1850
12 Feb 1853	Marie R. Sloan	James R	COOP 1155		1853
08 Apr 1819	John H. Snodderly		NODA 554	Page	1856
14 Feb 1828	Dr. H.C. Spears	George C	PETT 877	Cass	1854

Date	Name	Parents (origin)	Code	No.	County	Year
22 Jan 1816	William H. Stapleton	Thomas H & Eliza(Sheely)	HOCO	411		1816
23 Mar 1820	J.W. Steele	Rev. Brice & Elizabeth(Thornsbury)	Ire/Pa	1079		1847
05 Feb 1801	Elder O.C. Steele	Elder Brice & Elizabeth	CLPL	1118		1841
16 Jun 1838	John K. Stitfield		CLIN	148		1856
00 000 1795	Demetrius A. Sutton		ANPL	99		---
16 Mar 1819	Col. William F. Switzer	Simeon	BOON	943	Howard	1826
01 Aug 1811	James B. Taylor	Maj.Jonathan & Mary(Ashley)Va/Va	RAMA	691	Marion	1836
00 Nov 1836	Austin Thompson		RAY	793		1856
21 Jan 1845	John W. Thomson	Capt.Pike M & Elizabeth E **/**	SALI	633		1848
25 Aug 1819	Capt. Pike M. Thomson	Captain John & Ann	SALI	630		1819
10 Jun 1807	Robert W. Thorpson	Fulton & Martha(Lindsey) Pa/Pa	SCMW	703		---
10 Jun 1807	William B. Thompson		SCMW	702	Lincoln	1829
00 000 1790	David Todd		CHHO	195		---
00 000 1790	Judge David Todd		HOCO	249		---
00 000 0000	James W. Tolson		FGRU	350		---
01 Oct 1843	John W. Tompkins	Whitefield & Elizabeth(Ingles)Jessam	PLAS	606		1846
02 Dec 1818	John E.M. Triplett	Hedgemon & Margaret(Eddins)Va/Va	BOON	1166	Carroll	---
17 Jan 1827	Major Elijah True	William & Ellen(White) Va/**	PLAS	590		1831
31 Jul 1809	Jacob Walker	Henry	CLIN	177	Clay	---
29 Nov 1821	Rev.Joseph W. Wallace		CAUD	234		---
05 Oct 1845	Alfred O. Washington	Edward S & Ann E(Ellzey) 08/--	CALL	938	Montgomery	1849
10 May 1839	Marshall Washington	Edward S & Anna E(Elsea)	SCMW	950	Callaway	1849
12 Jun 1798	James D. Wason		NW	922	Clay	1837
20 May 1851	James W. Weldon	Dr. James & Margaret(McConnell)Pa/**SCMW		705		1859
15 Sep 1812	Jeremiah White		NW	1727		1834
03 Sep 1841	Henry A. Whitt		DAVI	810		1847
14 Apr 1840	John T. Whitt	-- & Rebecca(Patterson) Ky/Ky	CALI	424	Daviess	1844
13 Oct 1841	Abner Wilson	Benjamin R & Agnes W	MOSH	612	Randolph	1855
14 Jan 1829	George W. Wymore	Samuel & Eliza(Downing)	CLPL	371		1843
12 Jan 1800	John T. Young		RAY	765	Jackson	1827

FLEMING COUNTY

BIRTHDATE	NAME OF BIOGRAPHEE	PARENTS/BIRTHPLACE/BIRTHDATE	SOURCE/PAGE	FIRST MO.CO.	DATE
26 Jan 1831	William Adair	Abner J & Mary(Adkins) Ky/Ky	HSTC 660		c1841
04 Jan 1808	Priscilla Alexander	William & Cynthia	CALL 595		1829
10 May 1845	Joseph Anderson	Johnse Ky/--	CLPL 1043		1849
09 Sep 1855	J.H. Armstrong	H.J Ky/--	PETT 607	Lexington	1862
13 Feb 1831	Captain M. Bateman	Newton & Margaret	BOON 747		1864
11 Mar 1819	Andrew Beckner		GRUN 534		1841
23 Jul 1825	George W. Belt	Joseph C & Mary(Armstrong) Md/Ky	USBI 614	Platte	1839
20 Dec 1834	Samuel Boyd, Esq.	Wilson P & Susan E(Lacy)	SALI 771		1859
14 Nov 1829	Alfred A. Brown	James & Luannah(Secrest) **/**	NLBM 814		1870
12 Nov 1820	William Buckley	William & Permelia(Eaton) Md/Ky	CSBA 640		1866
27 Jul 1839	Elmo Campbell	James S & Frances J(Butler)**19/**13	NODA 524	Clay	1852
08 Jul 1829	Dr. W.H. Carpenter	William Ky/--	JOHN 309		1852
01 Nov 1830	James I. Cassity	William F Montgomery03/--	LINN 853		1851
20 Oct 1824	Ambrose D. Christy	Joseph K & Ann B(Crosthwait)Va/Va	USBI 649	Linn	1853
08 Aug 1850	J.M. Christy	Ambrose B & Elizabeth J(Fagan)**/**	CSBA 1122		1871
04 May 1845	Taylor P. Christy	Philip W & Nancy Ky/Ky	LINN 760		1853
15 Dec 1841	James V. Cowan	John H & Elizabeth(Harper)	VERN 500		1876
09 Jun 1843	Alfred L. Crain	William E & Elizabeth(Abrams)	MOSH 1049		c1860
03 Oct 1839	Joseph J. Crain		LINN 536		1870
04 Sep 1830	Thomas J. Crain		DAVI 529	Holt	1855
03 Nov 1820	William A. Crain	William Va84/--	RAY 528		----
06 Jan 1830	Lawrence T. Davis		JOHN 616		1866
00 000 0000	Washington F. Deatley		VERN 399		----
31 Jul 1821	John Denton	Joseph & Dradenna(Hunt) --/Tn	CSBA 490	Benton	1839
19 Dec 1839	William B. Douglass	Charles B & Rebecca	LAFA 611	Jackson	1844
16 Jan 1831	Samuel H. Fitch	Nathan & Mary(Fitzgerald) Ky/Ky	CSBA 556	Johnson	1867
00 000 1823	Andrew M. Fuqua	Col.Washington & Rebecca(Wilson	HSTC 1082	Osceola	1867
23 Jun 1850	James E. Fuqua	Andrew M & Malina(Gross)	HSTC 1082		1867
22 Jun 1852	Thomas F. Gatts	William & Susan(Tucker) Oh/Oh	MARI 927		1870

Date	Name	Relation	Parents	Origin	Code	No.	County	Year
24 Jul 1848	Henry W. Harris	Dr. N. W			HOCO	1095	Linn	1856
22 Apr 1820	John L. Harrison	James B			RAY	616	Callaway	1841
00 000 0000	Nancy Hobbs				SCMW	737		1846
27 Sep 1837	John H. Howe	J . D & Margaret A (Henderson)			CALL	667		1846
30 Jun 1814	Alexander M. Huls				NODA	571		1856
00 000 1829	Rev. John W. Hunt	James M			NW	1894		----
03 Dec 1797	Gen.Benjamin F. Jackson	Judge Wade M & Sarah M(Bass)			HOCO	550	Boone	c1822
04 Apr 1806	Gov.Claiborne F. Jackson	Dempsey & Mary(Pickett)			SALI	403	Howard	1826
00 000 1806	Thomas Jarvis	Daniel & Martha(Thompson)			FJWC	910	Saint Louis	1836
00 000 1806	Thornton Jarvis				SERD	1127		1845
21 Jul 1814	William Jones				NODA	993		1857
03 Oct 1834	William K. Jones				BUCH	1014	Buchanan	1860
12 Oct 1837	A. J. Lee	Joseph & Abigail		Va/Ky	GRUN	330		----
17 Sep 1824	Elizabeth Leeper	Samuel & Nancy(Prine)			NW	1486		1816
00 000 0000	Felix G. Logan				SCMW	737		1819
00 000 0000	Charles W. McIntyre				USBI	670	Boone	1858
03 Jan 1834	William Mangus				SALI	611		1858
05 Dec 1844	James P. Mayhew	Thomas & Rebecca(Smith)		**17/**22	NODA	1021		1858
20 Jul 1840	William H. Mayhew	Thomas & Rebecca(Smith)		**17/**22	NODA	1021		1858
13 Apr 1822	W.T. Mers	John & Nancy(Thompson)		Pa/Ky	CSBA	506		1857
06 Jun 1829	H. Metcalfe	John P & Rebecca			HOCO	456		1857
04 May 1832	Robert P. Metcalfe				LAFA	667	Howard	1878
22 Nov 1848	Prof. R.D. Moore	Thomas T & Delilah(Stout)		Md/--	HSTC	752		1854
29 May 1817	Col.Benjamin F. Northcott	Rev.Benj.&Martha(Odell)		NC70/--	LINN	771		1869
02 Mar 1850	C.W. Nute	Charles G & Elizabeth		NY/--	HOLT	466		1855
21 Sep 1847	Dr. Charles T.Pepper	Enoch S & Sarah R(Tebbs)		Va/Va	PIKE	585		1852
08 Jan 1845	Hon. Enoch Pepper				PIKE	717		1877
29 Dec 1838	Samuel G. Park	John H & Elizabeth(Shanklin)			HOAT	279		1850
09 Dec 1819	J.F. Pitts				BUCH	1016	Platte	----
00 000 1835	Thomas J. Porter	John S & Elvira(VanCamp)		Ky/Ky	PETT	715		1878
26 Feb 1815	Coleman Rawlings	Aaron & Sophia(Fouch)		Va/Ky	HOCO	977		1843
00 000 0000	Rebecca Rawlings				LAFA	600	Johnson	

BIRTHDATE	NAME OF BIOGRAPHEE	PARENTS/BIRTHPLACE/BIRTHDATE	SOURCE/PAGE	FIRST MO.CO.	DATE
00 000 0000	George W. Reams	John & --(Swain) Pa/--	BOON 1128		1839
25 Sep 1834	James P. Ringo	David D	BUCH 874	Platte	1844
22 Apr 1834	George W. Rose	Capt. James Ellis & Kitty(Robinson)	USBI 418	Platte	1856
20 Sep 1829	Major John T. Ross		JACK 879	Saint Joseph	1857
00 000 1840	William E. Seamans	Isaac Va00/--	JOHN 729		1849
13 May 1832	David B. Shepard	Robert & Lydia	RAY 641		1868
15 Jan 1827	Judge Jackson C. Summers		CLPL 965		1850
06 Nov 1843	Greenup Sutton		BUCH 1018		1855
21 Oct 1842	Lizzie Taylor		BUCH 1055		----
13 Nov 1816	Adam Terhune		NODA 842		1841
00 Nov 1836	Austin Thompson		RAY 793		1856
14 May 1819	Benjamin Tout		JASP 921		1881
30 Aug 1851	John W. Trimble	Robin & Susan(Triplett)	LINN 796		c1871
25 Apr 1816	Elijah Watson		BUCH 1018		1845
00 Oct 1829	Judge John T. Wells		HOAT 964		1857
09 Oct 1829	J.T. Wells	Jeremiah & Harriett	BATC 632	Holt	1861
21 Mar 1829	Nelson Williams		CLIN 217	Clay	1851
10 Jul 1822	W.T. Wilson		RAY 747		1842
30 Apr 1830	James D. Wyatt	Micajah & Mary(Denmen) Ky/Ky	BOON 733		1855

F L O Y D   C O U N T Y

BIRTHDATE	NAME OF BIOGRAPHEE	PARENTS/BIRTHPLACE/BIRTHDATE	SOURCE/PAGE	FIRST MO.CO.	DATE
06 Dec 1832	S. Akers	William N & Lucinda(Garrett)Ire/--	JACK 899	Cass	1837
27 Jun 1839	Alexander B. Cecil		CSBA 704		1868
00 000 1807	Roberson Morris	Daniel & Mary(Crosswight) Va/Va	ASPS 862		----

BIRTHDATE	NAME OF BIOGRAPHEE	PARENT'S/BIRTHPLACE/BIRTHDATE	SOURCE/PAGE	FIRST MO.CO.	DATE
12 Sep 1859	Jacob D. Allen	Richard N & Jannette	BATE 139		1875
01 May 1848	Dr. W.H. Allen	R. N	CSBA 1362	Carroll	1871
17 Jun 1811	Hon. Willis Anderson	Elijah & Rachel(Downing)**87/Garra89	LCKS 990	Marion	1824
10 Mar 1835	W.S. Bacon	Robert & Elizabeth(Jeffries)	GREH 879	Cooper	1854
00 000 1842	John H. Boyer		SALI 806		1871
10 Feb 1865	Clarence A. Brakeman		NW 840		----
26 Dec 1820	F. Brock		RAY 659	Clay	1827
09 Dec 1807	Benjamin J. Brown		RAY 544		1832
17 Dec 1823	Henderson Brown	L & Mary M(Kidd) Ky/Va.	HOCO 493		1829
01 Mar 1831	Samuel Calvert	Isaac & Mildred(Chambers) Va/Va	HSTC 732		1858
27 Aug 1826	Thomas N. Carpenter	Wilson D	JOHN 738		----
21 Apr 1818	Samuel Coffman		NW 1703		1822
04 Mar 1814	John C. Cole	Aquilla	FJWC 874		1818
00 000 1810	Jacob Cox	Thomas & Jane(Smith) Ky/Ky	MOSH 365		1836
13 Feb 1836	William R. Crockett	Dr. Samuel B & Anna(Instone)**/**	VERN 630	Cooper	1860
00 000 1844	Thomas V. Foster		LAFA 504	Saline	1851
13 Sep 1833	Dr. J. W. Frazier	Thomas & Lucy(McAtee) Ky/Ky	MARI 647	Ralls	1836
05 Jul 1840	P.A. Gibbs		SALI 783		1850
26 Dec 1841	George C. Goodnight	Thomas	JOHN 450		1849
00 000 1814	William L. Graves	John D & Catherine(Thomison)Md76/Scot	LCKS 749		1831
00 000 0000	Leroy C. Griffin		CALL 772		1824
11 May 1816	Dr.Richard T. Hawkins		PIKE 413		1839
06 Apr 1826	Judge Samuel F. Hawkins	William & Mary(Crockett)	CSBA 1293	Johnson	1857
00 000 1810	Col.B.F. Hickman		STLO 1476		----
08 Mar 1810	Col. Benjamin F. Hickman		BENC 432	Saint Louis	1841
10 Oct 1819	Capt. Edwin A. Hickman	William & Elizabeth(Dickins)Va/Ky	USBI ---		1840
13 Mar 1828	William P. Hubbell	Captain William D Ct97/--	RAY 563	Howard	1840
13 Mar 1828	William P. Hubbell	Captain William D Ct/--	NW 1095	Howard	1840

FRANKLIN COUNTY (CONT.)

BIRTHDATE	NAME OF BIOGRAPHEE	PARENTS/BIRTHPLACE/BIRTHDATE	SOURCE/PAGE	FIRST MO.CO.	DATE
11 Oct 1825	Warren M. Hudgins	William & Nancy(Blake)	CALI 975	Ray	1856
25 Nov 1850	William T. Hughes		DAVI 837		1885
00 Jul 1862	Hon. H.S. Julian		KC& 608		1832
20 Feb 1822	Durrett R. Lawrence	Alexander & Elizabeth(Laughlin)	CALL 869		1840
00 Jan 1824	Mattie A. Livingston	Thomas & Sallie(Riddle) Ky/Ky	JACK 741		1840
13 May 1833	Chapman H. McDonald	John & Elizabeth(Laughlin)	HSTC 716	Audrain	1838
03 Feb 1818	Anthony C. McKee		CLIN 142		1854
00 000 1826	Thomas J. McMahill	Charles F	---- 1904		----
10 Mar 1809	Benjamin P. Major		BENC 519	Lewis	1835
10 Aug 1835	Minor Major	Oliver T & Nancy **/**	SALI 648		1848
00 000 0000	Mrs. R.M. Major	John S & Lucinda S(Slaughter)	JACK 866		1868
04 Mar 1829	Dr. T.T. Major	Oliver T & Nancy T(Gunnell)Va/Ky	PETT 692	Saline	1848
19 Dec 1825	W. Boon Major		LAFA 590		1847
22 Sep 1804	Eli Mars	Samuel & Mary(Baker	BOON 777		1820
11 Aug 1848	David S. Miller	J.D & Mildred(Haggerty) Ky/Ky	JASP 358	Lafayette	1859
00 000 0000	Joseph D. Miller	Aaron & Mary(Zook) Pa/--	PLAS 564		1856
25 May 1811	Samuel Nash	Jeremiah Va/--	CLIN 196	Clay	1825
01 Jul 1817	Wilburn K. Nation	SC/--	DAVI 677	Callaway	1833
20 Mar 1829	George H. Nelson	John F & Susan(Lowen)	MARI 740		c1835
00 Sep 1800	Col. William M. Newberry		SERD 791	Madison	c1818
03 Jan 1818	Harrison Noble	William & Hannah(Miner) Va/Pa	HSTC 738	Harrison	1842
22 Oct 1819	Hon. Mordecai Oliver		USBI 675	Ray	1830
15 Jun 1820	James C. Pollard	Abner & Martha	SALI 613	Callaway	1838
08 Nov 1817	James L. Pruette		BOON 923		1861
27 Jul 1823	John Quinn		LCKS 816	Marion	1825
17 Dec 1815	Col. John B. Reddish	Ransom & Mary(Butler) Va/--	LCKS 1204		1830
05 Oct 1819	Thomas S. Richardson	James A	BENC 513		1829
00 000 1810	Richard F. Richmond	--/NC	BENC 451		1841

BIRTHDATE	NAME OF BIOGRAPHEE	PARENTS/BIRTHPLACE/BIRTHDATE	SOURCE	PAGE	FIRST MO.CO.	DATE
26 Jan 1815	O. Roberts		NODA	1026	Andrew	1843
12 May 1853	Frank E. Scrogin	Thomas D & America(Curry) Ky/Ky	AUDR	533	Pike	1856
28 Jul 1821	William H. Shannon	Lewis S & Elizabeth(Ellison)Woodf/Ky	CLPL	442	Clinton	1857
12 Apr 1825	John W. Shouse	John & Sarah(Slaughter)	NW	1258	Clay	1826
12 Apr 1825	John W. Shouse	John & Sarah(Slaughter)	CLPL	503		1827
20 Dec 1827	Dr.Achilles F. Sneed	Landon C & Elizabeth(Gibson)**/**	BOON	730		1853
30 Jan 1818	John S. Thomason	William & Sarah(McQuilty) Ky/Ky	NW	1128		1836
02 Dec 1818	John Triplett	Hedgemon & Margaret(Eddins)Va/Va	HOCH	1166	Carroll	1846
06 Dec 1830	Hon. G.G. Vest		USBI	521	Pettis	1852
12 Aug 1862	Dr. James A. Waterman	Rev. J. H	NW	1842		----
11 Dec 1828	Charles S. Williams	Andrew P **/**	LCKS	854	Marion	1830
02 Feb 1830	John W. Wilson		BUCH	942		1851
17 Jun 1832	P.V. Wise		BUCH	945		---
00 000 1850	Hon. John M. Wood	Richard J	LCKS	987		1855
00 000 0000	Richard J. Wood	William & Helen(Julian) Eng/--	LCKS	986		1855
00 000 1830	John H. Wright	John & Ann(Poague) **99/**04	LCKS	855		1840

FULTON COUNTY

BIRTHDATE	NAME OF BIOGRAPHEE	PARENTS/BIRTHPLACE/BIRTHDATE	SOURCE	PAGE	FIRST MO.CO.	DATE
15 Oct 1876	Herbert L. Boaz		SERD	1210		1902
09 Dec 1850	Dr. A.A. Bordurant	John S & Julia D(Edmiston)	SEGO	958		1875
27 Oct 1847	Judge James M. Douglass	Alexander T & Elizabeth(Mott)	SERD	571	Dunkin	1850
27 Oct 1847	Judge James M. Douglass	A. T & Elizabeth	DUNK	189		1850
12 Jul 1827	William R. Fields	Absalom & Lucy Ann(Hester) Tn/NCO?	SEGO	1193		1850
15 Feb 1860	Charles P. Hawkins	Dr. James M & Matilda(Harris)Tn/Ky	SEGO	1164		1871
22 Jun 1842	Collins B. Hodges	Samuel & Nancy(Cane) Va/Va	CLPL	947		----
07 Oct 1825	James Hodges	Samuel & Nancy(Roberts) Va/Ky	CLPL	946		1851
25 Nov 1850	William T. Hughes	Va/Ky	DAVI	837		1851
02 Jul 1842	Francis M. Lester	Lewis & Polly Ann(Gamble) Ga/Mis	SEGO	1164		1856
23 Dec 1871	John N. O'Connor		SERD	1239		---

G A L L A T I N C O U N T Y

BIRTHDATE	NAME OF BIOGRAPHEE	PARENTS/BIRTHPLACE/BIRTHDATE	SOURCE	PAGE	FIRST MO.CO.	DATE
19 Dec 1849	J.P. Bennett		BUCH	676		1869
01 Jun 1851	Andrew Craig	Albert G & Virginia J(Brooking)Ky/Ky	NODA	952		1871
11 Sep 1847	J.M. Craig	A.G & Virginia(Brooking) Ky/Ky	NODA	743		1873
01 Feb 1847	S.L. Craig		NODA	743		1873
01 Mar 1812	Moses Furnish	James & Keziah Ann(Ray)	ASPS	970		1841
00 000 1847	S.P. Gibson	John E & Cynthia A	JOHN	622		1855
04 Feb 1846	John W. Goode	Thomas J & Martha A(Callaway)Va15/Ky	ANDE	562	Cass	1847
00 000 1819	Mordecai A. Jackson	Mordecai & Nancy(Cook) Va/Scott	SEGO	873		----
30 Oct 1841	John F. Kenney	William N & Jane(White) Ky/Ky	CIPL	1063		1856
07 Jul 1835	William T. Marsh	William B & Maria(Hilton)	MARI	669	Saint Louis	1869
11 Sep 1846	Benjamin G. Matthews		HOCH	1209	Linn	1856
31 Jul 1833	G.W. Montgomery		RAY	659	Clinton	c1856
00 Feb 1864	Dr. R.E. Montgomery	G.W & Agnes(Clevenger)	NW	959		1852
22 Sep 1839	Lucretia Robinson		BUCH	970		----
00 000 1814	Willis B. Sale		LCKS	1112		1851
00 000 1849	H.B. Tunstall		LAFA	493		1864
14 Dec 1828	John G. Turner	George & Rebecca(Ramey)	NODA	847		1870

G A R R A R D C O U N T Y

BIRTHDATE	NAME OF BIOGRAPHEE	PARENTS/BIRTHPLACE/BIRTHDATE	SOURCE	PAGE	FIRST MO.CO.	DATE
00 Dec 1795	William M. Adams	John Va/--	HOCO	856		1816
18 Nov 1809	Francis Alexander		RAMA	685	Monroe	1836
01 Oct 1826	James R. Allega	John & Elizabeth(Singleton)	HOCH	715		1837
11 Mar 1825	Eastham Allen	Erasmus & Lucy Ky/Ky	JACK	930		1856

Date	Name	Parents	States	Code	No.	Location	Year
13 Sep 1829	N. F. Arbunkle	Drinkard & Lucretia(Maxey)	Ky/Ky	RAMA	989		1869
23 Feb 1823	George B. Arnold	Isaac & Jane(Bryant)	**/**	CSBA	529		1850
01 Aug 1829	George M. Austin			RAY	625	Cass	1856
05 Jan 1829	Eliza Baker			GRUN	632		----
00 000 1816	William R. Ballinger			RAY	593		1871
07 Jul 1818	H.P. Banks	Gerard & Elizabeth(Mills)	Va/Md	MARI	758		1830
07 Jul 1814	James M. Brasfield			ASPS	1041	Shelby	1839
20 Nov 1816	Dr. John M. Bryant	George S & Kesiah		USBI	810		1850
21 Jun 1828	Simeon A. Bryant			PIKE	842	Lincoln	1830
00 000 0000	Stephen Bryant			HAME	498		1851
00 000 0000	Thomas O. Bryant			HAME	497		1856
21 Nov 1824	W. S. Bryant			PIKE	843		1838
01 Oct 1853	G. D. Carpenter	Christian R & Elizabeth		GRUN	617		1854
28 Mar 1847	R. J. Carpenter			FGRU	377		1854
03 Jun 1825	Matthew Chandler	William & Frances(Coy)	Tn/Ky	AUDR	447		1866
00 000 0000	Charles Denny			HOCO	373		1816
05 Feb 1823	Rev. Willis E. Dockery	Alexander & Nancy(Ware)	Ky/Ky	CALI	1089		1834
00 000 1839	J. Russell Duncan	Alvis & Ann(Palmer)	Tn/Ky	CWMB	1110		1844
00 000 1794	Reuben Elliott			JASP	526		----
24 Mar 1825	John C. England	James & Nancy(Campbell)	**/**	CLPL	466	Grundy	1855
16 May 1845	Lewis L. Evans			BUCH	977	Clinton	1850
20 Mar 1809	Milton Findley	John & Margaret(Brown)		CALL	655	Warren	1832
00 000 1838	J.M. Gallemore	Jonathan R & Sarah B(Dismukes)	Va/Ky	HOCH	1079		1856
19 Dec 1829	John Gardner			SCMW	732		c1857
17 Dec 1827	Elijah Gates	John & Mary(Maupin)	Ky/Madison	NW	1923	Platte	1846
29 Jan 1795	John Graves	William	Va/--	CALI	1100	Boone	1818
12 Oct 1820	Mason Gulley			GRUN	584		1865
15 Dec 1843	John T. Harmon	Jacob I		CLPL	469		1849
22 Jun 1809	George Heard	John & Jane(Stevenson)		PETT	664	Saline	1817
00 000 0000	Silas Hombs			ASPS	1170		1818
00 000 1820	Abner Hubbard			NW	864	Boone	----
23 May 1825	Rev. James H. Hubbard			RAMA	1027		1825

BIRTHDATE	NAME OF BIOGRAPHEE	PARENTS/BIRTHPLACE/BIRTHDATE	SOURCE/PAGE		FIRST MO.CO.	DATE
03 Nov 1821	Thomas J. Hubbard		CLIN	158		1841
30 Jan 1836	F. Kennedy		CLIN	35		1854
00 000 1807	John Kerby		HOCO	592	Clinton	1829
21 May 1801	Adriel King		RAY	615	Boone	c1827
00 000 1823	Walter Lear		LCKS	1063		1853
00 000 0000	C.W. Long		LAFA	492		1878
22 Sep 1806	Alexander McMutry		MOSH	932	Ralls	1831
14 Jan 1818	Burl Masters		GRUN	589	Chariton	----
09 Mar 1819	W.F. Maxey	Boaz & Judith Va/Va.	MOSH	579		1831
20 Apr 1826	James A. Millan		BUCH	832	Marion	1831
18 Sep 1812	George W. Moberly		GRUN	461	Monroe	1832
30 Nov 1809	A.S. O'Bannon	William B & Susanah(Thompson)Va/Ky	CSBA	650		1856
24 Dec 1837	James S. Onsot	Levi & Judith(Ball) Ky08/Ky	NODA	811	Buchanan	1844
08 Oct 1837	Norman Porter	William & Sallie(Richardson)Ky/Tn	LINC	603		1859
02 Apr 1825	Stephen Pulliam	William & Elizabeth	GRUN	632		1851
02 Apr 1825	Judge John J. Price		JOHN	723	Saint Louis	1828
01 Oct 1825	John B. Reid	Col. Garland & Elizabeth(Woods)	RAMA	571		1839
11 Jul 1840	Dr. John T. Rothwell	Fountain & Jennie Va/Ky	BOON	675		1858
30 Jan 1829	Mary A. Rothwell	Dr. John & China.	CALL	822		1832
02 Sep 1831	Rev. William R. Rothwell	Dr. Charles & China(Renfro)Va/Va	USBI	320	Callaway	1831
19 Jan 1811	L.D. Sherrow	Reuben	GRUN	551		1852
26 May 1823	Elijah W. Shrewsbury	Drew & Anna.	CLCA	527		1842
02 Mar 1848	E.A. Simpson	Benjamin & Pauline(Arnold) **/**	LCKS	1123		1857
02 Mar 1848	J.W. Simpson	Benjamin & Pauline(Arnold)	LCKS	1123		1857
12 Nov 1819	Henry Smith		BUCH	995		----
22 Dec 1833	John A. Smith	Flavius J & Permelia(Long) **/Mad	LCKS	835	Monroe	1834
05 Aug 1828	Alexander F. Stephens	John L & Mary(Sams)	BOON	792		1838
17 Nov 1815	James L. Stephens	Elijah NC/Va	BOON	955		1819

BIRTHDATE	NAME OF BIOGRAPHEE	PARENTS/BIRTHPLACE/BIRTHDATE		SOURCE/PAGE		FIRST MO.CO.	DATE
25 Jun 1877	George Sutton	Mont & America		FGRU	734		----
06 Apr 1828	Eliza Terrill	Robert & Mary(Beasley)		MARI	627		1830
02 Apr 1820	Reuben Taylor	Dudley & Anna(Myes)	Va/Va	RAMA	603		----
00 000 0000	J. H. Terrill	-- & Catherine(Turner)		AUDR	543	Marion	1838
00 000 0000	James H. Terrill			MARI	766		1830
08 Jun 1850	Oliver Terrill	Henry T & Fannie		SALI	732	Boone	1878
17 Nov 1823	Judge Oliver T. Terrill	John & Sarah(Henderson)	Va/Va	MOSH	949		----
26 Feb 1844	William A. Terrill	Elijah J & Susan B(Smith)	--/Ky	VERN	560		----
22 Jul 1831	James T. Tracy			GRUN	636		1852
04 Aug 1844	N. R. Tracy	James B & Mary F		FGRU	798		1850
00 000 1839	James W. Turner			MOSH	1133	Marion	1840
10 May 1810	Col. Nathan M. Vance			CLIN	67		1833
00 000 0000	James Walkup			HOCO	584		1830
19 Nov 1819	Lysander West	Lysander & Lucy(Kemper)		CSBA	657		1856
23 Feb 1832	Dr. O. P. West			GRUN	519	Ralls	1858
30 Aug 1807	Alfred Wheeler			SALI	811		1819
00 000 1805	William Wheeler			SALI	675		1819
02 Feb 1830	John W. Wilson	G. B		BUCH	942		1851
24 Oct 1810	Mary Wooley	William & Mary(Sulton)	Va/Va	GRUN	624		1838
14 Sep 1804	Rev. John L. Yantis			SALI	859	Clay	1834
20 May 1825	Mason Yater			MARI	627		1831

GRANT COUNTY

BIRTHDATE	NAME OF BIOGRAPHEE	PARENTS/BIRTHPLACE/BIRTHDATE		SOURCE/PAGE		FIRST MO.CO.	DATE
21 Aug 1834	O. S. Barker			LCKS	707		1855
14 Jun 1852	Cash Blackburn	Hon. W.F & Charloote(Maddex)Ky/Ky		AUDR	432		c1862
09 May 1856	O. Bouscaren			JACK	742		1880
26 Sep 1812	George Buskirk	Lawrence & Mary A(Norton)		LCKS	1154		1841
04 Jul 1843	Judge James M. Clark	Eli & Mary E(Draper) **/**		LCKS	1157		1864

BIRTHDATE	NAME OF BIOGRAPHEE	PARENTS/BIRTHPLACE/BIRTHDATE	SOURCE/PAGE	FIRST MO.CO.	DATE
24 Nov 1813	Judge John C. Collins	Ralph & Margaret(Wharton)Eng/Pendle	LCKS	1158		1836
13 May 1823	John M. Crook	William & Nancy(McCann) Bourbon96/Va	LCKS	881		1866
23 Jul 1839	William F. Kennett	Martin & Mary(Brazier) Ky/Ky	MOSH	569		1854
19 Sep 1857	Millard F. Lemon		SALI	838		1875
08 Apr 1842	William A. McNees	P.F & Artemissa(Dejarnette)Ky/Ky	PETT	695	Lewis	1866
18 May 1838	Dr. Pryor N. Norton	George & --(Brumback) Ky/Va	CALI	409	Daviess	1855
17 Aug 1834	Samuel D. Norton	Archibald & Nancy(Nicholas)**97/**99	LCKS	1195		1854
19 Jul 1830	Theodophilus Sechrist		JACK	992		1856
08 Jun 1859	John W. Stewart	A.D & Mary C	GREH	872		----

G R A V E S   C O U N T Y

BIRTHDATE	NAME OF BIOGRAPHEE	PARENTS/BIRTHPLACE/BIRTHDATE	SOURCE/PAGE	FIRST MO.CO.	DATE
12 Apr 1846	T. Porter Eden	Thomas G & Lorenda(Howard)Ky14/Butler	LCKS	1033	Scotland	1853
12 Sep 1834	W. Benton Farr	James King & Rhoda N(Craig)	USBI	147	Johnson	1844
20 Apr 1837	James H. Fewell		HSTC	811		1839
27 Feb 1848	J. W. Gary	Sabe & Adeline Logan/Logan	SERD	1269		----
11 Oct 1874	Alfred W. Greer		SERD	1172	Butler	1891
22 Jan 1840	Fielding K. Gullion	William & Sarah A(Colter) Ky99/Ky16	SEGO	895		----
00 000 1831	James Hibbs	Isaac & Susan(McClennin) Ky/Ky	SEGO	1033	Mississippi	1851
25 Aug 1836	Capt.Dr. Benj.C.Jones	Reverend Eli S Va00/--	SERD	1165		----
00 000 1832	James A. Kennedy		SERD	1156		1879
25 Dec 1850	Andrew J. Scimmones	Thomas & Mary A(Mackvoy) Tn18/Ky	SEGO	910		----
30 Aug 1840	William H. Shelton	W.R & Elizabeth(Rhodes) Va/Va	SEGO	1174		----

| 06 Aug 1845 | Leonidas L. Steele | Richard B & Elizabeth M(Wilson)Tn/SC | SEGO | 1210 | | 1868 |
| 00 000 1862 | Dr. W.D. Turnbow | Thomas J & Mary(Cochram) | JOHN | 959 | | 1891 |

G R A Y S O N   C O U N T Y

BIRTHDATE	NAME OF BIOGRAPHEE	PARENTS/BIRTHPLACE/BIRTHDATE	SOURCE/PAGE	FIRST MO.CO.	DATE
03 Oct 1849	Charles P. Bowman	William & Bettie(Mooreman)	HOCH	921		1857
24 Sep 1825	F.A. Bratcher	Asa & Martha(Sands)	PIKE	924		1844
00 Mar 1807	Thomas Cleaver	Gen. Stephen & Rebecca(Smith)Va/--	MOSH	476	Ralls	1817
20 Jan 1837	Isham Downs		JASP	846		1867
26 May 1843	Richard G. Duncan	William S & M. E(Thomas)	RAMA	672	Marion	1852
15 Feb 1844	Pinkney Edwards	Gilbert & Rachel(Decker)	LINN	607		1858
29 Sep 1819	James A. Hagan	George W & Catherine(Simpson)Ky/Ky	HAME	542	Knox	1853
25 Sep 1839	Dr. Abraham Van Meter	Jacob R & Rhoda C(Hackley)Ky20/Ky	HPCD	956	Linn	1857

G R E E N   C O U N T Y

BIRTHDATE	NAME OF BIOGRAPHEE	PARENTS/BIRTHPLACE/BIRTHDATE	SOURCE/PAGE	FIRST MO.CO.	DATE
08 Dec 1808	Thomas L. Anderson	David & Jane R(Bullock) Va/Va	MARI	586	Saint Charles	1830
00 Feb 1824	Elder Wm. B.Anderson	Rev.Robert T & Martha(Lowry)Va/Va	RAMA	537		1847
08 Jul 1818	Gideon P. Balay	Perry & Tomsey(Warren)	GREH	628	Marion	1839
16 Jun 1837	John Barton	Samuel S & Margaret(Ward) Va/Ky	ANDE	487		1846
00 000 0000	Thomas Bass		FJWC	1023		1825
30 Apr 1813	Fisher R. Bennett		DAVI	821		1842
18 Aug 1816	Jesse Blevins		BUCH	1020	Jackson	1833
24 Oct 1812	Louis C. Bohannon		RAY	800	Pettis	1847
00 000 0000	Nancy Bottom		LCDW	947	Washington	----

G R E E N   C O U N T Y   (C O N T.)

BIRTHPLACE	NAME OF BIOGRAPHEE	PARENTS/BIRTHPLACE/BIRTHDATE	SOURCE/PAGE	FIRST MO.CO.	DATE
24 Oct 1834	Elijah S. Buckner	Robert R & Mary L(Tate) Ky/Ky	CALL 857		1844
29 Nov 1836	Dr. F. Buckner		CSBA 482	Callaway	1844
04 May 1863	William A. Cann	John M & Margaret(Calhoun)	VERN 628		1881
06 Feb 1822	Alexander Carter	Robert & Mary(Smith) Va/Va	AUDR 703	Callaway	1838
04 Jun 1818	Jasper P. Childress		JASP 620		1872
00 000 0000	Nancy Compton		FJWC 1023		1825
22 Nov 1809	Judge Cornelius		BUCH 1037		----
08 Jun 1823	Pleasant Daniel	Thomas & Chloe(Shofner) WV/Ky	HAME 516		1840
23 Jun 1816	Samuel Denison		CLCA 653	Carroll	1843
05 Jul 1837	J. H. Dicken	Isaac H & Elizabeth	BUCH 1025		1855
12 Mar 1831	Daniel C. Forbes		CSBA 1225	Pettis	----
31 Dec 1829	Samuel Y. Forbes	Yates & Margaret(Jackson) Va/NC	CSBA 1224		1854
10 Jan 1827	Richard Garland	Jesse & Elizabeth(Smith) Va/Va	HSTC 748	Benton	1836
23 Apr 1832	George W. Gilmer	John	SALI 541		1834
14 Aug 1824	James Gilmer	John & Elizabeth(Phillips) Va91/Va.	SALI 555		1834
23 May 1850	Joseph M. Green	David D & Nancy C(Phillips)NJ01/Ky16	COOP 505		1852
23 May 1850	Joseph M. Green	D. D & A. C(Phillips) NJ/**	SALI 551		1852
01 Mar 1840	James P. Hamilton		HAME 543	Daviess	1846
00 000 1818	J. C. Hinch		SEGO 643	Crawford	1823
00 000 1799	John Hughes	Blackmore Va/--	JOHN 860	Camden	1850
13 Jul 1823	Joseph U. Hutchason	Matthew & Nancy(Rogers) Va/Va	PLAS 181		1884
16 Jun 1820	Richard Kerby		JACK 981		1837
19 Dec 1795	Samuel Latimer		LCDW 947	Washington	----
29 Jan 1808	Benjamin M. Lisle		BENC 242		1831
13 Aug 1844	Henry C. McGasson		CLIN 141		----
05 Jul 1828	John F. McKinney		SALI 606		1850
22 Dec 1821	Judge John B. Mayes	John & Nancy H(Berry) Pa/**	JOHN 441	Lafayette	1834
26 Mar 1835	D. P. Ming	Charles A & Nancy(Lewis) Va/Ky	SALI 632	Callaway	----

BIRTHDATE	NAME OF BIOGRAPHEE	PARENTS/BIRTHPLACE/BIRTHDATE	SOURCE/PAGE	FIRST MO.CO.	DATE
03 Dec 1823	John Montgomery		BUCH 993		1838
02 Mar 1828	Samuel Montgomery		BUCH 993		1838
26 Oct 1812	George W. Murray		MARI 633		1835
31 Aug 1832	T. W. Phillips	James H.	PETT 794	Saline	1839
26 Nov 1839	W. T. Phillips	Thomas & Mary(McCorkle)	CMMB 1078		c1849
22 Jan 1822	Marcus M. Powers		MOSH 491	Ralls	1830
00 Nov 1809	Judge Cornelius Roberts		BUCH 1037	Jackson	1836
10 Jun 1833	Lemuel A. Rogers	David & Nancy(Cofey) **/**	RAMA 537		1842
06 May 1821	William Sallee	John	BUCH 880		1838
18 Apr 1838	John L. Samples	Charles & Anna(Young) Va/Taylor	VERN 837	Clay	1840
00 000 1838	Robert S. Sandidge	Aaron & Polly(Thompson)	PLAS 437		----
25 May 1816	Benjamin Stewart	Samuel S & Mary(Howard)	BUCH 1039	Platte	1841
02 Oct 1843	W. T. Stovall		DAVI 683		1868
15 Jan 1835	William Vineyard		JACK 858		----
11 Feb 1822	John W. Ward	Richard & Lotta(Belcher) Va99/**01	USBI 217		----
27 Sep 1817	Isaac Wilcox		NODA 903		1852
00 000 0000	John W. Williams		MOSH 611	Marion	1828
01 Aug 1802	Gen. David Willock	David & Rachael(McFarland)Scott/Scott	MARI 597		1830

G R E E N U P   C O U N T Y

BIRTHDATE	NAME OF BIOGRAPHEE	PARENTS/BIRTHPLACE/BIRTHDATE	SOURCE/PAGE	FIRST MO.CO.	DATE
11 Aug 1848	J. H. Black	Henry & Eliza(Bradshaw) Ky18/Ky19	JASP 508		1875
02 Jun 1817	Greenville Blankenship	John & Agnes	DAVI 730	Ray	1849
08 Mar 1842	Marion Brown	Piersol & Margaret(Thomas)	BJAS 258		----
00 000 0000	Lewis B. Chinn		CLPL 933		1840
26 Feb 1834	William H. Conner	Hon. William	CLIN 42		1852
23 Aug 1823	Greenville Cooper	Charles & Tabitha(Willis) Va66/--	CALI 894		1835
00 000 1839	William G. Crum	Thomas & Wilmoth A(Dickson)Va/Va	HSTC 566	Benton	1857

BIRTHDATE	NAME OF BIOGRAPHEE	PARENTS/BIRTHPLACE/BIRTHDATE	SOURCE/PAGE	FIRST MO.CO.	DATE
06 Nov 1835	William L. Culver		CLIN 187		----
08 Dec 1832	William D. Dixon	William & Unity(Hackworth)Va91/Va93	HSTC 568		1865
25 Jul 1808	William Dupuy		JACK 961		1853
10 Nov 1823	Eliza Ann Farmer	Jeremiah & Nancy	BATC 152	Platte	----
13 Sep 1833	L. Fuqua		--- ---		1836
14 Jul 1849	Dr. George D.Greenslate	Silas & Elizabeth	VADA 1020		1855
26 Nov 1816	James H. Hern	William & Mary Ky/Ky	JASP 966		1866
00 000 0000	Isaac N. Hockaday		CLIN 26		1842
19 Mar 1855	Joseph M. Long	George W & Mary Ann(Gray) 24/--	LCDW 791		1867
00 000 0000	Nicholas Pogue		NLBM 1083	Howard	1839
00 000 1847	John W. Pollard		SALI 687		1854
08 Mar 1826	Milfred Powers	Richard & Harriet(Poage)	MOSH 587		1831
18 Dec 1830	Dr. Charles R. Stewart	Price & Mariah(Remmeck) Ky/NY	HSTC 744	Sullivan	1851
30 Jun 1818	Thomas H. Talbot		CLPL 968		1837
01 Nov 1829	John R. Terrill	William & Ann(Calvin) Va/Ky	RAMA 433		1846
08 Apr 1845	George W. Thomas	J.M	RAY 611		1857
09 Feb 1834	William M. Williams	John D & Eleanor(McCosky)	DAVI 643		1841
04 Nov 1833	John T. Woodrow	John T & Mary(Cain)	JASP 1017		1857

HANCOCK COUNTY

BIRTHDATE	NAME OF BIOGRAPHEE	PARENTS/BIRTHPLACE/BIRTHDATE	SOURCE/PAGE	FIRST MO.CO.	DATE
03 Jun 1827	Benjamin B. Lamar	Benona & Nancy(Blincoe) Md/Va	CALL 675		1858

HARDIN COUNTY

BIRTHDATE	NAME OF BIOGRAPHEE	PARENTS/BIRTHPLACE/BIRTHDATE	SOURCE/PAGE	FIRST MO.CO.	DATE
11 Nov 1878	W. W. Ament	J. H & Rachel	DAGE 695	Caldwell	1881
19 Aug 1840	J. W. Anderson		CLIN 219	DeKalb	1850
09 Mar 1855	John L. Berry	William & Catherine(Lewis)	NW 775	Platte	1883
28 Mar 1829	Newton Bird	Jesse & Laodica(Ray) WV09/Marion09	ANDE 490		1855
00 000 1807	William C. Briscoe		LCKS 719		1833
31 May 1833	Kimbrel Carlton	John & Rachel(Spellman)	HOAT 463		1871
31 Oct 1833	William M Carroll	John	CALI 563		1852
00 000 1812	William P. Carson	James & --(Phillips) SC/SC	NLBM 907		1855
01 Feb 1829	Judge Joshua M.Cash	Abraham & Deborah	LINN 657	Chariton	1843
11 Mar 1840	Lee Cash	Abraham **99/--	HOCH 924		1844
27 Feb 1827	Loyd Cash	Abraham & Deborah	LINN 657	Chariton	1844
08 Feb 1839	Willis H. Crutcher		JASP 1021		1866
15 Oct 1832	Dr. W.H.H.Cundiff	Greenberg & Ann(Sutton) Va/Va	CSBA 487	Saint Louis	1853
27 Apr 1835	James C. Drake	William & Mary(Holland) Va/--	LCKS 1167		1855
31 Oct 1823	Thomas Duvall	Thomas & Hannah(Davis) Md/Ky	CSBA 643		1854
25 Dec 1865	Dr. James H. English	Robert S	SERD 754	Mississippi	1881
09 Feb 1830	William G. Farleigh		BUCH 742	Platte	1843
28 Jul 1847	C. C. Fogle	Samuel & Matilda(Smith) **20/**19	ASPS 1155	Scotland	1850
30 Mar 1822	Robert M. Funk	Alexander & Sarah(Watters) Ky/--	HSTC 573		1857
08 Feb 1831	William T. Gannaway		GRUN 582	Macon	1852
20 Jun 1846	Richard P. Giles	Granville T & Rosanna(Duncan)Va/Ky	USBI 647	Monroe	1848
15 Jun 1829	Andrew J. Greenawatt		RAY 666	Clay	1843
20 Dec 1817	Isaac Greenawatt		HAME 541		1855
19 Nov 1827	Alexander Greenwell	Robert & Dorcas(Gathage)	DAGE 512		1840
18 Dec 1826	John J Grigsby	Redman & Nancy(Keeling) Va00/Ky	NODA 1011		1859
18 Jan 1837	F. M. Handy		PIKE 970	Saint Louis	1865
00 000 1797	E. M. Haycraft	Rev.Presley N & Elizabeth(Kennedy)	LCKS 763		1835
00 Nov 1820	John Haywood		CLIN 92	Buchanan	1850

BIRTHDATE	NAME OF BIOGRAPHEE	PARENTS/BIRTHPLACE/BIRTHDATE	SOURCE/PAGE	FIRST MO.CO.	DATE
11 Oct 1827	Cyrus T. Helm	Judge John B & Jane	MARI 954		1854
00 000 1823	Dewitt Hoover		VERN 422		1871
16 Dec 1819	Dr. John B. Howard	John H & Sarah(Marrifield)	BUCH 777		c1849
19 Mar 1833	E.G. Jeffries	Elijah & Elizabeth(Marshall)Va03/**	VERN 472		----
15 Jun 1849	Charles Kerfoot	Albert & Eliza	JASP 1004		----
25 May 1858	William H. Kerfoot	Albien & Elizabeth(Cecil)	DAGE 558		----
03 Jul 1852	Joseph M. Knott	Samuel C & Sarah(Gates) Madison/Ga	USBI 149		1851
05 Jul 1850	Dewitt C Langley	Randolph H & Elizabeth(Calvin)	---- ---		----
25 Dec 1865	John P. Larue	Jacob & Rhoda F(Perry)	SERD 1111	Stoddard	1869
09 Dec 1838	Dr. Robert J. Larue	Jesse B & Latatia	AUDR 798	Boone	1860
00 000 1808	William Lasswell	Jesse & Jane W(Mitton) NC/Va	LCKS 913	Scotland	1846
28 Feb 1812	Major Andrew H. Linder		ASPS 988		1840
13 Oct 1848	J. W. McAntire	Aaron B & Sarah(Hills) Wash16/20	JASP 554	Scotland	1850
14 Oct 1848	William B. McAntire	William S & Elizabeth E Ky/Ky	USBI 743	Scotland	1849
00 000 0000	William B. McAntire	William S & Elizabeth(VanMeter)Ky/**	BJAS 269	Scotland	1847
14 Oct 1848	W. B. McAntire	W. S & Elizabeth E(VanMeter)Va16/Va23 JASP 555	Scotland	1849
01 Oct 1845	William J. McCullum	Macon & Jane(Miller)	HSTC 685	Scotland	1851
31 Dec 1805	Silas Mahurin		LINN 616		1858
27 May 1817	Thomas S. Mooreman		NODA 996		1859
11 Jul 1838	Gilbert F. Nall	A. J & Theodocia(Berry)	HSTC 752	Benton	1876
10 May 1830	Hon. J. L. Nall	William P & Elizabeth(Brumfield)Ky/Ky BJAS 419		----
09 Sep 1830	John L. Nolen	John & Mary(Miller) Md/--	MOSH 337		1852
05 Jul 1820	William Paul	George S & Elizabeth(Purcell)Pa66/--	HSTC 671		1842
09 Jun 1843	Lt.William Q.Purcell	James & Matilda(Metcalf)Breckin09/**	USBI 722	Saline	1855
00 000 1830	J.D. Raine	J. S & --(Dillord) Va/Ky	LCKS 944		1850
00 Oct 1834	C. Reno	William P & Lititia Ky/Ky	DAVI 737		1856
04 Sep 1800	David Rice	John & Patsy(Johnson)	BOON 672		1819
00 000 1824	Granville Scott		LCKS 828		1852

BIRTHDATE	NAME OF BIOGRAPHEE	PARENTS/BIRTHPLACE/BIRTHDATE	SOURCE/PAGE	FIRST MO.CO.	DATE
00 000 1805	Maj.B.W. Shacklett	Benjamin & Elizabeth(Ashcraft)Pa76/Pa	LCKS 1211		1853
17 Jan 1821	Hercules Smith	David & Mary Ann(Gray) Ky/Ky	LCKS 1215		1850
15 Dec 1850	Druey Stith	Henry & Elizabeth Ky/Ky	JASP 1013		----
00 000 1854	George H. Stith		SALI 804		1866
20 May 1846	Hardin N. Stovall	John D & Rachael(Newman) **/--	DAGE 951		----
07 Jun 1794	Major William Todd	Joseph & Ann(Crause) Pa/--	NW 936	Howard	1817
12 Jan 1844	John B.Van Metre	Nathan & Elizabeth(Bland) **/**	LCKS 848		1865
17 Apr 1812	Dr. William S. West	Isaac & Martha(Meeks) SC/Va	HOCH 850	C. Giradeau	1832
29 Jul 1829	John Whittle		SALI 590		1844
16 Jun 1842	L. James Wilkes	Samuel M & Margaret R	SALI 615	Holt	1843
17 Jun 1837	Dr. B. F. Wilson	George & Mary(Shepherd) Ky/Ky	BOON 1117	Lewis	1852
12 Apr 1838	H. H. Wooldridge	Jesse & Susan(Hays) Va/Ky	HOCO 1165		1858
09 Aug 1832	Charles G. Wortham		JOHN 911		1854
09 Jun 1840	Isaac J. Wortham	John & Mary(Grundy)	CSBA 690	Johnson	1867
28 May 1832	William P. Yeaman	Stephen M & Lucretia(Helm) Pa/--	BOON 972	Saint Louis	1870

H A R L A N   C O U N T Y

BIRTHDATE	NAME OF BIOGRAPHEE	PARENTS/BIRTHPLACE/BIRTHDATE	SOURCE/PAGE	FIRST MO.CO.	DATE
04 Nov 1839	Ira Creech	Henry & Mahala(Field) Ky18/Tn18	JASP 519	Dade	1854

H A R R I S O N   C O U N T Y

BIRTHDATE	NAME OF BIOGRAPHEE	PARENTS/BIRTHPLACE/BIRTHDATE	SOURCE/PAGE	FIRST MO.CO.	DATE
03 Sep 1845	Lucius D. Ashcraft	Ellis & Elizabeth(Keith) Ky/Pa	FJWC 854		----
22 Feb 1866	Ely D. Baird	Thomas & Kate(Michael) 29/Bourbon	SERD 985		----
00 000 1871	Francis M. Baird	Thomas & Kate(Michael)	SERD 1072	Dunklin	1897
27 Mar 1830	B. F. Bassett		CLIN 73		1857

H A R R I S O N   C O U N T Y   (C O N T.)

BIRTHDATE	NAME OF BIOGRAPHEE	PARENTS/BIRTHPLACE/BIRTHDATE	SOURCE	PAGE	FIRST MO.CO.	DATE
21 Jun 1848	W. F. Bassett		BUCH	673	Clinton	1861
00 000 0000	John Biggs		VERN	893		----
03 Sep 1841	John T. Boswell		CSBA	437		1843
03 Apr 1831	George W. Brannock	William & Mary(Craig)	CSBA	534		1855
03 Apr 1831	G. W. Brannock		JACK	995	Cass	1855
31 Dec 1821	William A. Brannock	James & Elizabeth(Shanks)Bour97/Bour	CSBA	533		1855
22 Dec 1817	W. H. Bumbarger	Michael Va/--	LCKS	722		1870
00 000 1820	B. F. Burns	Tarrance & Catherine(Jackson)	HAME	500		1844
23 May 1840	Granville J. Buzzard	Daniel & Elizabeth	JASP	959	Barton	1870
25 Apr 1814	Alfred N. Cake		NW	1389		----
00 000 1828	Judge John Callaway	Henry H & Annie(Sherman)**/Bourbon	LCKS	1009	Marion	1832
07 Feb 1820	Hon. Colin M. Campbell	Matthew & Dorothy(Martin)Pa/Md	LCKS	1010		1826
10 Oct 1843	Thornton Cash		JACK	932	Benton	1856
02 Feb 1839	William N. Cason	Granville & Matilda(Williams)	SCMW	840		1869
00 000 0000	John W. Chambers	George A & Mary E(Conner)	MOSH	961		----
25 Sep 1825	Elijah G. Chinn	Judge William S & Lucy A(Chinn)	MOSH	1159		c1830
22 Jan 1804	M. H. Craig	John & Margaret(McIlvain) SC/Va	CSBA	486	Morgan	1834
13 Aug 1800	George Criswell	James & Sarah(Maloneson) Ire56/Pa.	CALL	583		1827
29 Sep 1819	Perry A. Curry	John & Nancy	PIKE	966		1840
17 Jan 1839	J. M. DeMoss	Rev.Thomas & Catherine(Ricord)Ky/Ky	HOCH	938	Monroe	1856
19 Feb 1815	Alexander T. Downing	Alexander & Mary(Bracken) Pa/Pa	ANDE	558	Marion	1840
31 Aug 1827	Milton Forsyth		MOSH	464		1856
06 Nov 1828	William F. Garrett	Isaac & Elizabeth(Bell) Shelby/Va	CSBA	709	Jackson	1871
30 Jul 1806	Fincelius R. Gray		LAFA	514		1833
29 Jan 1825	Judge John W. Henry	Jesse & Nancy(Porter) Ky/Bourbon	USBI	639	Jackson	1845
29 Jan 1825	Judge John W. Henry		KC&	128		----
06 Apr 1842	Judge William Henry	William & Sarah A(Jones) **/**	USBI	498	DeKalb	1849
06 Apr 1842	Judge William Henry	William & Sarah A(Jones)	CLCA	368	DeKalb	1849

Date	Name	Parents / Spouse	Origin	Code	No.	County	Year
28 Sep 1834	--- Hickman			MOSH	326	Ralls	1845
01 May 1833	H. Hinkson		Ky/Ky	JACK	918	Lewis	1855
00 000 1822	George E. Hinson	George & Jane(Williams)		LCKS	769		----
05 Sep 1809	Samuel G. Holmes	Thomas & Nancy(Vance)	Va87/Va86	LCKS	1053	Marion	1848
02 Mar 1814	William Holmes	Thomas & Nancy(Vance)	Va/Va	USBI	45		1848
00 000 1832	William T. Humphrey	Henry M & Rebecca(Wallace)Ky09/Ky11		LCKS	773		1839
17 Oct 1820	Thomas W. Hurd	Judge Thomas & Martha(Stevenson)		MOSH	487		1832
10 Jul 1842	John R. Jones	Richard S & Verlinda	Ky/Ky	RAY	652		1872
23 Sep 1827	Rev. Nathan W. Keith	William & Elizabeth		GRUN	512		1839
23 Sep 1827	Reverend N. W. Keith			FGRU	404		1839
23 Jul 1837	Jackson King			MOSH	1143		1856
18 Oct 1833	Charles F. Lail	Paul & Mahala(Garrett)	Ky/Ky	CALL	924	Pike	1855
00 000 1810	James W. Leeper	John & Burzilla(Brown)		LCKS	786	Marion	1834
25 Sep 1831	Benjamin F. Lemmon	Benjamin F & Emily(Chandler)Ky/Ky		SALI	822		1876
00 000 1836	John T. Lewis	Benjamin	Ky/--	LCKS	1065		1846
06 Nov 1831	Hon. Archibald V. McKee	Archibald & Lilly(McClure)Va/BooneLINC			360		1854
06 Nov 1831	Archibald V. McKee	Archibald & Lillie(McClure)Va/Va		USBI	650	Lincoln	1854
13 Mar 1833	James C. Minteer	William & Sarah(Davis)	Pa/Ky	CALI	1129	Monroe	1856
14 Jul 1830	John W. Minteer	William & Sarah(Davis)	Pa/Ky	CALI	1129		1857
01 Jan 1837	Benjamin F. Moore			SCMW	519		1848
02 Dec 1814	John T. Nesbit			MOSH	583	Callaway	1824
00 000 0000	Robert Nesbit			MOSH	427		1819
09 Jul 1814	Elijah Orr	James & Catherine(Williams)Pa??/Va??		MOSH	1127	Anderson	1845
21 Apr 1855	Dr. David O. Ravenscraft	James & Minerva(Bailey)Ky/Ky		CSBA	470		1867
00 000 1830	Benjamin W. Roberts	Benjamin & Sarah(Henry)	Va/Ky	LCKS	823	Marion	1833
05 Jul 1824	Dr. M. M. Robinson			LAFA	496	Boone	1834
24 Feb 1823	Abraham Ruddle			GRUN	593		----
14 Feb 1834	George W. Shropshire Capt.M.P & Agnes(Pemberton)Ky/Ky			RAMA	978		1855
25 Feb 1813	Rev. William H. Sipple John			CALL	845		1867
21 Sep 1812	Milton Smith	Martin & Sarah(Spears)	Pa/Ky	AUDR	579		1879
03 May 1833	John M. Spears	Adam & Leah(Baxter) Bourbon/Bourbon		CALI	1257		1855
24 Oct 1839	O. P. Spears	Adam & Leah		VADA	1053	Livingston	1858

HARRISON COUNTY (CONT.)

BIRTHDATE	NAME OF BIOGRAPHEE	PARENTS/BIRTHPLACE/BIRTHDATE	SOURCE/PAGE	FIRST MO.CO.	DATE
00 000 0000	William F. Spears	Adam & Leah(Baxter) Ky/Ky	CALI 981		1855
00 000 0000	W. H. Steers	Rollins & Sarah E	SALI 868		1855
02 May 1828	Joseph I. Sterne	Thomas & Nancy(Ingles)	BOON 681		----
20 Jan 1854	Thomas W. Sterne	Joseph & Emma(Coleman)	BOON 681		1857
25 Feb 1813	Rev. William H. Supple John		CALL 845		1867
10 Apr 1818	Wilson F. Swinford	John & Polly(Adams) Ky/Ky	NODA 841		1857
30 Mar 1837	Elder John W. Tate	Joseph & Rachel(Foster)	CLPL 908	Jackson	1840
04 Jun 1833	D. M. Turney		CLIN 151		1853
23 Jan 1824	M. B. Underwood	Francis & Margaret(Jarvis) Eng/Ky	CSBA 655	Schuyler	1867
28 May 1812	Stephen Wheeler		SALI 810		1824
00 000 1851	Dr. James M. White	William M & Mary J(Davis) Ky/Ky	JASP 381		1870
00 000 0000	Thomas Whiteledge		PIKE 942		1840
20 Jan 1833	Richard T. Whitley	James & Phebe(Haley)	VERN 874		1872
15 Feb 1835	Samuel Yarnall		NODA 904		1854

HART COUNTY

BIRTHDATE	NAME OF BIOGRAPHEE	PARENTS/BIRTHPLACE/BIRTHDATE	SOURCE/PAGE	FIRST MO.CO.	DATE
10 Jun 1825	William Bennett	William & Sarah(McCubbin) Ky/Ky	CALI 647		1842
00 Sep 1847	George H. Bush		RAY 797		1864
12 Apr 1836	Thomas J. Davis		RAY 817		1853
07 Sep 1841	Vardaymon W. Dawson	Ky/Ky	SALI 741		1850
01 Feb 1847	Zachariah T. Denison	Zachariah & Mary(Isbel)	LCDW 1105		1848
01 Sep 1830	Fountain Donan	David C & Elizabeth(Gillaspy)Va/Va	HOAT 424		1856
00 May 1836	William Drury	T. B & Elizabeth(Walden) NY/Ky	HOAT 424		1868

HENDERSON COUNTY

BIRTHDATE	NAME OF NOMINEE	PARENTS/BIRTHPLACE/BIRTHDATE	SOURCE	PAGE	FIRST MO.CO.	DATE
04 Sep 1851	Rev. Henry Eubank	Reuben E & Martha H(Thompson)**/Ky	CHHO	592		1858
18 Jan 1865	W. R. Handy	David W & Mary(Cook) Va30/Pa	DAGE	449		1865
17 Feb 1833	John C. Hart	George P & Susan R Ky/Barren	CSBA	545		1857
10 Jan 1860	Edward L. Hawks	F. T & Amanda M(Overfelt) Ky/Ky	SERD	1185		1871
00 000 1824	J. P. Ketcham	Joseph & Jane(Sherl) Jefferson/Ky	HOCO	592		1846
00 000 0000	William M. Poynter		HOLT	343		----
00 000 0000	Micajah Sandidge		SALI	773		----
00 000 1854	Thomas G. Sturgeon	Isham & Delilah(Denison)	LCDW	1152	Phelps	1851
29 Sep 1851	C. L. Welden	Washington B & Mary M(Highbaugh)Va/Ky	ANDE	590		----
00 000 0000	William G. Welden	Jonathan & Sarah(Burch) Va/--	DAGE	758		1856
00 000 1843	James I. Weldon	Jonathan & Sallie	DAVI	851		1855
29 Nov 1835	W. G. Weldon	Jonathan & Sarah(Burch) Va/Va	DAVI	642	Harrison	1856
29 May 1842	John W. Whitlock	James B & Elizabeth(Gill) Ky/Ky	NLBM	891		1852
10 Mar 1828	Thomas D. Woodson	Robert S & Hylda A(Young) Va96/--	RAY	533		----
22 Mar 1835	Gen.Waddy Thompson		JOHN	736	Macon	1842
21 May 1824	William M. Matney		BUCH	1061		1845

BIRTHDATE	NAME OF NOMINEE	PARENTS/BIRTHPLACE/BIRTHDATE	SOURCE	PAGE	FIRST MO.CO.	DATE
11 Sep 1801	Adam Black		CALI	1004	Cooper	1819
30 Nov 1844	James S. Blackwell	James J & Mary(Jeffress) Va/Va	BOON	841		1879
01 Apr 1822	William A. Cannon		SALI	585		--
10 Jun 1837	L. W. Danforth	Leander F & Jane W(Jones) NY/Va	SERD	1256	Mississippi	1859
00 000 1856	Eugene C. Randolph	Malachi & Mary(Slaton) **28/**38	SEGO	946		1880
01 Jan 1853	William N.Randolph	Malachi F & Mary(Slaton) **/**	SEGO	994		1878
23 Jan 1813	Elias Turner		HOCH	779		1835
00 000 0000	Jack T. Weller		SALI	760		----
23 Oct 1856	George L. Wilkes		SERD	872	Pemiscot	----

BIRTHDATE	NAME OF BIOGRAPHEE	PARENTS/BIRTHPLACE/BIRTHDATE	SOURCE/PAGE	FIRST MO.CO.	DATE
04 Apr 1846	James P. Adams		SALI 719		1849
00 000 1834	Samuel A. Adams	George & Nancy(Simmons) Ky/Ky	ASPS 938		1870
29 Jul 1829	Alfred Banta	John & Nancy(List)	RAMA 1144		1844
00 000 0000	Mollie Bowen	B.J	AUDR 459		----
00 000 1813	George G. Burnett	Samuel	LCKS 723		1836
20 Apr 1837	James Campbell	John & Annie(Scott) **04/**09	LCKS 1012	Marion	1845
17 Aug 1833	C. R. Chinn	W.S	JASP 621	Shelby	----
16 Jan 1829	J. A. Clements	Zachariah & Virlinda(Bramlett)Mont/B	KC& 535	Clay	1855
08 Jul 1831	Judge John T.Coates	Judge Thomas P & Belinda(Darrett)Va/Va	RAMA 547		1835
13 May 1854	Madison B. Critchlow	Thomas & Martha(Nevill) Ky/Ky	LCKS 1028		1865
00 000 1823	William H. Cull	Nathan & Rebecca(Rawlings) **/**	LCKS 882		1850
25 Feb 1823	Joseph Duncan		CLIN 131	Clay	1842
15 Dec 1833	Stephen C. Duncan	Stephen & Lucy(Browning)Bour/Bourbon	CLPL 435	Saline	1838
16 Dec 1815	Henry S. Foree	Silas Va/--	CLIN 22	Caldwell	1860
22 Dec 1838	William H. Foree	Joseph & Caroline(Shrader)	MOSH 372		1848
19 Jul 1830	William D. Gardner	Wesley & Abigail(Dawson)	MOSH 983		1859
15 Oct 1843	David S. Hall		CLIN 190	Buchanan	1857
02 Aug 1839	John W. Hall		CLIN 189	Buchanan	1856
20 Dec 1816	Thomas Hall		CLIN 189	Buchanan	1859
29 Aug 1837	Thomas R. Hill		NW 2018		1857
30 Aug 1838	Thomas R. Hill		NW 1126	Clinton	c.1858
13 Nov 1856	G. N. Jackson		SALI 816		1881
12 Jul 1837	Barton A. Jones	M. M	LINN 446	Saline	1855
09 Mar 1814	Charles O. Jones	Va/Va	PETT 847		1845
23 Oct 1841	Mary A. Jones		BUCH 1023		----
00 000 1852	John W. Kerlin	Thomas & Nancy J(Jeffries) Ky/Ky	DAGE 806		1857
15 Jan 1822	J. N. Lindsey	Thomas & Keziah(Jones)	CLPL 525		1857
02 Mar 1842	John H. Logan	John H & Lorinda(Stewart)	VERN 589		----

Birth Date	Name	Parents		Code	No.	County	Death
01 Aug 1801	Levi McGuire			BOON	778		1818
09 Dec 1833	Taylor McKenzie	John	**/--	----	--		1858
16 Mar 1815	Aaron McPike	Edwin & Sarah(Van Cleve)	Va/--	AUDR	504	Marion	1838
02 Nov 1838	Benjamin T. McPike	James & Mary(Chiltor)		MARI	794		1840
14 Jul 1830	Edward McPike	James & Zerelda(Sudduth)		MARI	762	Pike	----
09 Dec 1832	William F. McPike	James & Zerelda(Sudduth)		MARI	761	Pike	1848
21 Jan 1827	John B. Maddox			CALL	680		1855
19 Mar 1851	George H. Magee	Tolbert & Mary J(Gibhany)		NW	1625		1852
09 Oct 1831	David M. Magruder	Alpheus & Sarah(Martinie)rd03/Ky12		LINC	572		1852
20 Feb 1833	Elias Magruder	Alpheus & Sarah(Martinie)rd03/Ky12		LINC	573		1852
05 Nov 1851	James L. Martin	Charles N		SALI	722		1854
05 Jan 1851	William H. Mead	Shannon & Mary(Voorhies)	Ky/Ky	CSBA	1348		----
22 Apr 1826	Dr. B. Meek	-- & Temperance(Lowden)	SC/Ky	HOAT	170		1851
16 Jan 1818	Samuel N. Miller	Ephraim & Jemima	Va/Va	DAVI	823		1865
00 000 0000	Thomas Moore			HAME	581		1860
25 Aug 1843	Isaac B. Newton			MOSH	955		1869
20 May 1822	James A. Owens	Nelson R & Nancy(Baber)		NW	670		1844
19 Sep 1835	John T. Owens	John S & Harriet B(Moore)		CLPL	1029		1845
19 Sep 1835	Joseph T. Owens	John S	Va/--	ANPL	153		1845
02 Aug 1827	William Robbins	John & Edie(Sanders)	Va/**	MARI	654		1840
00 000 1840	James Rollins	B. F & Elizabeth	**/**	LAFA	659	Saline	1856
06 Apr 1842	Hon.D.A. Rouner	Argyle A & Lucinda(Morris)Ky10/**11		LCKS	1110	Marion	1851
00 000 1807	Edward M. Samuel	Reuben	Va/--	RAMA	508		----
12 Oct 1807	Edward M. Samuel			STLO	1396	Randolph	1815
14 Aug 1855	Richard Powell			JACK	908	Buchanan	c1865
04 Jun 1810	George W. Samuel	Reuben		RAMA	512		----
04 Jun 1810	George W. Samuel			BUCH	881	Howard	1828
04 Jun 1810	George W. Samuel			USBI	412		----
05 Sep 1848	James T. Scott			HOCO	561	Monroe	1866
00 000 1844	E. D. Shannon			SALI	857		----
20 Jul 1823	Thomas G. Sims	Thomas A & Elizabeth(Morris)		BOON	608		1836
07 Oct 1843	Benjamin M. Smith	Ballard S & Julia(Shrader)**/Oldham		VERN	838	Bates	1879

HENRY COUNTY (CONT.)

BIRTHDATE	NAME OF BIOGRAPHEE	PARENTS/BIRTHPLACE/BIRTHDATE	SOURCE/PAGE	FIRST MO.CO.	DATE
30 Oct 1850	Henry C. Smith		SALI 840		----
13 Feb 1834	Nicholas J. Smith		SALI 849		----
17 Mar 1833	Robert T. Sparks	James P & Sallie(Threlkeld)	MOSH 1027		1839
00 000 1847	Thomas N. Spillman	Charles W Va/--	NW 998	Worth	1850
00 000 1836	Capt.William O. Stewart	Charles & Mary(McCracken)Va88/Ky99	LCKS 838		1881
08 Feb 1827	James Stoneum		CLIN 59		----
06 Aug 1850	Henry Strother		SALI 770		1874
16 Feb 1837	Judge John P. Strother		SALI 777		1858
29 Nov 1834	Jefferson Sullenger	John & Lucinda(Berry) Va89/Ky	LINC 618		1852
07 Sep 1837	A. S. Tilley	William & Mary Va/Va	JASP 714		1868
17 Nov 1813	John Tyler		PLAS 177		----
00 000 1810	Henry M. Vories		BENC 494	Buchanan	1844
00 000 0000	Henry M. Vories		BUCH 232		----
17 Aug 1863	Billy M. Winter	W. H & Amanda(Hunt) Franklin23/23	ASPS 934		1881

HICKMAN COUNTY

BIRTHDATE	NAME OF BIOGRAPHEE	PARENTS/BIRTHPLACE/BIRTHDATE	SOURCE/PAGE	FIRST MO.CO.	DATE
15 Aug 1851	Samuel Gardner		SERD 1155		1886
05 Sep 1845	George H. Mobley		VERN 476		1856
10 Apr 1831	Huldah A. Mott		DUNK 222		----
16 Apr 1840	William S. Nichol	David & Martha(Mitchell) Va98/Va08	LCDW 1136		1856
31 Jan 1838	Joseph R. Ridge	William	MOSH 1020		1852
06 Mar 1835	J. R. Taylor	John E & Rebecca(Edrington)	MARI 671		----

HOPKINS COUNTY

BIRTHDATE	NAME OF BIOGRAPHEE	PARENTS/BIRTHPLACE/BIRTHDATE		SOURCE/PAGE		FIRST MO.CO.	DATE
22 May 1827	Dr. James W. Brock	James	NC/--	JASP	763		----
07 Aug 1814	Daniel A. Brooks			HSTC	784		1874
15 Dec 1873	Thomas J. Brown			SERD	1046		1899
18 Jun 1850	Dr. Green B. Christian Robert B	William B & Sarah(Dever)	**45/**5C	NLEM	1060		1883
18 Jun 1850	Dr. Green B. Christian Robert B		Va/--	NLEM	1060		1883
20 Jan 1818	Marcellus D. Cook		Va/--	BOON	1022		1828
22 May 1833	William M. Cox	Howell B & Hanrietta(Steen)	NC/**	HSTC	1144		----
11 Sep 1818	James F. Finley	William & Leah(Dobbins)	NC92/Va	HPCD	808		1848
00 000 1791	James Leeper			CALI	1113	Chariton	1822
22 Aug 1842	M. G. Lovan			LCDW	951	Greene	1844
00 000 1839	Joseph P. Porter	William H & Maria(Carnahar.)		NLEM	970		1848
02 Mar 1841	Louis C. Rice	William & Paulina(Young)		CALI	1020		1869
00 000 0000	Silas M. Ross	John E & Jane(Martin)		FJWC	1010		1833
00 000 0000	James H. Tinsley	Boswell & Mary(Henry)	SC/Ky	CSBA	1218	Grundy	1840
00 000 1826	John N. Williams			SERD	1125	Stoddard	1842
10 Jun 1833	H. S. Witherspoon	Isaac	NC86/--	JOHN	741	Henry	1839

J A C K S O N   C O U N T Y   N O N E

J E F F E R S O N   C O U N T Y

BIRTHDATE	NAME OF BIOGRAPHEE	PARENTS/BIRTHPLACE/BIRTHDATE		SOURCE/PAGE		FIRST MO.CO.	DATE
06 Nov 1840	Leon J. Albert	Nicholas & Anna(Holn)	--/Fr	SERD	588	C. Giradeau	c1845
00 000 1840	Hon. Leon J. Albert	Nicholas	Fr/--	SEGO	741		1852
28 Jul 1834	Capt.Richard S.Alcoke	Robert H	Va/--	AUDR	420	Saint Louis	1852

-85-

BIRTHDATE	NAME OF BIOGRAPHEE	PARENTS/BIRTHPLACE/BIRTHDATE	SOURCE/PAGE	FIRST MO.CO.	DATE
00 000 1840	John Allen		JOHN 922		----
03 Dec 1849	Dr. Nicholas R. Alvey	Robert & Catherine Ky/Ky	MARI 906	Monroe	----
00 000 0000	Philip E. Ayres	Thomas & Elizabeth(Ebert) Va/Va	PLAS 554		----
28 Mar 1823	John D. Bell		VADA 928		1857
00 000 1836	M. M. Biven	Bozel	SALI 665	Johnson	c1847
29 Apr 1817	Dr. L. W. Boston		JOHN 839	Saint Louis	1837
00 000 0000	James H. Bridges		SEGO 959		1830
14 Oct 1840	J. H. Brown	Andrew & Jane(McDowell) Va/Va	GRUN 714	Chariton	1840
00 000 1785	Alexander Buckner		BENC 41	C. Giradeau	1818
07 Feb 1853	Charles W. Bullen	Samuel H **/--	PETT 624		1869
00 000 0000	William Buttrum	J. W	BJAS 349		1871
17 Feb 1817	J. F. Cassady	Thomas & Nancy(Finley) Va/Va	MARI 693		----
06 Feb 1824	Dr. Paschal H. Chambers		LAFA 615		1845
06 Feb 1824	Dr. Paschal H. Chambers	General George W & Sarah(Hickman)	PLAS 518		----
07 Apr 1840	John W. Cleaveland		JOHN 919		----
12 Apr 1860	George W. Conn	George W & Julia(Blankenbecker)**/**	CHHO 780		1880
18 Sep 1830	John Costin	Lewis & Catherine(Smock)	NW 1301		1850
10 Sep 1847	William C. Crawford	Peery & Era Ann	FGRU 511		----
09 Jun 1826	J. R. Daughtery	William Ky/--	CLIN 13	Buchanan	1854
11 Dec 1845	Thomas B. Dodge	Martin B & Lucinda E(Bacon)NY/Ky	SEGO 924	Mississippi	1860
25 Aug 1836	Thomas R. Dodge	William R Eng/--	AUDR 461	Saint Louis	c1849
00 000 0000	James Donaldson		CLCA 663	Macon	----
04 Jul 1803	Richard Earickson	Judge James & Rebecca(Malone)Md/Md	USBI 809	Chariton	1819
10 May 1816	William L. Earickson	Peregreen & Laranie(Stucky)Md/Ky	HOCO 439	Chariton	1819
25 Jan 0000	Capt.Charles S.Edwards	Capt. William & Elizabeth(Floyd)Md/	RAMA 948		1866
00 000 1828	William G. Ellis	William & Sarah(Cassedy) 04/05	LCKS 738		1836
21 Jun 1837	Henry Y. Field	Col.W.H & Mary(Young) Va/Ky	PETT 651		1853
00 000 0000	R. C. Friend	Fielding & Elizabeth(Sleeper)**/Pa	BJAS 516		----

Date	Name	Parents	Birthplace	Code	No.	County	Year
10 Aug 1811	Samuel Gaty			STLO	666		1828
28 Apr 1831	John W. Gosney	Alfred & Lucy(Haws)	Ky/Ky	CSBA	1215	Jefferson	1840
07 Mar 1842	Martin V. Graham	William & Elizabeth(Farmer)	Va/Va	CMMB	945	Morgan	1855
22 Aug 1859	Frank H. Gross	Theodore & Anna	Germany/Germany	LCKS	752		1872
00 000 1850	George K. Gwathmey			ANDE	562		1879
04 Mar 1817	Dr.Joseph S.Halstead	Alexander	NY/--	CALI	657		1860
18 May 1830	Dr. W. Hamilton	Judge Thomas & Rachel(Crowe)		CLCA	472		1832
10 Mar 1821	W. B. Howard	John & Annie C(Bullitt)	Md/Jefferson	KC&	314		1842
10 Mar 1821	W. B. Howard			JACK	952		1844
00 000 1853	J. F. Joyce	Michael & Mary(Ball)	Nd26/Md31	FJWC	913	Saint Louis	----
15 Sep 1835	Valantine A. Judd	Valentine W & Rachel(Crannells)		VADA	819		1850
16 Sep 1851	Edgar J. Kellogg	Alonzo & Nannie(Burt)	NY/Md	HOAT	471		1870
05 Nov 1796	Dr. Lewis F. Linn	Ashael & --(Hunter)	Md/Md	CLPL	485		1856
13 Sep 1845	John F. Llewellyn	Robert & Abbie(Knott)		CAUD	214		1869
13 Sep 1845	J. F. Llewellyn	Robert & Abbie(Knott)	Eng/Eng	AUDR	799		1869
23 Jan 1826	Benjamin L. Locke			AUDR	800	Callaway	----
23 Apr 1848	Stephen T. Lupe	James H & Annie E		PETT	920	Saint Louis	1858
26 Mar 1842	E. M. Lyons			CLIN	42		1863
08 May 1845	Robert J. McGowan	James & Ellen(Foulks)	Ky/Ky	VERN	664		1870
29 Oct 1825	Elijah T. Mapel			RAY	810		1854
03 Mar 1842	Henry Mayfield	James & Mahala	Ky/--	CALI	402	Daviess	----
21 Jun 1851	John B. Merrill	Andrew & Julia A(Davis)	Va/Va	RAMA	1024		1854
25 Feb 1809	Charles Miller			JACK	983		1870
00 000 1827	James H. Munson	James H & Elizabeth(Baxter)	Vt/Ky	MARI	966		1834
17 Dec 1856	G. A. Neal	Moses M & Letitia(King)	Ky/Ky	KC&	426		1881
18 Oct 1830	A. Netherton	John & Betsey(Wells)	Md/Md	CLPL	485		1856
01 Jul 1845	John H. North			USBI	497		1868
00 000 1792	Hon. John O'Fallon			FJWC	932		c1800
29 Dec 1859	Lee C. Phillips	Captain Thomas	Ky/--	SEGO	906		1855
22 Sep 1802	Shapley R. Phillips			SEGO	906		c1820
01 Dec 1806	Judge James B. Redd	John & Ann(Bullock)	Va76/Va74	MARI	796		1834
10 Jun 1810	Judge Amos Riley	Amose & Susan(Philips)	Md/Va	SEGO	908		1837

J E F F E R S O N   C O U N T Y   (C O N T.)

BIRTHDATE	NAME OF BIOGRAPHEE	PARENTS/BIRTHPLACE/BIRTHDATE	SOURCE/PAGE	FIRST MO.CO.	DATE
20 Dec 1840	William Riley	Amos	SEGO 909		1844
12 Apr 1824	John Shannon	Jeremiah & Jane(McClanahan)De97/Ky05	MARI 871		1845
15 Mar 1826	William Sherman	Charles R & Julia A(Porter)Md/Md	SEGO 999		1840
14 Mar 1874	E. W. Snyder	Christopher C & Mattie(Guill)	CLCA 784	Vernon	1875
05 Nov 1830	John N. Spickert	Nicholas & Mary A Fr/France	PETT 980		1866
17 Aug 1820	Richard F. Taylor	William & Elizabeth(Courts)Va56/Va	HSTC 598		1839
30 Sep 1834	James K. Tyler	Milton W & Mary(Seaton) **12/**14	JOHN 911		1856
02 Mar 1850	Milton W. Tyler	M. W **/--	PETT 830	Johnson	1869
28 Feb 1812	Milton W. Tyler		JOHN 911		1869
24 Jun 1825	Alfred Urton	James & Jane Va/Ky	GRUN 338		----
01 Feb 1828	Cain Urton		GRUN 649		----
00 000 0000	P. S. Winston		SERD 988		1878
00 000 0000	Isaac C. Withers		SALI 793	Knox	1851
14 May 1831	Marcus A. Wolff	Abraham B & Susan(Franklin)Eng/--	USBI 296		1844
07 May 1849	Fountain C. Yager	Dr. F. J & Alice(Smith) Ky/Ky	JASP 383		1875
14 Mar 1823	George Wheeler	Ignatius & Jennie(James)	CLPL 893		1855
26 Aug 1828	Joseph S. Wimp	William & Mariah **/--	SEGO 913		c.1835

J E S S A M I N E   C O U N T Y

BIRTHDATE	NAME OF BIOGRAPHEE	PARENTS/BIRTHPLACE/BIRTHDATE	SOURCE/PAGE	FIRST MO.CO.	DATE
10 Apr 1844	Hugh G. Allen	George W & Eliza(Sals) Va/Va	SALI 769		1860
10 Apr 1844	Hugh G. Allen	George W & Eliza(Sale) Va/Va	PIAS 248		1860
04 Dec 1845	Samuel P. Allen	George W & Eliza	SALI 644		1859
19 Nov 1831	Thomas J. Allen	George W & Eliza	SALI 631		1860

Date	Name	Parents	Origin	Abbr.	No.	County	Year
14 Feb 1830	Lucy J. Ballard	Dr. W. J & Elizabeth(Tapp)Va03/--		PLAS	186		----
06 Feb 1807	Levi Barkley			MARI	617		1829
00 000 1810	James M. Blackford			MOSH	1116		1832
29 Aug 1813	Jacob N. Brawner			CLIN	155	Clay	1831
02 Apr 1841	George S. Bryant			BOON	844		1850
29 Jul 1851	John D. Butler	John & Martha Ann		HOCO	922	Cass	1875
08 Jan 1808	Judge David W. Campbell			AUDR	698	Monroe	1838
19 Feb 1827	William Carter			LAFA	700		1869
24 May 1838	George W. Cassell			JACK	988		1848
00 000 0000	George W. Cassell	David & Mary(Corn) **14/Ky		KC&	645		1847
00 000 1828	Hugh H. Chrisman			SALI	727		1856
00 000 1833	William M. Chrisman			SALI	726		1849
11 Sep 1848	J. H. Christopher			JOHN	694	Cass	1850
08 Nov 1823	Capt. J. M. Collier	William & Susan(Higbee)	Ky/Ky	MOSH	896	Howard	1827
28 Feb 1852	T. B. Crutcher	Peter & Eliza		FGRU	645		----
10 Apr 1810	Benjamin P. Curd	James & Mary A(Perkins)	Va/Va	MARI	815		1834
00 000 1841	Andrew M. Dickerson	John & Paulina(Cravens)		PLAS	464		----
12 Jun 1821	Elizabeth M. Douglass	James & Hetty		DUNK	184		1850
03 Nov 1822	Nathaniel W. Dunn	Henry B & Nancy(Wilson)		MARI	732		1827
19 Jun 1824	Samuel F. Dunn	John & Elizabeth(Doak)		MOSH	908	Randolph	1824
28 Apr 1801	Williamson T. Dunn			MARI	759		1829
00 000 1830	James H. Faulconer			SALI	712	Pettis	1845
24 Feb 1833	William M. Featherston	Buzwell & Sarah(Wymore)		MOSH	435	Randolph	1841
10 Dec 1834	Robert J. Finney			MOSH	1122		1839
11 Feb 1816	Cyrus H. Frost	Simeon & Mary(Woods)		USBI	574	Washington	1821
00 000 1820	Hon. E. F. Frost	Simeon & Mary(Woods)	Ky89/Ky90	FJWC	892	Washington	1822
31 Dec 1833	Jacob R. Funk	John & Nancy(Rice)	Pa/--	CIPL	876		1855
25 Aug 1817	James Gooch	James & Deziah		MOSH	1123		1832
07 Jul 1831	D. Gregg			JACK	888	Clarke	1847
10 Nov 1834	Milton Grow	Peter & Sarah(Lewelen)	Ky/Ky	MOSH	561		1870
00 000 1821	Robert E. Hall			NW	927		1828
11 Feb 1833	George H. Hiffner			JACK	889	Clay	1857

BIRTHDATE	NAME OF BIOGRAPHEE	PARENTS/BIRTHPLACE/BIRTHDATE		SOURCE/PAGE		FIRST MO.CO.	DATE
00 000 0000	Susan Higbee	Joseph		NW	1834	Randolph	1855
16 Mar 1816	John Hightower			JACK	903		----
30 Jul 1846	George W. Holloway	Samuel & Jane P	Ky/Va	CSBA	497		1853
04 Apr 1820	Alfred Hoover			JACK	792		----
30 Jul 1846	George W. Holloway	Samuel & Jane P	Ky/Va	CSBA	497		1856
06 Nov 1850	Samuel W. Hoover			CSBA	451	Jackson	1840
27 Mar 1829	Dr. John H. Howard	Chichester & --(McGrath)		CALL	666		----
00 000 0000	John Hudson			BJAS	518		1820
11 Oct 1812	Major H. H. Hughes	Samuel & Nancy(Price)		HOCO	509		1822
30 Mar 1814	James Hughes	John & Elizabeth(Berry)	Pa??/--	USBI	79	Boone	1822
30 Mar 1814	James Hughes	John		NW	1174	Boone	1821
25 Jul 1817	Col. John T. Hughes	Samuel M & Nancy(Price)	--/**	CLIN	30	Howard	1820
21 Oct 1815	Joseph F. Hughes	Samuel M & Nancy(Price)	**/**	ANDE	568	Howard	1838
11 Jan 1820	Joseph S. Hughes	John & Elizabeth(Berry)		NW	876		1822
01 Jan 1820	Joseph S. Hughes	John & Elizabeth(Berry)		RAY	508	Boone	c1829
20 Apr 1827	M. R. Hughes			JACK	889	Howard	1869
03 Dec 1841	Robert M. Hunter	J. D & America(Bowen)	Ky97/--	RAY	663		1871
13 Jul 1827	William M. Jones	James & Eliza		HOCO	606		1844
05 Jun 1836	Jacob H. Kackley	Jacob		GRUN	586		1838
18 Dec 1812	Hon. John R. Keller			CLPL	342		1847
22 Apr 1827	Thomas Lessley			SALI	591	Randolph	1862
16 Nov 1830	James T. Mahin		Ky/--	JOHN	798		1869
24 Dec 1825	Henry Hoover	Jacob & Elizabeth(Rhorer)	Md/Md	CSBA	648		1853
09 Feb 1833	M. C. Masters			JACK	922		1829
29 Jun 1805	Colonel John Mays	Lindsey & Martha(Simpson)	Va/Va	MARI	629		1829
12 Mar 1818	Latham Mays	Lindsay & Martha(Simpson)	Va/--	MARI	794		1871
09 Jan 1846	John Messick			JASP	944		1870
10 Nov 1841	John Messick	John		CLPL	348		

Date	Name	Parents	Origin	County	No.	Location	Year
06 Jun 1829	H. Metcalfe	John P & Rebecca		HOCO	456		1857
16 Apr 1832	James H. Miller	Thomas & Nellie(Branham)		RAMA	493		1852
09 Apr 1818	John Minor	Thomas & Margaret(Garrison)Va/Va		MARI	652		1835
25 Nov 1802	Judge Alfred W. Morrison	William & Elizabeth(Williams)		HOCO	461		1820
00 000 0000	Edward G. Moseley	Edward & Lucy(Smith)	Ky/Ky	LCKS	931		1835
05 Sep 1826	John A. Mott	James & Hettie(Withers)	Va/**	SEGO	903		1852
00 000 0000	Catherine Nave			NW	1072		1848
20 Oct 1828	Charles M. Neet	Jacob & Sarah(Robb)		PLAS	479		----
00 000 0000	Frederick R. Neet	Jacob & Sarah(Robb)		PLAS	190		----
00 Aug 1833	F. R. Neet			IAFA	649	Saint Louis	1851
16 Oct 1824	Dr. W. C. Overstreet		Ky/Ky	PETT	1027		1847
25 Dec 1829	T. F. Peake	James L & Mary A(Francis)	Ky96/Ky10	MARI	868		1831
27 Dec 1813	Robert P. Peniston	Robert & Nancy(Nuttle)	Va/Md	CALI	1018	Daviess	1832
06 May 1812	Theodore Peniston	Robert P & Nancy(Nuttall)		DAVI	762		1831
00 000 1796	Major W. E. Price			CLPL	411		1824
13 Oct 1815	Montgomery M. Proctor			MARI	869		1830
00 000 0000	Dr. Thomas Proctor	Columbus		MOSH	341	Marion	1832
28 Apr 1816	Uriah Proctor	George M & Elizabeth(Beasley)Ky81/Ky	HPCD	598	Marion	1834
12 Oct 1840	Elijah H. Reid			CSBA	456	Cooper	1855
15 Apr 1806	Allen A. Rial	Richard & Parmelia(Dickerson)Va/Va		CALI	666	Marion	1830
00 000 1845	J. B. Robinsor	Benjamin & Virginia(Bryart)Ky/Ky		CSBA	594	Jackson	1851
06 Mar 1807	Hezekiah C. Roby	Thomas & Elizabeth(Cloud) Md/Ky		MARI	744	Monroe	1849
02 Oct 1813	William T. Rutherford	Shelton & Hannah(Roman)Fayette/Fayette	USBI	138	Randolph	1831
17 May 1833	J. T. Sale			JACK	908		1838
26 Apr 1817	Milton R. Singleton	Louis & Rebecca(Robards)	Ky/Ky	ANDE	535		----
00 Sep 1798	John S. Smith	Reverend George S	Va/--	USBI	299		----
17 Jul 1820	Thomas S. Smith	Thomas F & --(Lockett)	Va80/Va84	LCKS	1127	Buchanan	1837
16 Mar 1825	T. J. Sodowsky	James & Fannie S(Gatewood)Ky01/Ky99	CLIN	200		1845
18 Feb 1821	Dudley M. Steele			BUCH	901		----
18 Feb 1821	Dudley M. Steele	Samuel C & Elizabeth(Mitchum)		USBI	280	Andrew	1842
00 000 1857	J. D. Stipe			NW	833	Clinton	----
26 Jun 1856	R. J. Stipe	R. E & Ann(Long)	Ky/Ky	CLCA	495		1872

J E S S A M I N E   C O U N T Y   (C O N T.)

BIRTHDATE	NAME OF BIOGRAPHEE	PARENTS/BIRTHPLACE/BIRTHDATE	SOURCE/PAGE	FIRST MO.CO.	DATE
00 000 1818	James H. Sudduth	Francis & Sarah(Musick) Va/Va	LCKS 839	Ralls	1830
10 Feb 1841	Captain R. Todhunter		LAFA 542		----
00 000 1808	Lewis Tracy	-- & Sarah(Krisbaum) Ky/Ky	BUCH 920		----
00 Aug 1801	M. Treadaway	Daniel F & Esther(Organ) **/**	HSTC 793	Clinton	1867
08 Oct 1822	John Whitmore	Frederick & Mary(Hinds) Va/Va	RAMA 683		1845
27 Oct 1846	D. C. Wilmore	Jacob W & Mary J(Walter)	DAGE 594	Grundy	1879
03 Mar 1824	Capt. James M. Withers	Peter & Evalina(Price) Va/Va	PlAS 648		----
03 Mar 1827	J. M. Withers	Peter & Evaline	LAFA 684		1851
27 Sep 1819	William P. Withers		RAY 710	Howard	1843
23 Aug 1845	Dr. I. B. Woodson		JACK 865		1868
24 Oct 1828	Capt.Charles S. Wright	James G & Theresa(Anderson)Ky/NC	MARI 747		1836
00 000 1845	Thomas F. Yost	G.J & Elizabeth(Ritter) 06/13	CSBA 601	Jackson	1855
27 Jul 1839	William E. Yost	George & Elizabeth(Ritter) Md/Ky	CSBA 574	Jackson	1852
30 Sep 1829	Dr. Archibald L. Young		BOON 973	Callaway	1849
27 Jul 1824	Jessamine Young		CAUD 234		----

J O H N S O N   C O U N T Y

BIRTHDATE	NAME OF BIOGRAPHEE	PARENTS/BIRTHPLACE/BIRTHDATE	SOURCE/PAGE	FIRST MO.CO.	DATE
14 Feb 1846	Samuel Auxier	George W & Nancy(Prater)	ASPS 758	Buchanan	1868
00 000 1823	Isaac Preston	Isaac & Sarah(Downing) Va/Va	HPCD 836		1837

BIRTHDATE	NAME OF BIOGRAPHEE	PARENTS/BIRTHPLACE/BIRTHDATE	SOURCE/PAGE	FIRST MO.CO.	DATE
26 Apr 1847	Charles W. Batchelor	Joseph & Mary(Ashbrook) Pa/Ky	SCMW 833		----
00 000 0000	Juda Benson		BUCH 857	Clay	1837
15 Jul 1854	Nathan L. Burwell	John & Sarah M(Best)	LCDW 981		1881
02 Apr 1859	Caleb W. Dawley	James & Nannie H(Ambrose)	GREH 748		1867
16 Nov 1822	Mrs. Eliza J. Evans		SALI 587		1854
18 Feb 1861	Peter C. Glixner	John & Tracy(Felix) Germany/--	HPCD 893		----
00 000 1841	John R. Gosney		RAY 791	Lafayette	1869
22 Oct 1869	William H. Harrington	D. A. & Mary(Tobin) Ireland/--	JACK 785		1869
23 Dec 1823	John J. Johnson		BUCH 786	Saint Louis	1835
12 Dec 1805	John S. Pickett		BUCH 857	Clay	1837
05 Jul 1832	Sterling Powers	Richard C & Judah Va/Bourbon	LAFA 681		1852
24 Aug 1842	Samuel S. Rich		RAMA 427	Chariton	1876
25 Jan 1847	J. J. Sommer	J. J & Anna M(Bahlman) Germany/German	CWMB 892		----
00 000 0000	William Sparks		NW 1659	Platte	1860

BIRTHDATE	NAME OF BIOGRAPHEE	PARENTS/BIRTHPLACE/BIRTHDATE	SOURCE/PAGE	FIRST MO.CO.	DATE
03 Mar 1809	Samuel Cox	Frederick	CLIN 186	Buchanan	1873
06 Apr 1837	Ella S. Dorton	James B & Sallie B	RAY 640		1849
00 000 1836	James F. Dowis	Isaac & Elizabeth(Rogers) NC/NC	ASPS 1148	Nodaway	1854
20 Jul 1850	Jesse Engle	Campbell & Tempa S(Polly)	NW 921		1851

BIRTHDATE	NAME OF BIOGRAPHEE	PARENTS/BIRTHPLACE/BIRTHDATE	SOURCE/PAGE	FIRST MO.CO.	DATE
12 Nov 1819	Thomas G. Foley		DAGE	704		1833
29 Sep 1842	James M. Goodin	E. B & Jane(Fuson) Ky/--	HAME	701		1849
13 Oct 1833	James T. Green	Va/Ky	DAVI	804		1837
07 Aug 1846	Hezekiah Grisham	Joseph B & Johana(Gooding)	VADA	909	Putnam	1851
08 Jun 1811	Hon. Robert W. Jameson	Samuel & Rebecca(Rease) NJ/De	LCDW	854		1843
25 Dec 1830	David G. King	Joseph & Anna(Lauderdale) Pa90/--	HAME	700		1839
00 000 1827	Wesley McClure		PETT	791		1851
00 000 0000	Jane McIntosh	Jesse Tn/--	NW	1603		1852
30 Jun 1830	James G. Mackey	Elias & Sarah(Golden)Scotland/Tn	CALI	490		1841
00 000 0000	Tilford Moore		CLCA	720	Johnson	----
30 Dec 1836	Henry H. Moss	Joseph & Fanny(Pritchard)	CLPL	985	Daviess	1838
00 000 0000	John I. Peavler	Lewis & Kate(Head) Tn/Va	PLAS	394		----
09 Jul 1841	Dr. James F. Scott	Dr. Abraham C & Hannah(Denney)	JASP	711		1867
00 000 0000	William Sims		NLBM	880		1859
09 Sep 1838	Solomon S. Smith		JASP	1013		1879
22 Jun 1848	William S. Tuggle	Spencer H Va04/**12	DAVI	809	Clinton	1855
09 Dec 1809	Dr. James L. Wood	Capt. John & Margaret(Mane)--/Pa	RAMA	1080	Saint Louis	1845
17 May 1848	C. R. Woodson	Wade N	BUCH	983	Lafayette	1855
18 May 1819	Hon. Silas Woodson		USBI	277		1854
18 May 1819	Silas Woodson		BUCH	947		----
10 Sep 1841	William Word	Nelson & Margaret(Burch) Tn/Lincoln	CLCA	827		----

BIRTHDATE	NAME OF BIOGRAPHEE	PARENTS/BIRTHPLACE/BIRTHDATE	SOURCE/PAGE	FIRST MO.	CO.	DATE
12 Feb 1846	James Coy	John M & Siania	VADA 1083			1855
14 Feb 1853	T. A. Dunn	Philip & Lucinda J(Patterson)	HAME 519			1871
19 Jan 1826	Dr. Thomas Hodgen	Elder Jacob & Frances Park(Brown)	STLO 1534			1848
00 000 1829	Conrad Kaster	Nathan & Nancy⎰Gray⎱	ASPS 1177			1855
13 Feb 1824	James Kaster	Nathan & Nancy⎰Gray⎱	LCKS 780	Schuyler		1855
14 Jan 1847	William T. Marshall	Thomas & Jane(Rogers)	SEGO 988			1850
27 Mar 1852	E. C. Mudd		BATE 137			1873
28 Apr 1866	Henry M. Patterson		FGRU 708			----
22 Nov 1825	James A. Woodress		GRUN 600			----

BIRTHDATE	NAME OF BIOGRAPHEE	PARENTS/BIRTHPLACE/BIRTHDATE	SOURCE/PAGE	FIRST MO.CO.	DATE
00 000 1834	Charles Chesnut	Abraham	BUCH 705	Chariton	1850
23 Jul 1857	Hon.David A.Chesnut	William & Lucinda(Garrard;**26/Clay27NW	BUCH 2040	Platte	1859
04 Apr 1840	P. E. Chesnut	Abraham	BUCH 705	Platte	1859
12 May 1820	A. C. Chestnut		BUCH 1058	Daviess	1840
20 Jun 1856	Dr. S. W. Ewell	Richard L & Nettie(Ruke) Ky/Ky	CMMB 762		1883
31 May 1843	John M. Higgins	William & Sarah P(Owens) Ky/Ky	HAME 705		1854
00 000 1847	Meshach Hodge	Jeremiah & Frances(Freeman)	CMMB 1115		1853
11 Jun 1836	William R. Jackson	William & Lyda(Brock)	FGRU 304		----
15 Jul 1840	Jesse F. Parman	Frethias & Elizabeth(Curtis)Knox/KnoxCALI 520	Ray	1850
31 Mar 1831	Julian D. Smith	William & Sarah(Julian) Ky01/Tn	GREH 619		1838
06 Mar 1839	Samuel Stanbury	William & Malinda(Stansberry)	NLBM 884	Douglas	1846
10 Mar 1819	Remus Wise		LINN 629	Henry	1851
01 Jan 1862	Milton Wiser	William & Elizabeth Ky/Ky	CLCA 526	Mercer	1866

L A W R E N C E   C O U N T Y

BIRTHDATE	NAME OF BIOGRAPHEE	PARENTS/BIRTHPLACE/BIRTHDATE	SOURCE/PAGE	FIRST MO.CO.	DATE
11 Dec 1822	Reuben F. Cantebury	Reuben & Elizabeth(Lycan) Va/Va	CSBA 722	Marion	1836
17 Nov 1833	John M. Canterbury	Franklin P & Nancy	LAFA 531	Audrain	1835
28 Feb 1820	David D. Newman		CLPL 903		1836
01 Aug 1804	James L. Sperry		HOCO 581		1839
07 Dec 1839	J. B. Stafford		BUCH 1063	Platte	1842
19 Sep 1862	Rev. Marcus L. Stewart	Thomas H & Julia M	IMCD 298	Daviess	1864
12 Feb 1861	Granville Thompson	David J & Frances(Pennington)34/39	VERN 482	Platte	----
23 Jan 1834	Judge D.J.Thompson	Martin & Annie(Large) Va02/Va05	HPCD 782	Platte	1865

L E E   C O U N T Y   (N O N E)

L E S L I E   C O U N T Y   (N O N E)

L E T C H E R   C O U N T Y   (N O N E)

L E W I S   C O U N T Y

BIRTHDATE	NAME OF BIOGRAPHEE	PARENTS/BIRTHPLACE/BIRTHDATE	SOURCE/PAGE	FIRST MO.CO.	DATE
05 Feb 1845	Oliver A. Carr		BOON 846		1874
15 May 1832	Cynthia A. Davidson	Joseph & Nancy	NW 2010	Platte	1840
22 Feb 1826	Reverend I. D. Davis		BUCH 1012	Clay	1828

BIRTHDATE	NAME OF BIOGRAPHEE	PARENTS/BIRTHPLACE/BIRTHDATE	SOURCE	PAGE	FIRST MO.CO.	DATE
00 000 1840	James M. Fitch		JOHN	819		1865
00 000 0000	William Hackworth		SEGO	1100		1868
19 Nov 1823	John W. Jameson	John & Eliza Ky/--	LINC	558	Pike	1831
15 Apr 1844	Henry C. Lyons	William & Mahala(Bruce)Montg/Garrard	VERN	402		----
06 Jun 1827	Thomas H. Lyons	William Vt/--	VERN	402		----
10 Jun 1847	John F. Mitchell	Charles G & Mary J(Hendrickson)Ky/Oh	RAMA	1193		1858
00 000 1840	Judge Robert N. Thomson	Jchn & Jemima(Thomas) **13/--	LCKS	1221	Carroll	1853
22 May 1807	William Westhers	John & Henrietta(Carrington)Va/--	PETT	800		1842

L I N C O L N   C O U N T Y

BIRTHDATE	NAME OF BIOGRAPHEE	PARENTS/BIRTHPLACE/BIRTHDATE	SOURCE	PAGE	FIRST MO.CO.	DATE
19 Apr 1834	John A. Badgett	John R & America(Bosley) Ky/Ky	CSBA	1400		1877
17 Jan 1803	Dr. Thomas J. Bailey	John Va/--	GREH	596	Ralls	----
00 000 1795	George East		SEGO	743		c1827
12 Oct 1812	P. B. Bell	John T & Grace(Luckey)	PIKE	840		1830
07 Feb 1806	Greenbury Boyce		CALL	803		1829
10 Oct 1839	William H. Bright		RAY	760		1860
15 Nov 1835	Madison F. Brock	**/--	RAMA	1009		----
07 Jun 1831	W. S. Bryant	Edward G & Catherine(Kissenger)Ky/--	PIKE	843		1843
01 Jun 1831	C. T. Carter	James & Ann P(Estes) Ky/Mo	HOCH	1191		1836
29 Sep 1824	James Carter	Solonon & Sarah(Ballenger) Va/Ky	MARI	731		1849
24 Oct 1829	Jesse Carter	Pete= & Elizabeth(Nevin) Va/Ire	ASPS	1141		1837
26 Jan 1816	William Chapman	Richard & Elizabeth	SALI	863		1854
26 Jan 1829	Dr. E. M. Coffey	Richard N Va/--	CIPL	937		1849
17 Jun 1831	Capt.Alexander C.Cook	James Va/--	CLIN	129	Clay	1828
29 Feb 1828	Willis R. Cox	William B Va/--	NLBM	1062	Warren	1830
11 Jun 1811	Samuel Crutcher		SCMW	691		1831
16 Jul 1818	Thomas Crutcher	Charles & Elizabeth(Jones) Va/Va	MOSH	540		

LINCOLN COUNTY (CONT.)

BIRTHDATE	NAME OF BIOGRAPHEE	PARENTS/BIRTHPLACE/BIRTHDATE	SOURCE/PAGE	FIRST MO.CO.	DATE
22 Mar 1789	Tandy J. Davis	Thomas	SEGO 968		1845
11 Aug 1819	Capt. E. W. Dawson	Elijah & Sallie(Logan) Va/Ky	JOHN 783		1845
10 Dec 1840	George Delaney		CLIN 208	Harrison	1865
05 Apr 1832	G. E. Dickson		LAFA 539	Cooper	1838
11 May 1839	James M. Dinwiddie	Samuel & Patsy(McBride) Ky/Ky	BOON 758		1840
18 Dec 1833	William Dinwiddie	Samuel & Frances(Hughes)	BOON 584		1826
17 Jul 1831	John D. Dunn	Robert & Jane(Host)	HOCH 1074		1831
25 Apr 1827	P. P. Embree		JOHN 784	Cooper	1831
15 Feb 1817	Pembroke S. Epperson		SALI 605		1839
23 Jun 1834	Uriah Ferrell		LAFA 602	Saline	1839
00 000 1825	William J. Francis		CLPL 327	Gasconade	c1826
26 Dec 1814	George Gabbert	James & Polly(Sullivan)	CLPL 1056		1839
08 Oct 1817	William Gabbert	James & Polly S(Sullivan) Va/Va	CLPL 1048		1844
20 Nov 1796	H. J. Galbraith	Alexander	LAFA 660	Howard	1817
29 Oct 1829	John T. Garvin	James & Caroline(Thomas)	HOCO 533	Randolph	1836
16 Jun 1836	O. H. Gentry	Joseph & Elizabeth(Tribble)	KC& 362		1851
14 Dec 1837	Washington L. Gilbert	John C & Elizabeth(Huston)Va84/**	HSTC 1160	Johnson	1854
23 Sep 1839	Captain John W. Greenlee	Va/Md	JOHN 871		1842
19 Nov 1811	Thomas Hair	James & Elizabeth Ire/Ire	JACK 935		1865
16 Oct 1807	Joseph W. Hall	John & Rachel	SALI 870		1832
18 Jul 1822	Henry B. Hamilton	Thomas & Rachel	RAY 631		1832
27 Oct 1840	Charles D. Hocker	Philip S & Amanda(Duncan) Md/Va	NODA 919	Holt	1866
00 000 0000	John Hocker		BOON 720	Monroe	1830
00 000 0000	Larkin Hocker		JOHN 903		1835
20 Nov 1811	William Hocker	William & Sarah(Allnutt) Md/Md	HOCO 509		1824
08 Sep 1814	John Huntsman	Benjamin & Ann C(Darby) **88/**03	RAMA 656		1833
00 000 0000	Henry Hutchinson	William & Mary(Carpenter) Va/Ky	CALI 1034		----
25 Jan 1832	Adamantine Johnson	Major M & Betsey L(Jones) NC/--	HOCH 1204		1835

Date	Name	Parents / Spouse	Origin	Code	No.	County	Ref.
00 000 1808	Hugh Kelly			PETT	821		c1840
01 Jun 1849	John L. Level	A. T & Elizabeth J(Logan)	Ky/Ky	CIPL	857		1853
22 Apr 1851	William Logan	David & Nancy(Parks)		HSTC	778	Cooper	1826
24 Nov 1831	W. C. Logan			CLIN	140		1852
00 000 0000	Thomas McCanne			SCMW	879	Randolph	1830
18 Dec 1826	Charles L. McCormick			SALI	585		1850
13 Jan 1802	D. M. McCormick			SALI	609		1848
13 Jan 1802	Daniel McKinney			RAMA	658		1834
	Hiram McKinney			RAMA	658		1832
03 Aug 1837	Thomas L. McMullin	Dillord		JOHN	760		1840
00 000 1834	Daniel H. McQuerry			CLCA	765	Ray	1857
01 Jan 1845	William B. McRoberts	Hayden J & Lucinda R(Bruce)**10/**13		LCKS	799		1853
03 Jan 1816	William Magill	William		RAY	603		----
27 Nov 1814	John Mason			RAY	647		1836
00 000 1849	J. W. Meeker	Alfred & Lucinda(Allen)		CSBA	1408		1835
22 Sep 1830	William Moore	Samuel & Nancy		HSTC	---	Johnson	1874
08 Sep 1847	Mattie Myers			BOON	846		1855
00 000 1836	S. S. Neely			JACK	908		1876
24 Jun 1836	Dr. A. J. Norris			GREH	637		----
24 Apr 1847	Dr. S. A. Paxton	William & Matilda J 08/18		RAY	656	Pike	1855
30 Jan 1829	John T. Pendleton			JACK	826		1860
00 000 1847	J. C. Pendleton			JACK	878		1833
08 Apr 1811	Aytchmonde L. Perrin	Achilles & Jane(Smith)	Va/Va	CIPL	1029		1867
25 Feb 1818	William A. Pollock		Ire/--	JOHN	917		1846
30 Aug 1825	Tifny Sandidge			DAVI	574	Grundy	1834
00 000 1808	Elder John Shanks	John & Sarah(Gaines)		LCKS	830		1847
14 Jan 1842	Richard L. Shanks			JACK	1001		1849
18 Nov 1836	Hon.Jesse D. Skidmore	James C & Nancy(Adams)		LCKS	1214	Schuyler	1860
31 Dec 1841	Joseph Skidmore	Daniel & Elizabeth(Carman)**/Casey		NODA	921		1857
00 000 0000	David Smith	Elias	Va/--	CLIN	200		1854
02 Jun 1830	Edward H. Smith			LAFA	597		1867
10 Sep 1844	Judge William E.Smith	John C		NLBM	1089		----
00 Sep 1844	Judge William E.Smith	John C		IMCD	281		

LINCOLN COUNTY (CONT.)

BIRTHDATE	NAME OF BIOGRAPHEE	PARENTS/BIRTHPLACE/BIRTHDATE	SOURCE/PAGE	FIRST MO.CO.	DATE
25 Jan 1813	Joseph E. Sproul		MOSH 600		1829
19 Sep 1845	George W. Stansbury	William & Melinda(Stansberry)	NLBM 884	Barry	1846
00 000 0000	Henry D. Stringer	Thomas M & Nancy(Watkins) Ky/NC	PETT 739	Jasper	1874
25 Aug 1813	George Stults		JASP 856		1866
00 000 0000	Elizabeth Tankersley		BOON 720	Monroe	1830
17 Oct 1838	William P. Tate		SALI 727		----
12 Jan 1816	George M. Thompson	Nelson A	JACK 944		1852
00 000 0000	Jefferson S. Thurman		CLCA 479		----
19 Mar 1834	Jefferson S. Thurman	Willis S	NW 2012	Clinton	1856
12 Oct 1816	Dr. J. Warren	William & Lucretia(Taylor) Va/Ky	LAFA 660		1845
03 Sep 1838	Melinda J. Weldon	Andrew & Matilda(Ham)	GRUN 511		1839
00 000 1840	Henry M. Withers	James & Elizabeth(Carr) Va/Va	HOCO 977		1857
28 Sep 1808	Elijah Woods	John & Henrietta(Dunn) Va/--	HAME 757		1866

LIVINGSTON COUNTY

BIRTHDATE	NAME OF BIOGRAPHEE	PARENTS/BIRTHPLACE/BIRTHDATE	SOURCE/PAGE	FIRST MO.CO.	DATE
10 May 1867	James D. Brandon	John A & Fredonia(Burgess)	SERD 915	Dunklin	1891
00 000 0000	Edward L. Davis	William 11/--/--	SERD 959	Pemiscot	1880
06 May 1835	James J. Ray	James H & Hannah **05/**11	LAFA 519	Macon	1838
00 000 1865	William P. Robinson	James H Ky/--	SERD 1288		1890

L O G A N   C O U N T Y

BIRTHDATE	NAME OF BIOGRAPHEE	PARENTS/BIRTHPLACE/BIRTHDATE	SOURCE/PAGE	FIRST MO.CO.	DATE
00 000 0000	M. F. Adcock		JOHN 898	Morgan	1849
19 Sep 1842	Joseph R. Aingell	Presley & Carol(Rose) **/--	VERN 395		----
20 Jun 1830	Judge John W. Baker	William C & Mrs. Ann(Rayburn) Va/**	SEGO 1154	Dunklin	1859
00 000 0000	Commodore P. Barker	C. P & Nancy(Ragdale) Va/Ky	CSBA 1241	Henry	1866
14 Nov 1842	John Bennett	William & --(Ham) Ky/--	PETT 1068	Henry	1843
00 000 0000	James G. Bibb	Henry G & Elizabeth(Poe) Va/Va	RAMA 447		1853
07 Dec 1836	John A. Blanchard	Henry H & Mary W(Patton)	GREH 650		1839
00 000 1844	John B. Breathitt	Cardwell & Mary(Slaughter)	SALI 776	Cooper	1852
10 Dec 1827	F. M. Bradley	R. D & --(Baker) Fl/Ky	JOHN 932		1830
02 Apr 1824	Jefferson W. Britt	Bowling & Mary(Gautien) Va/Ky	CSBA 694		1849
03 Feb 1828	John W. Brown		LAFA 593		1829
00 000 1817	Edward Chastain		CSBA 1401	Benton	----
09 Aug 1836	Ellen Chastain	Jacob & Eleanor	HSTC 644	Benton	1837
13 May 1839	Dr. M.T. Chastain		SALI 758	Benton	1849
00 000 1813	William W. Chastain	William Va/--	NW 802	Benton	c1844
03 Sep 1823	Benjamin F. Clark	Samuel B & Elizabeth Ky/Ky	AUDR 448		1877
23 Apr 1834	Daniel W. Cloud	John & Catherine(Rutherford)	CSBA 1243	Lafayette	1852
00 000 0000	Elizabeth C. Crawford		AUDR 905	St. Francois	1855
27 Oct 1832	J. D. Cusenbary		JACK 887		1840
10 Jul 1812	Thomas W. Davis	Gen.Cornelius & Sally(Wilson)--/Va	CLPL 848	Saline	1822
05 Feb 1834	George W. Duncan	B. F & Sarah A	SALI 623	Howard	1837
19 Feb 1831	James P. Duncan	Benjamin F & Sarah A	SALI 604	Howard	1837
09 May 1859	James F. Dunscombe		SERD 952	Dunklin	1860
04 Oct 1851	Benjamin A. Duvall	Dr. Felix G & Hannah D(Ashburn)Nel/KyNLBM 828			----
30 Nov 1800	Chatman S. Ewing		LAFA 693		1821
14 Jul 1814	Hon. Major William C. Ewing Reuben & Mary(Hammor)Ky/DC		HOCO 1057		1819
20 Dec 1820	P. N. Grinter	John H & Nancy(Crewdson)	KC& 368		1849
02 Jan 1822	Jacob Hainley	Jacob & Bethla(Jenkins) NC/NC	SEGO 977		1838

-101-

BIRTHDATE	NAME OF BIOGRAPHEE	PARENTS/BIRTHPLACE/BIRTHDATE	SOURCE/PAGE	FIRST MO.CO.	DATE
26 May 1836	W. W. Hall		JOHN 755		1869
00 000 1833	Francis M. Ham	Joshua & Frances(Wood) NC/Ct	HSTC 582		1845
31 Jul 1824	Elisha G. Hayden	Elisha & Mary A(Harrison)	SCMW 927	Pike	1828
00 000 1816	Anthony G. Hickman		CMMB 952		1839
00 000 1835	E. S. Hite	E. S & Mary R(Butler) Va/Va	CMMB 777		1855
13 Sep 1853	M. P. Horn	N. D & Sarah F(Dawson) Ky14/Warren	NODA 1013		----
00 000 1816	Mathias Houx	Jacob	JOHN 824	Cooper	----
02 Jul 1826	James Hunter		JACK 794		1829
01 Jul 1838	Robert W. James		SALI 766		1865
08 Apr 1823	Thomas M. James	Thomas M & Polly(Poor) Va/Va	USBI 772		1854
20 May 1847	Francis M. Johns	J. H & Mary H(Glass) Tn/Shelby	AUDR 793		1880
17 Feb 1834	S. W. Judkins		HAME 556	Worth	1854
05 Oct 1829	Rev.Joseph W.Langston	R. N & Martha A(Galion)	GREH 695		1831
00 000 0000	Edward N. Larmon	Edward	CALI 437		1872
09 Aug 1851	John A. Lee	Nathaniel H & Frances(Evans)Va/Va	HOCH 972		1874
08 Apr 1830	William Loving	Willis	BUCH 814		1855
23 Feb 1816	Judge J.M. McCutchen	John & Anna(Matheral) Va/Tn	HOCO 1099		----
28 Aug 1838	George McIntire	William R & Rachel(McIntosh)	CALL 680		1853
15 Nov 1846	J. W. McIntire		CALL 679		1854
01 Jul 1814	R. G. Mabry		CMMB 725	Pettis	1841
20 Mar 1830	Judge Robert W.Mimms	John W & Mary(James) Ky/Va	CLPL 502		1856
31 Jan 1831	Joseph S. Moss		BOON 911	Greene	1838
00 000 1827	Charles B. Neal	Charles Va/--	HOCO 1041		1833
04 Dec 1853	Levi H. Orndorff	Ira & Nannie B(Grubbs) Ky/Ky	VERN 802		1872
18 Apr 1835	James L. Page	Lemuel J & Susan(Thomas) Va/Va	HSTC 671		1855
18 Mar 1823	Dr. Horace M. Parrish	Peyton & Mary A(Porter)	GREH 820		1837
10 Oct 1853	Dr. Solomon D.Preston		IMCD 309		----
07 Dec 1826	William H. Ragar	Peter C & Sarah(Simmons) Ky/Ky	MARI 742		1839

BIRTHDATE	NAME OF BIOGRAPHEE	PARENTS/BIRTHPLACE/BIRTHDATE	SOURCE	PAGE	FIRST MO.CO.	DATE
07 Apr 1825	Dr. David M. Simmons	John W & Sarah(Gallaway) NC04/NC	SEGO	1053		1860
25 Apr 1846	Felix B. Stenimons	J. M & Harriet	JASP	951	Lawrence	1853
04 Feb 1830	Jesse T. Swain	Cornelius & Martha(Tubbs) NC/Ky	HOCH	997		1851
11 Oct 1818	Benjamin F. Townsend		SALI	573	Cooper	1819
00 000 1832	John H. Townsend	George M & Nancy(Williams)Ky97/Ky02	SEGO	883		1841
00 000 1815	Winford G. Townsend	William & Mary(Langstone) **94/--	NLBM	1051	Greene	1832
05 Sep 1832	W. M. Townsend	William & Mary(Langston)	GREH	833		1832
00 000 0000	Emanuel Traughber		AUDR	905	St. Francois	1855
00 000 1828	B. F. Turner	Willis & Sarah(King) Va/Va	SEGO	1091		1856
29 May 1818	John C. Williams	Nathaniel & Nancy(Cross) Ky/Va	LINC	631		1820
06 Oct 1833	James Younger	William C Ky/-	LAFA	670		1857

L Y O N   C O U N T Y

BIRTHDATE	NAME OF BIOGRAPHEE	PARENTS/BIRTHPLACE/BIRTHDATE	SOURCE	PAGE	FIRST MO.CO.	DATE
19 Mar 1848	Dr. Frederick Cahn	Bernhart & Sarah	LINN	720		1876
11 Feb 1821	James A. Dobbins		SALI	801		1856
20 Jan 1854	James F. Evins	William S & Elizabeth(Winthrow)Ky/Ky	SEGO	925	Pemiscot	1856
06 Feb 1839	Mason H. Foley	Mason & Virginia **91/**04	SEGO	894		1861
00 000 1851	D. A. Glenn	William V & Sarah(Leech) Ga/Va	SEGO	758		1877
00 000 1843	Henry L. Machen		SERD	580	Scott	1877
13 May 1866	Lee Williams	Samuel & Harrett(Doom) --/Ky	SERD	1228	Dexter	1891

McCRACKEN COUNTY

BIRTHDATE	NAME OF BIOGRAPHEE	PARENTS/BIRTHPLACE/BIRTHDATE	SOURCE/PAGE	FIRST MO.CO. DATE
00 000 1839	Hon.James G.Donnell	Dr. Leander N & Rebecca(Ewing)Tn/Loga	SEGO 868	----
18 Aug 1842	William T. Fonville	Thomas T & Fannie(Murphy) NC/NC	SERD 1217	1861
06 Feb 1872	Edward D. Gillen	Edward & Loulie(Gardner) **33/**54	SERD 951	----
06 May 1851	Elijah W. Oglivie	Lemuel & Martha(Winstead) Tn97/Tn03	SEGO 992	1874
00 000 0000	R. R. Reynolds	Y. P & Mary E(Anderson) Ky/Ky	CHHO 425	1900
00 Jun 1837	John H. Smith		JOHN 765	Saint Louis 1839
23 May 1848	John W. Smith	William A & Mary R(Smith) Tn/Va	SEGO 1002	1875
14 May 1874	Julia Young	Thomas & Mollie	SERD 1260	----

McCREARY COUNTY (NONE)

McLEAN COUNTY

BIRTHDATE	NAME OF BIOGRAPHEE	PARENTS/BIRTHPLACE/BIRTHDATE	SOURCE/PAGE	FIRST MO.CO. DATE
07 Oct 1871	James W. Lynn	Rufus & Arabella(Van Horn)	SERD 1028	1880
00 000 1858	Daniel W. Roland		SERD 724	1903
21 Sep 1817	Absalom Vickers	John & Mary(Lands) NC96/Va	HSTC 793	1854

BIRTHDATE	NAME OF BIOGRAPHEE	PARENTS/BIRTHPLACE/BIRTHDATE	SOURCE/PAGE	FIRST MO.CO.	DATE
00 000 1816	Giles J. Adams	Joel & Mary Jane(Johnson) 97/VaOl	AUDR 910		----
05 Feb 1818	John W. Ammons	John L & Mary P(Irvin)	BOON 831		1822
13 Sep 1829	N. F. Arbuckle	Drinkard & Lucretia(Maxey) Ky/Ky	RAMA 989		1869
02 Jun 1815	James M. Armstrong	Mason Va/Ky	JASP 671		1855
16 Apr 1816	John M. Baber		CLIN 168	Clay	1836
19 Jun 1836	George S. Baker	Charles & Fannie(Saunders)	NW 1984	Buchanan	1846
11 May 1802	William M. Baker	Isaac & Jane(McCulley)	RAMA 643	Howard	1818
25 Jan 1835	William H. Ballard		CLPL 993		1858
18 Sep 1788	Elder James Barnes		BOON 1118	Howard	1800
08 Jan 1860	Thomas H. Barnes	Thomas H & Ann(Wingfield) **/Va	BOON 710		1866
07 Mar 1821	Camillus Barnett	Alexander & Elizabeth(Dinwiddie)	PLAS 572		----
00 Jul 1829	Capt.Joseph R.Barnett	Joseph & Elizabeth(Ryland) Va/Va	PLAS 192		1848
04 Aug 1814	Judge Robert A.Barnett	Alexander & Elizabeth(Dinwiddie)Va	PLAS 509		1835
23 Feb 1824	D. L. Beck		BUCH 1056	Lafayette	1840
01 Mar 1805	George L. Bennett	Joseph & Margaret(Davis) /	CALL 856	Boone	1818
20 Jul 1824	John R. Blackburn	Randolph & Frances(Jett) **81/**	KC& 483		1869
01 Mar 1805	George Bennett	Joseph & Margaret(Davis)	CALL 856	Boone	1818
08 Jan 1858	Edward Boen	James M & Phoebe A(Boggs)	NW 1187	Ray	1875
20 Dec 1840	Marcus A. Bogie	Daniel H & Emeline(Taylor)	USBI 566		----
20 Dec 1841	Dr. M. A. Bogie		JACK 742		1871
20 Dec 1841	Dr. Marcus A. Bogie	Daniel H & Emeline(Taylor) Ky/Ky	KC& 557		1871
26 Aug 1838	Thomas D. Bogie		RAY 515	Randolph	1859
19 Jun 1816	Capt.C. Bondurant	Edward Va/--	JOHN 776	Pike	1830
13 Jul 1820	Presley Boon		GRUN 731	Howard	1822
22 Feb 1795	Robert Boucher		RAMA 647	Howard	1818
00 000 1836	Thomas E. Brawner	George & Ann(Turner) --/**	LINN 424	Clay	1837
19 Jun 1835	Hon.Elbridge J. Broaddus	Andrew & Grace(Haskins)Va/Ky	CALI 1074		1868
14 Nov 1843	S. T. Broaddus		BATE 151		----

BIRTHDATE	NAME OF BIOGRAPHEE	PARENTS/BIRTHPLACE/BIRTHDATE	SOURCE	PAGE	FIRST MO.CO.	DATE
21 May 1848	Thomas M. Broaddus	George W & Elvira(Hocker) --/**	CSBA	1233		1873
15 Jul 1819	Isaac N. Brooks		BUCH	955	Johnson	1833
00 000 1811	Samuel H. Brown	James & Ann B(Clark)	HOCO	429		1815
30 May 1826	James R. Bryson	Andrew	BOON	714	Howard	1829
05 Feb 1809	James M. Burrus	Thomas & Mary A(Mills) Ky/--	HOCO	495		1816
15 Jul 1825	Harlan Butner	William & Nancy(Lowry) Va/--	MOSH	1155	Marion	1835
04 Apr 1831	John W. Butner	William & Margaret(Belcher)Ky/Ky	CALI	1076		1878
07 Nov 1811	D. I. Caldwell		JACK	869	Warren	1834
00 000 0000	Thomas J. Campbell	W. A **/--	NW	825	Clinton	1857
22 Mar 1820	William C. Campbell	William & Elizabeth(Snoddy)Va/--	CLPL	515		1834
18 Jan 1808	Hamilton Carson	Lindsey & Rebecca(Roberson)SC/Ky	HOCO	529		1811
00 000 1802	General John B. Clark		CHHO	196		1818
08 Mar 1822	David M. Clarke	Edward & Hannah(McIlvain)	CLPL	847		1826
20 Apr 1820	Charles Clarke	Edward & Hannah(McIlvain)	CLPL	848		1826
01 Jul 1808	Brutus J. Clay		AUDR	115		1873
03 Feb 1828	James W. Cochran	Samuel & Frances(Wood) NC/--	MOSH	1091		----
07 Nov 1821	Asa K. Collett	William & Jane(Hubbard) Va/--	ASPS	957	Howard	----
00 000 1802	Lewis Collier		CALI	1079	Howard	c1820
00 000 0000	Lewis Collier		USBI	819	Howard	1824
00 000 1790	William Collier	James	NW	1833		1827
15 Sep 1815	Andrew Collins		HOCO	603		1819
22 Sep 1789	Thomas Collins		NLBM	1061	Cooper	c1813
08 Jan 1815	Sanford Connelly	John & Elizabeth(Turner) Md55/**	BOON	754		1827
25 Dec 1842	Edward Cooper	Samuel & Nancy(Marcum) Ky16/Ky	FGRU	509		----
04 Dec 1800	Hendley Cooper		HOCO	531		1808
19 Feb 1814	Dr. James Cooper		GRUN	427	Boone	1837
30 Oct 1796	Joseph Cooper		HOCO	539		1808
17 Jan 1833	James W. Cosby	Winfield M & Amanda(Hudson)Va06/Va10	RAMA	687	Monroe	1867

Date	Name	Parents	Ky/Pa	Code	No.	County	Year
05 Nov 1803	Isaac Cox	Joseph & Sarah(Newland)	Ky/Pa	NODA	742	Buchanan	1842
08 Apr 1818	Hamilton Crews			HOCO	370		1834
05 Jan 1832	J. C. Crook			BUCH	1023		1848
05 Jun 1826	Isaac P. Davis	Charles & Elizabeth(Carter)Md/--		LCKS	1165	Montgomery	1834
00 000 0000	James M. Davis	Barnabas C & Julia(Davis) --/12		CALL	584		1815
12 Apr 1823	Marquis L. Davis			JASP	727	Cole	1828
23 Jun 1834	Joseph Dawes			NODA	565	Andrew	c1859
26 Dec 1811	Col.Bird Deatherage	Amos & Elizabeth(Howard)	Ky82/Ky90	HOCO	372		1817
00 000 0000	George W. Denham	Samuel		BOON	1087		1849
28 Oct 1838	R. B. Denny	Arthur & Frances(Rhodus)	Ky/NC	FJWC	739		1850
00 000 1835	Salem W. Dever	William & Jane(Clark)	**/--	CLIN	158		1857
29 Sep 1853	John H. Dillingham			NW	2046		c1855
04 Mar 1812	Robert S. Dinwiddie	Thomas & Sarah D(Moore)		PLAS	139		----
05 Jun 1829	James H. Douglass			KC&	665		1835
00 Apr 1825	William I. Douglass			JACK	901		1835
27 Aug 1803	Captain Dudgeon			HOCO	374		1836
27 Jul 1816	Daniel M. Dulany	Joseph S & Sarah(Maupin)		MARI	602	Howard	1816
20 Aug 1828	A. B. Dunn	James & Elizabeth(Burton)		CSBA	642		1856
20 Nov 1820	James W. Eastin			CLPL	465		1851
00 000 0000	George R. Estill	Daniel & Sallie(Broaddus) **90/**00		HOCO	440		1834
30 Jan 1819	James R. Estill	Wallace & Elizabeth		HOCO	504		1843
00 000 1841	John F. Evans	Green		CALL	563		----
06 Sep 1844	Thomas D. Evans	William & Paulina(Cornelliuson)Ky/Ky		LINN	722	Pettis	1856
30 Jan 1847	Solon H. Farrell	Daniel & Spicie(Irving) Ky/Ky		MOSH	464		1878
03 Nov 1822	Curtis Curtis Field	Curtis & Rosanna(Hardin) Va81/Ky91		PETT	649		1868
02 Mar 1858	John H. Field	Judge Curtis & Martha(Richardson)		AUDR	739		1868
00 000 1822	Thomas S. Foster			JOHN	902		1837
01 Jan 1829	Benjamin F. Fowler	Thomas & Emily(Tevis) Ky/Ky		CSBA	626	Cooper	1854
29 Jun 1819	R. P. Fox	Charles L & Nancy(Embry) Ky/Ky		PIKE	927		1841
19 Aug 1813	James M. Freeman	Jonathan & Anna(Coulton)		HOCO	1144	Boone	1825
02 Jun 1828	Robert Freeman			MOSH	555		1840
25 Jul 1813	Isom S. Gardner	Burket & Elizabeth(Linsey) Ky/Ky		BUCH	1028		1838

MADISON COUNTY (CONT.)

BIRTHDATE	NAME OF BIOGRAPHEE	PARENTS/BIRTHPLACE/BIRTHDATE	SOURCE/PAGE	FIRST MO.CO.	DATE
06 Jun 1797	Col. Joshua Gentry	Richard & Jane(Harris)	MARI 602	Howard	1816
21 Aug 1788	Gen. Richard Gentry	Richard Va/--	BOON 869	Saint Louis	1816
09 Sep 1807	Richard Gentry	Reuben E	PETT 937		1809
15 Apr 1815	George W. George		CLPL 397		1819
05 Jun 1812	Archibald Goin	Francis & Nancy	BOON 1089		1829
08 Dec 1825	Boyle Gordon		BOON 763		1826
00 000 1798	John B. Gordon	David & Jane(Boyle) NC/--	USBI 256		1826
00 000 0000	John B. Gordon	David NC/--	BOON 873		1826
00 000 0000	Squire Green		AUDR 882		1818
00 000 0000	Wesley S. Greene		HOCO 576		1819
26 Feb 1829	Abner Grinstead		JOHN 872	Callaway	1830
01 May 1827	Capt.David Guitar	John & Emily(Gordon)	BOON 764		1829
31 Aug 1827	Gen. Odon Guitar	John & Emily	BOON 877		1829
00 000 1793	Samuel T. Guthrie		CALL 590		1819
10 May 1818	Henry D. Guyer	John & Ellen(Hill) Va93/NC92	LINN 856	Cooper	1834
06 Aug 1828	Gideon Haines	Jonathan & Elizabeth(Wright)Ky/Ky	RAMA 633		1832
00 000 0000	Rev.Stephen Ham		SCMW 868		----
26 Oct 1854	Edgar M. Harber	Thomas B & Mildred(Phelps)	FGRU 775		----
26 Oct 1854	Edgar M. Harber		GRUN 448		----
00 Oct 1829	T. B. Harber		GRUN 446	Clinton	1857
13 Jan 1821	Dr. Joseph E. Harris		GRUN 446	Clinton	1854
00 000 0000	Josephus Harris		SEGO 639		----
25 Dec 1821	Thomas B. Harris	Tyre	CALL 658	Boone	1815
00 000 0000	John Harvey		HOCO 576		1817
00 000 0000	William Harvey		HOCO 577		1818
14 Jul 1828	A. J. Hawkins	John & Rebecca(Skinner)	BOON 590		1829
28 Feb 1813	Harrison Hawkins	James & Nancy(White) Va/Ky	HOCH 958	Boone	1834
10 Aug 1852	William H. Hawkins	Edward & Lucinda(Elder) Ky/Ky	NODA 773		1869

Birth Date	Name	Parents	Origin	Co.	No.	Location	Year
03 Mar 1825	James Henderson	John & Elsie(Quick)	Tn/NC	NODA	774		1857
03 Aug 1833	John W. Hendrix	Allen & Levina(Howard)	Ky90/Ky	RAMA	561		1840
00 000 1827	William J. Herndon		Va/--	SALI	709	Cooper	1830
00 000 0000	Overton Hern			HOCO	549	Pike	1830
09 Oct 1835	Columbus Higgerson		Va/Va	HOCO	985		1837
14 Jan 1813	William H. Holman	Joseph & Nancy I(Zachary)		RAMA	1165	Howard	1818
21 Feb 1822	Alexander J. Horn	William & Elenor(Barns)		NODA	534	Buchanan	1841
16 Nov 1817	Thomas Howard	Matthew& --(Tolson)	**94/Va96	HOCO	388		1844
28 Oct 1807	Fleming Hubbard			AUDR	888		1826
00 000 0000	Michael W. Hubbard			SERD	922		1861
07 Apr 1807	M. W. Hubbard	Greenvil & Mary(Jarman)	Ky/Ky	DUNK	206		1861
03 Oct 1840	Hon.Walter D.Hubbard	John H & Sarah A		GREH	760		1845
03 Oct 1840	Walter D. Hubbard	John H & Sarah A (Brooks)	**17/--	USBI	517		1845
13 Nov 1846	Merrill Hughes			SALI	604		1879
01 Jan 1831	John G. Hume	Reuben & Annie(Finks)	Va/--	HOCO	444		1844
06 Mar 1843	Lewis Hume			BOON	890		1819
00 000 0000	R. H. Hume			GRUN	450		1869
00 000 1790	Judge Frederick Hyatt			STLO	1472		1815
24 Jul 1823	William J. Jarboe			JACK	796		1834
20 Mar 1813	Talton Johnson	William & Catherine(Barnes)	SC/82	HOCO	390		----
02 Oct 1848	M. B. Jolly	Spear & Susan		FGRU	779		1865
00 000 0000	William E. Jones	Christopher H		BOON	662		1818
10 Aug 1849	Clifton T. Kerby	E. P & Elizabeth E(Baker)		RAMA	485	Howard	1859
22 Aug 1833	Daniel B. Kidd	Allen & Mildred(Gorland)	Va/Va	HSTC	1146	Boone	1834
00 Oct 1824	Thomas D. Kidwell			HAME	559	Gentry	1855
15 Dec 1828	John F. Kinkaid	Joseph & Roda(Baugh)		MARI	700		1830
15 May 1816	Colby Lanham			CLIN	139		1841
10 Feb 1818	James Leveridge	Joseph & Mary(Shields)	Ky91/Ky99	HOCO	392	Platte	1824
16 Nov 1798	James Lewis			JACK	892		1825
02 Feb 1811	John H. Lewis	Charles	Va/--	PETT	993		1838
21 Oct 1813	Joel Lipscomb	Nathan	SC/--	KC&	273		1839
16 Jun 1836	W. T. Long	L. D & Cynthia(Phelps)	Va09/**	NODA	874	Chariton	1847

BIRTHDATE	NAME OF BIOGRAPHEE	PARENTS/BIRTHPLACE/BIRTHDATE	SOURCE/PAGE	FIRST MO.CO.	DATE
21 Oct 1813	Joel Lipscomb		JACK 982		1839
01 Apr 1800	Ephraim S. McClain		SALI 638	Howard	1811
30 Jan 1832	B. F. McCord		LAFA 662		----
07 May 1822	Francis M. McCoyl	Jesse & Jane(Powell) NC/Tn	VERN 550	Henry	1865
15 Jun 1805	Thomas M. McMahan	Samuel & Sarah(Clark) Ky/Ky	HOCO 988		1811
21 Sep 1829	F. M. McVay	Patrick & Malinda(Austin) Va/Va	JACK 892	Pike	1833
08 Apr 1829	Sidney McWilliams	Alexander C & Jane C(Breedlove)**/Va	USBI 710	Caldwell	1857
08 Apr 1829	Sidney McWilliams	Alexander C & Jane C(Breedlove)**/Va	CALI 1164		1857
00 000 1839	Azariah Martin	Maston B & Lucinda(Hill) **09/**15	SEGO 1109		1845
00 000 1843	A. H. Martin	Lewis B & Elizabeth	SALI 614	Pike	----
03 Dec 1828	Hudson Q. Martin	Hudson & Lucy(Hill) Va/Va	HOCO 553		1829
13 Dec 1805	Merideth Martin	Tyree & Mourning(Jones) Va/WV	USBI 21	Boone	1816
30 Sep 1828	Dr. Thomas J. Mattingly	Ignatius & Mary(Daft) Md/Md	DAVI 635		1852
00 000 0000	William Maupin		BOON 905	Howard	1816
06 Apr 1821	Robert M. Maxwell	Thomas J Va77/Va80	JOHN 916	Howard	1826
19 Nov 1831	Dr.Robert T.Miller	James E & Harriet F **/**	PETT 701	Moniteau	1844
10 Oct 1819	Travis Million	Joel & Mary(Saunders)	MOSH 468		1838
17 Dec 1831	William C. Mings	George W & Pollie(Kanatzar)Wayne/Ky10LCDW 1187			----
08 Jan 1841	B. A. Moberly	Simon & Armentina(Banta) Ky/Ky	VERN 757	Clinton	1855
02 Aug 1835	C. D. Moberly	William & Susan(Davis) Ky/Ky	CSBA 650	Cooper	1853
00 000 1817	Martin S. Morris		NW 1449		1871
31 Dec 1811	Thomas Morris		LINN 842	Howard	1833
28 Apr 1813	Mathew Mullins	Richard & Susanna(Woods) Ky/Ky	HOCO 521	St. Charles	1813
01 Feb 1828	Phoebe A. Neal		NW 924		1832
00 000 1824	Allen Nickerson	John & Ruth	LINN 663	Howard	1835
05 Dec 1830	George W. Noland	Joshua & Sallie(McKinney) Ky/Ky	CLPL 863		----
00 000 1840	Napoleon B. Ogg		RAY 598		1868
15 Jun 1837	Thomas J. Ogg		RAY 597		----

Date	Name	Parents	Origin	County	Code	Number	Year
26 Apr 1826	F. B. Oldham	Enoch & Harriet	Ky01/Ky05		CSBA	592	----
07 Sep 1838	Cyrus Park				CLPL	357	1868
07 Mar 1818	John Park			Pettis	JOHN	908	1838
14 Nov 1822	Overton Park	James & Polly(Benton)		Benton	HSTC	753	1841
12 Oct 1842	Thomas W. Park	Elihu & Mary(Ballou)			NW	2049	1857
00 000 0000	Jonah Parke				STLO	1881	1807
06 Jul 1815	Edmond J. Parks				CLCA	504	c1833
00 000 0000	Rebecca Patton				CALL	546	----
00 000 1820	D. H. Payton	Yelverton & Mildred(White)	Ky90/**	Randolph	HOCO	596	1843
00 000 1815	Judge Yelverton W.Payton	Yelverton & Mildred(White)	**/**	Randolph	ASPS	1194	1843
12 Oct 1842	Thomas W. Park	Elihu & Mary(Ballew)	Ky/Ky		USBI	638	1857
25 Feb 1811	Rice Patterson	Thomas & Mary(Harvey)		Clay	HOCO	579	1817
16 Mar 1831	C. C. Perkins				CLIN	168	1836
00 000 1821	Robeson Perrin	James & Milkey(Paget)	NC/NC		RAMA	1000	1849
00 000 1819	Rev.William Perrin				HOCH	799	1821
26 Nov 1835	T. T. Phelps				CLIN	145	1857
19 Oct 1829	Charles H. Prather	Thomas & Polly(Cowan)	Ky/Va		BOON	603	1830
17 Mar 1836	John T. Redd	Samuel & Nancy(Cornell)	Va/Va		HOCO	990	1836
26 Jan 1843	Sanford Reed	Orestus			BOON	1095	----
15 Jan 1829	James I. Reid				CSBA	672	1873
00 000 0000	John M. Reid			Howard	HSTC	790	1809
11 Apr 1825	Meredeth Rice	James & --(Turner)			JOHN	943	1869
00 000 1830	Samuel Rice		Va/Va		JOHN	944	1853
04 Mar 1824	Thomas H. Richards	Reason & Elizabeth(Patterson)	**/*	Boone	HOCO	558	1827
13 Dec 1820	James Richardson	Thomas & Mary(Harris)	Va/Ky		HOCO	580	1859
12 Mar 1829	James F. Roberts	S & M(Park)	NC98/**09		CSBA	594	1859
09 Dec 1839	Jesse T. Roberts	A.J	**/--		RAY	695	1868
15 Dec 1817	John Roberts	William M & Martha	Ky/Ky		BOON	1130	1827
19 Apr 1812	Hon.James S.Rollins	Dr. Anthony W & --(Rodes)	Ky/Va		BOON	933	1830
17 Dec 1816	Craven P. Ross	John & Nancy(Peyton)			RAMA	1139	1817
06 Apr 1818	John H. Sampson	Richard & Mary(Watkins)	Md80/Va89	Howard	BOON	1052	c1839
06 Oct 1815	Thomas W. Sampson	Richard & Mary(Watkins)	Md80/Va89		BOON	1053	----

BIRTHDATE	NAME OF BIOGRAPHEE	PARENTS/BIRTHPLACE/BIRTHDATE	SOURCE/PAGE	FIRST MO.CO.	DATE
06 May 1824	J.H. Saunders	John	NODA	821	Buchanan	1843
21 Mar 1835	Richard Saunders	John & Nancy	NODA	822		1843
03 Feb 1822	Dr. James H. Shoot	Frederick & Rebecca(Taylor)Ky/Mo	JASP	588	Monroe	1838
12 Feb 1811	Meashek Sigler	John & Nancy(Hodge) Tn/Tn	LCKS	1212		1861
18 Sep 1835	Willis M. Simmons		CIPL	414		1857
04 Feb 1832	Alfred Sims	Abram & Gracie(Robards) Ky/Ky	BOON	608		1834
00 May 1844	B.H. Smith	James & Mary(Howard) **/**	CSBA	1412	Cooper	----
00 000 1806	David Smith		BOON	1098		1824
10 Feb 1794	David Smith	James & Margary Ire/Ire	HOCO	916		1816
20 Jul 1838	Judge James T.Smith		HOCO	408		1856
03 Apr 1842	Solon Smith		HOCO	408		1857
00 000 1794	Capt. William Smith		BOON	1097		1819
13 Feb 1831	David Stagner		BUCH	1063	Livingston	1854
20 Oct 1826	J.N. Stagner		BUCH	1063	Livingston	1849
15 Aug 1853	John T. Stagner	James C & Charlotte(Elledge)**/**	CALI	505		1857
00 Dec 1824	Major L.R.Stagner	Thomas & Nancy(Moppine) Ky/**	PLAS	171		----
18 Jul 1828	William T. Steele		BUCH	1038	Platte	1840
23 Apr 1834	Andrew T. Stephenson	Jesse & Elsus(Blankburn) Ky/Ky	NODA	839	Buchanan	1844
27 Jun 1822	-- Stephenson		NODA	836		1844
00 Mar 1845	Hon.Charles C.Tevis	Cyrus Ky/--	JOHN	769		1869
07 Nov 1803	Jesse Thomas		JACK	1002		1839
11 Nov 1829	William G. Thornton	William & Henrietta(Standley)Va95/Va	JOHN	910		----
26 Apr 1836	Levi Todd		DAGE	472		1869
04 Dec 1804	Neriah Todd	Thomas & Mary(Chenault) NC71/Ky75	HOCO	414		1816
28 Oct 1804	Robert Todd	Joseph & Cynthia(Williams)	ANPL	130		1817
00 000 1841	S.W. Todd	Isom F & Nancy(Woolery) Ky/Ky	NLBM	991	Dade	1878
16 Oct 1821	A.C. Tolson		HOCO	583	Calloway	1823
10 Jan 1816	Judge Ben H. Tolson	John & Rebecca(Howard) Va91/--	HOCO	414		1819

BIRTHDATE	NAME OF BIOGRAPHEE	PARENTS/BIRTHPLACE/BIRTHDATE	SOURCE	PAGE	FIRST MO.CO.	DATE
17 Feb 1819	Jeremiah Tomlinson	Ambrose D & Frances(White)**87/--	HOCO	1009	Morgan	1838
03 Mar 1805	James E. Turley	Samuel A & Sally Va69/Va70	CALL	574		1829
00 000 1812	Augustus Turner	Enoch & Susan(Tolson)	AUDR	906	Boone	1816
02 Nov 1791	Talton Turner	Philip & Abigail	USBI	452	Howard	1818
24 Aug 1791	Thomas Turner		AUDR	907	Boone	1825
23 Jan 1850	Cassius M. VanWinkle	John B & Patsy Jackson/Jackson	CLCA	525		1881
26 Aug 1839	Nancy Vaughn		DACE	472		1869
31 Mar 1813	Thomas B. Wallace	John & Elizabeth(Walker) Va83/Va84	LAFA	624		1819
31 Mar 1813	Thomas B. Wallace	John & Elizabeth(Walker) Va83/Va84	USBI	231		----
00 000 1812	William J. Wallace	Samuel & Anna(Snoddy)	CALI	935	Howard	1819
30 Mar 1830	Thomas J. Wherritt	Barton & Margaret(Peacock)	CSBA	549		1852
00 000 0000	George L. White	John R	PETT	1020		1871
10 Sep 1877	H. C. White	Durrett V & Sallie(Arvin) **36/**46	CHHO	386		1881
22 Jun 1876	J. T. White	Durrett V & Sallie(Arvin) **36/**46	CHHO	382		1881
12 Feb 1869	William S. White	Durrett V & Sallie(Arvine)	CHHO	432		----
23 May 1815	Dr. J. B. Winn	William & Mildred(Hurt) Va/Adair	USBI	637	Howard	1819
00 000 1797	James Winn		HOCO	608		1817
00 000 0000	Patrick Woods		HOCO	585		1816

MAGOFFIN COUNTY (NONE)

MARION COUNTY

BIRTHDATE	NAME OF BIOGRAPHEE	PARENTS/BIRTHPLACE/BIRTHDATE	SOURCE/PAGE		FIRST MO.CO.	DATE
20 Mar 1814	John Arthur	Barnabus & Nancy(Vaughn)	LCDW	1027	Franklin	----
16 Sep 1837	Capt. Marcus L. Belt	Dr. William M Jessamine/Va	PLAS	524		----

BIRTHDATE	NAME OF BIOGRAPHEE	PARENTS/BIRTHPLACE/BIRTHDATE	SOURCE	PAGE	FIRST MO.CO.	DATE
13 Feb 1830	A. L. Bickett	Anthony & Ann(Knott) Md83/In91	NODA	726		1857
16 Nov 1817	Edmund G. Bickett	Henry & Elizabeth(Graves) Md/Ky	NODA	725		1846
00 000 1807	James Bradford		LCDW	1096	Phelps	1827
24 Jan 1843	Charles W. Bullock	Samuel & Celia(Buckler) In/**	VERN	862		1876
00 000 1845	Richard Campbell		SALI	796		
00 000 0000	Joseph Cissell	Bernard Eng/Eng	SEGO	693		1803
06 Jun 1847	George A. Crowdes		NODA	527		1851
00 000 1827	W. B. Edelen	Leonard & Susan(Bruce)Washing/Lincoln	CSBA	582		1872
07 Jul 1857	W. B. Elliott	Berryman & Nancy J Ky/Ky03	HOCO	878		1860
28 Oct 1797	Judge John B. Helm	Judge John	MARI	608		1852
06 Feb 1831	Sally Inman		AUDR	876	Randolph	1854
14 Oct 1847	M. L. Lear	Thomas & Julia A(Nicholson)Ky/Ky	MARI	700		
00 000 1832	Benedict J. Lee	James & Sarah(Hayden) Ky03/Ky03	ASPS	836	Howard	1832
13 Jan 1843	Elijah Loyd	Ila M & Charity Ky/Ky	JASP	633		1861
00 000 1826	John C. McBride	Stephen & Elizabeth(McCauley)Nels/**	SEGO	713		
00 000 1828	John F. McMurray	William	----	---	Marion	1834
22 Apr 1837	Charles P. Medley	John S & Barbara A(Wathen) Ky/Md	SEGO	783		1848
09 Feb 1835	David W. Meriwether	James & Elizabeth(McMurray)Va05/**09	LCKS	1085		1839
09 Mar 1835	James L. Miller	Lewis & Agnes(Anderson)	CIPL	1002		1821
12 Apr 1797	Col.William Muldrow	John & Margaret(McElroy) Ire/--	MARI	625	Ralls	1859
00 000 0000	Charles C. Pierce		RAMA	1088	Randolph	1855
08 Jul 1839	John G. Rakes	Wilson P Va09/--	CMMB	881		
00 000 1836	Thomas W. Robinson	George C & Dorothy A	SEGO	727		
24 Apr 1827	R. M. Scott	George W & Sarah(Thurman) Ky/Ky	CSBA	700	Andrew	1854
29 Jun 1824	S. M. Scott	George S & Rachel(Miller)Cumber01/08	ANDE	533		1854
23 Sep 1818	Thomas Shelby	William & Nancy(Edmondson) Va/Va	PLAS	381		1836
23 Sep 1818	Thomas Shelby	William & Nancy(Edmondson) Va/Va	IAFA	365		1836
05 Jul 1839	James R. Shocklee	James M & Nancy A(Lee) Ky/Va	SCMW	945	St. Charles	1850

BIRTHDATE	NAME OF BIOGRAPHEE	PARENTS/BIRTHPLACE/BIRTHDATE		SOURCE/PAGE	FIRST MO.CO.	DATE
19 May 1813	Dr.James A.Shuttleworth	Allen & Anna(Washburn)	Va/Md	CSBA 516		1867
28 Dec 1839	Judge Oscar F.Smith	Judge Jacob & Frances P(Crews)	Ky/Va	HOCH 993		----
21 Oct 1816	Daniel H.Tucker			RAY 654		1835

M A R S H A L L   C O U N T Y

BIRTHDATE	NAME OF BIOGRAPHEE	PARENTS/BIRTHPLACE/BIRTHDATE		SOURCE/PAGE	FIRST MO.CO.	DATE
13 Jan 1854	William C. Graddy	Lewis W & Eliza(Carpenter)**21/24		SEGO 1075		----
09 Oct 1837	James O. Gray	Harrison & Mary	Ky/Ky	SEGO 975		1859
10 Oct 1847	Rufus B. Jones	James L & Sarah(Whitlock)		SEGO 1037		1865
23 Feb 1840	Haston Yales	John & Laura T(Butler)		SEGO 1010		----

M A R T I N   C O U N T Y   (N O N E)

M A S O N   C O U N T Y

BIRTHDATE	NAME OF BIOGRAPHEE	PARENTS/BIRTHPLACE/BIRTHDATE		SOURCE/PAGE	FIRST MO.CO.	DATE
09 Jan 1859	Henry W. Adamson	James M & Matilda(Krusor)		BATC 36	Holt	1874
13 Dec 1837	C. L. Allen	John & Elizabeth(Lyne)	Ky/Ky	HPCD 618	Scotland	1865
11 Mar 1835	George F. Allen	Samuel & Nancy(Fielder)	Ky/--	HOCH 1133		1867
03 Jan 1813	Joseph D. Anderson	George & Sally	79/81	NW 1032	Clay	1834
10 Feb 1814	N. W. Asbury			JACK 994	Pike	1829
01 Apr 1819	Judge James Baker	M & Margaret(Waters)		GREH 742		1864
06 Apr 1815	James H. Baldwin	James & Sarah(Harris)		ANPL 201		----

BIRTHDATE	NAME OF BIOGRAPHEE	PARENTS/BIRTHPLACE/BIRTHDATE	SOURCE/PAGE	FIRST MO.CO.	DATE
19 May 1817	Judge Jesse A.Boulton		BOON	749	1840
13 Oct 1871	W.A. Browning	L.Y & Henrietta(Ware) Ky/--	CHHO	636	----
05 Nov 1833	Judge Cavon D. Burgess	Henry D Md/--	LINN	422	Saint Joseph 1855
13 Oct 1851	H.G. Burgess	O.B & P. D(Kilgore)	CSBA	482	Clinton 1864
15 Aug 1820	O.B. Burgess		CLIN	206	Platte 1864
12 Mar 1830	J. Kate Burgess	John D & Lydia M(Wise) Md/Va	BUCH	695	1855
15 Jun 1828	Thomas J. Burgess		BUCH	693	1850
01 May 1810	William Buxton	William & Rachel(Trail) Ky/Ky	CLPL	390	1836
00 000 0000	James W. Coburn	Dr. John A & Elizabeth M(Wood)Ky/Ky	CLPL	1050	1866
00 Dec 1841	Capt.Richard A.Collins	Gen. Richard	LAFA	527	1857
03 Jun 1797	Major William C.Connett		BUCH	986	1839
09 Feb 1813	Richard S. Corwine	George & Nancy(Thornton) NJ/Va	HSTC	690	1872
18 Jan 1819	Benjamin P. Crawford	Crozard & Lavina(Reynolds) Ky/Ky	GRUN	716	----
19 Jun 1824	William G. Daulton	James & Naomi(Wakeman) Ky/NY	LINN	537	1829
00 Jan 1799	Greer W. Davis		BENC	27	1818
04 Nov 1844	Benjamin F. Dobyns		AUDR	730	c1855
11 Mar 1815	David P. Dobyns	James Reed	HOLT	357	----
04 Apr 1853	G.H. Dobyns	Henry M & Elizabeth(Allen)	HOCH	1147	1876
09 Jul 1808	Alexander W. Doniphan	Joseph & Ann(Smith) Va/Va	RAY	498	1830
09 Jul 1808	Gen.A.W. Doniphan		BUCH	251	1830
30 Jan 1836	Elza P. Donovan	James & Mary(West) Va/Va	CLPL	392	1855
00 000 0000	Charles Dougherty		ANPL	262	1842
17 Jul 1834	Jacob Downing	Charles & Susan **02/**07	CALI	655	Clay 1855
15 Feb 1834	James Dye	John & Parthenia(Gow) Pa99/Ky00	CLPL	1096	1851
26 May 1824	Jane Dye		BUCH	1036	----
00 000 0000	James Ellis		NW	660	----
28 May 1829	Alfred Fenton	John Va/--	BUCH	1012	1850
00 000 0000	Washington Fitzgerald		FJWC	748	Saint Louis 1818

Birth Date	Name	Parents / Notes	Code	No.	County	Year
20 Nov 1810	G. C. Fletcher		SALI	764	Pike	1830
00 000 1813	William Fletcher	John & Ellen	LAFA	495	Pike	1829
00 000 0000	Benjamin J. Franklin		ANPL	177		----
00 Aug 1844	Baldwin B. Gill	**/Ky	CALI	1096		----
13 Nov 1808	B. B. Gill	Baldwin & Lydia(Moss)	GRUN	324	Livingston	1855
20 Jul 1828	Charles I. Gooch	James & Elizabeth(Moss)	HSTC	691	Booneville	1851
17 Dec 1805	Arthur Gow	Charles I & Tabitha(Walton)Va/Ky	NW	1034		1830
29 Jan 1829	George W. Griffith	John & Mary A	JACK	934	LaFayette	1836
00 000 0000	Ewen C. Hale		NW	889	Clinton	----
00 000 0000	James Hale		NW	1052		1844
00 Sep 1836	Moses Henderson		RAY	811		1847
19 Feb 1806	Thomas M. Hickman		BUCH	1032	Saint Louis	1827
07 Jun 1834	E. H. Hord		CLIN	173		----
18 Mar 1834	Major E. Livingston Hord	Lewis	AUDR	781	LaFayette	1853
20 Oct 1819	Hon. James B. Hord		LAFA	606		1850
21 Oct 1823	Mason A. Hord		CLIN	29	Clay	1847
09 Sep 1818	J. J. Howe		JACK	1005	Clay	1855
15 Jun 1813	Walter S. Hull	James H & Clarinda(Chandler)Ky/Ky	CLPL	1100		1844
27 Apr 1849	Harvey W. Isbell	Rev.E. D & Sarah E(Wheat)Bourbon/--	VERN	650		1878
06 Nov 1818	Thomas R. James	Berryman & Mary	LAFA	669	Lexington	1840
31 May 1809	M. T. January	Thomas Thruston	VERN	650		----
30 Aug 1810	Elizabeth Jones		ANPL	91		1839
19 Jan 1805	Julia A. Kercheval	James	JACK	852	Boone	1834
30 Apr 1845	John B. Killgore		CLIN	138		1864
04 Jul 1833	Charles M. King	Elbert Jones & Lucy A(Thomas)	MOSH	1004	Ralls	1837
27 Oct 1810	Jacob Knaus	Pa/Pa	JOHN	794	Howard	1817
21 Apr 1848	Samuel B. Lashbrooke	Peter **92/--	USBI	729	Bates	1872
13 Jul 1813	James N. Layton		CLPL	1102		1843
23 Jul 1843	Henry Lightfoot	John & Keziah(Chapman)Allen/Monroe	HPCD	672		1853
19 Jul 1830	James M. Littlejohn	Daniel & Cynthia(Thompson) Va/Ky	CLPL	950		1850
08 Oct 1812	Robert T. Littlejohn		LAFA	600		1830
13 Apr 1866	H. S. Locke	William & Mary E(Savage) Scotland/--	CHHO	786		----

BIRTHDATE	NAME OF BIOGRAPHEE	PARENTS/BIRTHPLACE/BIRTHDATE	SOURCE/PAGE	FIRST MO.CO.	DATE
10 May 1820	John Machir	Henry A & Martha A(Woodson)	BOON	909	Saint Louis	1837
12 Mar 1842	Edward L. Martin	William & Margaret(Sheridan)Ire/Ire	USBI	509	Kansas City	1868
31 May 1835	S. O. Mason		RAY	590	LaFayette	c1837
25 Sep 1841	A. S. Masterson	George W & Eliza Ky/Ky	HSTC	1220	Platte	---
00 000 0000	John McAdow		CIPL	1105		1837
05 Nov 1844	Robert McElfresh	Wesley Md/--	JOHN	718		1877
24 Jan 1839	Thomas P. Meglasson	Wilson T & Carolina I(Anderson)	MOSH	1125	Marion	1852
19 Nov 1833	Charles S. Mitchell	Charles H & Elizabeth(Fowhe)	PLAS	516		---
00 000 0000	David R. Mitchell		LAFA	495		---
16 Nov 1852	George W. Mitchell	George W & Minerva	RAY	637		1858
22 Apr 1814	Ann T. Morris		CLIN	137		1859
11 Dec 1822	William B. Morris	James & Nancy(Bell) NJ/Va	STLO	1118		1855
19 Jan 1826	John Neal		CIPL	525		1837
04 Jun 1810	Col. John Nichols	Jack Va/Md	MARI	619		1832
06 Apr 1803	John Painter	John & Sarah(Downey) Va/Va	SEGO	789		1819
02 Mar 1819	William M. Paxton		CIPL	961		1840
14 Sep 1834	James N. Peed	William & Mary Ky/Ky	JASP	972		1866
22 Mar 1852	George H. Pogue	W. T & Sallie(Pickett)Greenup/Greenup	DAGE	752		---
20 Jan 1845	W. S. Pickett	Major B. O & Mary L. F(Bacon)Ky/Va	HPCD	608		1868
22 Mar 1860	W. C. Pogue	William T & Sallie P(Shanklin)Greenup	DAGE	388		---
19 Jun 1844	Joseph C. Prather	Ross & Mary	LINN	773		1880
23 Nov 1807	Thomas Prather	Ross & Nellie	LINN	773	Monroe	1836
03 Mar 1818	Hambury Pyles		BUCH	1036	Platte	1846
06 Apr 1823	Edward D. Rawlings	Jonathan & Nancy	LAFA	676		1843
04 Aug 1833	W. H. Richardson		BUCH	961		1857
00 000 1800	James Sanders		FJWC	1058		c1815
12 Jun 1830	John A. Scudder	Dr.Charles & Mary H NJ/Va	STLO	1118		---
08 Jul 1836	Joseph E. Sexton		NW	2053	Platte	1860

Date	Name	Parents	Birthplace	County	No.	Residence	Year
04 Jul 1828	Judge John W.Shotwell	Judge Jabez	Ky91/Ky97	RAY	519		1833
08 Dec 1811	Nathaniel Shotwell	John & Sarah(Burris)	NJ/Md	PIKE	1020		1831
01 Aug 1816	Gen.William V.Slack			BENC	137	Saint Louis	----
00 000 1814	Thomas H. Small			LAFA	683		1829
21 Jan 1813	Milton C. Smith			CLIN	148		1862
22 Apr 1810	Alfred Sower			CLPL	1118		1839
00 000 0000	John W. Spencer	Ephraim & Sarah E(Smith)		BJAS	220		1882
26 Aug 1832	John R. Starkey			RAY	693		1838
20 Apr 1828	Amos J. Stilwell		Ky/Ky	MARI	614		1848
04 Nov 1834	Randolph V.Sullivan	Austin & Catherine(Hiles)		MOSH	311	Marion	1867
23 May 1837	R. A. Sullivan	Austin B & Catherine(Hiles)		MARI	708		1857
00 000 1818	Judge Walker R.Tebbs	James & Elizabeth		LAFA	503		1843
11 Mar 1813	James H. Thompson	Archibald & Margaret(Blair)	Ire/Pa	LCKS	1134		1864
03 Jun 1818	Henry Thornton	Joseph & Judy(Asbury)	Ky/Ky	CALI	417	Boone	1838
24 Jan 1808	Richard A. Thornton	James & Mary(Lucas)	Va/Eng	PIKE	1023		1832
00 000 0000	George H. Tolle			GRUN	688		----
25 Aug 1831	John W. Waddell	William B & Susan C	Va/--	PLAS	629		
19 Jan 1836	J. White Waddell			LAFA	611		1845
04 Dec 1819	George R. Waddle		Va/--	PIKE	1025		1827
07 May 1835	Lewis S. Watts	George	Ire/--	MOSH	606		1874
27 Jan 1838	Col. J. S. White			LAFA	685	Ray	1857
29 Dec 1811	Major Nathaniel W.Wilson Ir.	Augustus N & Caroline	**/Va	BOON	795		1825
00 000 0000	Walter W. Wilson			AUDR	863	Boone	----
31 Jan 1846	Dr. J. T. Wood	John T & Rachel(Webb)	Oh/**	HOCO	542	Boone	1858
19 Nov 1830	William Woods	William & Ann(Shelton)	Ky/--	CALI	1162		1857
00 000 0000	Joseph Turner			USBI	792	Clarke	1838

M E A D E   C O U N T Y

BIRTHDATE	NAME OF BIOGRAPHEE	PARENTS/BIRTHPLACE/BIRTHDATE	SOURCE/PAGE	FIRST MO.CO.	DATE
02 Sep 1842	Murry Bennett	Louis & Sarah A(Clarkson) Va/Va	HOCH 920		1856
00 000 1865	Robert L. Calvin		SERD 1190		1883
18 Jun 1836	Thomas W.Chamberlain	Paul P & Elizabeth(Lampton)Va12/Va14	NODA 951	Andrew	1843
11 May 1829	Rev.B.H.Charles	William B & Elvira(Crutcher)Va/Ky	CALL 747		1867
00 Feb 1843	Nathan M. Griggs	David & Martha J(Staples) NY/Va	SEGO 976		1875
02 Jun 1834	William P. Jared	John & Hixie(Elliott) Va/Va	HOCH 966		1855
08 May 1835	Eli Kendall	James & Eliza Nelson04/13	CALI 873		1869
07 Aug 1845	Thomas J. Martin	John & Eliza C(Adams) Va/Va	HOCH 980		1858
25 Dec 1855	John W. Scott	John & Minerva(Ewing) Ky/--	MARI 765		1856
13 Aug 1848	Dr. George F. Smith	William & Mary(Smith) **/**	SALI 652		1875
21 May 1837	Isaac N. Smith	John & Jane(Peak) Ky/Ky	SEGO 1002		1855
08 Apr 1831	Benjamin G. Willett	Judson & Barbara(Shackett) Md/Pa	HOCH 1019		1855

M E N I F E E   C O U N T Y   (N O N E)

M E R C E R   C O U N T Y

BIRTHDATE	NAME OF BIOGRAPHEE	PARENTS/BIRTHPLACE/BIRTHDATE	SOURCE/PAGE	FIRST MO.CO.	DATE
00 000 1812	Judge J. D. Adams	David & Margaret(Dickson)	CMMB 905	Cooper	1819
04 Jan 1817	William Adams	John & Margaret(Durr) Ky/Va	CSBA 638		1842
02 Dec 1815	J. H. Alexander	Joshua Ga/--	BOON 577		1818
09 Mar 1826	Dr. James Allin		PETT 933	Brunswick	1847

Date	Name	Parents	Origin	Abbr.	No.	County	Year
23 Nov 1816	Alfred F. Barnet	Zacharius & Nancy(Burnett)		DAVI	522	Howard	1818
03 Mar 1842	William M. Bellew			CLPL	511	Pottawattomie	1864
16 May 1830	William Bishop			SALI	839		1858
12 Oct 1828	Benjamin P. Black	Daniel	Va/--	JOHN	689		1857
15 Apr 1825	Garrett Bohon			PETT	1014		1838
10 Mar 1790	W. R. Bohon	John		PETT	1015		1838
12 Oct 1856	John L. Bonta	Abram & Elizabeth	Ger/Ms	BATC	52	Buchanan	1867
01 Sep 1836	Henry Bottom	James & Mary(Nichols)	Ky/Ky	CSBA	1327	Johnson	1849
18 Dec 1854	Aaron C. Bradshaw	Frederick H & Sarah		SALI	626		1870
15 Jun 1829	George W. Bradshaw	Frederick & Sarah		SALI	614		1871
10 Jan 1823	Ambrose D. Bridges	William & Nancy(Davis)		SEGO	1156	Dunklin	1844
03 Jan 1810	James C. Bunnell	Samuel & Elizabeth		GRUN	701		----
16 Aug 1828	James C. Burford	John & Frances(Brown)		CSBA	438		1852
01 Feb 1842	Jefferson Burford			CSBA	438		1854
00 000 0000	William C.Burford			CSBA	439		1840
10 Jun 1814	Allen J. Burks	Allen & Elizabeth(Townsend)	Va/SC	NODA	732	Platte	1839
02 Feb 1814	George M. Crane	Tarleton L & Polly	Va/NC	MARI	731		1838
03 Nov 1816	Jacob S. Crow	John & Mary(Little)	Ky/Ky	MOSH	421	Pike	1824
00 Mar 1792	John Crow			PIKE	845	Boone	1824
11 Feb 1800	William Crow			PIKE	967		1830
25 Mar 1810	Nancy S. Curry			CALL	593		----
13 Dec 1852	Alfred N. Davis	Commodore Perry & Louisa(Elza)Ky/Va		VERN	864		1879
12 Jan 1799	Greer W. Davis			SEGO	753		1818
00 000 1792	George Dickson			VERN	865		1818
12 Nov 1819	Gen.John B.Douglass	William	Md75/--	BOON	853		1827
15 Oct 1815	George W. Dunn	Lemuel & Sarah R(Campbell)	Va/Va	USBI	337		1839
15 Oct 1815	Hon. George W. Dunn	Lemuel		RAY	502		1839
15 Oct 1815	Hon. George W. Dunn	Lemuel & Sarah(Reed)		CLIN	17	Ray	1839
02 Jan 1820	Lemuel Dunn	Lemuel & Sarah(Campbell)	Va/Va	USBI	141	Ray	1841
28 May 1808	William W. Fisher			PIKE	807	Ralls	1829
00 000 1825	James M. Freeman	Bayless & Mary		MOSH	916	Marion	1839
22 Jan 1803	Chesley Gates	James	Va/--	JOHN	845		1839

BIRTHDATE	NAME OF BIOGRAPHEE	PARENTS/BIRTHPLACE/BIRTHDATE	SOURCE/PAGE	FIRST MO.CO.	DATE
08 Jun 1824	John J. Gilmer	James & Nancy(Wilson) Va/Va	AUDR 154	Monroe	1831
00 000 0000	Major Albert D.Glover	John & Fannie(Taylor Va78/Va88	LCKS 747		1835
30 Sep 1830	John S. Graves		JOHN 846		1855
01 May 1827	Jesse J. Hale	Elias & Cynthia Ky99/Ky02	PETT 1090	Monroe	1837
00 000 1781	Dr. George C. Hart		HOCO 1060	New Madrid	1805
29 Jun 1819	Dr. James P. Henry	Jesse & Nancy(Porter)	KC& 127	Howard	1844
00 000 1818	Levi Holt		HAME 706		----
14 Feb 1836	John C. Hope		JACK 793		1854
15 Jun 1830	William Hulett	Edward & Rebecca	BOON 1035		1832
03 Oct 1820	William S. Jones	Joshua & Nancy(Saunders) Wayne/Va	KC& 119		1854
00 000 1796	Abraham Kirkland		AUDR 944	Cooper	1822
00 000 0000	William Kyle	Matthew & Elizabeth(Burris)Ky/Va15	CLPL 1101		1839
03 Dec 1820	Peter B.LeBertew	Asher & Bethesda(Browkaw) NJ/NJ	PLAS 537		1842
10 Jan 1848	William Lake	John & Charlotte(Brown) **16/--	CHHO 759		----
00 Aug 1827	W. F. Lancaster		RAY 589		1865
05 Dec 1827	James G. League	Richard & Susan(Anderson) Pa73/Ky	ANDE 516		1856
09 Aug 1822	William H. Lee	Samuel & Margaret(Mitchell)Va86/Ky96	MARI 864		1830
27 Sep 1806	Rev.James M.Lillard	Rev. David & Mary(Spencer) Va/Va	LCKS 790	Boone	1815
22 Nov 1813	Mary M. McAfee	George & Ann(Hamilton) Va/Va	CALL 856		1839
00 000 0000	Priestly H. McBride		BENC 526		----
23 May 1844	H. B. McDonald	Daniel & Martha(McMurtry)Wash/Washing	ANDE 518		1865
23 May 1844	H. B. McDonald	Daniel & Martha(McMurtry)Washing/Wash	NW 1708		1865
19 May 1832	R. L. McDonald		BUCH 820		1851
00 000 1799	Elizabeth T.McGee	John & Jane C(Curry)	AUDR 944	Cooper	1822
20 Oct 1819	J. J. McGhee		MOSH 574	Howard	1833
06 May 1817	David A. McKamey		MOSH 576		1828
10 Feb 1818	James I. McKarney	Robert & Susannah(McAfee) Pa79/Va	CALL 833	Howard	1826
03 Jun 1837	Col.Elijah Magoffin	Ebenezer & Margaret	SALI 650	Boone	1856

Date	Name	Parents / Spouse	Origin	Code	No.	County	Year
16 Oct 1837	W. J. Mann			JOHN	718		----
19 Nov 1826	W. J. Matherly	James B & Mary		NODA	967	Buchanan	1839
17 May 1834	I. N. Montgomery			JACK	922		1846
00 000 0000	Williamson Mosby	Levi S & Sophia W(Crum)		CMMB	1154	Callaway	1832
00 000 1802	Richard T. Murphy	Joseph		CALL	593		1828
04 Feb 1830	Dr. J.M.Overstreet			PETT	711		c1854
07 Dec 1861	John M. Overstreet	Robert & Jane(Lowery) Ky/Ky		VERN	741		----
08 May 1832	William S. Overstreet	Robert J & Mary(Frost)		VERN	803	Pettis	1864
00 000 1826	John Parr	Robert & Jane(Lowery) Fayette/--		CLGA	450		c1845
16 Jun 1823	George W. Parrish	Jollie S & Roxie A --/Va		VERN	492	Pettis	1833
08 Sep 1821	Jolly S. Parrish			PETT	1093		1832
00 000 1816	Col.Oliver P.Phillips	George M & Margaret(Johnson)Va64/Va66		ASPS	876	Howard	1836
19 Feb 1828	A. W. Pipes	Nathaniel & Margaret(Harmon)		CLPL	488		1855
17 Dec 1857	B. D. Proctor	Joseph & Mary		FGRU	835		1865
21 Jun 1849	J. H. Proctor	Francis M & Eliza(Baker)Jessa/Garrard		GRUN	632		----
17 Apr 1817	Major Z.S.Raglan	Robert & Nancy(Smith) Va88/Ky94		JACK	895		1869
25 Dec 1797	Archibald Robards	Captain George		MARI	991		1843
08 Mar 1820	William L. Robinson	Henry Va/--		PIKE	815	Ralls	1830
15 May 1822	William A. Ryan	David & Martha(Burford) Va/Ky		CSBA	456		1852
06 Oct 1810	John R. Sanford	John & Elizabeth(Ransdell)		MARI	633		1834
28 Sep 1815	Thomas S. Sanford	John & Elizabeth(Ransdell)		MARI	764		1839
00 000 1824	John W. Sevier	William & Mary(Richardson)		ASPS	894	Boone	1825
23 Nov 1819	Thomas R. Sevier	William & Mary(Richardson)		ASPS	893	Boone	1825
19 Nov 1809	L. P. Shirley			GRUN	594		----
13 Mar 1852	Thomas A. Smith	J. D		PETT	799		1873
27 Jun 1867	T. L. Smith	H. H & Emily(Bunnell)		FGRU	345		----
24 Apr 1797	William Smith	George W Ky/--		BOON	679	Saint Louis	1816
00 000 1816	Judge William P.Springate	William & --(Gritten)		FJWC	825	Saint Louis	1822
13 Sep 1801	W. C. Stagg			CLIN	232	Platte	1840
22 Feb 1800	Col. Enoch Steen	William Pa/--		USBI	712		----
00 000 1848	William R. Thomas	John H		PETT	741		1867
22 May 1825	Henry Tronier	Wesley B & Elizabeth(Jones)		SCMW	703	Pike	1830

-123-

M E R C E R   C O U N T Y   (C O N T.)

BIRTHDATE	NAME OF BIOGRAPHEE	PARENTS/BIRTHPLACE/BIRTHDATE	SOURCE/PAGE	FIRST MO.CO.	DATE
10 Aug 1819	Henry Tuny		BOON 1058		1842
25 Nov 1827	John G. Waddle	James H Va00/--	PETT 972		1866
25 Aug 1824	Dr. James M. Walker	Dr. W. W & Susan A (Schooling)Ky/Ky	HOCO 480	Boone	c1833
00 Jul 1828	Israel Walkup		PETT 1035	Howard	1830
08 Apr 1853	Dr. James L. Warden	D. S & Susan(Adams) Ky/Ky	CSBA 525		1855
30 Mar 1807	Joseph Wilcoxson	Isaac	HOCO 419		1818
13 Feb 1822	Harvey Wilson		PIKE 988		1824
09 Oct 1819	Ephraim B. Wood	Gideon & Mary(Boyce)	MOSH 1112	Saint Louis	1834
08 Sep 1797	James Wood		MOSH 616		1834
27 Mar 1810	Dr.Joseph M. Wood		USBI 890	Clay	1832
25 Mar 1809	Hon.William T.Wood	William & Sallie(Thomas) Va/Va	PLAS 495	Boone	1829
25 Mar 1809	Hon.Judge William T. Wood	William & Sallie(Thomas)	USBI 232	Boone	1829

M E T C A L F E   C O U N T Y

BIRTHDATE	NAME OF BIOGRAPHEE	PARENTS/BIRTHPLACE/BIRTHDATE	SOURCE/PAGE	FIRST MO.CO.	DATE
17 Jan 1863	Scott Alexander	J. J & Mary(Tandy)	SEGO 953		1887
12 Jan 1871	John F. Grant	Flournoy & Frances(Tupman)	SERD 1001		1886
20 Feb 1835	Joseph B. Stockton		SALI 840		1852

M O N R O E   C O U N T Y

BIRTHDATE	NAME OF BIOGRAPHEE	PARENTS / BIRTHPLACE/BIRTHDATE	SOURCE/PAGE	FIRST MO.CO.	DATE
12 May 1812	Gilbert Apperson	Frances & Nancy(Spears) NC/NC	HOCO 1015	Platte	1830
24 Mar 1842	J. A. Bailey		BUCH 1009		1843
30 Oct 1818	G. T. Biggerstaff	William	CLIN 7		1842
05 Apr 1823	J. B. Biggerstaff	William	CLIN 7		1846
15 Aug 1824	Samuel Biggerstaff		LAFA 537	Clinton	1831
20 Aug 1808	S. G. Biggerstaff	Aaron	CLIN 5		1857
28 Mar 1816	W. L. Biggerstaff	William	CLIN 6		1860
24 May 1850	James Birge	John & Liddie(Headrick) Ky/--	DAGE 760		1855
05 May 1839	L. J. Brown		CSBA 721		1855
27 Apr 1845	William H. Cunningham	E. B Tn/--	CMMB 705		1835
09 Jul 1826	John Daniel	Marmaduke & Elizabeth(Gibson) Tn/Tn	CSBA 1304	Osage	1852
08 Nov 1845	Samuel N. Jackson	James A	CLPL 522		----
14 Jan 1860	Thomas M. Jackson		SERD 686		1846
04 Sep 1824	Dr. James T. Means	James & S(Mayfield) NC/--	GREH 787	Lawrence	1848
00 000 1822	Dr. Thomas J. Means	Thomas & Mary(Mulkey) Pa72/Tn78	NLBM 1039		1869
00 000 1837	William M. Morehead	John & Priscilla(Payne) Va11/**13	ASPS 860		1856
00 000 1830	Judge Addison Payne	Reuben & Sarah(Norman) Tn05/Tn11	ASPS 871		1858
00 000 1844	Caleb Payne	Reuben & Sarah(Norman) Tn05/Tn11	ASPS 871		1883
00 000 1822	Enoch Payne	David & Martha Va80/Tn83	ASPS 873		1856
22 Oct 1851	Reuben Payne	Addison & America(Bradburn)**/--	ASPS 874		1857
04 Dec 1825	Jackson Sympson	Henry & Catherine(Cantrel) Ky/Ky	HSTC 597	Montgomery	1845
24 Aug 1845	Madison W. Webb	Washington & Priscilla(Marshall)Tn00/	ASPS 931		

BIRTHDATE	NAME OF BIOGRAPHEE	PARENTS/BIRTHPLACE/BIRTHDATE		SOURCE/PAGE		FIRST MO.CO.	DATE
11 Dec 1810	J. O. Abbott	Joseph & Rhoda(Masterson)	Ky/Ky	CLPL	1088		1842
19 Jun 1819	Thomas J. Berry	John & Polly(Coon)		CSBA	476		1857
23 Jan 1822	William W. Berry	John & Polly(Coons)	Tn/Tn	CSBA	532		1869
24 Aug 1814	Judge William B.Beshears	Robert & Elizabeth(Whitton)Va/Md		AUDR	429	Pike	1833
08 Feb 1830	Dr. Francis J. Bruton			BOON	712		1853
11 Oct 1810	Louisa Cheatham	James & Elizabeth		CALL	812		1836
06 Jul 1818	Col. Henry C. Chiles	William & Nancy(Pugh)	Va/Ky	PLAS	571		----
06 Jul 1818	Hon. H. C. Chiles			LAFA	692		1859
21 Apr 1821	William P. Chiles	William & Nancy(Pugh)		USBI	677		1860
27 Dec 1844	G. W. Clark			FGRU	454		1865
27 Dec 1844	G. W. Clark	James M & Elizabeth	Ky04/Ky16	GRUN	539		----
22 Oct 1850	John Clark	James M & Elizabeth(Clyce)	04/16	FGRU	378		1866
07 Jun 1825	Martin J. Clark	James & Eliza(Burroughs)	--/Va	MOSH	475		1852
09 Jun 1834	John R. Clements	Jonathan & Nancy(Williams)	Ky/Ky	CLPL	934		1855
22 May 1821	Silas E. Combs	Ennis & Mary S(Hinde)	Va/Ky	CSBA	641	Saline	1842
03 Apr 1842	Jesse M. Daniel	Milton & Mary B(Williams)		HOCO	968		1867
15 Dec 1837	Mahala Dickey	Daniel & Martha(Cummins)		HOCH	802		1868
21 Oct 1824	Judge James F.Downing	Dennis & Mary(McCormick)	**/--	USBI	686	Grundy	1854
25 Oct 1841	R. C. Dunlap			BUCH	1026		1843
22 Aug 1827	Edwin Edmonson			MOSH	1054		1881
05 May 1825	Archibald B.Ficklin	William & Fannie(Walker)	Ky/Va	AUDR	879		----
00 000 1813	William H. Forman	John & Susan(Caldwell)		MOSH	550		1831
18 Jul 1837	John W. Fox	William C & Sophia(Hensley)		AUDR	744		1858
19 Sep 1842	William H. Fox	Thomas L & Martha(Ingram)	Ky/Ky	AUDR	744		1865
30 Jun 1818	Joseph T. Frakes			BUCH	1027		1840
24 Jun 1820	William H. Garrett	Murdock T & Ann(Smith)	Va/Ky	LINN	444	Boone	1844
01 Jul 1837	C. S. Glover	Charles & Elizabeth	Va/Va	JASP	1057		1858
30 Jun 1819	Dr. J. E. Goodson	Samuel & Elizabeth(Beck)		RAMA	1155		1836
27 Sep 1863	Dr. Robert L.Green	Beal & Corine(Ratliff)	Ky/Ky	KC&	471		----

Date	Name	Parents	Origin	Code	No.	Location	Year
29 Nov 1839	John J. Greenwade	Thomas & Sarah(King)	**18/Pa19	JASP	628		1877
02 Oct 1828	D. W. Fainlane			PETT	820		1867
12 Oct 1819	Harden Hainlane			BUCH	1030		1844
16 Apr 1843	W. F. Fainline			PETT	894		1870
23 Nov 1818	Joel C. Ham			PETT	972	Callaway	1835
26 Jun 1800	Albert G. Harrison			CALL	281		1827
26 Jun 1800	Albert G. Harrison			BENC	65	Callaway	1827
11 Oct 1832	Jilson E. Harrison	Capt. M. Y & Dilcenia M(Bledsoe)		CALL	602		1834
00 000 1846	J.T.Fensley	James & Theney(Anderson)	**/**	CSBA	1282		1869
28 Oct 1839	Col. Eli Hodge			BOON	883		1857
25 Nov 1817	Thomas B. Howe	Isaac P & Jeanetta(Boyd)	Ky/Ky	RAMA	1167	Callaway	---
09 Feb 1789	Andrew S. Hughes	Davil & Margaret(Frame)	Va56/--	ANPL	57	Clay	1829
10 Mar 1828	James Furst			JACK	795	Columbia	1852
22 Nov 1824	Prof.William P.Hurt	John P & Elizabeth(Pebworth)		BOON	887		1852
00 000 1798	John Jamieson			BENC	185		1825
24 Jul 1845	Jacob F. Johnson	Phillip & Mary(Combes)		CLPL	523		1868
26 Jan 1837	James F. Jones	Davil & Mary(Jamison)	Va/--	CLPL	948		1869
06 Nov 1817	Col. J. F. Jones			CALL	867		---
14 Nov 1861	W. Z. Jones	James H & Fannie(Ragan)	35/--	NW	2052		1869
13 Aug 1842	Thomas W. Judy	Jeremiah V & Lucella(Aller)	Ky/Ky	HSTC	1114	Cooper	1843
05 Feb 1799	Simeon Kemper			BUCH	790		1837
00 000 0000	Samuel McCauley			BOON	597		1819
06 Dec 1825	John T. McClure	John & Mary(Redman)	78/--	CALL	567		1829
18 Dec 1830	James A. McCormick	Rev. S. M & Jane(McClellard)	Flemin/--	CIPL	858		1858
15 Apr 1848	Dr. Joseph H. Leslie	Preston H & Louisa(Black)		USBI	812	Saint Louis	1875
22 Jul 1857	E. S. Marshall			JACK	815	Cass	1865
01 Oct 1808	Luther Mason			JACK	968		1838
01 Mar 1836	B. F. Mitchell			JACK	819		1850
27 Sep 1834	William H. Moore			JACK	893		1852
00 000 1811	Ezekial A. Mounce	Henry & Ann E(Downing)		LINC	583	Saint Louis	---
00 000 1820	Rev.Benjamin F.Northcutt	Hosea	Va/--	LCKS	1096	Ralls	1828
04 Nov 1831	William W. Northcutt	William	Va/--	AUDR	950	Boone	1873

BIRTHDATE	NAME OF BIOGRAPHEE	PARENTS/BIRTHPLACE/BIRTHDATE	SOURCE/PAGE	FIRST MO.CO.	DATE
24 Jun 1838	Judge Bellvard J.O'Rear	Catlett & Sarah R(Caldwell)Va/--	SALI 643		1843
02 May 1829	Benjamin F. O'Rear	John D & Mariam B(Calbreath)	AUDR 816		1859
19 Mar 1831	Elias O'Rear	Marcus & Edna(Gardiner) **/Clark	CSBA 1267		1868
09 Jan 1827	Jesse O'Rear	Ross & Melinda	SALI 632		----
28 Sep 1834	John W. Pace	Wyatt & Frances(McDonald) Va06/Ky	CALL 693		1835
18 Feb 1801	Judge William Penix	John & Patsy(Walker) Va/Va	PIKE 1017		----
15 May 1819	Luke D. Priest	Elias	RAY 624		1835
27 Mar 1823	S. C. Ragan		JACK 984		1837
25 Jan 1823	Judge Legrand Ratekin	John & Mary(Smart) Ky/Ky	CALL 799		1828
22 Jan 1840	John W. Redmon	S. P & Elizabeth J(Berry)Clark/**	CSBA 1269		1866
07 Oct 1817	Sarah B. Riggs		JACK 921		1829
20 Dec 1809	Hamilton Shouse	Abraham & Frances(Prichett)	MOSH 1098		----
21 Apr 1829	Amanda C. Smart	Thomas A Va/--	JACK 776		1837
00 000 1819	Robert G. Smart		BENC 407		1828
00 000 1795	Enoch Smith		HOCO 410		1851
17 Nov 1825	Amos D. Spratt	Robert & Sena(Wilkerson) Ky/Ky	AUDR 902		1847
00 000 1835	Patterson Stewart		USBI 814	Kansas City	1855
00 000 0000	William Stewart		JACK 1002		1836
03 Sep 1821	Judge William H. Stewart	James & Henrietta(Hensley)Ky/Ky	AUDR 846		1853
27 Feb 1843	George W. Stith		BATE 127	Johnson	1868
06 Feb 1801	Mason Summers	John Va/Va	CLIN 256	Clay	1836
02 Sep 1823	Hugh Tolin	Porterphine & Rebecca(Vallandigham)	CALI 580	Ray	1837
00 000 0000	A. C. Tracy		LAFA 492		----
01 Feb 1819	Eliza J. Trimble	Robert & Elizabeth	RAMA 642		1835
16 Nov 1800	John B. Wells	Hasten & Tabitha(Davis)	CIPL 1084	Marion	1833
27 Oct 1836	Samuel G. West		BUCH 1040		1848
00 000 0000	Dr. Achilles Wilkerson		CALL 737		1830
19 Dec 1827	Judge W. H. Wilkerson	Hon. William & Elizabeth(Clark)	CALL 739		1830

BIRTHDATE	NAME	PARENTS/BIRTHPLACE/BIRTHDATE	SOURCE	PAGE	FIRST MO.CO.	DATE
28 May 1805	John R. Whittsett	James	Md/Clark	KC&	309		----
25 Oct 1822	William Williams	Amos & Rebecca(Couch)	Va/Va	CSBA	701	Jackson	1857
28 Oct 1824	Reuben C. Wilson	Joseph & Ann(Hopwood)		CSBA	1325		1868
21 Apr 1830	James Wise	Richard & Patsy(Gilmore)	Va/Ky	CALL	874		1839
05 Nov 1823	William T. Wise	Richard	Va/--	CALL	801		1839
07 Sep 1828	Anna L. Wolrath	Jacob & Mary		CALL	940		1872
13 Oct 1845	George M. Wood	William & Lucretia	Ky/Ky	JASP	717	Lafayette	1870
20 Aug 1801	Samuel Wythe			CALL	812		1836
05 Feb 1826	Harvey Yocum	Jonathan & Rachel(Williams)**03/**08		HOCO	805		----
05 Feb 1826	Harvey Yocum	Jonathan & Rachel(Williams)**03/**08		HOCO	805		----
27 Jan 1827	Stewart C. Summers			LAFA	644		1836

M O R G A N   C O U N T Y

BIRTHDATE	NAME OF BIOGRAPHEE	PARENTS/BIRTHPLACE/BIRTHDATE	SOURCE/PAGE		FIRST MO.CO.	DATE
28 May 1859	Rufus G. Humphrey	Rufus & Catherine	VADA	575	Scotland	1884
25 Sep 1830	James A. Kirk	Alexander & Elizabeth(Nickell)Ky/Ky	HSTC	1134	Linn	1863
22 Jun 1826	Wiley Maddex		----	---	Cooper	1837
15 Feb 1819	Dr. John Martin	Lewis	Ky/-- DAVI	602		1845
06 Mar 1833	Rev.Ambrose Nickell		LINN	863		1857
13 May 1855	Jasper Wheeler		HOCO	1046	Lawrence	c1859

M U H L E N B E R G   C O U N T Y

BIRTHDATE	NAME OF BIOGRAPHEE	PARENTS/BIRTHPLACE/BIRTHDATE	SOURCE	PAGE	FIRST MO.CO.	DATE
00 000 1814	Dr. D. Dobyns	Dr. Lew & Ann(Anderson) Va/Va	HPCD	732	Cooper	1856
04 Mar 1804	Thomas Elliott		HOCH	738		1828
15 Jan 1812	Henry Rhoads	John & Elsie(McQuarry) Pa/Tn	MARI	743		1827
11 Jan 1821	Judge Alney Rhoads	Jacob & Elizabeth(Ripple) Ky86/Pa88	HSTC	537	Pettis	1854
25 Oct 1840	R. H. Tolbart	Oliver & Harriet(Smith) **/**	NLBM	992		1879
27 Apr 1840	Lafayeete B. Walker		GRUN	487		1841
02 Dec 1841	Dr.Charles T.Widney	James H Pa/--	PETT	832	Saint Louis	1870

N E L S O N   C O U N T Y

BIRTHDATE	NAME OF BIOGRAPHEE	PARENTS/BIRTHPLACE/BIRTHDATE	SOURCE	PAGE	FIRST MO.CO.	DATE
29 Jul 1813	Peter T. Abell		BENC			1828
12 Apr 1817	Hon. I. G. Beal		SEGO			
31 Dec 1810	Philip Bennett		LCDW			
22 Feb 1810	Jerome C. Berryman	Gerard B & Ailsie(Quisenberry)	SERD	725		1847
22 Feb 1810	Jerome C. Berryman	Gerard B & Ailsie(Quisenberry)	FJWC	970	Iron	1839
00 000 1836	John H. Bland	Bryant & Margaret(Bridwell)Ky/Ky	LCKS	715		1825
10 Aug 1819	Dr. W. W. Bland	James & Mary(Wyatt) --/Ky	CLIN	183	Warren	1848
07 Nov 1808	Judge John R.Chenault Stephen		BENC	354	Jasper	c1834
08 Sep 1815	Zachary G. Cooper	John & Mary(Duncan) Va/Va	KC&	554		----
00 000 1821	Jonathan W. Crume	John & Jane(Kirkland) Va81/Ky83	LINC	522		1820
02 Nov 1817	Judge John M. Davis	Robert S & Lucinda(Mason) Va/Va	HOCH	735		1820
29 Nov 1811	William H. Davis		BENC	491		1842
12 Dec 1818	John Dixon		MOSH	410		1808
12 Apr 1791	Major John Dougherty		NW	644		

Date	Name	Parents	Code	No.	Place	Year
09 Jun 1844	C. C. Duke	James A & Elizabeth(Pannabaker)	CSBA	1126	Morgan	1845
02 Nov 1835	I. W. Duncan		JACK	887		1873
01 Feb 1815	John S. Duncan	George & Nancy(Connelly) Va/Va	MOSH	907		1840
00 000 1829	J. W. Duncan	Seth & Jane(Carter) Va/Ky	CSBA	685	Jackson	1857
27 Nov 1823	Dr. Joshua A. Gore		BUCH	757	Monroe	1845
00 000 0000	Joseph Grow		CALL	164		----
11 Apr 1829	George Harned	Benjamin & Ellen(Lee) Ky/Ky	HOCO	972		----
24 Jul 1852	Henry C. Heffley	M. L & Susan E(Randall)	JASP	1000		1877
31 Oct 1833	Valorus Hughes		JOHN	792		1856
13 Jul 1823	William O. Huston		MOSH	1062	Ralls	1825
04 Jun 1830	D. M. Jarboe		JACK	796		1834
00 000 1842	William N. Jenkins	George W & Martha(Cravens) 09/20	LCKS	775	Scotland	1861
00 Feb 1839	N. S. Langsford	Daniel & Rebecca(Stallard) Ky/Ky	CSBA	1138		1870
00 000 1826	Warren Lesley	David & Annie(Craven) Pa/Va	LCKS	787	Scotland	c1852
00 000 1833	Shelby H. Lewis		SERD	742		----
11 Jan 1842	William B. Lewis		JASP	785		----
00 000 0000	Rev.John J.Lilly	John H & Mary C(Moore)	PLAS	647		----
21 May 1815	Allen B. McGee	James H & Nellie(Fry) Ky/Va	KC&	197		1827
21 May 1815	Allen B. McGee	James H	USBI	317	Clay	1827
21 May 1815	A. B. McGee		JACK	811	Clay	1827
00 000 0000	George Marks		SEGO	656		----
00 000 0000	J. W. Marshall	Joseph B	PETT	849		1869
00 000 1853	J. W. Mason	J. W & Mollie(Kirk) Henry/In	LCKS	920		1856
00 000 0000	David Masterson	Medad Ky/--	SEGO	783		----
05 Apr 1826	Willis Metcalf		NODA	910		----
14 Feb 1804	Richard Miles		MOSH	334	Callaway	1826
12 Aug 1821	Judge Alexander P.Miller	Alexander & Sarah(Phillips)Va/Ky	PIKE	814	Marion	1835
00 000 1854	William H. Napper		SERD	1043	C. Giradeau	1857
00 000 1816	James D. Nourse		STLO	1595		----
02 Jan 1842	H. C. Parrish	Benjamin F & Minerva A(Hamilton)Ky/Ky	VERN	781	Callaway	1826
07 Dec 1827	William J. Pike	Bernard & Mary L(Shircligg)	MOSH	418		1853
23 Dec 1823	Anthony J. Reed	Judge A. F & Ellen C(Ewing)**/**	HOCO	1074		1826

N E L S O N   C O U N T Y   (C O N T.)

BIRTHDATE	NAME OF BIOGRAPHEE	PARENTS/BIRTHPLACE/BIRTHDATE	SOURCE/PAGE	FIRST MO.CO.	DATE
11 Apr 1835	Dr. Robert Reddish	Joseph E & Jacyntha E(King)	CLPL	525		1857
00 Dec 1828	William Ricks	William & Susan	PETT	852		1841
01 Aug 1826	Dr. Elijah T. Scott	Rev.William & Sarah H(Tate) SC/Ky	CALL	711		1837
00 000 1811	Fieldin L. Shaw		PLAS	653		----
19 Jun 1842	Hon.George H.Shields	George W & Martha(Howell)	USBI	428		1865
10 Mar 1827	Dr. William D. Strother	John D & Nancy A(Slaughter)Va/Va	KC&	119		1882
24 Nov 1841	Robert Vowels	Henry & Elizabeth J(Ice) Ky/Ky	SEGO	1007		1860
16 Jun 1816	Dr.Matthew F. Wakefield		ANDE	539		----
17 Feb 1821	James E. Weller		BUCH	1064		1844
10 Jun 1816	Joseph Wells	Thomas & Mary(Hoskins) Pa/Ky	LCKS	980	Lewis	1837
00 000 0000	John Williams		PIKE	1037		1818
08 Dec 1811	W. G. Woodsmall		LCKS	1228	Lewis	1836

N I C H O L A S   C O U N T Y

BIRTHDATE	NAME OF BIOGRAPHEE	PARENTS/BIRTHPLACE/BIRTHDATE	SOURCE/PAGE	FIRST MO.CO.	DATE
27 Nov 1824	Jesse P. Allen	Jesse & Martha(Craig)Mason/Bourbon	VERN	861	Monroe	1848
00 000 0000	John T. Bannister	Judge Nathaniel	RAY	564		1843
00 000 0000	Martin Basket		CALL	171		1821
01 Mar 1824	J. A. Brown		GRUN	732	Adair	1843
15 Sep 1830	John T. Brown	David	----	---		----
18 Aug 1834	William H. Brown		DAGE	957		----
27 Dec 1802	Judge Eldridge Burden	James & Mary(Brain)	USBI	160		1833
27 Dec 1802	Judge Eldridge Burden	Rev. James --/Va	LAFA	613		----
27 Jun 1818	Thomas H. Caldwell	Thomas & Eleanor(Boyd)Bourbon92/NC88	CALL	580		1826

Birth Date	Name	Parents / Spouse	Birthplace	Code	No.	County	Year
00 000 0000	Samuel Clark	James & Polly	Ky/Ky	MARI	814		1828
11 Jul 1847	William Clark	John L & Mary(Norton)	**/**	CIPL	308		1858
11 Jul 1847	William Clark	John L & Mary(Norton)		NW	1119		1858
16 Jan 1848	Thomas Conway			SALI	780	Saint Louis	1852
16 Sep 1849	William A. Conway			SALI	779	Ray	1853
00 Mar 1833	N. M. Corbin	Joshua		SALI	738		1859
04 Mar 1840	William B. Couchman	Andrew & Julia(Henderson)	**10/**03	HPCD	875		1857
00 Mar 1824	Alexander B. Crawford	Alexander B & Charlotte(Riggs)	Md/Md	CIPL	434	Lafayette	1859
00 000 0000	Moses G. Dale	Mathew & Elizabeth(Baker)	Md94/Ky96	NW	850		----
11 Nov 1834	Jeremiah S. Dorsey			BOON	852		1854
00 000 1837	Benjamin F. Dougherty			CLCA	508		
25 Jan 1825	E. Feeback	Gilbert & Millie(Richey)	Ky/Ky	CSBA	644		1865
12 Sep 1825	David A. Foster	David & Priscilla G(Piper)	Ky/--	RAMA	1047		1866
14 Feb 1841	Joshua M. Gibbs	John W & Rachel(Dean)	Oh/Oh	MARI	927		1868
00 Feb 1831	John H. Glenn			CALL	563		1859
24 May 1826	Robert P. Glenn	Moses T & Elizabeth(Cowen)	Fleming/--	BOON	761	Audrain	1858
00 000 1844	George M. Hardin	R. W & Delpha(Beard)	Va/Ky	CSBA	1131		----
00 000 0000	Gen.Bela M. Hughes	Gen. Andrew S & --(Metcalfe)		BUCH	241		----
23 Jun 1831	William B.Kincaid	Samuel B & Nancy	Ky/--	SALI	612	Cass	1854
06 Feb 1845	Levi Moler	John	--/Va	CSBA	1359		1869
20 Sep 1827	O. T. Orr	John & Nancy(Steerman)	Ky01/Ky	HOCO	1104		1874
18 Apr 1834	John W. Payton	Joseph M & Lucinda(Caldwell)	Harris CIPL	CMMB	730		1867
27 Oct 1842	Richard L. Raymond	Hon.John M & Sarah(Griffith)		CIPL	358		1856
20 Feb 1826	Col.W.P.Robinson	George & Clarrisa(Holladay)	Ky/--	HAME	610		----
18 Jan 1820	William M. Selby	Joshua & Mary(Riggens)	Md/Md	HAME	617		1853
00 000 1844	Joseph W. Sharp			LCKS	832		1839
27 Sep 1834	William L. Smith	William & Eliza A(Shannon)		PLAS	563		1850
09 Aug 1809	William L. Thomas	Lawson & Sarah(Riley)	Ky/Md	HSTC	1125	Saline	1885
00 000 1861	Francis Usher	James H & Frances(Sanford)	Chri/Chri	BOON	955		1845
19 Aug 1818	William L. Victor	William & Eleanor		CSBA	794		1871
15 Dec 1851	Dr. James T. Walls			CSBA	1164		1877
11 Sep 1823	William M. Walls	Zachariah & Tempe(Osborn)	Va/Clark	CSBA	1232	Butler	

NICHOLAS COUNTY (CONT.)

BIRTHDATE	NAME OF BIOGRAPHEE	PARENTS/BIRTHPLACE/BIRTHDATE	SOURCE/PAGE	FIRST MO.CO.	DATE
26 Nov 1832	James H. Waugh	Archer S & Matilda G(Piper)Ky/Ky	BOON 3		1854
20 Jul 1836	Lewis W. Wernway	Thomas D	LAFA 546	Ray	1844

OHIO COUNTY

BIRTHDATE	NAME OF BIOGRAPHEE	PARENTS/BIRTHPLACE/BIRTHDATE	SOURCE/PAGE	FIRST MO.CO.	DATE
09 Feb 1837	Judge Charles C.Bland	Edward & Margaret(Nalle) Ky/Ky	LCDW 977		1851
19 Aug 1835	Hon.Richard P. Bland	Stouton E & Margaret(Nall) Ky/Ky	LCDW 694	Wayne	1855
00 000 1822	William M. Chapman	Willis & Nancy(Render) SC75/Va80	SEGO 962		1849
02 Feb 1819	J. J. Cooksey		LAFA 587		1855
07 Mar 1808	Wayman Crow	Joshua & Mary(Wayman) Va60/--	STLO 871		----
18 May 1814	Philip Fulkerson	Adam & Rebecca(Wakeland) NJ/Ky	CSBA 741		1855
00 000 0000	John L. Greer	William & Sarah P(Cox) **/**	SEGO 976		1859
09 Feb 1841	Charles W. Hoskinson	Charles C & Tamer(Ashby) Ky/Ky	CALI 1033		1869

OLDHAM COUNTY

BIRTHDATE	NAME OF BIOGRAPHEE	PARENTS/BIRTHPLACE/BIRTHDATE	SOURCE/PAGE	FIRST MO.CO.	DATE
18 May 1849	George W. Ball	John D & Nancy	VADA 1066		1857
13 May 1827	Robert H. Berry	Jonathan T & Eleanor M(Taylor)Hen/JefHSTC	630		1835
10 Mar 1819	Joseph M. Blades		MOSH 518		1852
07 Jan 1833	Harris Felps	Harris & Nellie E(Laurence)Ky95/Ky97	RAMA 687	Marion	1833

BIRTHDATE	NAME OF BIOGRAPHEE	PARENTS/BIRTHPLACE/BIRTHDATE	SOURCE/PAGE	FIRST MO.CO.	DATE
15 Feb 1855	Charles E. Fowler	Thomas C & Hattie(McFadden)Vt/Ky	HSTC 766	Carroll	1856
01 Aug 1827	Abraham C. Hitt	Joel & Sarah(Kellar) Ky/Ky00	AUDR 942		---
17 May 1841	Amos G. Mount	Amos & Charlotte(Woodsmall)	GREH 658	Scotland	1865
26 Jan 1853	Dr.T.O.Pendleton	George T & Catherine(McGruder)Jeff24/HOCO	HOCO 1106		1855
07 Sep 1816	Judge John T. Redd	John & Ann(Bullock) Ky76/--	MARI 593		1834
14 Oct 1830	John C. Risk	Moses M & Fannie(Crosby) Scott/--	LCKS 820		1842
00 000 1836	John J. Romjue	Judge John H	RAMA 974	Scotland	1836
03 Nov 1848	Lizzie Satterwhite	Mortimer & Jane	NW 1737		1887
09 Jul 1844	James P. Shrader	Philip & Mary(Blevins)Bourb/Bourbon	MOSH 594		1854
08 Dec 1840	J. W. Silvey	William G & A. P	JASP 1062	Newton	1867
13 Sep 1848	George T. Taylor	John & Mariah F(Barber)Jefferson/Va	SALI 848		1881
18 Aug 1818	William R. Taylor	Fitzhugh & Caroline M(Fitzhugh)Va/Va	HSTC 597		1838
08 Jul 1826	John F. Thornton	Samuel & Lucinda(Muster)Shelby33/**13	HSTC 599		1840
00 000 1833	James W. Washburn	Gibson & Amanda(Hardin) Ky/Ky	LCKS 851		c1856
00 000 1839	Hammet L. Wilholt		VERN 762	Lafayette	1838
05 Sep 1843	W. A. Wilholt		CIPL 1009		1855
01 Oct 1831	John R. Yeager	Elijah & Elizabeth(Redd) Va/Ky	MARI 801		1835
26 Aug 1843	R. L. Yeager	Elijah & Elizabeth(Graham) Va/Ky	KC& 441		---

OWEN COUNTY

BIRTHDATE	NAME OF BIOGRAPHEE	PARENTS/BIRTHPLACE/BIRTHDATE	SOURCE/PAGE	FIRST MO.CO.	DATE
00 000 1800	Edwin G. Adkins	Edwin G & Elizabeth(Garvey)Ky/Ky	ANPL 107	Lewis	1834
07 Dec 1830	Hon. James Adkins	J.J & Mary(Tandy) Ky/Ky	CIPL 992	Lewis	1834
17 Jan 1863	Scott Alexander		SEGO 953		1887
11 Aug 1847	Joseph M Caldwell	William M & Catherine(Minor)	DAGE 904	Platte	1852
28 Feb 1847	Jesse Davis	George W & Priscilla(Caldwell)**/**	RAMA 946	Adair	1868
03 Dec 1825	Oliver Elmore	John Va/--	PETT 870		---
17 Dec 1842	John L. Fant	Linn J & Sophia(Yancy) Scott/Scott	CALL 861		1858

O W E N   C O U N T Y   (C O N T.)

BIRTHDATE	NAME OF BIOGRAPHEE	PARENTS/BIRTHPLACE/BIRTHDATE	SOURCE/PAGE	FIRST MO. CO.	DATE
07 Nov 1830	James S. Frank		NODA 757		1851
20 Nov 1831	John B. Hancock	George W & Jane(Settles) Va/Ky	HSTC 516		1854
27 Oct 1824	Prof.C.B.Johnson	William C & Harriet B(Dillon)Oh/Ky	HOCO 1096		1856
06 Aug 1840	Thaddeus C. Jones	James D & Sarah(Wood)	CLPL 1101		1860
20 Nov 1813	Dr.J.R.McKinney	William & Sarah(Randolph) Va86/NJ	SEGO 1108		----
03 Oct 1825	Jacob Maddox	Sherwood Ky/Va	CALL 871		1830
00 000 1837	Joseph W. Mason	Samuel & Felicia(Neal) 01/08	HOCO 595		1845
18 Dec 1817	Samuel J. Morgan	Samuel	LAFA 607		1855
00 000 0000	Hon.Braxton Pollard		MOSH 1075		1845
17 Oct 1826	Judge James M.Pollard	Thomas & Nancy(Marsh) Ky/NC	MOSH 489		1840
24 Nov 1834	Judge Daniel J.Stamper	Squire Hiram & Sallie(Cobb)**/**	RAMA 626		1855
08 Apr 1812	Squire Hiram Stamper	Jesse & Nancy(Sebantin) NC/NC	RAMA 625		1855
14 Jun 1833	George W. Smith		PIKE 982		1843
28 Jan 1845	James W. Thompson		SALI 601		----
00 000 1831	R. A. Towles	Oliver & Ellen(White) Va/Va	ASPS 1031	Lewis	1840
05 Dec 1838	L. B. Wright		RAY 787	Lafayette	1849

O W S L E Y   C O U N T Y

BIRTHDATE	NAME OF BIOGRAPHEE	PARENTS/BIRTHPLACE/BIRTHDATE	SOURCE/PAGE	FIRST MO. CO.	DATE
29 Apr 1818	Mary A. McCoy		GRUN 460		1819

P E N D L E T O N   C O U N T Y

BIRTHDATE	NAME OF BIOGRAPHEE	PARENTS/BIRTHPLACE/BIRTHDATE	SOURCE/PAGE	FIRST MO.CO.	DATE
25 Oct 1849	James M. Bonar	Washington F & Patsy(Ervin)Ky/Ky	HOCO 1016		1875
01 Dec 1821	John Ewing	Elijah & Sausanna(Makamson)Ky/Ky	LCKS 887	Lewis	1835
18 Mar 1818	Robert P. Forsythe	John & Isabella(Anderson) Pa/Pa	MARI 733		1840
02 Feb 1827	Henry H. Fugate		LCKS 1172	Lewis	----
00 000 1821	David N. Glaves	Michael & Patsy(Clarkson)Va/Bourbon	LCKS 746		1857
00 000 0000	James R. Glaves	Thomas T & Elizabeth(Dance)Va92/Ky00	LCKS 746		1864
24 Aug 1846	Dr.Walter S.Hall	Jefferson Y & Cynthia	VADA 851		----
00 000 1838	Dr. W. R. Hopkins		ASPS 976	Shelby	1859
00 000 1833	John W. Johnson	Jeremiah & Jane(Humphrey) **09/**09	LCKS 778		1885
15 Mar 1807	Luther M. Kennett	Press G	STLO 686		1825
00 000 0000	Alexander C.Levengood	Rev.Feter & Catherine(Orr)Bourbon/BouLCKS 787		Scotland	1860
13 Dec 1844	Joseph M. Lowe	Moses & Nancy W(Porter) **05/Ky97	KC& 626	Clinton	1868
13 Dec 1844	Joseph M. Lowe	Moses & Nancy W(Porter) **05/Ky97	CLIN 41		----
16 Sep 1850	Robert S. McCandless	Mitchell M & Priscilla(Orr)Ky/Ky	LCKS 1191		1857
00 000 1803	Samuel Miller		MOSH 1168	Marion	1818
03 Dec 1806	Judge John B. Morris		CAUD 262	Callaway	1830
21 Oct 1852	L. C. Shomaker	Landers & Catherine(Metcalf)	HSTC 771	Buchanan	1855
00 000 1814	Joseph B. Wallace	Graham & Elizabeth(Makemscm)Fay89/HarlCKS 851			----

P E R R Y   C O U N T Y

BIRTHDATE	NAME OF BIOGRAPHEE	PARENTS/BIRTHPLACE/BIRTHDATE	SOURCE/PAGE	FIRST MO.CO.	DATE
00 000 1822	Archibald Youd	Samuel & Mary(Newton)	NC74/NC77 ----	----	1841

P I K E   C O U N T Y

BIRTHDATE	NAME OF BIOGRAPHEE	PARENTS/BIRTHPLACE/BIRTHDATE	SOURCE/PAGE	FIRST MO.CO.	DATE
03 Oct 1849	William B. Auxier	George W & Nancy(Prater)	ASPS 758	Buchanan	1868
05 Jun 1854	W. H. Deskin	W. H & Louisa(Atkins) Ky/Ky	DAVI 630		1861

P O W E L L   C O U N T Y

BIRTHDATE	NAME OF BIOGRAPHEE	PARENTS/BIRTHPLACE/BIRTHDATE	SOURCE/PAGE	FIRST MO.CO.	DATE
19 Nov 1808	James Hall		BUCH 1030	Jackson	1837
19 Nov 1844	M. L. Hall		JACK 917		1868

P U L A S K I   C O U N T Y

BIRTHDATE	NAME OF BIOGRAPHEE	PARENTS/BIRTHPLACE/BIRTHDATE	SOURCE/PAGE	FIRST MO.CO.	DATE
22 Aug 1825	John Baber	John	CLPL 896		1841
12 Dec 1844	Dr. P. J. Barron	Walker	NODA 946		1871
00 000 1840	Charles Bishop		SALI 709	Pettis	1851
00 000 0000	Dr. Galen E. Bishop	Va/--	BUCH 678	Platte	1843
00 000 1841	John M. Buster	John T & Mary(Bryant)	QMMB 756	Andrew	1847
00 000 0000	Francis B. Clare	Daniel & Jane(Hansford) Va91/Ky92	LINC 518		1826
17 May 1819	Judge William Collins	William & Sarah(Porterfield)Va84/Va90	HSTC 1172		1854
21 Jun 1820	John G. Cowan	William G & Sarah(Gilmore) Va/Va	HOAT 271	Lafayette	1842
25 Jan 1825	Judge Samuel D.Cowan	John W & Fannie(Dysart)	BUCH 712		1854
01 Apr 1832	William L. Crain	James A & Catherine	SALI 865		1855

Date	Name	Parents (Origins)	Code	No.	County	Year
05 Jul 1833	George W. Daughtery	Joseph & Elizabeth(Lee)	RAMA	1034		1839
14 Feb 1826	William K. DeBord	Jonathan & Patience(McKinney)Va93/Va	ANDE	500		1852
16 Jul 1846	Dr.Zachariah C.DenneySimeon & Elizabeth J (Pumphrey)NC/23		NLBM	919		1878
00 000 1827	Hiram Doolin		NW	1111	Howard	1837
00 000 0000	T. J. Fitzpatrick		SALI	650		1846
07 Nov 1865	John F. Floyd	Monroe **/--	PLAS	350		1871
15 Jun 1841	Monroe Floyd	John & Matilda	SALI	653		1873
08 Jul 1824	Dr. B. G. Ford		NODA	756		1853
27 May 1819	Marshall Ford	Reuben & Elizabeth(Petty) Va86/Va90	NODA	867		----
23 Apr 1823	William C. Garrett		RAY	630	Jackson	1838
03 Apr 1845	Dr. Milton Godbey	Rev. Josiah & Sena(Kelly)	LCDW	1044	Cooper	1852
01 Feb 1824	John B. Griffin	William & Susan(Buster) Va/Va	RAMA	1121	Ralls	1828
13 May 1803	William G. Griffin	James & Delphia(Adams) Va/--	RAMA	653	Ralls	1838
18 May 1838	T. H. Hail	Micajah & Elizabeth(Vaughan)Va/Va	BUCH	762	Andrew	----
00 000 0000	Henry Hardgrove		RAMA	1070		1840
27 Mar 1815	Edmond Hart	Israel & Usley Ky/Ky	CSBA	1318	Saint Louis	1839
08 Aug 1819	J. Craig Hays	Isaac & Catherine A Va/Va	SALI	655		1837
27 Oct 1837	James M. Hays	Charles & Elizabeth	SALI	656		1838
00 000 1807	William Hays	Isaac & Catherine Va/Va	SALI	653		1841
00 Mar 1830	Anderson Hunter	Thomas & Polly	SALI	654		1830
25 Dec 1846	George W. Hutchison	D & Nancy(Corbet)	NODA	961		1852
03 May 1840	Joseph W. Johnson	Andrew R & Elizabeth Va/Ky	ANDE	512		1858
00 000 0000	Oliver P. Lee		RAMA	962		1834
26 Nov 1842	J. C. McClure		JOHN	760		1867
01 Mar 1831	James McDowell	Granville & Lucy(Bullock)	HOCH	795		1859
27 Jul 1832	Francis McGuinnis		CLIN	103		----
00 000 1801	Rev. Abraham Norfleet		CMMB	988	C. Giradeau	1827
00 000 1848	James Parkey	Peter & Martha(Linville) Ky16/Ky	ASPS	870		1854
03 Feb 1837	P. M. Paschal	Alvah & Sarah(McQuary) Va/NC	HOAT	233		1864
03 Feb 1827	P. M. Paschal	Alvah & Sarah(McQuary) Va01/NC02	NODA	1024	Holt	1864
15 Mar 1824	Samuel H. Prather	Thomas & Mary E(Cowan)	BOON	784	Callaway	1832
05 Oct 1837	Peter Randall	Payton & Elizabeth(Renick) NC/-	CSBA	1237		1857

P U L A S K I   C O U N T Y   (C O N T.)

BIRTHDATE	NAME OF BIOGRAPHEE	PARENTS/BIRTHPLACE/BIRTHDATE	SOURCE/PAGE	FIRST MO.CO.	DATE
00 000 1833	Hon.Joseph P.Raney	William & Lucy(Graves)	LCDW 1197	Macon	1859
21 Sep 1807	Thomas Smith	Robert NC/--	ANDE 585	Howard	----
00 000 1824	Rev.Jonathan Spencer	James & May(Gadbery) **/--	NLBM 984		1874
30 Mar 1851	Prof.L.J. Spencer	William & Louisa J(Cooper) Ky/Ky	JASP 645		1882
00 000 1833	Fountain Stacy	James Ky/--	JOHN 876	Macon	1836
10 Feb 1814	Judge P. M. Stacy	Simon & Elizabeth(Hull) Oh/Oh	RAMA 1105	Saline	1835
00 000 1843	Conrad Stringer	James M & Elizabeth(Starns)	ASPS 907		1851
00 000 1848	Dr.D.K.Stringer	Jefferson & Hannah(Starns)**12/**22	ASPS 908		1851
00 000 1839	James M. Stringer	James M & Elizabeth(Starns)**08/**18	ASPS 907		1852
11 Jan 1843	Caleb Thomas	Lorenzo D & Rebecca(Bobbitt)Ky/22	CHHO 424		
30 Mar 1823	Benjamin F. Todd	Thomas & Mary(Vanhook)	ASPS 1113	Scotland	1864
00 000 0000	F. H. Warren		BJAS 267	Vernon	----
20 Feb 1843	Nancy J. Warren	John K & Nancy(Griffin) Ky99/--	FGRU 748		
04 Apr 1818	Rev. J. A. Whitely		JASP 922		1877
09 Jun 1848	J. J. Wood		CSBA 750	Andrew	1867
08 Jun 1845	John S. Wood		NODA 559	Andrew	1850
04 Dec 1854	H. L. Zachary	B. J & Nancy(Paschal)	HOAT 436		1864

R O B E R T S O N   C O U N T Y   (N O N E)

R O C K C A S T L E   C O U N T Y

BIRTHDATE	NAME OF BIOGRAPHEE	PARENTS/BIRTHPLACE/BIRTHDATE	SOURCE/PAGE	FIRST MO.CO.	DATE
10 Jul 1817	Francis M. Brittain	Parks & Sarah(Price) Pa/NJ	GRUN 693		1856
00 000 1831	John C. Brooks	Richard & Nancy(Merriman) Va/Va	ANDE 551		1855
05 Feb 1847	Dr. John J. Brown	John & Ellen(Henderson)	GREH 651		----

BIRTHDATE	NAME OF BIOGRAPHEE	PARENTS/BIRTHPLACE/BIRTHDATE	SOURCE	PAGE	FIRST MO. CO.	DATE
12 Dec 1812	Joseph Carson		NW	1645		c1848
19 Dec 1823	William L. Craig		BUCH	716		1855
23 Apr 1823	Dr. W. F. Crawford		CLIN	80	Andrew	1840
22 Dec 1817	Col. James Dysart	Colonel Johnson	BUCH	988		1853
29 May 1840	John B. Dysart	William L & Permelia(Evans)**09/Pulas	ANDE	501		1849
23 Dec 1841	Nicholas Kirtley	Larkin & Nancy(Dysart) Scott05/**06	ANDE	514		----
19 Apr 1833	Benjamin F. Merryman	John H & Jemima Va/Ky	GRUN	651		1843
21 Oct 1841	John H. Merryman	John H & Jemima	GRUN	651		1844
21 Oct 1841	John H. Merryman	John & Jemima Va/Ky	FGRU	412		----
00 000 0000	Judge William Metcalf		GRUN	587	Randolph	1835
00 000 1818	Granville L. Owens		ANPL	150		----
19 Feb 1843	Andrew C. Swinney	Robert & Lydia Ky/Ky	GREH	660		1873
01 Aug 1850	R. H. Swinney	Robert & Lydia Ky/Ky	GREH	661		1877
29 Oct 1854	Leander Todd	Benjamin F & Julia A(Bowman)	ASPS	1115	Scotland	1863

R O W A N   C O U N T Y

BIRTHDATE	NAME OF BIOGRAPHEE	PARENTS/BIRTHPLACE/BIRTHDATE	SOURCE/PAGE	FIRST MO. CO.	DATE
17 Jan 1868	Dr. Thomas L. Hodges	William S & Elizabeth(Humprey)1835/-	SERD 859		----

R U S S E L L   C O U N T Y

BIRTHDATE	NAME OF BIOGRAPHEE	PARENTS/BIRTHPLACE/BIRTHDATE	SOURCE/PAGE	FIRST MO.CO.	DATE
00 000 1837	Sidney Antle	Jacob F & Sarah(Stepp) Adair13/16	NLBM 1011	Daviess	1851
00 000 1837	James K. Belk	John & Nancy(Stanton) Vall/Ky15	HPCD 857	Buchanan	1839
07 Apr 1829	Enoch Callicotte	Jordan 00/--	JOHN 882		----
27 May 1827	Henry F. Callicotte	Jordan & Frances(Dubar) NC/--	CLPL 931		1856
27 May 1827	Henry F. Callicotte	Jordan & Frances(Dubar) NC/--	ANPL 214		1856

-141-

BIRTHDATE	NAME OF BIOGRAPHEE	PARENTS/BIRTHPLACE/BIRTHDATE	SOURCE/PAGE		FIRST MO. CO.	DATE
28 May 1829	W. H. Chapman		BUCH	986		1851
00 000 1833	Henry T. Cook	Edward & Nancy(Ellis) Ky/Ky	QMMB	758		1846
07 Jun 1821	Thomas M. Easley	Jesse & Bettie	VADA	1050		1855
20 Oct 1841	H. H. George	H & Jane(Wilson)	LCDW	904	Miller	1842
14 May 1830	Harbert W. Haynes	John & Elizabeth(Harlem) Va/Ky	ANDE	564		1858
14 May 1821	Harbert W. Haynes		NW	1155		1857
13 Sep 1826	Thomas M. Jackman	Alexander & Polly(Jones)	NLBM	845		----
00 000 1805	Thomas P. Lair		SALI	674	Marion	1830
09 Jan 1838	Judge Anderson McFall	Lindsay & Mary(Bradley) Ky08/Ky	LCDW	733		1870
00 000 1834	James H. McKinney	Solomon & Ann(Cane) Ky/--	HSTC	1207		1853
23 Oct 1847	Willis Warner	Willis & Martha(Vigels)	NLBM	888	DeKalb	1851

S C O T T   C O U N T Y

BIRTHDATE	NAME OF BIOGRAPHEE	PARENTS/BIRTHPLACE/BIRTHDATE	SOURCE/PAGE		FIRST MO.CO.	DATE
09 Oct 1821	Darwin J. Adkins	Judge Robert & Mary(Snell) Va/Ky	CLPL	289	Howard	1825
09 Mar 1835	James A. Allen	Alfred & Amney(Thomas) Ky/Ky	CLPL	1089		1842
01 Jan 1828	M. S. Alligaier		CLIN	4	Platte	1857
03 Feb 1819	Erasmus L. Benton		LAFA	606		1836
09 Aug 1856	Dr. Thomas D. Bedford	Greene & Caroline(Chinn) Ky/Ky	KC&	401	Lafayette	1867
06 Jun 1830	G. A. Bradford	Austin & Levina	BOON	751		1836
12 Jun 1828	James N. Bradley	Granville C & Maria(West) 02/Md02	CSBA	1355	Callaway	c.1833
13 Oct 1811	Milton Bradley	Stephen & Margaret(Duncan) Ky/Scotland	MARI	909		1830
09 Sep 1835	Alfred L. Brashear	Otho M & Jenetta(Suggett) Ky/--	CALL	536		1836
31 Jan 1808	L. S. Brashear	Judge & Elizabeth(Leach) Md/--	HOCO	493		1816

Date	Name	Parents / Spouse	Birthplace	Code	No.	County	Year
24 Apr 1832	Capt.Henry C.Brooking			JACK	988		1838
24 Apr 1832	Henry C. Brooking Judge	Alvin & Permelia **97/--		KC&	324		1838
18 May 1828	Dr. Leoridas B. Brown	James & Dorcus(McCalla)		BOON	752		1835
05 Jan 1824	William R. Burch	Milton & Martha(Viley)		RAMA	581		1847
17 Mar 1809	Franklin Burt	William & Sallie(Greenup)	Va/Md	CALL	858		1835
09 Mar 1835	Sarah C. Calvert			BUCH	1032		----
00 000 0000	Benjamin Cason			CALL	582	Boone	1816
00 000 0000	Henry Cave			CALL	764		----
05 Jan 1823	John T. Cavins	William & Margaret(Gorham)	Ky/Ky	RAMA	582		1835
00 000 0000	Napolear.B. Christian			USBI	115	Randolph	1830
01 Jan 1823	P.Jones Christian	Paul		RAMA	671		1830
02 Feb 1817	William S. Christian	Paul & Mary K(Sutton)	Va/Va	RAMA	391		1832
01 May 1818	John Clark			LCKS	1018	Saint Louis	1824
01 Sep 1817	John T. Cooper	Samuel & Jane(Tarlton)	Ky/Ky	MOSH	897		1842
00 000 1832	Alfred Coppage	Paton & Jane(Barlow)	Va/Ky	HOAT	878		1867
00 Nov 1820	W. G. Ccx			NW	2006	Platte	1855
19 Oct 1811	W. T. Craig	Scott		CALL	748		1837
28 Oct 1826	L. M. Dehoney			JACK	989		1847
23 Jan 1814	John A. Delaney			MOSH	545		1831
13 Mar 1818	John T. Douglass	Jerry & Susan		PIKE	1010		1821
27 Aug 1840	Robert H. Drennon	George W & Sarah(Williams)	Ky/Ky	USBI	336	Randolph	1855
08 Jan 1854	John H. Duncan	Harvey & Mary(Bowden)		GREH	749		----
00 000 0000	Ralph Dunn			CALL	586		1825
04 Jun 1840	Dr. G. E. Elley	Robert P & Cassandra B(Quinn)--/**		CSBA	686	Howard	1841
00 000 1812	Robert Elley			CLPL	997		1842
15 Jan 1824	James A. Emison	Benjamin & Catherine(Briscoe)**/Md02		PLAS	149		----
00 000 0000	James A Emison	Benjamin **01/--		LAFA	503		1850
15 Sep 1839	Dr. Oscar D. Fitzgerald			CLIN	243	Clay	1844
16 Jul 1817	Valentine Fcwkes	Gerard & Nancy		MOSH	550	Clay	1830
22 May 1803	Jefferson Garth	John & Sally(Griffith)		BOON	867		1836
24 Apr 1827	Col.Thomas J. Gibbs	Samuel C & Charlotte(Kenney)		CALL	885		1829
00 000 0000	James H. Gough			MOSH	984		1835

BIRTHDATE	NAME OF BIOGRAPHEE	PARENTS/BIRTHPLACE/BIRTHDATE	SOURCE	PAGE	FIRST MO.CO.	DATE
29 Mar 1797	William Grimes	Turner R & Sarah Ann(Loyd)	HOCO	380		1819
12 Sep 1811	Joel H. Haden	Turner & Rebecca(Cave)	BOON	765	Boone	1828
12 Sep 1811	Joel H. Haden	Charles W	USBI	198	Marion	1828
00 000 1818	Charles W. Hall	Braxton P & Catherine(Fulton)Ky/--	SALI	674	Saline	1835
00 000 1816	George W. Hall	Braxton P & Catherine(Shroyer)	PLAS	612		1828
00 000 1814	Hon. John J. Hall	Nathanial & Sallie(Duley)	PLAS	533		1831
00 Oct 1812	Capt. P. Hamilton		AUDR	735	Callaway	1821
14 Mar 1812	Edward D. Henry		BOON	766		1826
10 Mar 1801	Edward S. Herndon	David & Charity(Sinclair)	CALL	828		1840
14 Apr 1829	James P. Hinton	Albert & Patsey(Shannon} Ky/Ky	MARI	955		1867
00 000 1819	Dr. A. G. Houston	Charles C & Julia(Yager)	HOCH	1179	C. Giradeau	1842
04 Jun 1825	J. P. Hubbell	Captain W. D	BOON	889	Howard	1839
31 Dec 1834	Hon.Harvey C.Ireland	John J & Martha(Glenn) Ky/--	CALI	1105		1866
29 Jan 1809	James E. Johnson	William & Elizabeth(Entrekin)	BOON	892		1833
00 000 1824	Dr. W. S. Johnson	John S & Lucinda(Poague) **92/Mercer	LCKS	777	Marion	1828
20 Aug 1823	William Jones	Lewis P & Sarah(Graves) Va94/Frankl	USBI	480		1833
21 Jan 1817	Alfred Keene	John G & Fannie(Snell)	BOON	772		1826
21 Nov 1821	Robert W. Keene	Richard T & Priscilla(Wilmot)Md/Va	PLAS	593		----
20 Dec 1806	Dr. William Keith		PLAS	592		1840
21 Aug 1853	J. L. Kenney	-- & Polly A(Glass) Ky/Ky	CIPL	1063		1856
00 000 0000	George Kitchen	Weston Va/--	NW	895		1839
30 Jan 1818	Loyd Leach	Burton Ky/--	--	---	Platte	1847
23 Jul 1840	William B. Leach		CIPL	478	Platte	1847
25 Dec 1795	Richard C. Lindsay	Anthony & Alice Va/Va	CLIN	37		1856
23 Apr 1846	Leslie A. McMeekin	John & Margaret A(Graves)	PLAS	346		----
08 Jan 1822	John Maston	Thomas & Elizabeth(Wright)	MARI	701	Ralls	1832
14 Jan 1844	Dr.Walter T.Medford	David F & Martha(Samuels)**01/Mercer	KC&	530		----
09 Mar 1834	E. J. Montague	James M & Frances R(Threldkel)Va/Va	JASP	359		----

Date	Name	Parents/Spouse	Origin	Code	No.	County	Year
20 Apr 1833	George S. Moore	George & Sarah Ann(Mills)	Ky/Ky	CLPL	1003		1840
00 000 1810	Robert Morris			LCKS	803		----
20 Mar 1821	John Mosby	James & Eliza(Robards)	Ky/Ky	AUDR	512	Callaway	1828
01 Jun 1824	Dr. William W. Mosby	James	Va/--	RAY	549	Callaway	1828
01 Jun 1826	Dr. William W. Mosby	James & Elizabeth(Robards)	Va/Mercer	USBI	597		1828
16 Jan 1826	Clinton T. Nash			LINC	591		1844
21 May 1844	Dr. L. C. Nichols	William M & Naomi M(Menifee)	Va/Ky	LAFA	493		1872
26 Sep 1806	James F. Overton			CALL	569		1829
00 000 1807	Orville Pack			NW	939	Platte	1837
25 Feb 1831	Dr. C. N. Palmer			RAY	663	Jackson	1831
11 Oct 1834	Dennis Fayne			LAFA	529		1841
00 Apr 1839	John L. Peak			PJAC	129		----
20 Sep 1838	James Pence	Joseph & Sallie(Chism)		CLPL	1073		1849
00 000 1825	Captain William H. Pence	Adam & Annie(Snell)		CLPL	487		1825
00 000 1834	John T. Plummer			NW	846		1831
00 000 0000	John T. Plummer			CLCA	400		1856
00 000 1811	William Plummer			CMMB	879	Callaway	1827
00 000 1840	S. G. Polk	Daniel		CLIN	49	Platte	1858
06 Mar 1813	Thomas S. Pratt	William & Susie(Redding)	SC/Va	CLPL	880		1847
03 Oct 1813	Granville Read	Samuel & Nancy(Baldwin)		AUDR	820	Boone	1831
25 Nov 1804	Moses M. Risk	John		LCKS	819		1842
00 000 0000	Robert L Samuel	Reuben		CALL	707		1828
00 000 0000	Joel Scott	-- & --(Hawkins)	**/Mason	SALI	558	Boone	1832
28 Feb 1829	Joel Scott	Ezekiel & Dorothy(Hawkins)	**/Ky	PLAS	258		1832
05 Jul 1824	John C. Scott			SALI	813		1836
08 Oct 1837	Dr. Robert J. Scott	Thomas W & Adeline(Johnson)		LINN	560		1866
00 000 0000	Dr. J. V. Scruggs			CLIN	253	Clay	1858
08 Sep 1802	Elias Shannon	E & Nancy	Ky/Woodford	SALI	549		1844
15 Nov 1822	Loudon Snell	John & Nancy(Hamilton)	Ire/--	CALL	897		----
22 May 1819	Samuel B. Spence	Andrew & Rebecca(Lemon)		BOON	790		1824
00 Feb 1840	John W. Stone			JOHN	735		1865
00 000 0000	Manlius P. Suggett	Milton & Aurora.		SALI	658		----

SCOTT COUNTY (CONT.)

BIRTHDATE	NAME OF BIOGRAPHEE	PARENTS/BIRTHPLACE/BIRTHDATE	SOURCE/PAGE	FIRST MO.CO.	DATE
00 000 0000	Martha E. Suggett	Thomas & Mary	CALL	586		1825
18 Dec 1818	William W. Suggett	Rev.James & Sarah(Redding) 75/78	CALL	596		----
16 May 1803	Capt. John C. Swon	Md/--	STLO	1106		----
18 Apr 1821	Judge William S. Thomas	Benedict & Ann(Smith)DC89/Ky97	USBI	725	Lafayette	1830
00 000 0000	William S. Thomas	Benedict & Nancy(Smith) Va/Ky	PLAS	599		----
15 Nov 1847	John D. Thomason		SALI	637		1868
09 Mar 1811	Mentor Thomason		PETT	741		1834
01 Jan 1796	Judge John W. Viley	David Va/--	RAMA	580		1824
09 May 1817	William A. Waller	George & Martha Va/Va	MOSH	606		1838
09 Jun 1824	Edward West	John & Susan Va80/Va	JACK	863		1842
03 Dec 1830	June Williams		HOCO	485		1853
15 Nov 1820	Turner Williamson	Anderson & Hester(Johnson) Va/Va	PLAS	313		----
17 Jul 1807	Judge Hiram Yates		LCKS	856		1836

SHELBY COUNTY

BIRTHDATE	NAME OF BIOGRAPHEE	PARENTS/BIRTHPLACE/BIRTHDATE	SOURCE/PAGE	FIRST MO.CO.	DATE
00 Sep 1824	William Achor	Abram & Nancy(Ellis) Va/Ky	LINC	499		1846
00 000 1827	Reid Alexander	John & Anna(Reid) **/**	LINC	499		1833
17 Apr 1832	William P. Bailey		JACK	911	Clay	1843
31 Oct 1843	Thomas P. Bashaw	Philip T & Elizabeth	MOSH	512	Saint Louis	1866
14 Oct 1855	Charles T. Basket	W. C & Amanda(Yeager)	CLCA	755	Saline	1872
00 000 1809	Horatio N. Baskett	Job & Sarah(Mitchell) Va/Va	LINC	891		1843
00 000 1809	Horatio N. Baskett	Job & Sarah(Mitchell) Va/Va	LINC	505		1841
00 000 1841	William H. Baskett	Horatio N & Almeda(Griffith)**/--	LINC	505		1841

Date	Name	Parents	Birthplace	County	No.	County2	Year
04 Apr 1845	Coleman Bayse	Elijah & Susan(Brown)	Va/Nelson	NLBM	810		1885
03 Jan 1850	J. N. Berkley	H.M & Caroline F(Moore)	**/**	CLIN	75		1855
08 Jan 1828	Thomas H. Blakemore			BOON	1080		1863
20 Jun 1802	Rev. Hampton L. Boon	William		HOCO	361	Montgomery	1818
28 Jun 1827	G. S. Britt			PIKE	869	Lincoln	1829
30 Mar 1823	R. A. Brittain	Samuel		BUCH	687		1852
14 Feb 1814	Daniel Brumley	William	Ky/--	BUCH	1023		1843
01 Jun 1816	Joseph W. Burton	May & Nancy(Woolfolk)		RAMA	670		1819
00 000 1824	James S. Busbey			LCKS	1155		1854
15 Oct 1841	Henry C. Chinn	Achilles & Dorothy(Longest)Ky/Va		LCKS	727		1857
10 Mar 1851	E. B. Christie	J. B & Letha(Bohannon)	Ky/Ky	DAVI	630		1853
02 Jun 1839	Henry B. Christie	Israel & Elizabeth(Cook)	Va96/Ky99	HAME	507		1849
06 Mar 1829	James T. Churchill			BUCH	706		1853
23 Feb 1837	W. B. Churchill			BUCH	706		1855
00 000 0000	Abram S. Collings			HAME	682		----
13 Sep 1828	Dr. Spencer Collings			NODA	527	Mercer	1848
04 Jan 1834	Rev.Joshua F.Cook			LCKS	731		1852
17 Oct 1846	Thomas J. Cook			CLIN	207	Buchanan	1861
25 Jun 1836	Peter Courtney	Peter		PETT	916	Jackson	1840
00 000 1817	Benjamin E. Cowherd	William & Celia(Estes)		MOSH	365		c1833
02 Jan 1834	Thomas T. Crittenden	Henry & --(Allen)		USBI	878		1857
24 Aug 1835	Samuel H. Daniel			CLIN	207	Buchanan	1843
12 Jul 1824	Joseph Ditto	Abraham & Martha(Force)	Md/Md	CLPL	464		----
01 Feb 1841	Dr. John S. Drake	Samuel & Margaret(South)		MOSH	369		----
29 Apr 1842	Benjamin F. Duncan			RAY	576	Daviess	c1851
07 May 1818	Judge Thornton T.Easely	Woodson & Sallie(Tirsley)		LINN	437		1843
19 Mar 1823	Isaac Ellis			LINC	534		1850
00 Apr 1833	William Fibble	William & Melinda(Grundy)Oldh/Woodfor	LCKS	744		1859
28 Mar 1841	Thomas M. Fisher	Horace H & Hannah M(Bads)	Md/**	LINC	539		1842
27 Nov 1818	Squire T.Fitzgerald	Silas & Susan(Tyler)	Va/Va	PIAS	109		----
10 Oct 1847	Warner Ford	Silas		HOCH	947		1865
13 Sep 1816	Judge William F.Ford	William W	SC/--	VERN	467	Andrew	----

SHELBY COUNTY (CONT.)

BIRTHDATE	NAME OF BIOGRAPHEE	PARENTS/BIRTHPLACE/BIRTHDATE	SOURCE/PAGE	FIRST MO.CO.	DATE
21 Jun 1840	Dr, H. T. Garnett		HOCH 950		1866
00 000 1805	Major J. W. George		SALI 855		1869
06 Jul 1806	Lewis H. Gillaspy		MOSH 1137	Marion	1825
26 Jan 1816	John Gott	John D & Gracie	GREH 884		1845
24 Aug 1812	Joseph Gott	John S & Grace (Stubbins)	GREH 754		1845
07 Jul 1806	Richard S. Gott		GREH 884		1842
04 Aug 1825	William S. Gregory	Robert & Elizabeth(Ballard)	USBI 523		1844
00 000 1828	Joel Guthrie	Caleb **/--	CAUD 248		1853
26 Nov 1860	E. J. Harlow	James & Hulda(Nichols) Ky24/In28	DAGE 394		1867
08 Oct 1854	J. Sam Harlow	James & Hulda(Nichols) Ky24/--	DAGE 393		1867
19 Jan 1850	Jordan L. Harlow	William H & Parmelia J(Tilberry)**/**DAVI	DAVI 805	Livingston	1854
28 Sep 1823	George W. Harlan	George Ky/--	COOP 977		c1839
00 000 0000	William Hall		CALL 821		1816
22 Feb 1844	William C. Hedden	Lee & Susan	CSBA 1377	Vernon	1866
27 Feb 1830	James R. Hickman	Thomas J & Harriet(Taylor) Va/Ky	CSBA 496	Jackson	1844
15 Jan 1810	R. J. Holmes		JACK 790		1846
13 Aug 1847	Dr. T. H. Hudson	Musker L & Rebecca(Green) Ky/Ky	KC& 455	Cass	1870
20 Apr 1854	C. G. Jesse	James M & Amanda(Tinsley) Ky/Ky	HOAT 168		1874
00 000 1848	G. W. Johnson	J. D	CLIN 192	Platte	1854
00 000 1859	W. S. Johnson		NW 1255		1874
25 Jul 1833	John P. Jones		JACK 891		1843
26 Sep 1810	Luke Lewis		PIKE 973		1832
08 Feb 1829	Thomas K. Hanna	John S & Jane(King) Ky/Ky	USBI 70		1849
08 Aug 1840	Francis A. Logan		PETT 1054		1871
17 Jun 1832	Larz A. Logan		CLPL 482		1857
14 Dec 1854	James D. Lowry	Dr. James & Helen(Bullitt)Irel6/Ky	FJWC 1002		1875
04 Apr 1838	A. W. McCampbell		HOCH 975		1857
07 Jul 1811	Rice F. McFaden	John & Elizabeth(Hollandsworth)	LCKS 1074	Marion	1822

Date	Name	Parents / Spouse	Origin	Co.	No.	County	Year
25 Dec 1817	Mabillon McGee	James H & Eleanor(Fry)	Va/93	JACK	811	Clay	1827
14 Sep 1836	Ambrose Mann	Jesse P & Mary(Thorp)		KC&	496	St. Charles	1859
28 Jan 1815	Charles N. Martin	Peter & Sallie(Neal)	Va/--	SALI	721		1855
24 Jan 1815	Charles N. Martin	Peter & Sallie(Neal)	Va/--	PLAS	535		----
00 000 1821	Robert Miller	Abner & Betsy	Va/Va	JASP	638		1859
07 Oct 1828	William F. Miller			CLIN	106	Daviess	1855
11 Oct 1818	Thomas Mitchell	Rev.Thomas & Rebecca(Ketcham)--/Md		MOSH	937		1855
00 000 1817	Rufus Montgall			KC&	330		1840
19 Mar 1831	Joseph S. Muster	William & Mary(Jones)	Ky/Ky	AUDR	659		1849
29 May 1815	Judge William K. Neugent			MOSH	584		1856
16 Aug 1843	George N. Nolan	Wm.McMahon & Mildred(King)	Ky/Ky	USBI	426		1865
25 Jun 1829	George 3. Ogle	Adam & Polly		PIKE	975		c1831
26 Jan 1811	James D. Oldham	James T & Maggie R(Davis)	Va/Scott	CIPL	356		1869
16 Mar 1827	Dr. D. T. Pace	Joseph & Ann(Magee)	Va/**99	SEGO	788	Pike	1837
25 Feb 1825	Nuson Pace			PIKE	976		----
22 May 1808	James W. Patterson	William & Mary(Allen)	Va/Va	HOCO	399		1824
23 Jan 1813	B. C. Porter			BUCH	860		1837
19 Jan 1829	H. C. Price			PIKE	902	Lincoln	1856
24 Oct 1832	R. M. Price			SALI	779		1867
21 Sep 1846	Thomas T. Puckett	R & Barbara		LAFA	668		1850
00 000 1820	James V. Richardson		Pa/--	RAMA	1005	Howard	1821
00 000 1823	Benjamin F. Robertson	Horatio & Nancy(Gill)	Va/Va	LINC	609		1826
29 Nov 1830	E. F. Rogers			JACK	834	Cass	1857
00 000 1824	John B. Sanders	Culvin & Mary M(Fore)	Va/Ky	----	---	Marion	1850
30 Apr 1828	Dr. C. L. Sharp			CLIN	115		1866
00 000 1825	Capt. Lafayette Shindler	George & Susan		SALI	661	Lafayette	1850
00 000 1843	Horatio F. Simrall	James & Cynthia(Fritzlen)		CIPL	365		1869
21 Nov 1812	R. H. Smith			CLIN	231		1855
10 May 1831	Col. Henry G. Snider	Richard & Elizabeth(Gray)	Va/**	VERN	871	DeKalb	1851
07 Sep 1815	William Staples	Samuel & Mary(Hughes)	Va/Va	HOCH	996	Monroe	1847
22 May 1831	Joel Thomas	Nathan & Martha		USBI	345		1878
00 000 1819	Thomas J. Threlkeld	William G & Mary(Churchill)**/**	Va/**	ASPS	1219		1842

S H E L B Y   C O U N T Y   (C O N T.)

BIRTHDATE	NAME OF BIOGRAPHEE	PARENTS/BIRTHPLACE/BIRTHDATE	SOURCE/PAGE	FIRST MO.CO.	DATE
27 Sep 1852	Dr. W. A. Tichenor		CALL	721	1867
07 Sep 1832	A. S. Tilley	William & Mary(McDowel) Va/Va	BJAS	475	----
23 Feb 1808	Edwin Toole		BUCH	917	----
28 Mar 1818	Judge W. C. Toole		BUCH	919	----
27 Jan 1813	G. H. Triplett		LCKS	1222	1854
00 000 1842	Rev.William M.Vardeman		SALI	730	1878
24 Oct 1831	Richard P. Wall	Preston H **00/--	PLAS	307	----
17 Sep 1811	Granville Weakley	Thomas	CLIN	202	1853
01 Nov 1830	J. C. Weakley	Thomas Va/--	CLIN	202	1849
29 Oct 1833	Alfred Weeks	Alfred & Clarissa(Dowdle) Va/Va	LINC	625	1851
00 000 0000	Morgan B. White	Morgan B & Mary A(Marmaduke)	SCMW	706	Callaway 1822
10 Oct 1804	William Whiteside	Isaac & Linnie(Ellis) NC/Shelby	LINC	627	1828
00 000 1810	Elizabeth Wilcox		BOON	1028	1836
06 Feb 1845	Lemuel P. Willis	John & Julia P(Hunter) **/**	MCSH	612	1856
00 000 0000	Richard Wornall		---	---	1844
21 Aug 1820	J. C. Yantis	Aaron & Martha	CALL	743	Saint Louis 1847
15 Nov 1851	James T. Yates		RAY	795	----
02 Aug 1816	Jeptha Yates	Benjamin	CALL	874	c1837
04 Dec 1829	George W. Young		BUCH	998	----
26 Mar 1803	Hon.William Young	James & Ann F(Booker)	LINC	360	1827

S I M P S O N   C O U N T Y

BIRTHDATE	NAME OF BIOGRAPHEE	PARENTS/BIRTHPLACE/BIRTHDATE	SOURCE/PAGE	FIRST MO.CO.	DATE
25 Jan 1828	P. H. Alderson	William & Margaret(Boren) SC95/SC94	CSBA	602	1856
11 May 1833	James C. Anderson	John D & Nancy(Couther) Tn/NC	ANPL	203	1842

Date	Name	Parents & Spouse	Birthplace	Code	County	No.	Year
17 May 1833	James C. Anderson	John D & Nancy(Couther)	Tn/NC	CLPL		1090	1842
08 Jan 1819	Rev. C. J. Barr	Silas & Sarah(Headelston)	NC/NC	HSTC		1142	1856
02 Feb 1847	J. B. Brizendine			JACK		912	1871
24 Sep 1832	Harben N. Bullock	J. B & Mary P(Clark)		CSBA	Johnson	721	1835
09 Jan 1836	Edwin L. Clark	Christopher & Permelia(Usery)	Ky/Ky	CSBA		723	1841
05 Feb 1830	J. M. Dishman	Jeremiah & Cynthia A(Smith)	Va/**	GREH		910	1855
29 Jul 1835	Samuel Dishman		Ky/Ky	GREH		910	---
27 May 1830	Benjamin A. Gilliland	Robert & Annie(Moore)	Ky10/Ky09	LINC		543	1830
20 Feb 1843	Joseph S. Halcomb			CSBA		646	1856
00 000 0000	Cynthia Hambright			KC&		249	---
24 Apr 1836	M. M. Herrington			LINC	Dade	918	1856
17 Mar 1821	Hilliard H. Hudson	Richard & Elizabeth(Harris)	NC/Ky	CMMB	Boone	958	1825
22 Feb 1822	Robert N. Hudspeth			JACK		904	1828
00 000 1833	Judge John A. Lockhart			LAFA	Morgan	488	1840
26 Oct 1809	Brightberry M'Alester	James G & Tempest(Jackson)		BOON	Howard	913	1828
07 Nov 1830	Dr. W. C. McAninch	Samuel & Margaret(Mires)	Ky/Pa	CSBA	Jackson	1249	1832
12 Oct 1846	S. C. McCutchen	J. N & Julia A(Copeland)	**/**	CSBA		1267	1881
16 Nov 1846	Rev. S. H. McElvain	S. A		JOHN		827	1857
23 Jan 1813	Elberton E. Mallory	William & Catherine(Harris)	Va/Va	AUDR		894	1837
00 000 0000	David M. Milliken			SERD	Jackson	1244	---
24 Sep 1824	V. J. Moore	John & Mary A(Christman)	Va/Ky	HSTC		670	1865
04 Mar 1810	Jesse Morrow			JACK		907	1829
12 Sep 1849	Judge James C. Phillips	James & Mary F(Black)	Ga/--	HSTC	Henry	1120	1872
29 Apr 1829	Samuel Simpson	George & Nancy M(Cutcheon)	Ky/Ky	CSBA	Jackson	517	1833
00 000 0000	Reuben Smith			FJWC	Cooper	1060	---
29 Jul 1871	O. H. Swearingen			PJAC		105	1881
15 Aug 1823	Wright Taylor		Ky/Ky	DAVI	Clay	841	1827
10 Jan 1836	William F. Thompson	Tillman & Adaline(Barnest)	Eyll/--	HSTC		1195	1840
19 Oct 1856	Thomas E. Tribble	Nelson & Henrietta(Reed)		SERD		1083	---
25 Sep 1835	Garland C. Turner	John & Elizabeth(Bluette)	Ky/Ky	HSTC	Henry	1223	1870
00 000 1859	H. B. Turner	Richard O & Susannah J(Blewette)	Ky/Ky	HOCO		608	---
09 Dec 1835	Judge Albert G.Williams William J		Tn92/--	KC&		199	1852

SIMPSON COUNTY (CONT.)

BIRTHDATE	NAME OF BIOGRAPHEE	PARENTS/BIRTHPLACE/BIRTHDATE	SOURCE/PAGE	FIRST MO.CO.	DATE
09 Dec 1835	Judge Albert G. Williams	Judge William J Tn/--	JACK 928		1852
00 000 1815	Enoch Williams	James	NLBM 891	Stone	1837
00 000 1835	Enoch Williams	John B & Elizabeth(Hufhines)Ky/Ky	NLBM 1054	Stone	1837
25 Dec 1819	Crittenden Wyatt		JACK 929		1850
15 Jan 1833	D. G. Young		JACK 929	Clay	1863

SPENCER COUNTY

BIRTHDATE	NAME OF BIOGRAPHEE	PARENTS/BIRTHPLACE/BIRTHDATE	SOURCE/PAGE	FIRST MO.CO.	DATE
29 Feb 1836	Joseph L. Bennett	Joseph H & Susan(Overton) NJ99/DC98	ANDE 489		1856
27 Sep 1820	Judge Milton Brewer	George W & Sarah(Fox) Md/Va	SEGO 688		1841
00 000 1827	Benjamin Carter	John & Millie(Mason)	HPCD 725		1869
08 Nov 1824	James H. Davis	John M & Eliza(Sterling) Ky/Ky	CSBA 642	Johnson	1860
04 Mar 1824	Thomas E. Hagan	Simon & Rebecca(Newman)	MARI 952	Carroll	1844
20 Jul 1839	Thomas Howard	Zadoc & Nancy	SALI 616	Lewis	1851
29 Feb 1830	Payton H. Jones	Enoch & Polly(Wiggendean)	MOSH 999		1875
06 Oct 1845	Dr.Moses B.Kincheloe	Almanyor & Elvira(Buckner)**16/**21	HSTC 1114		1879
31 Oct 1849	A. F. Money		JACK 923		1881
00 000 0000	John Stark	Adam & Elenor(Stillwell)	PETT 738		1872

T A Y L O R   C O U N T Y

BIRTHDATE	NAME OF BIOGRAPHEE	PARENTS/BIRTHPLACE/BIRTHDATE	SOURCE/PAGE	FIRST MO.CO.	DATE
15 Feb 1844	Wilson H. Bledsoe		HSTC	499	1868
13 Jul 1829	J. T. Buckner	R. R & Mary(Tate) Ky/Ky	CALL	857	1844
26 Jan 1853	William L. Guyton	Stephen & Mary(Miller)	SCMW	792	1853
14 Jun 1852	Thomas B. Morris		LINN	770	1860
05 Mar 1848	Sanford G. Richeson	Joseph E & Margaret A(Turner)	RAMA	504	---
14 Jan 1833	John C. Rivers	James & Mary I(Short) Ky/Green02	HSTC	790	1856
09 Sep 1848	Stephen F. Sublett	James A & Elizabeth(Moore)Ky14/--	CHHO	667	---

T O D D   C O U N T Y

BIRTHDATE	NAME OF BIOGRAPHEE	PARENTS/BIRTHPLACE/BIRTHDATE	SOURCE/PAGE	FIRST MO.CO.	DATE
01 Jan 1827	John M. Alexander	Andrew & Jane Ky/Ky	CALI	940		1865
15 Feb 1834	Joseph F. Allison	Abraham & Sarah(Wagster) Va/NC	HPCD	620		1857
08 Feb 1840	J. W. Asbury		RAY	661	Dade	1843
27 Feb 1843	Dr.Charles D.Black	James & Mary(Martin) Va/**	NODA	663		---
04 Mar 1832	George I. Brown	A. H & Lucinda(Isbell)	NLBM	815		1837
27 May 1827	James Ccrdry	James & Margaret(Murphy) Ky95/Ky	HOCO	1002		1830
01 Jul 1826	Washington W. Drew		CLPL	518		1843
15 Jan 1816	William L. Cordry	James	COOP	887		1830
10 May 1827	Hon.C.L. Ewing		IAFA	689		1844
00 May 1819	Ephraim B. Ewing	Rev. Finis	BENC	172	Cooper	1820
23 Oct 1823	James B. Francis	Elisha & Theresa(Huff)	CALI	1009	Miller	1872
00 000 1834	James W. Gartin		BUCH	1070	Clay	1835
28 Oct 1822	George A. Gordon		RAY	678		1850
25 Sep 1840	Capt. J. T. Gorrell	John B & Mary H	CSBA	1375	Pettis	1848

BIRTHDATE	NAME OF BIOGRAPHEE	PARENTS/BIRTHPLACE/BIRTHDATE	SOURCE/PAGE	FIRST MO.CO.	DATE
04 Oct 1822	Samuel G. Greenfield		CLPL	436	1842
18 Apr 1820	Robert M. Hall	Cornelius H	NLBM	1068	1838
14 Oct 1840	Dr. Milton G. Hatcher	C H & Ann W(Gill) **/**	SEGO	895	1870
13 Apr 1840	J. C. Hill		JOHN	904	Saline	1855
21 Apr 1844	William H. Hill	Marshall & Frances	SALI	866	1854
26 Dec 1831	Thomas P. Hooser	George W & Mary W(Ring) Ky/Ky	VERN	801	Saline	c.1865
01 Sep 1837	Rev. H. D. Kennedy	Urban E & Lavina(Bryan) Ky/Ky	HOCO	1125	Lawrence	1871
27 Dec 1820	Robert H. Martin	Nathan & Mary(Hill) Ky/Ky	BOON	665	1838
08 Aug 1814	Judge Hazel P. Mobley	Richard SC/--	VERN	672	1857
22 Jan 1840	James A. Murphy	John & Letitia(Landers) Ire03/--	HOCO	1006	1842
00 Mar 1810	Thomas Murphy	William & Mary A(Kates) SC/--	HOCO	1006	----
21 Aug 1849	William D. Painter		RAY	589	----
15 Feb 1826	Curtis W. Pendleton		SALI	826	1836
14 Dec 1840	Clark E. Ritter	Burwell C & Editha(Maxey) Ky/Ky	NLBM	874	Boone	1881
21 Dec 1839	Judge A.H.Shelton	Charles C & Emiline(Scott)	NW	947	Ray	1842
26 Dec 1844	William Shirrod	John & Julianna	JASP	951	1865
15 Sep 1826	Samuel H. Stephenson		RAY	700	1833
00 000 1838	R. M. Taylor		LAFA	687	1878
28 Feb 1823	Col. Gideon W. Thompson	Robert & Eveline NC/--	CLPL	881	Cooper	1825
00 000 0000	Edward Winders		HOCO	957	1829
01 Jan 1808	J. C. Thompson	Gideon & Jane	NW	1954	Cooper	1826

T R I G G   C O U N T Y

BIRTHDATE	NAME OF BIOGRAPHEE	PARENTS/BIRTHPLACE/BIRTHDATE	SOURCE/PAGE	FIRST MO.CO.	DATE
25 Jun 1818	Henry Cooper	David NC/--	JOHN	884	1832
12 Aug 1849	Hon.Charles G.Daniel	Andrew B & Matilda(Greening)Va/Ky	AUDR	456	1854

BIRTHDATE	NAME OF BIOGRAPHEE	PARENTS/BIRTHPLACE/BIRTHDATE	SOURCE	PAGE	FIRST MO.CO.	DATE
10 Dec 1854	George W. Dariel	Andrew B & Matilda(Greening)Va/Ky	AUDR	458		1854
13 Jan 1838	Albert Dunning	S & Ada(Morris) Va/Va	HSTC	757		1839
10 May 1821	Dr.William A.Gordon	George H & Martha(Boyd) Tn96/99	LAFA	616		1832
10 May 1821	Dr.William A.Gordon	George H & Martha(Boyd) Tn96/99	USBI	532	Lafayette	1832
28 Apr 1829	Michael Gore	M & Elizabeth(Mitchell) Va/Ky	HSTC	1132		1881
15 Jan 1819	F. C. Holland	Whitemill & Jane(Alexander)NC94/Ky	HSTC	680		1837
00 000 1849	William E. Nance	Barton G & Lavica S(Harrison)Tn/Owen	HPCD	762		1851
00 000 1842	Francis M. Pitts	Barney & Catherine Ky06/NC	HPCD	688		1848
20 May 1830	G. M. Roper	H. C & Nancy W Va96/Va93	JASP	708		1867
19 Mar 1844	Rev.G.B Sergeant		HOCO	1079		----
09 Nov 1841	William M. Stuart	Wiley & Frances(Ferell) Va/Va	VERN	426		----
16 Oct 1857	Rev.David Q.Travis	John W Marshall/--	FJWC	951	Saint Louis	1881

T R I M B L E   C O U N T Y

BIRTHDATE	NAME OF BIOGRAPHEE	PARENTS/BIRTHPLACE/BIRTHDATE	SOURCE	PAGE	FIRST MO.CO.	DATE
03 Aug 1846	Joseph E. Adcock	Elijah & Susan	NW	1737		1887
02 May 1839	J. S. Cornell	James H & Malinda(Messick)	--	--		----
00 000 1831	M. N. Dougherty	Col.Robert S & Elizabeth(Pearce)90/00--	--	--		----
02 Jan 1842	George D. Ewing	Fulton & Rachel W(Robbins)Henry/--	DAGE	958		1845
22 Dec 1838	William H. Fallis	John & Sarah S(Stratton) Ky10/Ky16	JASP	528	Gentry	1875
01 Nov 1848	John H. Hardin		LCKS	757		1857
01 Aug 1832	Judge Marion Houghland		MOSH	1095		1843
25 Nov 1839	Daniel L. Hughes	James & Elizabeth(Lane)	ASPS	979	Macon	1884
24 Jul 1849	Dr. William A.Metcalfe	Sanford & Louisa A(Spilman)Va/Ky	ANDE	573		1884
00 000 0000	Dr. Jere T. Muir		VADA	1163		----
19 Feb 1852	Henry C Orr	Alexander & Editha(Wright)Garrard/**	CLCA	493		1866
00 000 1826	Samuel Pice		NW	1587		1842
08 Apr 1824	Simeon F. Rowlett		PETT	723		1854
06 Jan 1836	Joseph F. Simmons	Samuel & Amanda(Williams) Ky/Ky	NLBM	980		1860

U N I O N   C O U N T Y

BIRTHDATE	NAME OF BIOGRAPHEE	PARENTS/BIRTHPLACE/BIRTHDATE	SOURCE/PAGE	FIRST MO.CO.	DATE
27 Mar 1856	J. L. Ashby	E. R　Ky/--	JOHN 836	Pettis	1866
22 Dec 1846	William T. Buckham	James & Lucinda	BATC 86		1859
00 000 1845	Henry C. Churchill	Col. A. L & Rebecca(Catlett)Jeffer/--HSTC 564	Johnson	1866
04 Mar 1842	Jacob Curray	Benjamin & Elizabeth(Morgan)Va/Va	MOSH 1092		1882
30 Jan 1824	Dr. William C. Duval	Claiborne　　Va/--	NLBM 1064	Hickory	---
03 Apr 1839	Nathaniel A. Floyd		JASP 336		1855
27 Jul 1830	E. E. Gittings		NODA 699		1874
00 000 0000	Benjamin Hall		SEGO 966		1843
00 000 0000	Samuel M. Hewitt		MOSH 924	Marion	1855
00 000 0000	Sarah Holman		SEGO 966		1843
00 000 1855	Dr. W. W. Hull	James & Mary(Simpson)　In21/--	FJWC 907	C. Giradeau	1858
14 Jan 1827	Capt.John D.Piercall	Joseph & Elizabeth(Able)　Md/Md	MOSH 416		---
02 Feb 1868	Samuel L. Ramsey		SERD 1248		1872
11 Jan 1827	Edward R. Threlkeld	Benjamin & Julia A(Kercheval)Va/MasonUSBI 60	Boone	1834
20 Oct 1808	Hon.Nathaniel F.Givens	Samuel & Ann(Harris)　Va/Md	USBI 626	Saint Louis	1837

W A R R E N   C O U N T Y

BIRTHPLACE	NAME OF BIOGRAPHEE	PARENTS/BIRTHPLACE/BIRTHDATE	SOURCE/PAGE	FIRST MO.CO.	DATE
07 Dec 1816	Ira D. Anderson	Abraham	LAFA 509		1836
25 Oct 1815	John H. Allison		BUCH 1009	Lafayette	1826
28 Feb 1843	Judge J. B Barnett		HPCD 624		1861
04 Jul 1825	Col. A. G. Blakey		COOP 572		1836
17 Sep 1820	Benjamin T. Blewett	Edward	STLO 1878		----
15 Jun 1819	James J. Boyce	Willis P	BOON 1081		1819

Date	Name	Parents/Spouse	Birthplace	Code	No.	County	Year
05 Nov 1819	Benjamin M. Briggs	Robert & Jane(Cook)	Va/Va	MARI	910	Ralls	1823
16 Oct 1830	Willis Eagle			JASP	867		----
10 Jun 1813	Giles C. Clardy	Norman S & Rachel(Johnson)	Va/Va	CIPL	433	Carroll	1836
00 000 0000	Giles C. Clardy	Norman S & Rachel(Johnson)	Va74/87	ANPL	263		1840
18 Oct 1822	John Claypool	Jeremiah & Rebecca	Ky/Ky	GREH	614	Polk	1839
07 May 1837	Pleasant P.Collier			AUDR	557	Pettis	1858
27 Mar 1817	Mordecai M. Cooke			LAFA	583		1844
00 000 1830	Caleb J. Cox			SCMW	919	Montgomery	1854
00 000 0000	Dr. A.C. Davidson	A. L & Mary J(Adams)		HSTC	1213	Hickory	1865
26 Jun 1841	J. H. Davidson			HPCD	585		1866
00 000 0000	James M. Davis			LCDW	705		1840
01 Mar 1843	William N. Davis	James W & Syrena(Witherspoon)	Ky19/--	NLBM	917		1844
00 000 1831	Capt. William Dunn	John H & Charlotte P	Va/Ky	ASPS	1149		1858
00 000 0000	Abner W. Dyer	Abner & Mary		VERN	638	Saint Louis	1818
02 May 1807	Didama Dyer	M. W		IAFA	697		1828
20 Aug 1837	James D. Dyer	Manoah W		JOHN	919	Lafayette	1844
22 Dec 1838	M. A. Dyer			LAFA	607		1840
13 Mar 1856	John M. Earp	Rev. J. D & Dorcus C(Cox)	New Eng/Ky	HPCD	887	Montgomery	1857
00 Jun 1833	William N. Evans	John & Rebecca(Osburn)	SC/NC	CSBA	555	Lafayette	1843
00 000 1822	John Finney	John & Elizabeth(Heart)	Ky/--	FJWC	747	Warren	1832
00 000 1846	Dr. Theo.F.Frazer	Alexander & Zuriah(Atchison)	Ky97/Ky	O3SEGO	926		1866
00 000 0000	E. E. Gilmore	Samuel		CSBA	1193		1859
16 Jan 1838	Mordecai M. Gladden			LAFA	522		1841
22 Jul 1836	James E. Gladdish			LAFA	510		1841
22 Jul 1836	James E. Gladish	Elijah & Elizabeth(Cooke)	**/Va	PLAS	522		1841
25 Dec 1809	Joseph H. Harmett	Elijah & Mary(Snodgrass)	SC/Ky	RAMA	469	Howard	1825
25 Dec 1809	Joseph H. Harmett	Elijah & Mary(Snodgrass)	SC/**	USBI	186	Randolph	1827
07 Aug 1815	Vincent K. Hines	William & Betsey(Adams)	Va/Va	HSTC	582		1866
23 Oct 1851	Virgil H. Hires	Vincent K & Ann M(Stone)	**15/**19	LCDW	1113	Johnson	1867
14 Aug 1850	Prof.J.H. Hirton	Joseph & Mary V(Billingsley)	Ky/Ky	CSBA	1378		1881
03 May 1827	James O. Hogan	Alexander & Mary(Hatcher)	Va/Va	PLAS	229		----
00 000 1802	Elizabeth Hudspeth			FJWC	1058		c1815

BIRTHPLACE	NAME OF BIOGRAPHEE	PARENTS/BIRTHPLACE/BIRTHDATE	SOURCE/PAGE	FIRST MO.CO.	DATE
19 Jan 1830	Joseph J. Johnson	Benjamin C & Catherine B(Curd)--/Jess	VERN 733	Marion	1830
13 Mar 1826	Richard M.Johnson	Benjamin C & Catherine(Curd)85/96	MARI 818		1829
01 Oct 1830	J. A. Justice		SALI 790		1853
00 000 0000	D. Kimble		SCMW 736		----
06 May 1831	William Kirby		JACK 906		----
12 Oct 1812	John E. Lankford	Nathan D & Nancy(Embly) Va/Va	NLBM 852		1839
00 000 1811	James C. LeGrand		NLBM 1033	Lawrence	1840
15 Sep 1836	W. H. Lively	William Va/--	JOHN 892		1863
26 Jan 1843	John W. Morgan	Jonathan & Nancy(Simpson) Va/Va	HSTC 648		----
00 Jan 1817	Granville R. Page	Axel H & Sarah(Ennis) Va/Va	PLAS 617	Platte	1836
00 000 1813	Joseph H. Page	Alexander H & --(Ennis) Va/Va	PLAS 208		----
16 Apr 1813	Joseph H. Page		LAFA 547		1827
08 Jan 1848	Benjamin T. Poe	Alvin & Rebecca	SALI 860		----
00 000 0000	Anna E. Potts		SEGO 803		----
15 Mar 1837	James H. Prather		HOAT 844		1850
07 Jul 1820	Dr.Robert C.Prunty	Thomas & Sarah(Rives)	GREH 689		1857
27 Mar 1827	P. P. Reed	John & Ida(Lowe) NC/Ky	SEGO 1049		1839
00 000 1856	Fred B. Reynolds	Admiral & Elizabeth(Griffith)Ky/--	NLBM 975		1837
00 000 1803	Jeremiah Russell		LCDW 749		1881
00 000 0000	James Sears		RAMA 1029		1837
20 Jul 1840	Henry C. Shields	Egbert O & Ellen(Brent) Va18/--	HOCO 408		1819
20 Jul 1840	Judge Henry C.Shields	E. O & Ellen(Brent) Va18/--	CHHO 448		----
07 Jan 1839	John Shobe	Absalom & Jane(Dunn) Va03/**	HSTC 542	Pettis	1868
03 Jan 1844	Monroe I. Simpson		CLIN 254		1859
15 Sep 1823	David Smith	James Ky/Ky	PETT 1034		1865
00 000 1815	William C. Smith		SEGO 803		1850
00 000 1834	S. H. Strother	Robert D & Elizabeth(Hampton)	CMMB 1014		1846

BIRTHDATE	NAME OF BIOGRAPHEE	PARENTS/BIRTHPLACE/BIRTHDATE		SOURCE/PAGE		FIRST MO.CO.	DATE
20 Aug 1842	William M. Tarrant	John M & Nancy(Potter)	**20/--	HPCD	842		1843
00 000 1828	Martin G. Thompson	John & Mary(Wilkinson)	Ky84/Ky84	LINC	620		1828
03 Nov 1836	Rev. Thomas Toney	Jesse & Mary(Elliott)	Va95/Va	HPCD	844		c1885
06 Dec 1834	M. M. Tucker	William F & Nancy P(Wentlow)Va/Ky		CSBA	1187		1840
02 Sep 1831	A. J. Turner	Andrew & Mary(Harris)		BOON	611		1838
24 Jun 1812	Samuel W. Vanlandigham	Samuel W. Vanlandigham Lewis		MARI	823		1818
10 Oct 1817	William H.Vanlandigham	William H.Vanlandigham		MARI	624		1818
00 000 1837	Elizabeth Walker	Robert & Nancy(Allen)	Ky09/Ky18	SEGO	949		---
25 Jan 1824	George Wood	George & Winnie(Lawny)	Va/NC	LCDW	763		---
09 Jun 1821	David H. Woodson	Shadrack & Martha(Haynes)	Va/Va	CALL	939	Marion	1825
25 Dec 1826	William M. Wright	J. B & Mary G(Wallace)	Ky/Ky	CMMB	741		1838
07 Oct 1870	Charles A. Young	John & Sarah E(Hudnell)	**49/Ky	----	---		---

WASHINGTON COUNTY

BIRTHDATE	NAME OF BIOGRAPHEE	PARENTS/BIRTHPLACE/BIRTHDATE		SOURCE/PAGE		FIRST MO.CO.	DATE
13 Aug 1807	Edward G. Berry	Richard & Mary(Ewing)	Va71/---	CALL	535		1820
13 Apr 1818	Maj. Robert M.Berry	Richard & Polly(Ewing)		CALL	902		1820
12 Aug 1838	Paris Brown	Wesley & Elizabeth(Peters)		HSTC	1076	Washington	1848
07 Nov 1826	Nathan J. Charter			NODA	692		1869
08 May 1813	J. S. Clark	Benjamin & Polly(Head)	Va77/Md77	ANDE	496		1866
29 Feb 1844	Judge George W.Cotton	James & Ann(Carrier)		----	---		1849
26 Nov 1832	S. H. Crane	Talton	Va/---	MARI	694		1839
18 May 1824	William Crane			MARI	731		1839
23 Feb 1823	George W. Crowder			JASP	844		1873
06 Feb 1831	Thomas Downey			AUDR	876	Randolph	1854
01 Nov 1826	Luke Ellis	Thomas & Mildred(Jenkins)	Ky/Ky	RAMA	994	Chariton	1836
11 Mar 1832	Buford Farris	Isaiah & Elizabeth(McDowell)Ky/Ky		NODA	756		1874
06 Nov 1822	Henry H. Fields	John & Elizabeth(Wiseheart)Md/Ky		MOSH	549		1855

WASHINGTON COUNTY (CONT.)

BIRTHDATE	NAME OF BIOGRAPHEE	PARENTS/BIRTHPLACE/BIRTHDATE	SOURCE/PAGE	FIRST MO.CO.	DATE
21 Jan 1827	Squire Wilson T.Fields		MOSH	444	1858
25 Apr 1823	John S. Flournoy	James & Martha O(Halloway)Md/JessaminRAY		769	Clay	1851
23 Dec 1824	William H. Flournoy		RAY	798		1843
04 Apr 1840	W. C. Fullilove	Lewis B & Cordelia(Head)	MARI	618	Pike	1854
15 Mar 1844	Thomas B. Gannaway	William & Martha(Berry)	MOSH	555		1852
10 Mar 1842	Edward R. Gibbons	Edward R & Sarah(Noel) 05/11	NW	1712	Andrew	1843
00 000 0000	William Gillihan		NW	1149	Daviess	1855
14 Mar 1816	Col.Amos Graham		NODA	763	Andrew	1842
26 Aug 1832	Orville Graves	James & Ruth Va/Va	HOAT	375		1851
00 000 1817	Dr. Matthew W. Hall		SALI	851		1845
15 May 1847	Dr. Matthew W. Hall	Rev.Nathan H & Annie(Crawford)Va/Ky	PLAS	199		----
00 000 1817	Dr. Matthew W. Hall	Reverend Nathan	---	---		1817
01 Dec 1816	J. B. Howell		BUCH	777	Andrew	1839
22 Oct 1826	John K. Humphrey	William & Elizabeth Ann(Pettit)**/Va.	LCKS	1178	Lewis	1841
18 Apr 1812	Dr. Silas McDonald		BUCH	822	Howard	1836
00 000 1832	Hugh L. McElroy		KC&	213		1868
02 Jan 1839	William R. Mattingly	Philip & Elizabeth(Mudd)	LINC	574		1848
15 Jan 1845	John H. Miles	William F & Nancy W(Jackson)	MOSH	1008		1850
01 Sep 1823	Charles W.Montgomery	William P & Mary(Yates)	MOSH	415		----
00 Aug 1844	John Montgomery	Dr. T. S & Emily(Flournoy) Ky/Ky	PETT	705		1857
20 Jan 1850	Jesse N. Moore	Walter B & Marion(Pope) Ky/Ky	LCKS	927	Andrew	1857
10 Aug 1844	Dr. James R. Mudd	-- & Elizabeth(Janes) Md/Ky	SCMW	414		1849
09 Oct 1817	Robert Mudd	Nicholas & Martha(Janes) Md/Ky	LINC	587		1843
01 Apr 1836	Ina Peter	Richard & Lucy Ky/Ky	HOAT	402		1852
31 Mar 1811	Judge David Pipes		BOON	1051		1817
31 Oct 1808	Cyrus Powel	Charles & Leah(Goldman) Va/NC	MARI	741		1833
04 Sep 1805	John Reed	John & Jane(McMurray)	BOON	786		1825

-160-

BIRTHDATE	NAME OF BIOGRAPHEE	PARENTS/BIRTHPLACE/BIRTHDATE	SOURCE/PAGE	FIRST MO.CO.	DATE
10 Jan 1820	George Riley	Bailey & Pollie(Bridewell) Va/Va	NODA 878	Howard	1855
29 Feb 1813	Joseph Robertson		PETT 967		1816
01 Sep 1824	Robertson M. Royalty	Thomas & Margaret(Robertson)97/--	KC& 824		1853
23 Mar 1811	Edmund Rutter	Edmund & Elizabeth(Phillips)	MOSH 1106	C. Giradeau	1817
12 Sep 1812	Samuel D. Sandusky	John & Martha(Huntley) Ky/Va	LINN 472	Platte	1843
17 Dec 1819	Sarah J. Shuck		HAME 515	Ralls	--
22 Feb 1817	Jesse J. Summers	Greenberry & Nancy(Elliott)Ky/Ky	LINN 806		1839
17 Jan 1836	Calvin H. Sweeney	Nelson & Jane(Taylor)	HOCH 1109		1870
14 Aug 1851	C. W. Wright	Nathaniel & Elizabeth 06/13	HSTC 1157		--
27 Jul 1858	Charles W. Wright	Richard W & Angeline E(Moore)	MOSH 1040		1883
04 Jul 1844	George W. Wright	Morgan & Elizabeth(Hickerson)Ky/Ky	HSTC 1188		1870
23 Dec 1844	Dr. James P. Wright	Nathaniel & Matilda(Moore) Va/Va	HSTC 1188		1871
20 Dec 1836	Dr. John W. Wright	Nathaniel & Elizabeth(Parker)06/Val3	HSTC 1157		1870
01 May 1849	Dr. Nathaniel P.Wright	Nathaniel & Elizabeth(Parker)06/Va	HSTC 1165		1868
00 000 0000	Judge James B.Yager	Ananias & Rachel(Brumfield)Va/Va	JACK 898	Callaway	1837
00 000 1832	George W. Young	Jacob & Elizabeth(Stump) NC/Ky	ASPS 1134	Ralls	1826

W A Y N E   C O U N T Y

BIRTHDATE	NAME OF BIOGRAPHEE	PARENTS/BIRTHPLACE/BIRTHDATE	SOURCE/PAGE	FIRST MO.CO.	DATE
25 Dec 1825	James G. Baker	William & Rhoda(Summers,	RAMA 442		1827
12 Jul 1814	Matthew S. Baker		LCDW 975	Osage	1835
29 Jan 1844	Harvey Ballou	Linsey & Marina	SALI 601		1849
00 000 1823	Elizabeth Barnes		CALI 519	Daviess	1857
08 Jan 1842	Benjamin W. Bond	William P & Clara Tn/**	NLBM 901		1866
12 Apr 1838	Thomas Brooks		RAMA 542		1832
12 Jul 1807	Aaron F. Bruce	William & Sarah(Vandever) Va/NC	SALI 531		--
27 Jul 1842	Margaret T. Davenport	Samuel B & Minerva	BATC 162		--
26 Sep 1816	Rev. Oliver D. Davis	Major Drury & --(East) 87/--	COOP 727	Howard	1817

-161-

W A Y N E   C O U N T Y   (C O N T.)

BIRTHDATE	NAME OF BIOGRAPHEE	PARENTS/BIRTHPLACE/BIRTHDATE	SOURCE/PAGE	FIRST MO.CO.	DATE
16 Sep 1816	O. P. Davis	Major Drury	HOCO 1118	Howard	1817
21 Feb 1825	Judge John Denny	Benjamin	Va/--	LCDW 838		1836
00 Nov 1842	Reuben S. Dodson	John & Sarah(Burnett)	Va/Va	ASPS 797		1842
18 Mar 1868	Dr. Lee J. Eads	William T	NW 1475		----
23 Sep 1838	Benjamin F. Fleming	E. D & Dorcus(Vickery)	Ky/Va	HOAT 199		1867
23 Oct 1830	James B. Francis	Elisha & Theresa(Huff)	CALI 1099	Miller	1832
00 Apr 1806	Lewis Green		RAMA 1110		1825
00 000 0000	Tandy A. Greenup	Christopher B	CMMB 852		----
16 Nov 1851	Joseph W. Grubbs	Abraham & Polly	Tn10/Tn10	JASP 626	Greene	1869
07 Jan 1820	Samuel C. Hamilton	Joseph H & Nancy(Kiggin) 99/02	RAMA 1050		1843
12 Oct 1834	James C. Hancock	Benjamin & Elizabeth(Vickery)SC79/Ky	JASP 629		1860
00 000 1834	Joseph W. Hatfield	Andrew & Mary A(Miller) **01/--	ASPS 1167	Randolph	1837
14 May 1822	Capt.Thomas Higginbotham	John & Sallie(Dowell) Ky/Ky	HPCD 653		1845
07 Dec 1866	Lewis Hughes	Oliver & Emaline	VADA 1013		1868
10 Aug 1832	John P. Jones	George & Gracie Ann(City) Ky/Ky	RAMA 1095	Putnam	1857
28 Oct 1838	C. F. Kerr	James & Catherine(Simpson) Ky/SC	CLCA 607		1858
20 Apr 1826	John Koger		BUCH 1004	Gentry	1846
00 000 1825	Elias Lankford		CALI 519	Daviess	1857
17 Oct 1819	William Lunsford	Isam & Rhoda NC/NC	HOAT 394	Crawford	1833
07 Mar 1851	J. K. McBeath	Robert S & Mary J(Kerr) Ky/Ky	CLCA 459		1856
25 May 1816	James McHenry	John & Margaret(Hines) **/**	CSBA 1183		1841
19 Sep 1833	William F. McKinney		---- ---	Andrew	1849
18 Jul 1824	Michael Majors	Elisha & Catherine(Hufaker)Ky/Ky	HSTC 1220	Clay	1837
12 Oct 1831	William H. Marlow	Ga/Ga	CALI 1016	Cole	1832
05 Feb 1829	Benjamin F. Mills	Charles E & Betsy(Bell)Va/Fayette97	CSBA 540	Lafayette	1841
15 Feb 1816	W. L. Mills	Caleb W & Erzilla(East) Va/**	LCKS 1187	Monroe	1827
30 Aug 1828	Perry Millsaps	H. Esq. & Rebecca(Hoofacre)**02/**	HSTC 1197	Lincoln	1829
14 Mar 1822	Henry Minton	Isaac & Ruth(Blevins) Ky/Ky	HOAT 397	Franklin	1835

Date	Name	Parents	Birthplace	Code	No.	Place	Year
23 Dec 1823	Thomas Moody	James & Jane(Mercer)	NC/Ky	RAMA	1019		1844
06 May 1843	James H. Morris			CALI	332		1878
23 Sep 1853	Harrison Morrow			BUCH	1015		1873
30 Sep 1815	Larkin Norfleet		Va/Va	PLAS	517		---
10 Mar 1826	William S. Norfleet	James & Elizabeth		GREH	791	Polk	1838
17 Oct 1843	V. C. Reese	David & Elizabeth(Shacklefcrd)		BUCH	871		1874
06 Aug 1810	A. Rice		Va/Va	RAMA	636		1830
20 Jun 1843	Elijah E. Rice	Thomas & Margaret(Thong)	Va/Va	CHHO	852		---
15 Sep 1803	Dr. Samuel C. Rubey	Preston & Charlotte(Coger)	**18/Ky12	USBI	803	Cooper	1820
22 Sep 1810	Dr. H. P. Sanders	Thomas		CLIN	215		1859
08 Mar 1822	William H. Sheeks	& Rosa	95/--	ASPS	1018	Randolph	1828
20 Jul 1840	Judge Henry C.Shields	E. O & Ellen(Brent)	Va18/--	CHHO	448		---
06 Oct 1822	George W. Shumate	James & Jane		SALI	601		1837
12 Feb 1876	Mathew D. Sloan	William & Artie(Cooper)	Ky/Ky	CLCA	603	Marion	1886
27 Jan 1836	John R. Smith	David & Charlotte(Havine)	NC/Tn	NLBM	881		1836
08 Jan 1839	Isaac C. Stephens	Gordon C & Sallie(Crockett)		RAMA	1209		1844
12 Oct 1828	Judge John H.Sullens	Thomas & Martha(Boner)	Ky/Ky	CSBA	1299	Cole	1828
18 Dec 1876	Joseph M. Summers	Jereniah & Elizabeth(Baker)		RAMA	628		1818
00 000 0000	John S. Walker			NLBM	887		1854
00 000 1828	Alexander C. Tarlton			SERD	699	C. Giradeau	1843
30 Oct 1808	William Terry	Josiah & Nancy(Thomas)	Tn/Tn	RAMA	531		1837
18 Aug 1829	Allen J. Vickrey	Abner & Nancy	Va/Ky	RAMA	1098		1829
00 Apr 1849	James E. Walker	George W & Polly(Coughrr)	**/**	CMMB	821		1872
00 000 1811	Joseph Wolfskill	George & Mary(Ross)		CALI	1161		---
22 Jun 1829	Allen Wright	C & Rebecca(Vestal)		RAMA	1108		1829
22 Oct 1806	Martin Wright			RAMA	1107		1829
07 May 1851	Simeon Weaver	S. A & Margaret P	Ky/Ky	CSBA	737	Cooper	1823

WEBSTER COUNTY

BIRTHDATE	NAME OF BIOGRAPHEE	PARENTS/BIRTHPLACE/BIRTHDATE	SOURCE/PAGE	FIRST MO.CO.	DATE
03 Mar 1863	James H. Doris		SERD 722		----

WHITLEY COUNTY

BIRTHDATE	NAME OF BIOGRAPHEE	PARENTS/BIRTHPLACE/BIRTHDATE	SOURCE/PAGE	FIRST MO.CO.	DATE
20 Jan 1817	Levi P. Cox	Levi & Cynthia	DAGE 454		1840
16 Dec 1828	Major Samuel P. Cox		DAVI 527		1839
00 000 0000	Rev. Grant Creekmore	F. B & Sarah(Snyder)	DAGE 1027		1878
07 May 1833	James L. Farris		RAY 522		1856
03 May 1822	David Girdner	David & Elizabeth(Perman) Pa/Pa	CALI 1010		1834
05 Mar 1850	Christina Nix	John & Mary(Raines)	NW 1704	Andrew	1852
00 000 1854	Salaba J. Siler		NW 1451	Daviess	1854
04 Sep 1843	James M. Snyder	John & Diana Ky/Ky	HAME 747		1850
21 Oct 1814	Joshua Tye	Joshua & Elizabeth(Cummins)NC/Ky	CALI 1023		1856
00 000 0000	James Witt	Samuel	VERN 429		----

WOLFE COUNTY

BIRTHDATE	NAME OF BIOGRAPHEE	PARENTS/BIRTHPLACE/BIRTHDATE	SOURCE/PAGE	FIRST MO.CO.	DATE
27 Aug 1837	William F. Hanks	Cudmillion & Millie A(Garrett)Ky/Ky	CSBA 1130		1872

BIRTHDATE	NAME OF BIOGRAPHEE	PARENTS/BIRTHPLACE/BIRTHDATE	SOURCE/PAGE	FIRST MO.CO.	DATE
14 Apr 1835	Presley D Anderson	Spencer & Catherine(Hicks) Ky/Ky	CLPL 455		1852
25 Apr 1842	Robert S. Anderson		CLPL 456		c1851
00 000 1807	W. H. Arnold	Fauntleroy	CLPL 457		1828
14 Sep 1827	T. J. Ashford		BUCH 667	Andrew	1853
29 Sep 1800	Thomas J. Ayres	John & Agnes Va/Va	PIKE 960		1830
00 000 0000	Francis A. Blackburn	Dr. Churchill & Eleanor M	SALI 663		----
23 Mar 1823	H. B. Bohannon		JACK 886		1880
16 Jan 1800	Ephraim Bondurant		PIKE 961		1830
00 000 1831	Charles L. Bounds	Thomas J & Hester A(Furnell)Md00/Md04	ASPS 948	Marion	1832
06 May 1840	Evaline Bradley	William	NW 1362		----
09 Nov 1822	Jefferson Bridgford		MOSH 526		1836
13 Mar 1849	Henry H. Craig	Henry H & Emily C	JACK 757		1869
08 Sep 1844	John H. Craig	Herman B	LINN 432		1855
21 Jan 1817	Madison Dale	LeRoy & Jemima(Gill) Va/Va	CLPL 1095		1843
00 000 1800	James Driskell		CALL 911		1825
03 Sep 1807	William F. Dunnica	William H & --(Harper)	HOCO 436		1824
03 Sep 1807	William F. Dunnica	William H & --(Harper)	USBI 591		1824
22 Oct 1834	Joel H. Duvall	Jonathan C & Elizabeth(Roberts)**/Mon	HSTC 590	Marion	1835
00 000 1838	William H. Edwards		IAFA 680		----
09 Mar 1822	John Elliott	Isaac Ky/--	PETT 1070		1835
26 Mar 1824	Thomas J. Ford	John & Sarah(Berry) Va/--	KC& 286		1848
23 Feb 1830	Sarah Gaines		ANPL 186		1849
20 Nov 1825	John P. Gibbs	Robert & Fanny(Pemberton) Ky/Ky	CALL 822	Boone	1831
10 Nov 1858	Pres. Frank Gwynn	William S & Angelina L(Kear.)	CMMB 1055		1884
00 000 1814	Mark Hammond	Va/NC	JOHN 926		1855
18 Jul 1816	John Hamon	Ezra & Hanna(Farra) Pa/--	CLPL 854		1842
10 Dec 1825	Elder T. W. Hancock		SALI 665		1855
08 Oct 1811	Henry Harrison	Henry & Polly(Malone) Va/--	RAMA 609		1839

BIRTHDATE	NAME OF BIOGRAPHEE	PARENTS/BIRTHPLACE/BIRTHDATE	SOURCE/PAGE	FIRST MO.CO.	DATE
00 000 0000	Lewis C. Hawkins		LCKS 761		1827
26 Mar 1851	Joseph C. Hearne	Frank P & Catherine Ky/Ky	MARI 604		1867
00 Oct 1837	Dr. J. F. Hedges		PETT 872		1871
02 Oct 1817	Robuck Hudson	Thomas & Jemima(Cavender) --/17	HOCO 389	Boone	1826
29 Nov 1832	W. C. Johnson		BUCH 785		1858
28 Feb 1838	Marion M. Johnstone	Joseph B & Sally	JACK 966		1874
00 Dec 1803	Capt.Asariah Kennedy	James & Nellie(Quinn) Ky/Ky	HOCH 748		----
23 Dec 1874	James L. Kinkead		LAFA 507		1878
00 000 1821	Thomas Lyne	Thomas & Mary(Connelly) Va83/--	SALI 596		1853
00 000 1821	Thomas Lyne	Thomas & Mary(Connelly)	PLAS 627		----
14 Sep 1827	Richard McCarty	Dennis & Ellen(Tombling) Va/Va	HSTC 684	Howard	1830
00 000 1827	Dr.James C.McCown	John & Eliza J(Easton)Mercer/**	SEGO 1082	Ralls	1864
22 Jul 1810	James McFerrin		JASP 815	Ralls	1831
22 Sep 1831	Lucien M. Major		LAFA 605		1847
00 000 1811	Elijah Martin	Joseph M	NW 1646	Andrew	1836
28 Jun 1865	Hon.Ernest D.Martin	Dr. & Catherine(Pinkerton) Ky/Va	PLAS 330		----
00 000 1825	Dr. S. D. Martin		SALI 851		----
23 Jun 1797	Jeremiah A. Minter	Joseph Va/--	MARI 738		1830
17 Dec 1798	Gideon Mitchell	Charles & Mary(Barnett) Va/Va	MARI 652		1851
12 Dec 1811	Madison W. Mitchell	George K & Elizabeth(Watts)Va/Va	CLPL 1067	Boone	1838
00 000 1829	Albert G. Mosby		CLPL 406		1833
26 Mar 1822	John Mosley	James & America(Lewis)	PIKE 1017		1832
00 000 0000	Nicholas Mosby		NW 1122	Clay	1833
00 000 1803	A. P. Moss		RAY 669		1845
20 Dec 1807	Dr.Joseph G.Norwood	Charles & Mildred(Dale) Va53/--	USBI 879		1858
20 Dec 1807	Dr.Joseph G.Norwood	Charles	BOON 917		1858
05 Aug 1837	Benjamin F. Paul	Henry L & Catherine(McKee)	SALI 721		1854
00 Sep 1806	Samuel Ramsey		LCKS 817		----

Date	Name	Parents	Birth	Code	No.	County	Year
22 Apr 1824	Henry L. Routt	Rodham & Phoebe(Blanton)	Va/Va	USBI	794		----
15 Jun 1850	Williar D. Rusk			BUCH	878		----
17 Jun 1819	D. P. Ryley			JACK	1000	Callaway	1854
07 Nov 1820	William Scearce	Laban & Jane(Ashurst)	**/Fayette	CSBA	715		----
25 Jun 1816	U. T. Shipp			CLIN	167	Jackson	1836
29 Jul 1843	Hon.Benjamin F.Shouse	B. F & Margaret(Farra)		CLPL	1031		1844
14 Jun 1811	B. P. Shouse			CLCA	813	Platte	1832
00 000 0000	Lewis Shouse			CLPL	1116		1843
00 000 0000	William O. Shouse			---	---		1839
14 Oct 1820	Henry C. Smith			RAY	758		1841
12 Oct 1823	Alexander T.Stevenson	William & Jane(Gardiner)	**/Va	MARI	707	Ralls	1830
14 Mar 1842	Sidney Summers	Adam H & Dolly(Flemming)	Va/--	CLPL	528		1858
02 Jun 1806	Verdner Suter	J. W		MARI	822		1839
06 Oct 1834	John W. Taylor	Richard & Caroline(Whittier)	**07/**	HSTC	688		1860
00 000 1796	Rev. Eppe Tillery			CLIN	62	Clay	1819
03 Jul 1818	James Tillery	James		CLIN	258	Clay	1821
07 Oct 1814	Rev. W. W. Tillery	James		CLIN	201	Clay	1821
25 Sep 1843	F. J. Walker			RAY	791	Clay	1855
10 Oct 1835	Charles C. Wallace	Henry & Elizabeth(Carly-e)	Ky/Va	PLAS	543		----
18 Aug 1823	Hon.Henry C. Wallace	Henry & Elizabeth(Carly-e)		PLAS	580		1844
18 Aug 1823	Hon.Henry C. Wallace	Henry & Elizabeth(Carly-e)		LAFA	632		1844
18 Aug 1823	Henry C. Wallace	Henry & Elizabeth(Carly-e)	Ky92/Ky	USBI	227		1825
00 000 1804	Martha Wallace			CALL	911		1858
03 Dec 1844	Frank S. Ware	H. P & Eliza J(Watkins)	Ky/Ky	HSTC	548		1820
28 Jan 1796	Gen. Nathaniel W. Watkins			BENC	37	C. Giradeau	
30 Oct 1806	Walter L. Watkins	Benjamin & Jane(Minter)	Va75/Va81	USBI	740	Clay	1830
30 Oct 1806	Walter L. Watkins	Benjamin & Jane(Minter)	Va/Va	CLPL	504		1831
00 000 0000	W. L. watkins			RAY	689	Clay	----
07 Jun 1825	Churchill J.White	William & Mildred(Blackburn)Henry/Ky		USBI	847		1842
16 Nov 1809	Prudence B. White	William & Mildred(Blackburn)	Md/--	NW	1132		1834
13 Apr 1814	H. Whittington	William	Va/Ky	CLIN	68	Clay	1835
06 Jun 1834	R. J. Wickersham	Isaac & Nancy(Wiggs)		LCDW	762	Saint Louis	1849

W O O D F O R D   C O U N T Y   (C O N T.)

BIRTHDATE	NAME OF BIOGRAPHEE	PARENTS/BIRTHPLACE/BIRTHDATE	SOURCE/PAGE	FIRST MO.CO.	DATE
00 000 0000	Ambrose D. Wiggs		CALL 734	Lincoln	1843
24 May 1857	Benjamin S. Wilson	William S & Matilda (Hearn) Ky31/I132	BOON 798		1874
26 Sep 1821	Robert A. Wood	Edward B Va/--	RAY 767		1852
07 Mar 1825	Thomas Young	James R & Elizabeth Ky95/Ky84	MARI 825		1830

Anderson (cont.)
Martha(Lowry) 71
Martha[Shobe] 16
Mary E[Reynolds] 104
Mary A(Roberts) 19
Nancy(Couther) 150, 151
Presley D. 165
Rachel(Downing) 63
Robert S. 165
Robert T. 71
Sally 115
Spencer 165
Susan[Grant] 24
Theney[Hensley] 127
Theresa[Wright] 92
Thomas L. 71
Thomas V. 19
W.B. 19
William 19
William B. 71
William H. 37
Willis 63
Anson, Elizabeth[Taylor] 32
Antle, Jacob F. 10, 141
Sarah(Stepp) 141
Sidney 141
Apperson, Frances 125
Gilbert 125
Nancy(Spears) 125
Arbuckle, Drinkard 105
Lucretia(Maxey) 105
N.F. 105
Arbunkle, Drinkard 67
Lucretia(Maxey) 67
N.F. 67
Armstrong, H.J. 60
J.H. 60
James M. 105
Margaret[Lindley] 41
Mary[Belt] 60
Mason 105
Nancy[Hopkins] 37
Arnold, E.C. 49
Fauntleroy 165
George B. 67
Isaac 67
Jane(Bryant) 67
Lewis 21
Louis M. 49
Margaret(Throckmorton) 21
Matthew R. 21
Pauline[Simpson] 68
W.H. 165
Arthur, Barnabus 113
John 113
Nancy(Vaughn) 113
Arvin, Sallie[White] 113
Arvine, Sallie[White] 113
Asbury, J.W. 153
Judy[Thornton] 119
N.W. 115
Ashbrook, Mary[Batchelor] 93
Ashburn, Hannah D[Duvall] 101
Ashby, E.R. 156
J.L. 156
Tamer[Hoskinson] 134
Ashcraft, Elizabeth(Keith) 77
Elizabeth[Shacklett] 77
Ellis 77
Lucius D. 77
Asher, Narcissa[Robertson] 49
Ashford, T.J. 165
Ashley, Elizabeth(Montgomery)
39
James M. 39

John 39
Mary[Taylor] 59
Ashurst, Jane[Searce] 167
Askew, Elizabeth[McReynolds]
35
Atchison, Catherine(Allen) 54
David R. 54
William 54
Zuriah[Frazer] 157
Atkins, Elizabeth[Martin] 51
James M. 17
Louisa[Deskins] 138
Atkinson, C.A[Browning] 10
Rhoda[Howard] 33
Atteberry, Aden C. 14
Mary(Miller) 14
Susanna(Clemons) 14
Thomas 14
William 14
Zephemiah 14
Austin, George M. 67
Malinda[McVay] 110
Auxier, George W. 92, 138
Nancy(Prater) 92, 138
Samuel 92
William B. 138
Avitt, Andrew 33
J.R. 33
James R. 33
Jane(Helm) 33
Ayres, Agnes 165
Charlotte A(Lutton) 21
Elizabeth(Ebert) 86
Harmon 21
Harmon D. 21
John 165
Philip E. 86
Sallie(Turner) 21
Thomas 86
Thomas J. 165
Will T. 21

Baber, John 138
John M. 105
Nancy[Owens] 83
Bacon, Elizabeth(Jeffries) 63
Lucinda E[Dodge] 86
Mary L.F[Pickett] 118
Robert 63
W.S. 63
Badgett, America(Bosley) 97
John A. 97
John R. 97
Bahlman, Anna M[Sommer] 93
Bailey, Alfred 30
Cyrene(Baker) 30
Elijah B. 39
Elizabeth(Foster) 14
J.A. 125
Jasper N. 38
Jessee 38
John 97
Joseph P. 14
Margaret(Webb) 38
Minerva[Ravenscraft] 79
O.P.W. 30
Rebecca 39
[Ridge] 11
Thomas D. 30
Thomas J. 97
William 14
William P. 146
Bainbridge, A[Clay] 22

Baird, Barzilla A. 37
Caroline[Cox] 14
Ely D. 77
Frances M. 77
Hannah[Cox] 14
Kate(Mitchell) 77
Margaret[Prater] 18
Mary M(Scanland) 37
Thomas 77
William T. 37
Baker, Ann(Rayburn) 101
Charles 105
Cyrena[Bailey] 30
Eliza 67
Eliza[Proctor] 123
Elizabeth[Dale] 133
F. 21
Fannie(Saunders) 105
George 42
George S. 105
George W. 19, 42
H.B. 32
Isaac 32, 105
James 115
James G. 161
Jane(McCulley) 105
John W. 101
Julia A. 19
Lucretius 48
Lydia[Lewis] 48
M. 115
Margaret(Waters) 115
Martha A. 42
Martin 21
Mary[Taylor] 27
Matthew S. 161
Nancy W[Miller] 19
Rebecca J. 19
Rhoda[Summers] 161
Samuel 48
Sarah(Delay) 21
Thomas 21
Thomas J. 21
William 161
William C. 105
William M. 105
Balay, Gideon P. 71
Perry 71
Tomsey(Warren) 71
Baldwin, James 115
James H. 115
Nancy 145
Sarah(Harris) 115
Ball, Alonzo C. 54
George W. 134
John D. 134
Judith[Onsot] 68
Mary[Joyce] 87
Nancy 134
Ballard, Eliza
Elizabeth[Gregory] 148
Lucy J. 89
Nancy[Pickerell] 36
Polly[Willis] 47
W.J. 89
William H. 105
Ballenger, Sarah[Carter] 97
Ballew, Mary[Park] 111
Ballinger, William R. 67
Ballou, Harvey 161
Linsey 161
Marina 161
Mary[Park] 111
Banks, Elizabeth(Mills) 67
Gerard 67

Bibb, Elizabeth(Poe) 101
  Henry G. 101
  James G. 101
Bickett, A.L. 114
  Ann(Knott) 114
  Anthony 114
  Edmund G. 114
  Elizabeth(Graves) 114
  Henry 114
Biddle, Anna W[Lydick] 25
Biggerstaff, Aaron 125
  G.T. 125
  J.B. 125
  S.G. 125
  Samuel 125
  W.L. 125
  William 125
Biggs, Elizabeth(McCune) 21
  George K. 21
  John 78
  William 21
Billingsley, Mary V[Hinton]
  157
Birge, James 125
  John 125
  Liddie(Headrick) 125
Bishop, Charles 138
  David 43
  Galen E. 138
  Judith(Booth) 43
  Levin 43
  William 121
Black, Adam 81
  Benjamin P. 121
  Charles D. 153
  Daniel 121
  Eliza(Bradshaw) 73
  Henry 73
  J.H. 73
  James 153
  Louisa[Leslie] 127
  Mary(Martin) 153
  Mary F[Phillips] 151
Blackburn, Cash 69
  Charloote(Maddex) 69
  Churchill 165
  Eleanor M. 165
  Elsus[Stephenson] 112
  Frances(Jett) 105
  Francis A. 165
  John R. 105
  Mildred[White] 167
  Randolph 105
  W.F. 69
Blackford, James M. 89
Blackwell, James J. 81
  James S. 81
  John 13
  John S. 81
  Mary(Jeffress) 81
  Rachel(Lawrence) 13
  Sallie[Reynolds] 46
Blades, Joseph M. 134
Blair, Francis P. 54
  Margaret[Thompson] 119
Blake, Nancy[Hudgins] 64
Blakely, Hannah(Hardin) 40
  John 40
  Samuel J. 40
Blakemore, Thomas H. 147
Blakey, A.G. 156
Blanchard, Henry H. 101
  John 40
  Samuel J. 40
Bland, Bryant 130
  Charles C. 134
  Edward 134
  Elizabeth[Van Metre] 77

James 130
John H. 130
Margaret(Bridewell) 130
Margaret(Nall) 134
Mary(Wyatt) 130
Richard P. 134
Stouton E. 134
W.W. 130
Blankenbecker, Julia[Conn] 86
Blankenship, Agnes 73
  Greenville 73
  John 73
Blanton, Phoebe[Routt] 167
Bledsoe, Dilcenia M[Harrison]
  127
  Elizabeth[Emerson] 50
  Hiram M. 21, 50
  Mariah[Edwards] 39
  Susan T(Hughes) 21
  Wilson H. 153
Blincoe, Nancy[Lamar] 74
Biven, Bozel 86
  M.M. 86
  Martha[Waltrip] 51
Blevins, Jesse 71
  Mary[Shrader] 135
  Ruth[Minton] 162
Blewette, Benjamin T. 156
  Edward 156
  Susannah J[Turner] 151
Bluette, Elizabeth[Turner]
  151
Blythe, A.D. 54
  Jemima(Lay) 54
  Samuel 54
Boaz, Herbert L. 65
Bobbitt, Rebecca[Thomas] 140
Boen, Edward 105
  James M. 105
  Phoebe A(Boggs) 105
Bogard, A.C. 34
  Clifton 34
  Eliza(Webb) 34
Boggess, Henry 13
Boggs, Jane[McPherson] 20
  Phoebe A[Boen] 105
  Thomas A. 54
Bogie, Daniel H. 105
  Emeline(Taylor) 105
  M.A. 105
  Marcus A. 105
  Thomas D. 105
Bohannon, H.B. 165
  Letha[Christie] 147
  Louis C. 71
Bohon, Garrett 121
  John 121
  W.R. 121
Bolling, Beverly D. 30
  Elizabeth[Greenwood] 30
  James P. 30
  Lucinda(Kenley) 30
Bomer, Martha[Sullens] 163
Bonar, James M. 137
  Patsy(Ervin) 137
  Washington F. 137
Bond, Benjamin W. 161
  Clara 161
  Julia H[Lindsay] 38
  William P. 161
Bondurant, A.A. 65
  C. 105
  Edward 105
  Ephraim 165
  John S. 65
  Julia D(Edmiston) 65
Bonta, Abram 121
  Elizabeth 121

John L. 121
Boon, Hampton L. 147
  Presley 105
  William 147
Boone, Elizabeth[Nelson] 57
  Lavinia[Scholl] 47
Booth, Christopher C. 21
  Mary(Congleton) 21
  Stephen 21
Boothe, Elijah 54
  Sarah(Woods) 54
Boren, Margaret[Alderson] 150
Bosley, America[Badget] 97
Boston, L.W. 86
Boucher, Euphrates 11
  Gabriel 11
  Harrison 11
  John G. 11
  Mary(Smith) 11
  Robert 105
  William 11
  Zarilda(Woolsey) 11
Boswell, John T. 78
Bottom, Henry 121
  James 121
  Mary(Nichols) 121
  Nancy 121
Botts, John 10
Bouldin, E. Clark 40
Boulton, Jesse A. 116
Bounds, Charles L. 165
  Hester A(Purnell) 165
  Thomas J. 165
Bouscaren, O. 69
Bowden, Mary[Duncan] 143
Bowen, America[Jones] 90
  B.J. 82
  Mollie 82
Bowles, Benjamin P. 21
  David 21
  Elizabeth(Martin) 21
Bowlin, Margaret[Hutson] 48
Bowling, Jane C(Neal) 21
  John 21
  Robert 21
Bowman, Bettie(Mooreman) 71
  Charles P. 71
  Elizabeth A(Wilkerson) 39
  Elizabeth E(Dickerson) 54
  Parker T. 54; Julia A. 141
  Robert T. 54
  William 39, 70
  William G. 39
Boyce, Gabriel 54
  Greenbury 97
  James J. 156
  Mary[Wood] 124
  Willis P. 156
Boyd, Eleanor[Caldwell] 132
  Jane 40
  Jeanetta[Howe] 127
  Josiah 40
  Martha[Gordon] 155
  Mary[Barnes] 17
  Mary[Libbee] 37
  Samuel 60
  T.J. 40
  Susan E(Lacy) 60
  Wilson P. 60
Boyer, Henry 54
  John H. 63
Boyle, Jane(Forman) 43
  Jane[Gordon] 108
  James 43
  John W. 43
Bozarth, Alfred M. 40
  Milton J. 40
  Minerva 40

Bracken, Mary[Downing] 78
  Sarah E[Hatler] 11
Brackin, Abigail[Ginn] 37
Bradburn, America[Payne] 125
Bradford, Austin 142
  G.A. 142
  James 114
  Levina 142
Bradley, John J. 22
  John W. 14
  Layton 22
  Mary[McFall] 142
  Mary(Ratcliffe) 14
  Matilda S[Thompson] 42
  Nancy(Delany) 22
  Richard 14
Bradshaw, Aaron C. 121
  Eliza[Black] 73
  Frederick 121
  Frederick H. 121
  George W. 121
  Sarah 121
Brady, Harriett[Stephens] 21
Brain, Mary[Burden] 132
Brakeman, Clarence A. 63
Bramlett, Virlinda[Clements]
  82
Brandenburg, Elizabeth[March]
  45
Brandon, Fredonia(Burgess) 100
  James D. 100
  John A. 100
Branham, Nellie[Miller] 91
Brannock, Elizabeth(Shanks) 78
  George W. 78
  James 78
  Mary(Craig) 78
  William 78
  William A. 78
Brashear, Alfred L. 142
  Elizabeth(Leach) 142
  Jenetta(Suggett) 142
  Judge 142
  L.S. 142
  Otho M. 142
Brasher, Margaret[Wooldridge]
  42
  I.S. 40
  J.P. 40
  R.E(Petty) 40
Brawner, Ann(Turner) 105
  George 105
  Jacob N. 105
  Thomas E. 105
Breathitt, Cardwell 101
  John B. 101
  Mary(Slaughter) 101
Breckinridge, A. 22
  Adam A. 22
  Fannie[Sparks] 28
  J.D. 22
  John 22
  Mary[Caldwell] 17
  Rebecca(Wilmot) 22
Breeding, Jane C[Nunn] 10
Brent, Ellen[Shields] 158,
  163
Brewer, George W. 152
  Milton 152
  Sarah(Cox) 152
Bridewell, Pollie[Riley] 161
Bridges, Ambrose D. 121
  James H. 86
  Nancy(Davis) 121
  William 50, 121

Bridgford, Jefferson 165
Bridwell, Margaret[Bland] 130
Briggs, Benjamin M. 157
  Elizabeth[Tomlinson] 18
  Jane(Cook) 157
Bright, George 11
  James G. 43
  Manuel B. 11
  Nancy(Burton) 11
  William H. 97
Brinton, Bryant 30
Briscoe, Catherine[Emison] 143
  William C. 75
Britt, Bowling 101
  G.S. 147
  Jefferson 101
  Mary(Gautin) 101
Brittain, Francis M. 140
  Parks 140
  Samuel 147
  Sarah(Price) 140
Brizendine, J.B. 151
Broaddus, Andrew 105
  Elbridge J. 105
  Elvira(Hocker) 106
  George W. 106
  Grace(Haskins) 105
  S.T. 105
  Sallie[Estill] 107
  Thomas M. 106
Brock, F. 63
  James 85
  James W. 85
  Lyda[Jackson] 95
  Madison F. 97
Brockman, Albert C. 43
  Asa 43
  Carey 10
  Jacob 43
  Jacob E. 43
  James W. 43
  John H. 43
  Narcissa(Quisenbury) 43
  Rebecca(Perkins) 10
  Shelby 10
  Susan A(Hugnely) 43
Bromson, [Allen] 39
Brooking, Alvin 143
  Henry C. 143
  Permelia 143
Brooks, Daniel A. 85
  Evaline 165
  F.M. 101
  Granville 142
  Isaac N. 106
  James 54
  James N. 142
  John C. 140
  Margaret(Duncan) 142
  Maria(West) 142
  Milton 142
  Nancy(Merriman) 140
  R.D. 101
  Richard 140
  Sarah A[Hubbard] 109
  Stephen 142
  Tabitha[Pemberton] 36
  Terry 54
  Thomas 161
  William 165
Browkaw, Bethesda[LeBertew]
  122
Brown, A.H. 153
  Alexander 17
  Alfred A 60

Andrew 86
  Ann B(Clark) 106
  Anna(Harrison) 54
  Arthur 33
  Benjamin J. 63
  B. Gratz 54
  Burzilla[Lail] 79
  Charlotte[Lake] 122
  David 132
  Dorcus(McCalla) 143
  Ellen(Henderson) 140
  Elizabeth(Peters) 159
  Frances[Burford] 121
  Frances P[Hodgen] 95
  George I. 153
  Henderson 63
  J.A. 132
  J.H. 86
  James 60, 106, 143
  James D. 22
  Jane(McDowell) 86
  John 22, 140
  John J. 140
  John T. 132
  John W. 101
  L. 63
  L.J. 125
  Leonidas B. 143
  Lucinda(Isbell) 153
  Luannah(Secrest) 60
  Margaret(Thomas) 73
  Marion 73
  Mary M(Kidd) 63
  Mason 54
  Matilda J. 33
  Nancy A(Davis) 22
  Piersol 73
  Rebecca[Mitchell] 12
  Ruth J[Hedges] 17
  Samuel H. 106
  Samuel S. 54
  Sarah(Dever) 85
  Susan[Bayse] 147
  Thomas J. 85
  William 54
  William B. 85
  William B.C. 33
  William H. 132
Browning, C.A(Atkinson) 10
  Caleb 32
  Eli 22
  Francis C. 43
  Henrietta(Ware) 116
  James 43
  John M.S. 22
  John N. 32
  L.Y. 116
  Lucy[Duncan] 82
  Mary[Moore] 57
  Nancy(Johnson) 43
  Napoleon B. 43
  Octavia(Kennedy) 22
  Penelope 32
  W.A. 116
  W.T. 10
  William D. 10
Bruce, Aaron F. 161
  Durrett 54
  Lucinda R[McRoberts] 99
  Lucy N(Ryle) 19
  Mahala[Jameson] 97
  Richard I. 19
  Sarah(Vandever) 161
  Silas 19
  Susan[Edelen] 114

Bruce (cont.)
William 161
Brumfield, Elizabeth[Nall] 76
Rachel[Yager] 161
Brumley, Daniel 147
William 147
Bruner, Stephen 43
Bruton, Francis J. 126
Sallie[Hullen] 18
Bryan, Alexander 14
Eliza 30
Eliza(Weaver) 14
Enoch 54
James P. 30
Jane(Turner) 54
John P. 30
Lavina[Kennedy] 154
Moses A. 14
Bryam, A.W. 17
Emily(Robinson) 17
T.C. 17
Bryant, Bertha[Harlan] 31
Catherine(Kissinger) 97
Edward G. 97
Eliza[Reeves] 14
George 67
George S. 89
John 89; Jane[Arnold] 67
John M. 67
Kesiah 67
Laurence 40
Martha A. 89
Mary[Buster] 138
Mary[Hampton] 45
Morgan W. 40
Simeon A. 67
Stephen 67
Thomas O. 67
Virginia[Robinson] 91
W.S. 67, 97
Bryson, Andrew 106
James R. 106
Buchanan, George 22
Buckham, James 156
Lucinda 156
William T. 156
Buckler, Celia[Bullock] 114
Elvira[Kincheloe] 152
Buckley, Permelia(Eaton) 60
William 60
Buckner, Ann W[Thornton] 29
Alexander 86
Elijah S. 72
F. 72
J.T. 153
Mary L(Tate) 72, 153
R.R. 153
Robert R. 72
Bullen, Charles N. 86
Samuel H. 86
Bullitt, Annie C[Howard] 87
Helen[Lowry] 148
Bullock, Ann[Redd] 87, 135
Celia(Buckler) 114
Charles W. 114
Harben N. 151
J.B. 151
J.M.C. 40
J.S. 40
Jane R[Anderson] 71
Lucy[McDowell] 139
Martha[Clark] 52
Mary P(Clark) 151
Samuel 114
Bumbarger, Michael 78

W.H. 78
Bunnell, Elizabeth 121
Emily[Smith] 123
James C. 121
Samuel 121
Burbridge, Elizabeth(Ferguson) 43
John B. 43
Thomas 43
Burch, Margaret[Word] 94
Martha(Viley) 143
Million 143
Sarah[Welden] 81
William R. 143
Burden, Eldridge 132
James 132
Mary(Brain) 132
Burdett, [Shaw] 42
Burgess, Cavon D. 116
D(Kilgore) 116
Fredonia[Brandon] 100
H.G. 116
Henry D. 116
J. Kate 116
John D. 116
Lydia M(Wise) 116
O.B. 116
Thomas J. 116
Burford, Frances(Brown) 121
James C. 121
Jefferson 121
John 121
Martha[Ryan] 123
William C. 121
Burke, John L. 35
Burks, Allen 121
Allen J. 121
Elizabeth(Townsend) 121
Burnett, George G. 82
Nancy 121
Samuel 82
Sarah[Dodson] 162
Burns, B.F. 78
Catherine(Jackson) 78
Tarrance 78
Burris, Eliza[Clark] 43
Elizabeth[Kyle] 122
J.P. 19
Rebecca(Pulley) 19
Sarah[Shotwell] 119
Seth 19
Burroughs, Eliza[Clark] 126
Susan[Judy] 45
Burrus, James M. 106
Mary A(Mills) 106
Mildred[Paxton] 13
Thomas 106
Burt, Nannie[Kellogg] 87
Sallie(Greenup) 143
William 143
Burton, Elizabeth[Dunn] 107
Elizabeth(Stepp) 10
Hutchins 10
John J.G. 10
Joseph W. 147
May 147
Nancy[Bright] 11
Nancy(Woolfolk) 147
William Z. 10
Burwell, John 93
Nathan L. 93
Sarah M(Best) 93
Busbey, James S. 147
Busby, Eliza 17
Lewis 17

Sarah 10
William 10
William C. 17
William F. 10
Bush, E.B. 14
J. Porter 43
Jeremiah 43
Daniel 54
George H. 80
Frances(Sears) 54
Jane(Monroe) 43
John W. 54
Mary[Reed] 46
Nancy(Neal) 43
Nancy H(Gentry) 43
Nelson 43
Owen M. 43
Philip W. 43
R.N. 43
Sarah(Mathews) 14
William T. 14
Buskirk, George 69
Lawrence 69
Mary A(Norton) 69
Buster, John M. 138
John T. 138
Mary(Bryant) 138
Susan[Griffin] 139
Butler, John D. 89
Laura T[Yales] 115
Lucian[Robinson] 27
Mary R[Hite] 102
Butner, Harlan 106
John W. 106
Margaret(Belder) 106
Nancy(Lowry) 106
William 106
Buttrum, J.W. 86
William 86
Buxton, Rachel(Trail) 116
William 116
Buzzard, Daniel 78
Elizabeth 78
Granville J. 78
Bybee, Alfred 43

Cabness, J.B. 51
Louisa(Roland) 51
Milford 51
Cain, Mary[Woodrow] 74
Cahn, Bernhart 103
Frederick 103
Sarah 103
Calahan, Jane[Sharp] 58
Calbreath, Mariam B[O'Rear] 128
Caldwell, Andrew S. 40
Catherine(Minor) 135
D.I. 106
Eleanor(Boyd) 132
Eva(Stiles) 43
Isaac 40
James E. 35
James R. 22
John P. 17
Joseph M. 135
Lucinda[Payton] 133
Mary(Breckinridge) 17
Priscilla[Davis] 135
Sarah R[O'Rear] 128
Susan[Forman] 126
Thomas 22, 132
Thomas H. 132
Thomas J. 35

Christian (cont.)
Mary[Collins] 55
Mary K(Sutton) 143
Napoleon B. 143
P. Jones 143
Paul 143
William S. 143
Christie, E.B. 147
Elizabeth(Cook) 147
Henry B. 147
Israel 147
Letha(Bohannon) 147
Christison, Adam 30
Melinda[Hill] 10
Christman, Mary A[Moore] 151
Christy, Ambrose B. 60
Ambrose D. 60
Ann B(Crosswait) 60
Elizabeth J(Fagan) 60
J.M. 60
Joseph K. 60
Nancy 60
Philip W. 60
Churchill, James T. 147
W.B. 147
Cissell, Bernard 114
Joseph 114
City, Gracie A[Jones] 162
Clare, Daniel 138
Francis B. 138
Jane(Hansford) 138
Clardy, Giles C. 157
Norman S. 157
Rachel(Johnson) 157
Clark, A.D. 48
Ann B[Brown] 106
Benjamin F. 101
Bennett 52; Champ 13
D.R. 52;Deborah[French] 41
Eliza(Burris) 43
Elizabeth 101, 126
Elizabeth(Clyce) 126
Elizabeth[Hon] 18
G.W. 126
Hannah(Henderson) 40
J.C. 40;Elizabeth[Wilker-
J.L. 40   son] 128
James 22, 43, 126
James A. 52
James C. 40
James M. 126
Jane[Dever] 107
Jane[White] 13
John 40, 126, 143
John B. 106
John L. 133
Logan 40
Marion(McKiney) 52
Martha(Bullock) 52
Martin J. 126
Mary(Becket) 22
Mary(Norton) 133
Mary P[Bullock] 151
Permelia(Usery) 151
Polly 133
Robert P. 43
Samuel 133
Samuel B. 101
Sarah[McMahan] 110
William 52, 133
Clarke, Charles 106
David M. 106
Edward 106
Hannah(McIlvain) 106

Clarkson, Cynthia A(Small) 51
Elijah S. 22
Jabez 51
James 51
Martha[Eidson] 33
Mary(Smith) 22
Mildred[Lowry] 33
Patsy[Glaves] 137
Sarah A[Bennett] 120
William 22
Clawson, D.B. 43
Clay, Brutus J. 106
Charles 22
Charles V. 22
George 22
George W. 22
Green 22
James M. 22
L.B. 22
Polly(Hatheman) 22
Rebecca(Winn) 22
Clayton, Charles C. 55
Sarah[Smith] 36
Clemens, Jeremiah 30
James 30
Clements, John R. 126
Jonathan 126
Nancy(Williams) 126
Pamelia[Scrivner] 53
Clemons, Susanna[Atteebery] 14
Clevenger, Agnes[Montgomery]
66
Clifford, Sarah[Hall] 56
Clinkenbeard, George W. 22
Jonathan 22
Clinkinbeard, Andrew L. 43
John 43
Sally(Strode) 43
Cloud, Catherine(Rutherford)
101
Daniel W. 101
Elizabeth[Roby] 91
John 101
Cloudas, M.P. 19
Pitman 19
Clyce, Elizabeth[Clark] 126
Coates, Charles 10
Kinsey 10
Nancy(Royce) 10
Cobb, Sallie[Stamper] 136
Coburn, Elizabeth M(Wood) 116
James W. 116
John A. 116
Cochram, Mary[Turnbow] 71
Cochran, Frances(Wood) 106
James W. 106
Samuel 106
Coffey, E.M. 97
Elizabeth(Riffe) 39
Jesse 39
Osborn N. 39
Richard N. 97
Coger, Charlotte[Rice] 163
Colbert, George 11
John 11
Orpha(Sultzer) 11
William 11
Cofey, Nancy[Rogers] 73
Cole, Joshua 34
Mary A[Pendleton] 50
Cockrill, Clinton 55
Felix G. 55
Fielding 55
Joseph 55

Nancy(Lucas) 55
Coleman, Emma[Sterne] 80
Collett, Asa K. 106
Jane(Hubbard) 106
William 106
Colley, Cyrus 35
George W. 35
Collier, Andrew 106
James 106
James G. 106
Lewis 106
Thomas 106
William 106
Collings, Abram S. 147
Spencer 147
Collins, Ancel 52
Fannie[Parker] 27
James 55
John M. 55
Lewis P. 17
Lucinda[Ferguson] 11
Lucy[Neal] 26
Mary(Christian) 55
Michael 52
Rachel 22
Rebecca(Noland) 52
Richard 116
Richard A. 116
Robert W. 22
Sarah(Porterfield) 138
William 22, 138
Colter, Sarah A[Gullion] 70
Combes, Mary[Johnson] 127
Combs, Benjamin 43
Ennis 126
Fielding 43
Mary(Foreman) 43
Mary S(Hinde) 126
Nancy[Edwards] 44
Silas E. 126
Compton, Elizabeth[Parr] 31
Congleton, Mary[Booth] 21
Connelly, Elizabeth(Turner)
106
John 106
Mary[Lyne] 166
Nancy[Duncan] 134
Sanford 106
Conner, James 43
John W. 43
Margaret F(Conkwright) 43
Moses S. 43
S. 43
Connett, William C. 116
Connors, Frances[Whitaker] 21
Conway, Thomas 133
William A. 133
Cook, Alexander C. 97
Edward 142
Elizabeth[Christie] 147
Elizabeth[Dawson] 34
George B. 14
Henry T. 142
James 97
James W. 55
Joel D. 14
Joshua F. 147
Mary[Handy] 81
Nancy(Ellis) 142
Nancy(Howel) 14
Nancy[Jackson] 66
Thomas J. 147
Cooksey, J.J. 134
Cooley, George T. 39

Cooley (cont.)
Letitia(Anderson) 39
Thomas H. 39
Coon, Polly[Berry] 126
Coonrod, Ragan 55
Coons, Elizabeth(Nelson) 55
J.N. 55
Joseph 55
Polly[Berry] 126
Cooper, Albert J. 40
Artie[Sloan] 163
Edward 106
Eliza J(McDonald) 40
Hendley 106
Isaac M. 40
James 106
Jane[Tarlton] 143
John 130
John T. 143
Joseph 106
Louisa J[Spencer] 140
Mary(Duncan) 130
Nancy(Marcum) 106
Samuel 106, 143
Zachary G. 130
Copeland, Julia A[McCutchen] 151
Coppage, Alfred 143
Jane(Barlow) 143
Paton 143
Philip B. 51
Conkwright, Margaret F[Conner] 43
Corbet, Nancy[Hutchinson] 139
Corbin, Joshua 133
Lucy[Myers] 10
N.M. 133
Cornelius, Elizabeth(Haynie) 44
Isaiah 44
Richard 44
Corneliuson, Paulina[Evans] 107
Cornell, J.S. 155
James H. 155
Malinda(Messick) 155
Nancy[Redd] 111
Cornett, Charlotte(Calliham) 48
Moranda 55
Robert 48
William 48
William C. 55
Corwine, George 116
Nancy(Thornton) 116
Richard S. 116
Cosby, Amanda(Hudson) 106
James W. 106
Winfield M. 106
Couch, Rebecca[Williams] 129
Couchman, Andrew 133
Catherine[Letton] 25
Julia(Henderson) 133
William B. 133
Coughron, Polly[Walker] 163
Coulter, Mary[Powell] 31
Coulton, Anna[Freeman] 107
Courtney, Peter 147
Courts, Elizabeth[Taylor] 88
Couther, Nancy[Anderson] 150, 151
Cowan, Elizabeth(Harper) 60
Fannie(Dysart) 138
James V. 60
John G. 138

John H. 60
Mary E[Prather] 139
Polly[Prather] 117
Rachel[Pierce] 49
Sarah(Gilmore) 138
William G. 138
Cowden, Martha[Dysart] 56
Cox, Andrew S. 14
Carolina(Baird) 14
Daniel 55
David P. 55
Francis M. 14
Frederick 93
Hannah(Baird) 14
Isaac 107
James N. 55
Joseph 107
Lewis A. 14
Lydia(Hurst) 55
Margaret(McFarland) 51
Meredith 51
Moses 14
Pleasant M. 51
S.M. 14
Samuel 93
Sarah(Newland) 107
Sarah P[Green] 134
W.G. 143
William B. 97
Willie 97
Coy, James 95
John M. 95
Siania 95
Crabtree, Elizabeth(Pyle) 41
Emsley 41
Mary I[Lowe] 15
William J, 41
Craig, Antoine G. 37
J.T. 37
John S. 37
L.W. 38
Laurinda(Peak) 38
Letitia(Tandy) 37
Lewis E. 37
Louis N. 38
Martha[Allen] 132
Rhoda N[Farr] 70
Scott 143
W.T. 143
Walton 38
William L. 141
Crain, Alfred L. 60
Catherine 138
Elizabeth(Abrams) 60
James A. 138
Joseph J. 60
Thomas J. 60
William 60
William A. 60
William E. 60
William L. 138
Crane, George M. 121
James 30
Polly 30, 121
Rebecca[Pendery] 16
Tarleton L. 121
Tarlton L. 30
Crannells, Rachel[Judd] 87
Cowen, Elizabeth[Glenn] 133
Cowherd, Benjamin E. 147
Celia(Estes) 147
William 147
Crause, Ann[Todd] 77
Craven, Annie[Lesley] 131
Cravens, Martha[Jenkins] 131

Crawford, Alexander B. 133
Annie[Hall] 160
Benjamin P. 116
Charlotte(Riggs) 133
Crozard 116
Elizabeth C. 101
George 50
John 50
John E. 50
Lavina(Reynolds) 116
Martha(Robinson) 50
Crawley, J.T. 14
Mary(Stallsworth) 14
William 14
Cress, Elizabeth[Smith] 28
Crenshaw, Joseph 34
Martha(Wagner) 14
May J(Moore) 34
Richard 34
Thompson 14
W.T. 14
Crewdson,Nancy[Grinter] 101
Crews, Frances P[Smith] 115
Hamilton 107; W.H. 15
Crim, Enoch 44
J.W. 55
John R. 44
Margaret 55
Martin 55
Samuel M. 55
Crissman, Parmelia 49
Crittenden, (Allen) 147
Henry 147
Thomas T. 147
Crockett, Mary[Hawkins] 63
Sallie[Stephens] 169
Croft, Fairfield B. 41
Crook, J.C. 107
Crosby, Fanny[Risk] 135
Cross, Nancy[Williams] 103
Crosswright, Mary[Morris] 62
Crosthwait, Ann B[Christy] 60
Fannie[Price] 53
Croswhite, Frances(Hughes) 22
James 22
John H. 22
Mary(Hagerty) 44
Robert 44
William 44
Crow, Jacob S. 121
James 51
John 51, 121
Josephine[Sherman] 44
Joshua 134
Mary(Little) 121
Mary(Wayman) 134
Rhoda(Stemmons) 51
Wayman 134
William 121
Crowdes, George A. 114
Cruce, George W. 49
James 49
Lafayette 49
Nancy(Harrison) 49
Richard 49
Crum, Sophia W[Montgomery] 123
Crumbaugh, Henry 55
John 55
Mary(Snyder) 55
Crume, Jane(Kirkland) 130
John 130
Jonathan W. 130
Cruthcher, Charles 97
Elvira[Charles] 120

Ann(Palmer) 67
B.F. 101
Benjamin F. 147
Emory F. 11
Frances[Read] 12
George 131
George W. 101
Harvey 143
J.W. 19, 131
J. Russell 67
James F. 15
James P. 101
Jane(Carter) 131
John 19, 23
John H. 143
John S. 131
Joseph 82
I.W. 131
Lucy(Browning) 82
M.E(Thomas) 71
Margaret[Bradley] 142
Mary(Bowden) 143
Mary[Cooper] 130
Nancy(Connelly) 131
Richard G. 71
Rosanna[Giles] 75
Ruth A[Scott] 28
Sarah A. 101
Seth 131
Stephen 82, 173
Stephen C. 82
William S. 71
Dunlap, Harriet[McClanahan]
    57
R.C. 126
Dunmire, George T. 48
John H. 48
Viana M(Phillips) 48
Dunn, A.B. 107
Charlotte P. 157
Elizabeth(Burton) 107
Elizabeth(Doak) 89
George W. 121
Henrietta[Woods] 100
Henry B. 89
James 107
Jane(Host 98
Jane[Shobe] 158
John 98
John D. 98
Lemuel 121
Lucinda J(Patterson) 95
Mary[Hogan] 15
Nancy(Wilson) 89
Nathaniel W. 89
Philip 95
Ralph 143
Robert 98
Samuel F. 89
Sarah(Campbell) 121
Sarah(Reed) 121
T.A. 95
William 157
Williamson T. 89
Dunnica, William F. 165
William H. 165
Dunning, Ada(Morris) 155
Albert 155
S. 155
Dunscombe, James F. 101
Dupuy, William 74
Durr, Margaret[Adams] 120
Duval, Claiborne 156
William C. 156

Duvall, Benjamin A. 101
Elizabeth(Roberts) 165
Felix G. 101
Hannah(Davis) 75
Hannah D(Ashburn) 101
Joel H. 165
Jonathan C. 165
Nancy[Ellis] 56
Thomas 75
Dye, James 116
Jane 116
John 116
Parthenia(Gow) 116
Dyer, Abner 157
Abner W. 157
Didama 157
M.A. 157
M.W. 157
Manoah W. 157
Mary 157
James D. 157
Dysart, Fannie[Cowan] 138
James 56, 141
John B. 141
Johnson 141
Martha(Cowden) 56
Nancy[Kirtley] 141
Nicholas 56
Permelia(Evans) 141
William L. 141

Eades, Horatio 23
Margaret(Mosterman) 23
W.H. 23
Eads, Hannah M[Fisher] 147
Lee J. 162
William T. 162
Eales, Benjamin N. 23
George 23
Margaret C(Northcutt) 23
Earickson, James 86
Laranie(Stucky) 86
Perequen 86
Rebecca(Malone) 86
Richard 86
William L. 86
Earls, Sarah 19
Earnest, Adaline[Thompson] 151
Earp, Dorcus C(Cox) 157
J.D. 157
John M. 157
Easeley, Bettie 142
Jesse 142
Easely, Sallie(Tinsley) 147
Thornton T. 147
Woodson 147
East, [Davis] 161
Erzilla[Mills] 162
Eastin, James W. 107
Easton, Eliza J[McCown] 166
Eaton, Permelia[Buckley] 60
Ebert, Elizabeth[Ayres] 86
Ecton, Lucy[Lawrence] 45
Eddins, Margaret[Triplett]
    59, 65
Edelen, Leonard 114
Susan(Bruce) 114
W.B. 114
Eden, Lorenda(Howard) 70
T. Porter 70
Thomas G. 70
Edmiston, Julia A[Bondurant]
    65

Edmondson, Nancy[Shelby] 114
Edmonson, Edwin 126
Edrington, Benjamin 10
Emily 10
Rebecca[Taylor] 84
William 10
Edwards, B.B. 39
Charles S. 86
D.N. 39
Eliza[Neville] 16
Elizabeth(Floyd) 86
Gilbert 71
J.W. 44
John 23
John H. 23
John M. 23
Mariah(Bledsoe) 39
Margaret(Keller) 23
N.M. 41
Nancy(Combs) 44
Pinkney 71
Polly(Garrard) 23
Rachel(Decker) 71
Thomas W. 44
William 86
William B. 39
William H. 165
Egleston, Debora[Jayne] 37
Eidson, James L. 33
Martha(Clarkson) 33
William A. 33
Elder, Lucinda[Hawkins] 108
Elgin, Elizabeth M. 58
Elledge, Charlotte[Stagner]
    112
Elley, Cassandra B(Quinn) 143
G.E. 143
Robert 143
Robert P. 143
Elliott, Berryman 114
Eliza C. 23
Hixie[Jared] 120
Hubert 10
Isaac 165
John 165
Joseph 23
Mary[Toney] 159
Nancy[Summers] 161
Nancy J. 114
Reuben 67
Susan 10
W.B. 114
W.R. 23
William 10
Ellington, Jesse B. 50
Mary A(Perkinson) 50
Samuel D. 50
Ellis, Edward L. 23
Eleanor[Northcutt] 26
Eleazer 15
Hezekiah 56
Isaac 147
James 116
Jane(Todd) 23
Lettie[Jackson] 32
Linnie[Whiteside] 150
Luke 159
Mildred(Jenkins) 159
Nancy[Achor] 146
Nancy[Cook] 142
Nancy(Duvall) 56
Mary[Depp] 15
R.B. 23
Robert H. 23

-180-

Ellis (cont.)
Samuel 23
Sarah(Cassedy) 86
Thomas 159
William 86
William G. 86
Ellison, Elizabeth[Shannon] 65
Ellzey, Anne E[Washington] 59
Elza, Louisa[Davis] 121
Elmore, John 135
Oliver 135
Elsberry, Lydia P(Owen) 23
Robert T. 23
William N. 23
Elsea, Anna E[Washington] 59
Embly, Nancy[Lankford] 158
Embree, John M. 44
Martha(Vivian) 44
P.P. 98
Tarleton 44
William L. 44
Embry, Nancy[Fox] 107
Patsey[Tibble] 42
Emerson, Ann[Lane] 45
Elizabeth(Bledsoe) 50
Samuel R. 50
Thomas A. 50
Emison, Benjamin 143
Catherine(Briscoe) 143
James A. 143
England, James 67
John C. 67
Nancy(Campbell) 67
Engle, Campbell 93
Jesse 93
Tempa S(Polly) 93
English, James H. 75
Robert S. 75
Ennis, Sarah[Page] 158
Entrekin, Elizabeth[Johnson] 144
Epperson, Pembroke S. 93
Ervin, Patsy[Bonar] 137
Estes, Abel G. 23
Ann P[Carter] 97
Celia[Cowherd] 147
Elizabeth(Griffith) 23
Robert 23
Estill, Daniel 107
Elizabeth 107
George R. 107
James R. 107
Sallie(Broaddus) 107
Wallace 107
Eubank, Charles L. 44
Henry 18, 81
James 15
Maria(Garnett) 15
Martha(Thompson) 15
Nancy(Berkley) 44
Reuben B. 15, 81
Stephen 44
Evans, Ann[Calmes] 43
Eliza J. 93
Frances[Lee] 102
Green 107
John 157
John F. 107
Lavina[Muir] 46
Lewis L. 67
Margaret[Treadway] 29
Paulena(Corneliuson) 107
Permelia[Dysart] 141

Rebecca(Osburn) 157
Thomas D. 107
William 107
William N. 157
Eve, Elizabeth[Lawrence] 45
Everman, Daniel B. 44
John W. 44
Josephine(Crow) 44
Evins, Elizabeth(Winthrow) 103
James F. 103
William S. 103
Ewalt, Henry 23
John 23
Mary A[Thomas] 29
Ewell, Nettie(Ruke) 95
Richard L. 95
S.W. 95
Ewing, C.L. 153
Chatman S. 101
Elijah 37
Ellen C[Read] 131
Ephraim B. 153
Finis 153
Fulton 155
George D. 155
John 137
Mary[Berry] 159
Mary(Hammon) 101
Minerva[Scott] 120
Polly[Berry] 159
Rachel W.(Robbins) 155
Rebecca[Donnell] 104
Reuben 101
Sausanna(Makamson) 137
William G.

Fagan, Elizabeth J[Christy] 60
Fallis, John 155
Sarah S(Stratton) 155
William H. 155
Fant, James L. 135
Linn J. 135
Sophia(Yant) 135
Farhis, Mary[Rock] 16
Farleigh, William G. 75
Farmer, Eliza A. 74
Elizabeth[Graham] 87
Jeremiah 74
Nancy 74
Farr, James K. 70
Rhoda N(Craig) 70
W. Benton 70
Farra, Margaret[Shouse] 167
Farrell, Daniel 107
James 50
Solon H. 107
Spicio(Irving) 107
Farris, Alvin 48
Buford 159
Chloe[Campbell] 50
Elizabeth(McDowell) 159
Isaiah 159
James L. 164
Faulconer, James H. 89
Faulkner, Martha[Morrison] 15
Featherston, Burwell 56, 89
Sarah(Wymore) 56, 89
Walter T. 56
William M. 89
Feeback, E. 133
Gilbert 133

Millie(Richey) 133
Felix, Tracy[Glixner] 93
Felps, Harris 134
Nellie E(Laurence) 134
Fenton, Alfred 116
John 116
Ferguson, Elizabeth[Burbridge] 43
Francisca 15
Hannah 15
John B. 56
Lucinda(Collins) 11
Obadiah 11
William 15
William H. 15
Ferrell, Frances[Stuart] 155
Uriah 98
Ferrill, James 44
Martilius 44
Fewell, James H. 70
Fibble, Melinda(Grundy) 147
William 147
Ficklin, Archibald B. 126
Charles L. 17
Fannie(Walker) 126
Joseph 44
Mary(Young) 17
Thomas 17
William 126
Fidler, Nancy[Allen] 115
Field, Ambrose 32
Curtis 107
Elizabeth(Reeder) 32
Henry R. 32
Henry Y. 86
John H. 107
Mahala[Creech] 72
Martha(Richardson) 107
Mary(Young) 86
Rosanna(Hardin) 107
W.H. 86
Fielder, Nancy[Allen] 115
Fields, Elizabeth(Wiseheart) 32
Frederick R. 30
Henry H. 159
James 30
Absalom 65
John 159
Lucy(Hester) 65
William R. 65
Wilson T. 160
File, Jacob W. 23
Finch, Robert H. 23
Findley, John 67
Margaret(Brown) 67
Milton 67.
Fink, Charles H. 56
John 56
Matilda(Hammond) 56
Finks, Annie[Hume] 109
Finley, James F. 85
Leah(Dobbins) 85
Nancy[Cassady] 86
William 85
Finney, Elizabeth(Heart) 157
John 157
Robert J. 89
Fishback, Adolphus P. 15
Elizabeth(Button) 15
John M. 15
Sarah[Morin] 26
Fisher, Hannah M(Eads) 147
Horace H. 147
Mary A(Petty) 23

Fuqua (cont.)
L. 74
Washington 60
Furnish, James 66
Keziah A(Ray)66
Moses 66
Fuson, Jane[Goodin] 94

Gabbert, George 98
James 98
Polly(Sullivan) 98
William 98
Gadbery, May[Spencer] 140
Gaines, Benjamin W. 20
Elizabeth[Miller] 31
Sarah 165
Sarah[Shanks] 99
Galbraith, Alexander 98
H.J. 98
Galbreath, Catherine(Graham) 41
David 41
Tokle 41
Galion, Martha A[Langston] 102
Gallaway, Sarah[Simmons] 103
Gallemore, J.M. 67
Jonathan R. 67
Sarah B(Dismukes) 67
Gamble, Ann[Lester] 65
Gannaway, Thomas B. 160
William T. 75
Garden, Mary[Ramsey] 46
Gardner, Abigail(Dawson) 82
Edna[O'Rear] 128
Isom S. 107
John 15, 67
John L. 67
Letty(Woods) 15
Loulie[Gillen] 104
Samuel 84
Wesley 82
William D. 82
Gardiner, Jane 167
Garland, Elizabeth(Smith) 72
Jesse 72
Richard 72
Garner, Belle[Noland] 46
Chris T. 44
Dorcia(Trigg) 44
Jesse W. 44
John 24
John C. 44
Stephen 44
Susan(Canada) 24
William 24
Garth, Jefferson 143
John 143
Sally(Griffith) 143
Gartin, James W. 53
Garnett, Emily(Willis) 15
H.T. 148
Henry 20
James F. 15
James M. 15
Josephine 15
R.W. 15
Susan(Skinner) 20
Maria[Eubank] 15
William I. 15, 20
Garrard, Lucinda[Chesnut] 95
Polly[Edwards] 23
Garrett, Ann(Smith) 126
Elizabeth(Bell) 78
Isaac 78
Lucinda[Cecil] 62

Mahala[King] 79
Millie A[Hanks] 164
Murdoch T. 126
William C. 139
William F. 78
William H. 126
Garrison, Margaret[Minor] 91
Garvey, Elizabeth[Adkins] 135
Garvin, Caroline(Thomas) 98
James 98
John T. 98
Gary, Adeline 70
J.W. 70
Sabe 70
Gateley, Susan[Jenkins] 35
Gates, Chesley 121
Elijah 67
James 121
John 67
Mary(Maupin) 67
Sarah[Knott] 76
Gatewood, Fannie S[Sodowsky] 91
Joseph 44
Lucy C(Winn) 44
William L. 44
Gathage, Dorcas[Greenwell] 75
Gatten, Rebecca[Tanner] 21
Gatts, Susan(Tucker) 60
Thomas F. 60
William 60
Gaty, Samuel 87
Gaugh, James P. 56
Gautien, Mary[Britt] 101
Gay, Caleb W. 56
John 44
Rebecca 44
Robert B. 44
Gee, John T. 49
Gentry, D.H. 98
Elizabeth(Tribble) 98
Jane(Harris) 108
Joseph 98
Joshua 108
Martha[Wagers] 53
Nancy H[Bush] 43
Reuben E 108
Richard 108
George, Arreneous(Walker) 13
David 13
George W. 108
H. 142
H.H. 142
J.W. 148
Jane(Wilson) 142
Reuben E. 108
Richard 108
Thomas D. 13
Gibbons, Edward R. 160
Sarah(Noel) 160
Gibbs, Charlotte(Kenney) 143
Fannie(Pemberton) 165
John P. 165
P.A. 63
Robert 165
Samuel C. 143
Thomas J. 143
Gibhany, Mary J[Magee] 83
Gibson, Cynthia A. 66
Elizabeth[Daniel] 125
Elizabeth[Sneed] 65
James 20
John E. 66
Margaret(Current) 20
Parenia[Lindley] 41

Thomas J. 48
W.T. 20
Gilbert, Elizabeth(Huston) 98
John C. 98
Sally A[Holmes] 56
Washington 98
Giles, Elizabeth[Jones] 50
Granville T. 75
Richard P. 75
Rosanna(Duncan) 75
Gill, Ann W[Hatcher] 154
Baldwin 117
Baldwin B. 117
B.B. 117
Elizabeth(Moss) 117
Elizabeth[Whitlock] 81
James 117
Jemima[Dale] 165
Lydia(Moss) 117
Nancy[Robertson] 149
Gillaspy, Elizabeth[Donan] 80
Lewis H. 148
Gillen, Edward 104
Edward D. 104
Loulie(Gardner) 104
Gillihan, William 160
Gilliland, Annie(Moore) 151
Benjamin A. 151
Robert 151
Gilmer, Elizabeth(Phillips) 72
George W. 72
James 72, 122
John 72
John J. 122
Nancy(Wilson) 122
Gilmore, E.E. 157
Patsy[Wise] 129
Sarah[Cowan] 138
Ginn, A.E. 37
Abigail(Brackin) 37
John 37
Gillstrap, Jane[Barrow] 54
Girdner, David 164
Elizabeth(Perman) 164
Gittings, E.E. 156
Givens, Ann(Harris) 156
Nathaniel F. 156
Samuel 156
Gladden, Mordecai M. 157
Gladdish, Elijah 157
Elizabeth(Cooke) 157
James E. 157
Glass, Mary H[Johns] 102
Polly A[Kenney] 144
Glaves, David N. 137
Elizabeth(Dance) 137
James R. 137
Michael 137
Patsy(Clarkson) 137
Thomas T. 137
Glendenning, S[Palmer] 27
Glenn, D.A. 103
Elizabeth(Cowen) 133
John H. 133
Martha[Ireland] 144
Moses T. 133
Robert P. 133
Sarah[Leech] 103
William V. 103
Glixner, John 93
Peter C. 93
Tracy(Felix) 93
Glover, Albert D. 122
C.S. 126

-183-

Gross, Anna 87
Frank H. 87
Malina[Fuqua] 60
Theodore 87
Grow, Joseph 131
Milton 89
Peter 89
Sarah(Lewelen) 89
Grubbs, Abraham 162
Joseph W. 162
Nannie B[Orndorff] 102
Polly 162
Grundy, Mary[Wortham] 77
Melinda[Fibble] 147
Guerin, Bertrand 56
Edwin T. 56
Frances(Hickey) 56
Guill, Mattie[Shanks] 58
Guitar, David 108
Emily(Gordon) 108
John 108
Odon 108
Gulley, Mason 67
Gullion, E.D. 38
Fielding 70
George P. 38
Leah(Scott) 38
Sarah A(Colter) 70
William 70
Gum, Polly E[Roberts] 53
Gunnell, Elizabeth(Major) 41
John T. 41
Nancy T[Major] 64
Thomas A. 41
Gupton, Mary(Miller) 153
Stephen 153
William L. 153
Guthrie, Caleb 148
Joel 148
Samuel T. 108
Guy, John 13
R.L. 10
Guyer, Ellen(Hill) 108
Henry D. 108
John 108
Gwathmey, George R. 87
Gwynn, Angelina L(Kean) 165
Frank 165
William S. 165

Hackett, David D. 17
Maudalina(Hicks) 17
Samuel 17
Hackley, Rhoda C[Van Meter]
71
Haden, Charles A. 24
Joel H. 24
Lucy[Sale] 33
Martha(Smith) 24
Hagans, Elizabeth 11
Hagerty, Mary[Croswhite] 44
Haggard, Elizabeth[Lander]
41
Jane[Owen] 51
P.J. 44
Haines, Betsey[Woodson] 52
Hale, Mahala(Ledford) 17
Matthew 17
Thomas A. 17
Haley, Ambrose 56
John T. 56
Malinda(Snyder) 56
Phebe[Whitley] 80
Richard[McIntyre] 26

Haligan, Robert B. 56
Hall, Andrew 56
Frankie(Rice) 24
G.W. 24
James 24
James F. 24
Jesse 24
John 15
Joseph W. 30
Mary(McDonald) 15
Robert R. 56
Sarah(Clifford) 56
Sarah E(Gardner) 24
William 15, 148
Halloway, Martha O[Flournoy]
160
Halyard, George 41
Sarah(Chesis) 41
W.B. 41
Ham, [Bennett] 101
Matilda[Weldon] 100
Stephen 108
Hamilton, Ann[McAffee] 122
Ashby 17
Charles G. 31
Ellen 17
Isaac 31
Minerva A[Parrish] 131
Nancy[Snell] 145
Hammon, Mary[Ewing] 101
Hammond, Matilda[Fink] 56
Hampton, D.T. 44
David 44, 45
Elizabeth[Strother] 158
George 44
George W. 44, 45
Kittie(Routt) 44
Mary(Bryant) 45
Nancy(Jones) 44
Polly[Piggs] 46
Hanna, Jane(King) 148
John S. 148
Thomas K. 148
Hannah, Joseph 24
Mary(Sparks) 24
William J. 24
Handy, D.W. 15
Robert A. 15
Rosana 15
Hansford, Jane[Clare] 138
Happy, Elijah 56
Harvey 56
James 56
Harber, Edgar M. 108
Mildred(Phelps) 108
T.B. 108
Thomas B. 108
Harden, Elizabeth R[Dodson]
14
Hardin, Amanda[Wilhoit] 135
Daniel S. 24
Rosanna[Field] 107
W.T. 17
Harding, Mildred C[Chick]
32
Hare, C.C. 34
Harlan, Bertha(Bryant) 31
George 148
George W. 148
Henry 31
Jerry 31
Harlow, E.J. 148
Hulda(Nichols) 148
J. Sam 148
James 148

Jordan L. 148
Parmelia J(Tilberry) 148
William H. 148
Harmon, Clayton 10
Margaret[Pipes] 123
Sarah(Pendleton) 10
William 10
Harned, Job 41
Harper, [Dunnica] 165
Elizabeth[Cowan] 60
Harris, Catherine[Mallony]
151
Fannie(Hill) 52
J.C. 52
Jane[Gentry] 108
John 52
Lucy[Shanks] 58
Mary[Richardson] 111
Mary[Turner] 157
Matilda[Hawkins] 65
Patience[Maphet] 37
Rachel[Kelley] 15
Sarah[Baldwin] 115
Harrison, Anna[Brown] 54
Elizabeth(Hill) 15
Frances(Crutcher) 31
Frank 31
Frank M. 31
James 24
John 24
Joseph E. 108
Josephus 108
Lavica S[Nance] 155
Nancy[Cruce] 49
Reuben 15
Samuel T. 15
Thomas B. 108
Tyre 108
Virginia[Castleman] 55
Hart, Elizabeth 56
Harvey, John 108
Mary[Patterson] 111
William 108
Haskins, Grace[Broaddus] 105
Hatcher, Mary[Hogan] 157
Hatheman, Polly[Clay] 22
Hatler, Michael 11
Oliver 11
Sarah E(Bracken) 11
Havins, Charlotte[Smith] 163
Hawkins, A.J. 108
Cynthia(Castleburry) 35
Dorcas(Fletcher) 17
Dorothy[Scott] 145
Edward 108
Elizabeth[Hon] 17
Felix 17
Gregory F. 17
Harrison 35, 108
Henry H. 35
James 108
Jane(Robinson) 35
John 108
Jordan 17
Lewis 17
Lucinda(Elder) 105
Madison C. 17
Nancy(White) 108
Rebecca(Skinner) 108
Sarah(Cannon) 17
W.M. 45
William G. 45
William H. 108
Haws, Lucy[Gosney] 87

Hayden, Benjamin 24
  John G. 41
  John H. 38
  Martha A(Griffith) 24
  Peyton R. 24
  Sarah[Lee] 114
  T.J. 24
Haydon, James D. 20
  Jarvis 20
Hayes, Eliza[Offutt] 57
Haynes, Narcissa[Daley] 51
  Martha[Woodson] 159
Haynie, Elizabeth[Cornelius]
    44
Hays, Eleanor S[Jones] 36
  Mary[Shelman] 34
  Susan[Wooldridge] 77
Hazelrigg, Dillard 45
  Sallie(Renick) 45
Head, Cordelia[Fullilove]
    160
  Kate[Peavler] 94
  Polly[Clark] 159
Headelston, Sarah[Barr] 151
Headrick, Liddie[Birge] 125
Heart, Elizabeth[Finney] 157
Heaverin, Elizabeth[Taylor]
    33
Hedden, Lee 148
  Susan 148
  William C. 148
Hedges, Catherine[Moreland]
    26
  James F. 17
  John S. 24
  Ruth J(Brown) 17
  T.S. 24
  W.L. 17
Held, Jehoidia H. 14
  Lurana(Sams) 14
  Peter 14
Helm, Lucretia[Yeaman] 77
Helms, Jane[Avitt] 33
Henderson, D.P. 56
  Ellen[Brown] 140
  James 56
  John T. 51
  Joseph W. 24
  Harry 51
  Julia[Couchman] 133
  Margaret(White) 56
  Sarah[Terrill] 69
Henry, Frank G. 24
  Mary[Tinsley] 85
  Sarah[Roberts] 79
Hensley, Elbert B. 17
  Henrietta[Stewart] 128
  Sophia[Fox] 126
Henson, Melinda[Murphy] 39
Herndon, Cha lotte[Warren]
    29
  Eliza E[Riddle] 20
  John M. 52
Hersman, Charles C. 56
  Joseph 56
  Margaret(Scott) 56
Hester, Lucy A[Fields] 65
Hibler, Mary[Johnson] 25
Hickerson, Elizabeth[Wright]
    161
Hickey, Frances[Guerin] 56
Hickman, Ann[McGavock] 34
  Anthony G. 12
  Cuthbert H. 45

Harriet(Taylor) 148
  J.M. 12
  James L. 56
  James M. 12
  James R. 148
  John J. 56
  Mary(Dearing) 12
  Thomas J. 148
Hicks, Catherine[Anderson]
    165
  Maudalina[Hackett] 17
Hieronymous, Charles R. 45
  John 45
Higgins, Azariah 56
  Elizabeth K. 56
  Harvey J. 56
Highbaugh, Mary M[Welden] 81
Hiles, Catherine[Sullivan]
    119
Hill, Amanda B[Whalen] 19
  Ellen[Guyer] 108
  Elizabeth[Harrison] 15
  Fannie[Harris] 52
  George 10
  Lucinda[Martin] 110
  Lucy[Martin] 110
  Melinda(Christison) 10
  James W. 35
  Martha(Wade) 35
  Mary[Martin] 154
  Vandiver 10
  William 35
Hills, Sarah[McAntire] 76
Hillix, William W. 24
Hinde, Mary S[Combs] 126
Hinds, Mary[Whitmore] 92
Hines, Martha[Anderson] 19
Hisaw, Frederick 50
Hocker, Elvira[Broaddus] 106
Hodge, Nancy[Sigler] 112
Hogan, David 20
  John 15
  John M. 15
  Mary(Dunn) 15
  Thomas A. 20
  Virginia(Watts) 20
Holladay, Clarrisa[Robinson]
    133
Holland, Mary[Drake] 75
  W.S. 12
Hollandsworth, Elizabeth[Mc-
    Faden] 148
Holliday, Nancy(McCune) 25
  William H. 25
Hollyman, Jane(Langdon) 56
  John 56
  Thomas 56
Holman, Eliza J(Harris) 52
  George W. 52
  T.W. 52
Holmes, Daniel B. 56
  John 56
  R.J. 148
  Sally A(Gilbert) 56
Hon, Elizabeth(Clark) 18
  Elizabeth(Hawkins) 17
  Israel 17
  J.C. 17
  J.V. 17
  John 17
  John C. 18
  Peter 18
Honey, Josephine 25
  Margaret P(Stephens) 25

William 25
Hopkins, Ambrose B. 48
  Gennethen 37
  George W. 48
  John R. 48
  John T. 37
  Joseph 18
  N.O. 18
  Nancy(Armstrong) 97
  Margaret(Murphy) 18
  Sarah(Looney) 48
Hopson, Mary[Greer] 41
Hopwood, Ann[Wilson] 129
Hornback, Sabrina[Thatcher]
    29
Hoskins, Mary[Wells] 132
  Priscilla B[Jenkins] 34
Host, Jane[Dunn] 98
Houser, Mary[Nelson] 16
Howard, Elizabeth[Bedford]
    33
  Elizabeth[Deatherage] 107
  James H. 33
  Lorenda[Eden] 70
  Mary[Smith] 112
  Mary[Stewart] 73
  Rebecca[Tolson] 112
  Rhoda(Atkinson) 33
  William 33
Howel, Nancy[Cook] 14
Howell, Martha[Shields] 132
Howerton, Henry T. 25
Howlett, Eliza(Lee) 34
  John L. 34
  Luke 34
Hoy, Jones 53
Hubbard, Jane[Collett] 106
Hudnell, Sarah E[Young] 159
Hudson, Amanda[Cosby] 106
  Musker L. 148
  Rebecca(Green) 148
  T.H. 148
Huff, Benjamin 33
  Theresa[Francis] 153
  William D. 33
Hufford, Elizabeth C[Link] 25
Hughes, Andrew S. 25
  Charles J. 25
  Frances[Croswhite] 22
  Frances[Dinwiddie] 98
  John M. 13
  Lucy(Neal) 25
  Margaret 25
  Mary[Beard] 54
  Mary(Sweasey) 13
  Mary A[Risk] 58
  Susan T[Bledsoe] 21
  William 13, 25
  Mary[Staples] 149
Huguely, Susan A[Brockman] 43
Hukel, Narcissa(Schooler) 45
  R.J. 45
  William L. 45
Hulen, C.B. 18
  John C. 18
  Sallie(Bruton) 18
Hulett, Pauline 45
  R.F. 45
  Silas 45
Hull, Elizabeth[Stacy] 140
Hume, Benjamin B. 25
  Charles 25
  Lucy 25
Humphrey, Jane[Johnson] 137

Level (cont.)
  John L. 99
Levengood, Alexander C. 137
  Catherine(Orr) 137
  Peter 137
Leveridge, James 109
  Joseph 109
  Mary(Shields) 109
Lewelen, Sarah[Grow] 89
Lewis, America[Mosley] 166
  Charles 109
  James 109
  John H. 109
  Luke 148
  Mary H[Dawkins] 38
  Shelby H. 131
  William B. 131
Libbee, Edward L. 37
  Mary(Boyd) 37
  Silas 37
Lightfoot, Barbara(Lambert)
  12
  Henry 117
  Henry J. 12
  John 12, 117
  Keziah(Chapman) 117
  Sarah[Pope] 12
Lilliard, David 122
  James M. 122
  Mary(Spencer) 122
Lillicrap, Kate 36
Lilly, John H. 131
  John J. 131
  Mary C(Moore) 131
Lincoln, George 57
  John K. 57
  Thomas 57
Linder, Andrew H. 76
Lindley, David J. 41
  Jacob 41
  Jahu 41
  John 41
  Margaret(Armstrong) 41
  Margaret(Carr) 41
  Parenie(Gibson) 41
Lindsay, Alice 144
  Anthony 144
  David H. 38
  Julia H(Bond) 38
  Richard C. 38, 144
Lindsey, Amos 35
  J.N. 82
  Keziah(Jones) 82
  Lycurgus 35
  Martha[Thompson] 59
  Mary(Madison) 35
  Thomas 82
Link, Eli J. 25
  Elizabeth C(Hufford) 25
  Israel 25
Linn, Ashael 87
  Elizabeth V. 15
  John 15
  John G. 15
  (Hunter) 87
  Lewis F. 87
  Nancy(DePoyster) 15
Linseg, Rebecca[Smith] 37
Linsey, Elizabeth[Freeman]
  107
Linville, Martha[Thompson]
  139
Lipscomb, Joel 109, 110
  Nathan 109

Lisle, Benjamin M. 72
  Sallie A[Berkley] 43
List, Nancy[Banta] 82
Lithacumb, Thomas 34
Little, Mary[Crow] 121
Littlejohn, Cynthia(Thompson)
  117
  Daniel 117
  James M. 117
  Robert T. 117
Lively, W.H. 158
  William 158
Livingston, Mattie A. 64
Llewelyn, Abbie(Knott) 87
  John F. 87
  Robert 87
Loafman, Ellen(Pulliam) 12
  James E. 12
  William F. 12
Loan, Benjamin F. 33
Lobb, John A. 31
Lockard, Bedford B. 33
  Boyle D. 33
  Rhoda B(Trent) 33
Locke, Benjamin L. 87
  H.S. 117
  Mary E(Savage) 117
Lockett, [Smith] 91
Lockhart, John A. 151
Logan, David 99
  Elizabeth J[Level] 99
  Felix G. 61
  Francis A. 148
  John H. 82
  Larz A. 148
  Lovinda[Stewart] 82
  Nancy(Parks) 99
  Sallie[Dawson] 98
  W.G. 99
  William 99
Long, Ann[Stipe] 91
  C.W. 68
  Cynthia(Phelps) 109
  George W. 74
  Joseph H. 74
  L.D. 109
  Mary A(Gray) 74
  Permelia[Smith] 68
  W.T. 109
Longest, Dorothy[Chinn] 147
Longmore, Mary[Pew] 58
Looney, Sarah[Hopkins] 48
Lovan, M.G. 85
  Maria(Carnahan) 85
  William H. 85
Loving, William 102
  Willis 102
Lowden, Temperance[Meek] 83
Lowe, Caleb 15
  Daniel 45
  Delita(Barber) 45
  Joseph M. 137
  Joseph R. 15
  Mary P(Crabtree)
  Moses 137
  Nancy W(Porter) 137
  Obadiah 137
Lowen, Susan[Nelson] 64
Lowery, Daniel O. 36
  Elizabeth[McChristy] 45
  Jane[Overstreet] 123
Lowry, Helen(Bullitt) 148
  James 148
  James D. 148

  Martha[Anderson] 71
  Mildred(Clarkson) 33
  Nancy[Butner] 106
  Richard B. 33
  Thomas 33
Loyd, Charity 114
  Elijah 114
  Ila M. 114
  Sarah A[Haden] 144
Lucas, Charles H. 31
  Hannah F. 31
  John H. 31
  Mary[Thornton] 119
  Nancy[Cockrill] 55
  William C. 31
Luckey, Grace[Bell] 97
Lunsford, Isam 162
  Rhoda 162
  William 162
Lupe, Annie E. 87
  James H. 87
  Stephen T. 87
Lutton, Charlotte A[Ayres] 21
Lycan, Elizabeth[Cantebury]
  96
Lydick, A.W. 25
  Anna W(Biddle) 25
  John 25
  Nancy[Triplett] 29
Lyne, Elizabeth[Allen] 115
  Mary(Connelly) 166
  Thomas 166
Lynn, Arabella(Van Horn) 104
  James W. 104
  Rufus 104
Lyons, E.M. 87
  Henry C. 97
  Thomas H. 97
  William 97

McAdams, Dicey(Carter) 15
  I. 12
  James 15
  James M. 15
  William 12
McAdow, John 118
McAfee, Charles B. 57
  Martha(Cavanaugh) 57
  Martha(Kavanaugh) 57
  Robert 57
  Susannah[McKarney] 122
McAffee, Mary M. 122
McAlester, Brightberry 151
  James G. 151
  Tempest(Jackson) 151
McAninch, Margaret(Mires) 151
  Samuel 151
  W.C. 151
McAntire, Aaron B. 76
  Elizabeth(Van Meter) 76
  J.W. 76
  Sarah(Hills) 76
  William B. 76
  William S. 76
McAtee, Lucy[Frazier] 63
McBeath, J.K. 162
  Mary J(Kerr) 162
  Robert S. 162
McBride, Charles 31
  Elizabeth(McCauley) 114
  J.O. 57
  John C. 114
  Mattie J(Randall) 57

McKinney, Ann(Cane) 142
  David 99
  Hiram 99
  J.R. 136
  James H. 142
  John F. 72
  Patience[DeBord] 139
  Sallie[Noland] 110
  Sarah(Randolph) 136
  Solomon 142
  William 136
  William F. 162
McLean, David 53
  Elijah 53
  Elizabeth[Forbis] 41
  Leanora(Oldham) 53
McLeod, James S. 26
  Mary(Stark) 26
  William 26
McMahan, Samuel 110
  Sarah(Clark) 110
  Thomas M. 110
McMahill, Charles F. 64
  Thomas J. 64
McMeekin, John 144
  Leslie A. 144
  Margaret A(Graves) 144
McMonigle, Aaron B. 53
  Sarah J(Allison) 53
  William H. 53
McMullin, Dillord 99
  Thomas C. 99
McMurray, Elizabeth[Meri-
    wether] 114
  Jane[Reed] 160
  John F. 114
  William 114
McMurtry, Alexander 68
  Martha[McDonald] 122
McNees, Artemissa(Dejar-
    nette) 70
  P.F. 70
  William A. 70
McPherson, Alexander W. 20
  Jane(Bogg) 20
  Julia A. 45
  Mark 20
  William M. 20
McPike, Benjamin T. 83
  Edward 83
  James 83
  Mary(Chilton) 83
  Sarah(Van Cleve) 83
  William F. 83
  Zerelda(Sudduth) 83
McQuary, Sarah[Paschal] 139
McQuarry, Elsie[Rhodes] 130
McQuilty, Sarah[Thomason]
    65
McQuerry, Daniel H. 99
McReynolds, Anna[Roten] 12
  Benjamin K. 35
  Benjamin S. 35
  Elizabeth(Askew) 35
  William A. 35
McRoberts, Hayden J. 99
  Lucinda R(Bruce) 99
  William B. 99
McVay, F.M. 110
  Malinda(Austin) 110
  Patrick 110
McWhorter, Richard H. 10
McWilliams, Alexander C.
    110
  Jane C(Breedlove) 110

  Sidney 110
Mabry, R.G. 102
Machen, Henry L. 103
Machir, Henry A. 118
  John 118
  Martha A(Woodson) 118
Mackey, Elias 94
  James G. 94
  Sarah(Golden) 94
Mackvoy, Mary A[Scimmones] 70
Maddex, Charloote[Blackburn]
    69
  Wiley 129
Maddox, Barbara(Vaughn) 37
  Charles 37
  Elisha B. 37
  Henly J. 26
  Jacob 136
  James 26
  John B. 83
  Mahala 26
  Martha E. 34
  Sherwood 136
Maddux, Basil 26
  Frances 26
  William T. 26
Madison, Mary[Lindsey] 35
Magee, Ann[Pace] 149
Magill, William 99
Magree, George H. 83
  Mary J(Gibhany) 83
  Tolbert 83
Magruder, Alpheus 83
  David M. 83
  Elias 83
  Sarah(Martinie) 83
Magoffin, Ebenezer 122
  Elijah 122
  Margaret 122
Mahin, John T. 90
Mahurin, Silas 76
Major, Elizabeth[Gunnell] 41
  John S. 64
  Joseph M. 166
  Linda S(Slaughter) 64
  Lucien 166
  Minor 64
  Nancy T(Gunnell) 64
  Oliver T. 64
  R.M. 64
  T.T. 64
  W. Boon 64
Majors, Catherine(Hufaker)
    162
  Elisha 162
  Michael 162
Makemsom, Elizabeth[Wallace]
    137
Makemson, Sausanna[Ewing] 137
Mallony, Catherine(Harris) 151
  Elberton B. 151
  William 151
Malone, Martha[Forest] 15
  Rebecca[Earickson] 86
  Polly[Harrison] 165
Maloneson, Sarah[Griswell] 78
Mane, Margaret[Wood] 94
Mangus, William 61
Mann, Ambrose 149
  Eliza[Noel] 39
  James B. 123
  Jesse P. 149
  Mary 123
  Mary(Thorp) 149
  W. J. 123

Mansfield, Mary[Reese] 49
Napel, Elijah T. 87
Maphet, John 37
  Patience(Harris) 37
March, Absalom 45
  Elizabeth(Brandenburg) 45
  James 45
Marcum, Nancy[Cooper] 106
Margason, Elizabeth(Griggs)
    45
  John 45
  Martillus 45
Markland, Elizabeth[Adams] 17
Marks, George 131
  Lucinda[Thompson] 51
Marlow, William H. 162
Marmaduke, Mary A[White] 150
Marrifield, Sarah[Howard] 76
Mars, Eli 64
  Mary(Baker) 64
  Samuel 64
Marsh, Maria(Hilton) 66
  Nancy[Pollard] 136
  William B. 66
  William T. 66
Marshall, Charles E. 20
  E.S. 127
  Elizabeth[Jeffries] 76
  J.W. 131
  Jane(Rogers) 95
  Joseph B. 131
  Priscilla[Webb] 125
  Thomas 95
  William T. 95
Martin, A.H. 110
  Ann J. 45
  Azariah 110
  Caleb 45
  Catherine(Pinkerton) 166
  Charles N. 83, 149
  Dorothy[Campbell] 78
  Edward L. 118
  Elijah 166
  Eliza 39
  Eliza C(Adams) 120
  Elizabeth 110
  Elizabeth(Atkins) 51
  Elizabeth[Bowles] 21
  Elizabeth[Taylor] 46
  Ernest D. 166
  G. Thomas 45
  Hudson 110
  Hudson Q. 110
  James L. 83
  James T. 46
  Jane[Rice] 85
  Jesse 39
  John 26, 45, 51, 129
  John W. 26
  Lewis 129
  Lewis B. 110
  Louis 110
  Lucinda(Hill) 110
  Lucy(Hill) 110
  Margaret(Sheridan) 118
  Mary[Black] 153
  Mary(Hill) 154
  Maston B. 110
  Merideth 110
  Mourning(Jones) 110
  Nancy(Delaney) 45
  Nathan 154
  Peter 149
  R. Newton 26
  R.P. 39

Martin (cont.)
  Robert B. 46
  Robert H. 154
  S.D. 166
  Sallie(Bedford) 26
  Sallie(Neal) 149
  Samuel 45
  Samuel D. 46
  Susan(Pearson) 46
  Thomas J. 120
  Tyree 110
  William 118
  Zachary T. 46
Martinie, Sarah[Magruder]
    83
Mason, Clemency[Warriner]
    40
  Elizabeth[Shelton] 49
  Felicia(Neal) 136
  J.W. 131
  John 41, 99
  Joseph W. 136
  Lucinda[Davis] 130
  Luther 127
  Millie[Carter] 152
  Mollie(Kirk) 131
  S.O. 118
  Samuel 136
Masters, Burl 68
  M.C. 90
Masterson, A.S. 118
  David 131
  Eliza 118
  George W. 118
  James 57
  Medad 131
  Rhoda[Abbott] 126
  Robert 57
Maston, Elizabeth(Wright)
    144
  John 144
  Thomas 144
Matheral, Anna[McCutcheon]
    102
Materly, W.J. 123
Mathews, Sarah[Bush] 14
Matney, William M. 81
Matthews, Benjamin G. 66
Mattingly, Elizabeth(Mudd)
    160
  Ignatius 110
  Mary(Daft) 110
  Philip 160
  Thomas J. 110
  William R. 160
Maupin, Mary[Gates] 67
  Sarah[Dulany] 107
  William 110
Maxey, Boaz 68
  Edith[Ritter] 154
  John T. 15
  Judith 68
  Lucretia[Arbuckle] 105
  Luckretia[Arbunkle] 67
  W.F. 68
Maxwell, James 36
  Robert M. 110
  Thomas J. 110
Mayes, John B. 72
  Nancy H(Berry) 72
Mayfield, Henry 87
  James 15, 39, 87
  Mahala 87
  Mary(Johnson) 39

S[Means] 125
  William R. 39
Mayhew, James P. 61
  Rebecca(Smith) 61
  Thomas 61
  William H. 61
Mays, John 90
  Latham 90
  Lindsay 90
  Lindsey 90
  Martha(Simpson) 90
Mead, Mary(Voorhies) 83
  Shannon 83
  William H. 83
Means, James 125
  James T. 125
  Mary(Mulkey) 125
  S(Mayfield) 125
  Thomas 125
  Thomas J. 125
Medley, Barbara A(Wethen) 114
  Charles P. 114
  John S. 114
Meek, B. 83
  Temperance(Lowden) 83
Meeker, Alfred 99
  J.W. 99
  Lucina(Allen) 99
Meeks, Martha[West] 77
Meglasson, Carolina L(Ander-
    son) 118
  Thomas P. 118
  Wilson T. 118
Menifee, Naomi M[Nash] 145
Mercer, Jane[Moody] 163
Merrill, Andrew 87
  John B. 87
  Julia A(Davis) 87
Mers, John 61
  Nancy(Thompson) 61
  W.T. 61
Merideth, Willis 52
Meriwether, David W. 114
  Elizabeth(McMurray) 114
  James 114
Merryman, Benjamin F. 141
  Jemima 141
  John 141
  John H. 141
Messick, John 90
  Malinda[Cornell] 155
Metcalf, Catherine[Shomaker]
    137
  Matilda[Purcell] 76
  William 141
  Willis 131
Metcalfe, [Hughes] 133
  H. 61
  John P. 61, 91
  Louisa A(Spilman) 155
  Rebecca 61, 91
  Robert P. 61
  Sanford 155
  William A. 155
Michael, Kate[Baird] 77
Middaugh, Timothy 26
Middleton, Elizabeth(Wright)
    34
  John 34
  Thomas 34
Miles, John H. 160
  Nancy W(Jackson) 160
  Richard 131
  William F. 160

Millan, James A. 68
Miller, Aaron 64
  Abner 149
  Agnes(Anderson) 114
  Alexander 131
  Alexander P. 131
  Betsey 149
  Charles 87
  David S. 64
  Elizabeth(Gaines) 31
  Harriet F. 110
  Hettie A[McKim] 26
  Hezekiah 50
  J.D. 64
  James 26
  James E. 110
  James H. 91
  James L. 114
  James M. 26
  John D. 50
  Joseph D. 64
  Lewis 114
  Mary[Attebury] 14
  Mary[Gupton] 153
  Mary[Nolen] 76
  Mary(Zook) 64
  Mary A[Hatfield] 162
  Mildred(Haggerty) 64
  Nancy W(Baker) 26
  Nellie(Branham) 91
  Rachel[Scott] 114
  Robert 149
  Robert T. 110
  Sallie[McCarty] 45
  Samuel 137
  Sarah(Phillips) 131
  Thomas 91
  William 31
  William B. 31
  William F. 149
Million, Joel 110
  Mary(Saunders) 110
  Travis 110
Mills, Benjamin F. 162
  Betsy(Bell) 162
  Caleb W. 162
  Charles E. 162
  Elizabeth[Banks] 67
  Erzilla(East) 162
  Mary A[Burrus] 106
  Sarah A[Moore] 145
Millsaps, H. 162
  Perry 162
  Rebecca(Hoofacre) 162
Mimms, John W. 102
  Mary(James) 102
  Robert W. 102
Miner, Hannah[Noble] 64
Ming, Charles A. 72
  D.P. 72
  Nancy(Lewis) 72
Mings, George W. 110
  Polly(Kanatzar) 110
  William C. 110
Minor, Catherine[Caldwell]
    135
  Daniel 57
  Elizabeth(Vance) 57
  Ephraim 32
  John 91
  Margaret(Garrison) 91
  Preston H. 57
  Thomas 91
Minteer, James C. 79

Mullins, Anthony 46
  Mary[Wilson] 47
  Mathew 110
  Moses G. 46
  Richard 110
  Susanna(Woods) 110
Munson, Elizabeth(Baxter)
    87
  James H. 87
Murdock, Charles T. 26
  John T. 26
  Nancy(Chinn) 26
Murphy, Eliza[Poage] 30
  Fannie[Fonville] 104
  James A. 154
  John 154
  Letitiia(Landers) 154
  Margaret[Hopkins] 18
  Margaret[Cordry] 153
  Mary A(Kates) 154
  Melianda(Henson) 39
  Richard T. 123
  Robert 39
  Thomas 154
  William 39, 154
Murray, George W. 73
Murrell, George 15
  George A. 15
Musick, Sarah[Sudduth] 18,
    92
Muster, Joseph S. 149
  Lucinda[Washburn] 135
  Mary(Jones) 149
  William 149
Myers, Charlotte[Knoble] 57
  Jacob 18
  Lewis 18
  Lucy(Corbin) 18
  Mattie 99
  May 20
Myes, Anna[Taylor] 69

Nall, A.J. 76
  Gilbert F. 76
  Elizabeth(Brumfield) 76
  J.L. 76
  Margaret[Bland] 134
  Theodocia(Berry) 76
  William P. 76
Nalle, Margaret[Bland] 134
Nance, Barton G. 155
  Lavica S(Harrison) 155
  William E. 155
Napper, William H. 131
Nash, Clinton T. 145
  Jeremiah 64
  Naomi M(Menifee) 145
  Samuel 64
  William M. 145
Nation, Wilburn K. 57, 64
Nave, Catherine 91
Naylor, Francis M. 18
  George T. 18
  Ignatius 18
  Mary A(Jones) 18
  Northcut 18
  Susan(Kerns) 18
Neal, Charles 102
  Charles B. 102
  G.A. 87
  Felicia[Mason] 136
  Jane C[Bowling] 21
  John 118
  John B. 26

John T. 26
  Letitia(King) 87
  Lucy(Collins) 26
  Lucy[Hughes] 25
  Moses M. 87
  Nancy[Bush] 43
  Phoebe A. 110
  Sallie[Martin] 149
Neely, S.S. 99
Neet, Charles M. 91
  F.R. 91
  Frederick R. 91
  Jacob 91
  Sarah(Robb) 91
Nelson, Elizabeth(Boone) 57
  Elizabeth[Coons] 55
  George B. 57
  George H. 64
  James 57
  Jesse 16
  John H. 16
  Mary(Houser) 16
  Eliza[Robertson] 27
  Susan(Lowen) 64
Nesbit, Jane 26
  John 26
  John T. 79
  Robert 79
  T.B. 26
Netherton, A. 87
  Betsey(Wells) 87
Neugent, William K. 149
Nevill, Martha[Crtichlow] 82
Neville, Carroll 16
  Eliza(Edwards) 16
  M.E. 16
Nevin, Elizabeth[Carter] 97
Newberry, William M. 64
Newell, Americus B. 16
Newland, J.W. 16
  Sarah[Cox] 107
Newman, David D. 96
  Rachel[Stovall] 77
  Rebecca[Hagan] 152
Newton, Isaac B. 83
  Mary[Youd] 137
Nichol, David 84
  Martha(Mitchell) 84
  William S. 84
Nicholas, Nancy[Norton] 70
Nichols, E.J. 16
  Huldah[Harlow] 148
  Jack 118
  J.W. 26
  James 26
  L.C. 145
  Margaret(Wallace) 26
  Mary[Bottom] 121
  Mary(McCoy) 26
  Robert 57
  William 26
  William H. 26
Nicholson, Julia A[Lear] 114
Nickell, Ambrose 129
  Elizabeth[Kirk] 129
Nickerson, Allen 110
  John 110
  Ruth 110
Nix, Christina 164
  John 164
  Mary(Raines) 164
Noble, Hannah(Miner) 64
  Harrison 64
  William 64

Noe, Catherine(Smith) 57
  George 57
  J.W. 57
Noel, B.S. 39
  Clark W. 39
  Eliza(Mann) 39
  Nancy 39
  Sarah[Gibbons] 160
  W.H. 39
  Willis B. 39
Nolan, George N. 149
  Mildred(King) 149
  William 149
Noland, Belle(Garner) 46
  George W. 110
  John 46, 53
  Joshua 110
  Levi 46
  Rebecca[Collins] 52
  Sallie[McKinney] 110
  W.W. 53
Nolen, John 76
  John L. 76
  Mary(Miller) 76
Nolley, Daniel 26
  John 26
  Nancy(Dance) 26
Norfleet, David 163
  Elizabeth 163
  Elizabeth(Shackleford) 163
  James 163
  Larkin 163
  William S. 163
North, John H. 87
Northcott, Benjamin 61
  Benjamin F. 61
  Martha(Odell) 61
Northcutt, Benjamin 26
  Benjamin F. 127
  Cornelia[Langston] 25
  Eleanor(Ellis) 26
  Eli 26
  George E. 26
  Hosea 127
  J.K. 26
  Margaret C[Eales] 23
  William 127
  William W. 127
Norris, A.J. 99
  Kinzea H. 26
  Sarah(Stevens) 26
  William J. 26
Norton, Archibald 70
  (Brumback) 70
  George 70
  Mary[Clark] 133
  Mary A[Buskirk] 69
  Pryor N. 70
  Samuel D. 70
Norwood, Charles 166
  Joseph G. 166
  Mildred(Dale) 166
Nourse, James D. 131
Nunn, James W. 10
  Jane C(Breeding) 10
  John M. 10
Nute, C.W. 61
  Charles G. 61
  Elizabeth 61
Nuttall, Nancy[Peniston] 91
Nuttle, Nancy[Peniston] 91

O'Bannon, A.S. 68
  Susanah(Thompson) 68

-195-

O'Bannon (cont.)
William B. 68
O'Connor, John N. 65
O'Dell, Mary[Northcott] 61
Oden, Alfred 26
Sally[Thomas] 29
Offitt, J.M. 27
Offutt, Alfred W. 57
Eliza(Hayes) 57
Otho 57
Samuel R. 57
O'Fallon, John 87
Offatt, Amanda[Downing] 55
Ogg, Napoleon B. 110
Thomas J. 110
Ogle, Adam 149
George B. 149
Polly 149
Oglivie, Elijah W. 104
Lemuel 104
Martha(Winstead) 104
Oldham, Enoch 111
F.B. 111
Harriet 111
James 31
James D. 149
James T. 149
Leanora[McLean] 53
Lucy(Graves) 31
Maggie R(Davis) 149
William G. 31
Oliver, Cynthia A(Lawrence) 46
Henry B. 46
Isaac 39
Jane(Christian) 57
John 46
John C. 57
Mary(Downey) 39
Mordecai 64
Presley T. 57
William D. 39
O'Neal, R. 38
Onsot, James S. 68
Judith(Ball) 68
Levi 68
Oots, Joseph S. 57
Mary 57
Sampson 57
O'Rear, Bellvard J. 128
Benjamin F. 128
Catlett 128
George 57
Jeremiah 57
Jesse 128
John D. 128
Lydia(Westbrook) 57
Marcus 128
Melinda 128
Ross 128
Sarah R(Caldwell) 128
Organ, Esther[Treadway] 92
Orndorff, Ira 102
Levi H. 102
Nannie B(Grubbs) 102
Orr, Alexander 155
Catherine[Levengood] 131
Catherine(Williams) 79
Editha(Wright) 155
Elijah 79
Henry C. 155
James 79
John 133
Nancy(Steerman) 133

O.T. 133
Priscilla[McCandless] 137
Osborn, Tempe[Walls] 133
Osburn, Rebecca[Evans] 157
Overfelt, Amanda M[Hawks] 81
Overton, Susan[Bennett] 152
Overstreet, J.M. 123; Jas.145
Jane(Lowery) 123
John M. 123
Mary(Frost) 123
Robert 123
Robert J. 123
W.C. 91
William S. 123
Owen, Amsley 27
Crayton 46
Dorcus[Patrick] 58
Lydia P[Elsberry] 23
Martin B. 51
Mastin V. 51
Nancy(Layson) 27
Stephen 27
Owens, Elijah 27
Granville L. 141
Harriet B(Moore) 83
James A. 83
John 27
John S. 83
John T. 83
Joseph T. 83
Mary 27
Nancy(Baber) 83
Nelson R. 83
Ownby, Canada 27
Elizabeth[Wright] 11
Hannah 27
Joseph 27
Oxford, Elizabeth(Spurlock)48
John 48
Jonathan 48

Pace, Ann(Magee) 149
D.T. 149
Fannie[Allen] 49
Frances(McDonald) 128
J.D. 52
John W. 128
Joseph 149
Nuson 149
Wyatt 128
Pack, Orville 145
Packwood, Sally[Bartlett] 49
Page, Alexander H. 158
Axel H. 158
Granville R. 158
James L. 102
Joseph H. 158
Lemuel J. 102
Sarah(Ennis) 158
Susan(Thomas) 102
Paget, Milkey[Perrin] 111
Painter, John 118
Sarah(Downey) 118
William D. 154
Palmer, Ann[Duncan] 67
C.N. 145
Elizabeth(Foster) 46
George F. 27
Henry 46
Joel 46
S(Glendenning) 27
Thomas 27
Pannabaker, Elizabeth[Duke] 131

Parado, Nancy[Tribble] 18
Park, Cyrus B. 111
Elihu 111
Elizabeth(Shanklin) 61
James 111
John 61, 111
M[Roberts] 111
Mary(Ballew) 111
Mary(Ballow) 111
Nancy[Logan] 99
Overton 111
Polly(Benton) 111
Samuel G. 61
Simpson 53
Thomas W. 111
Parke, Jonah 111
Parker, David 13
Elizabeth[Wright] 161
Fannie(Collins) 27
G.W. 16
Howard S. 57
Rebecca E(McConnell) 57
W.H. 27
William 27
William O. 57
Parkey, James 139
Martha(Linville) 139
Peter 139
Parks, Edmond J. 111
Lucy[Adkisson] 33
Mary A[Denham] 15
Susan[Turner] 29
Parman, Elizabeth(Curtis) 95
Frethias 95
Jesse F. 95
Parnell, Elizabeth[Tandy] 38
Parr, Elizabeth(Compton) 31
James R. 31
John 31, 123
Parrish, Benjamin F. 131
Callaway 27
George W. 123
H.C. 131
Horace M. 102
Jolly S. 123
Mary A(Porter) 102
Nancy(Shropshire) 27
Peyton 102
Paschal, Alvah 139
Nancy[Zachary] 140
P.M. 139
Sarah(McQuary) 139
Patrick, Dorcus(Owen) 58
Hezekiah E. 58
Robert 58
Patterson, Abraham 32
Abraham P. 32
Elizabeth[Richards] 111
Henry M. 95
Jane C(Chisolm) 32
Jane M 27
James W. 149
Lucinda J[Dunn] 95
Mary(Allen) 149
Mary(Harvey) 111
Priscilla[Dawson] 32
Rebecca[Whitt] 59
Rice 111
Thomas 111
William 149
Patton, Mary W[Blanchard] 101
Polly[Halley] 44
Rebecca 111
Thomas D. 27

Paul, Benjamin F. 166
  Catherine(McKee) 166
  George S. 76
  Henry L. 166
  Elizabeth(Purcell) 76
  William 76
Paxton, B.F. 10
  Matilda J. 99
  Mildred(Burrus) 136
  Richard H. 13
  Richard S. 13
  S.A. 99
  William 99
  William M. 118
Payton, D.H. 111
  John W. 133
  Joseph M. 133
  Lucinda(Caldwell) 133
  Mildred(White) 111
  Yelverton 111
  Yelverton W. 111
Payne, Addison 125
  America(Bradburn) 125
  Caleb 125
  David 125
  Dennis 145
  Edward 42
  Enoch 125
  J.E. 42
  James E. 42
  M.J. 42
  Martha 125
  Mary A(Callaway) 42
  Priscilla[Morehead] 125
  Reuben 125
Peacock, Margaret[Wherritt] 113
Peak, Jane[Smith] 120
  John L. 145
  Laurinda[Craig] 38
Peake, James L. 91
  John L. 91
  Mary A(Francis) 91
  T.F. 91
Pearce, Elizabeth[Dought-ery] 155
Pearson, Susan[Martin] 46
Peavler, John I. 94
  Kate(Head) 94
  Lewis 94
Pebworth, Elizabeth[Hurt] 127
Peddicord, Nancy(Dawson)46
  Nathan 46
  Thomas L. 46
Pedigo, James A. 16
Peed, James N. 118
  Mary 118
  William 118
Pemberton, Agnes 79
  Agnes[Shropshire] 79
  Fannie[Gibbs] 165
  George M. 36
  Harvey W. 46
  Jesse B. 36
  John 46
  Lucy(Vivion) 46
  Tabitha(Brooks) 36
  Thomas B. 36
Pence, Adam 145
  Annie(Snell) 145
  James 145
  Joseph 145
  Sally(Chism) 145

  William H. 145
Pendery, James 16
  Rebecca(Crane) 16
  Richard T. 16
Pendleton, Catherine(McGruder) 135
  Curtis W. 154
  George L. 50
  George T. 135
  J.C. 99
  J.T. 50
  John T. 99
  Martha A(Cole) 50
  Sarah[Harmon] 10
  T.O. 135
Peniston, Nancy(Nuttall) 91
  Nancy(Nuttle) 91
  Robert 91
  Robert P. 91
  Theodore 91
Penix, John 128
  Patsy(Walker) 128
  William 128
Penn, Elizabeth[Russell] 28
Penney, Eli 13
Pennington, Frances[Thompson] 96
Pepper, Charles T. 61
  Enoch 61
  Enoch S. 61
  Sarah R(Tebbs) 61
Perkins, C.C. 111
  Mary A[Curd] 89
  Rebecca[Brockman] 10
Perkinson, Mary A[Ellington] 50
Perman, Elizabeth[Girdner] 164
Perrigan, Martha[Forbis] 56
Perrin, Achilles 99
  Atchemonde L. 99
  James 111
  Jane(Smith) 99
  Milkey(Paget) 111
  Robeson 111
  William 111
Perry, Berry 13
  John T. 13
  Polly(Searcy) 13
  Rhoda F[Larue] 76
Peter, Ina 160
  Lucy 160
  Richard 160
  Sherwood T. 31
Peters, Elizabeth[Brown] 159
Pettit, Elizabeth A[Humphrey] 160
Petty, Elizabeth[Ford] 139
  Mary A[Fisher] 23
  R.E[Brasher] 40
Pew, Edward C. 58
  John 58
  Mary(Longmore) 58
Peyton, Nancy[Ross] 111
Phelps, Cynthia[Long] 109
  Mildred[Harber] 108
  T.T. 111
Philips, Susan[Riley] 87
Phillips, A.C[Green] 72
  Allen 31
  [Carson] 75
  Elizabeth[Gilmer] 72
  Elizabeth[Rutter] 161
  Elizabeth M(Doswell) 31

  George M. 123
  James 151
  James C. 151
  James H. 73
  Jeremiah W. 31
  Lee C. 87
  Lucy T. 13
  Margaret(Johnson) 123
  Mary(McCorkle) 73
  Mary F(Black) 151
  Mary J(Terrell) 13
  Nancy C[Green] 72
  Oliver P. 123
  Sarah[Miller] 131
  Shapley R. 87
  T.W. 73
  Thomas 87
  Viana M[Dunmire] 48
  W.T. 73
Piatt, James R. 20
  John J. 20
  Orpheliaw(Riddell) 20
Pickerell, J.M. 36
  James 36
  Nancy(Ballard) 36
Pickett, B.O. 118
  John S. 93
  Mary[Jackson] 61
  Mary L.F(Bacon) 118
  Sally[Pogue] 118
  W.S. 118
Piercall, Elizabeth(Able) 156
  John D. 156
  Joseph 156
Pierce, Charles C. 114
  David C. 49
  Harriet[Carver] 38
  Joel 18
  Jonathan 27
  Louis 49
  Mordecai 27
  Philadelphia(Ledford) 18
  Peter 18
  Rachel(Cowan) 49
  Sarah(Barnard) 27
Pigg, David H. 46
  Lewis 39
  Polly(Hampton) 46
  William 46
Pike, Bernard 131
  Mary L(Shireligg) 131
  William J. 131
Piner, Joseph A. 20
  Presley 20
Pinkerton, Catherine[Martin] 166
Piper, Matilda G[Waugh] 134
  Priscilla G[Foster] 133
Pipes, A.W. 123
  Allen 31
  David 31, 160
  George 31
  (Jackman) 31
  Margaret(Harmon) 136
  Nathaniel 123
Pitchford, Alpheus 16
  Fleming 16
  Susan(Russell) 16
Pitts, Barney 155
  Catherine 155
  Francis M. 155
  J.F. 61
Plummer, John T. 145
  William 145

Poage, Eliza(Murphy) 30
  Harriet[Powers] 74
  Hugh A. 30
  Jacob M. 30
Poague, Ann[Wright] 65
  Lucinda[Johnson] 144
Poe, Alvin 158
  Elizabeth[Bibb] 101
  Benjamin T. 158
  Rebecca 158
Pogue, George H. 118
  Nicholas 74
  Sallie(Pickett) 118
  Sallie P(Shanklin) 118
  W.T. 118
  William T. 118
Poindexter, Fountain 13
  Robert 13
Points, Arthur 27
  Ellen 27
  J.W. 27
Polk, David 145
  S.G. 145
Pollard, Abner 64
  Braxton 136
  James C. 64
  James M. 136
  John W. 74
  Martha 64
  Nancy(Marsh) 136
  Nancy W[Deaton] 10
  Thomas 136
Pollock, William A. 99
Polly, Tempa S[Engle] 93
Polson, Benjamin 39
  Harrison P. 39
  Sarah(Wall) 39
Pond, Alfred 27
Poor, Polly[James] 102
Pope, Abraham 31
  Elizabeth[Smith] 31
  John C. 12
  Marion[Moore] 160
  Nathan K. 12
  Sarah(Lightfoot) 12
Porter, Elvira(Van Camp)
  61
  John S. 61
  Joseph P. 85
  Julia A[Sherman] 88
  Mary A[Parrish] 102
  Nancy[Henry] 78, 122
  Nancy W[Lowe] 137
  Norman 68
  Pauline(Young) 85
  Sallie(Richardson) 68
  Thomas J. 61
  William 68, 85
Porterfield, Sarah[Collins]
  138
Potter, Nancy[Tarrant] 159
Potts, Anna E. 158
Powel, Charles 160
  Cyrus 160
Powell, Golston 31
  Isham 31
  Jane[McCoyl] 110
  Mary(Coulter) 31
  Richard 83
Powers, Harriet(Poage) 74
  Judah 93
  Marcus M. 73
  Milfred 74
  Richard 74

Richard C. 93
  Sterling 93
Poynter, William M. 81
Prater, Isaac 18
  Margaret(Baird) 18
  Nancy[Auxier] 92
  William L. 18
Prather, Charles H. 111
  James H. 158
  Joseph C. 118
  Mary 118
  Mary E(Cowan) 139
  Nellie 118
  Polly(Cowan) 111
  Ross 118
  Samuel H. 118
  Thomas 111, 118, 139
Pratt, Susie(Redding) 145
  Thomas S. 145
  William 145
Preston, Francis A. 31
  Isaac 92
  L.W. 31
  Mary(Sedore) 31
  Sanford J. 46
  Sarah(Downing) 92
  Solomon D. 102
Prewett, James M. 27
  Joel 27
  Mattie(Bedford) 27
  Robert T. 27
  William H. 27
  William W. 27
Prewitt, Elizabeth M(Elgin)
  58
  Mildred(Ellis) 58
  Robert C. 58
  Vaul A. 58
  William C. 58
Price, Evalina[Withers] 92
  Fannie(Crosthwait) 53
  H.C. 149
  John E. 11
  John J. 68
  Morton M. 53
  Nancy[Hughes] 90
  R.M. 149
  Sarah[Brittain] 140
  Sarah A(Smoot) 27
  W.E. 91
  William G. 53
  William S. 27
Prichett, Frances[Shouse] 128
Priest, Elias 128
  George S. 27
  Luke D. 128
Prine, Nancy[Leeper] 61
Pritchard, Fanny[Moss] 94
Proctor, Alexander 58
  B.D. 123
  Columbus 91
  Diana(Chapman) 58
  Eliza(Baker) 123
  Elizabeth(Beasley) 91
  Francis M. 123
  George M. 91
  J.H. 123
  Joseph 123
  Mary 123
  Montgomer M. 91
  Rowland T. 58
  Thomas 91
  Uriah 91
Prowell, David 11

James 11
  Margaret(Fletcher) 11
  Robert 11
Pruette, James L. 64
Pruitt, Emily 12
  Moses 12
Prunty, Robert C. 158
  Sarah(Rives) 158
  Thomas 158
Puckett, Barbara 149
  R. 149
  Thomas T. 149
Pulley, Rebecca[Burris] 19
Pulliam, Ellen[Loafman] 12
  Elizabeth 68
  Stephen 68
  William 68
Pumphrey, Elizabeth J[Denney]
  139
Purcell, Elizabeth[Paul] 76
  James 76
  Matilda(Metcalfe) 76
  William Q. 76
Purnell, Hester A[Bounds] 165
Purvis, Philip 18
Pyle, Elizabeth[Crabtree] 41
Pyles, Hambury 118

Quesenberry, John P. 16
Quick, Elsie[Henderson] 109
Quinn, Cassandra B[Elley] 143
  John 64
  Nellie[Kennedy] 166
  William J. 53
Quisenberry, Ailsie[Berryman]
  130
  Colby 46
  Elkanah 46
  Philip 46
  William 46
Quisenbury, Narcissa[Brockman]
  43

Rackerby, Georgiana(Dudley) 36
  John H. 36
  Thomas W. 36
  W.C. 36
Ragan, Fannie[Jones] 127
  S.C. 128
Ragdale, Nancy[Barker] 101
Ragar, Peter C. 102
  Sarah(Simmons) 102
  William H. 102
Raglan, Nancy(Smith) 123
  Robert 123
  Z.S. 123
Railsback, Annie C. 53
  Daniel 53
  David 53
  James T. 53
  Martha E(Tuggle) 53
  Mary A(Reed) 53
  William A. 53
Raine, J.D. 76
  J.S. 76
  (Dillord) 76
Raines, Adam B. 13
  James S. 13
  Mary[Nix] 164
  Melinda 13
Raker, Polly[Williams] 47

Riddell, Orphelia W[Piatt]
    20
Riddle, Eliza E(Herndon)20
    Fountain 20
    J.L. 20
    Sallie[Lawrence] 64
Ridge, (Bailey) 11
    Benjamin C. 11
    Isaac M. 11
    Joseph R. 84
    Sophia(Dillingham) 11
    William 11, 84
Riffe, Christopher 39
    Elizabeth(Casey) 39
    Elizabeth[Coffey] 39
    Peter B. 39
Riggens, Mary[Selby] 133
Riggs, Charlotte[Crawford]
    133
    Sarah B. 128
Rigney, Levi N. 39
Riley, Amos 87, 88
    Amose 87
    Bailey 161
    George 161
    Pollie(Bridewell) 161
    Samuel 27
    Sarah[Smith] 133
    Susan(Philips) 87
    W.C. 27
    William 88
Ring, Mary W[Hooser] 154
Ringo, David D. 62
    James P. 62
Ripperdam, Sarah[Fields]30
Ripple, Elizabeth[Rhoads]
    130
Risk, Fannie(Crosby) 135
    John 145
    John C. 58, 135
    Moses 135
    Moses M. 145
    Mary A(Hues) 58
    T.F. 58
Ritter, Burwell C. 154
    Clark E. 154
    Editha(Maxey) 154
    Elizabeth[Yost] 92
Rives, Sarah(Prunty)158
Roach, Dudley 53
Roark, Joseph 16
    Josiah 16
    Ruth(Campbell) 16
Robards, Archibald 123
    Elizabeth[Mosby] 145
    George 123
    Gracie[Sims] 112
    Rebecca[Singleton] 91
Robb, Sarah[Neet] 91
Robbins, Edie(Sanders) 83
    John 83
    Rachel W[Ewing] 155
    William 83
Roberson, Milton T. 31
    Rebecca[Carson] 106
Roberts, A.J. 111
    Benjamin 79
    Benjamin W. 79
    Cornelius 73
    Elizabeth[Duvall] 165
    George 53
    J.M. 53
    James F. 111
    Jesse 111

John 111
M(Park) 111
Martha 111
Mary A[Anderson] 19
Nancy[Hodges] 65
O. 65
Polly E(Gum) 53
S. 111
Sarah(Henry) 79
William M. 111
Robertson, Benjamin F. 149
    David A. 49
    David T. 27
    Eliza(Nelson) 27
    Horatio 149
    Joseph 161
    Malinda[Jolly]
    Margaret[Royalty] 161
    Nancy(Gill) 149
    Narcissa(Asher) 49
    R.G. 16
    Rebecca[Moore] 41
    Solomon 27
    William 34, 49
    William H. 27
Robinson, Benjamin 91
    Clarrisa(Holladay) 133
    Dorothy A. 114
    E.W. 20
    Eliza A[Cash] 40
    Emily[Byram] 17
    Emily(Waller) 20
    F.F. 20
    Fannie(Berry) 58
    George 133
    George C. 114
    Henry 123
    J.B. 91
    J.V. 58
    James H. 100
    Jane[Hawkins] 36
    John 58
    Kitty[Rose] 62
    Lucretia 66
    Martha[Crawford] 50
    N.M. 79
    Thomas W. 114
    Virginia(Bryant) 91
    W.P. 133
    William L. 123
    William P. 100
Robey, Hezekiah 27
Robnett, Margaret E[DeGroff]
    23
Roby, Elizabeth(Cloud) 91
    Hezekiah C. 91
    Thomas 91
Rock, J.M. 16
    John M. 16
    Joshua 16
    Mary(Farhis) 16
Rockwell, Wealthy[Ryan] 47
Rodes, [Rollins] 111
Rogers, Betsey(Reed) 47
    David 73
    E.F. 149
    Elizabeth[Dowis] 93
    Frances 58
    Henry 47
    J.A. 47
    Jane[Marshall] 95
    Joseph K. 58
    Lemuel A. 73
    Nancy(Cofey) 73

Nancy[Hutchason] 72
T.G. 48
William 58
Roland, Daniel W. 104
    Louisa[Cabness] 51
Rollins, Anthony W. 111
    B.F. 83
    Elizabeth 83
    James 83
    James S. 111
    (Rodes) 111
Roman, Hanah[Rutherford] 91
Romjue, John H. 135
    John J. 135
Roper, G.M. 155
    H.C. 155
    Nancy W. 155
Rose, Carroll[Aingell] 101
    George W. 62
    James E. 62
    Kitty(Robinson) 62
Ross, Cassandra[Miller] 18
    Craven P. 111
    Erastus M. 20
    Franklin J. 39
    John 111
    John T. 62
    John W. 20
    Mary[Wolfskill] 163
    Nancy(Graves) 20
    Nancy(Peyton) 111
    Silas M. 85
Roten, Anna(McReynold) 12
    John 12
    Thompson 12
Rothwell, Charles 68
    China 68
    China(Renfro) 68
    Fountain 68
    Jennie 68
    John T. 68
    Mary A. 68
    William R. 68
Rounder, Argyle A. 83
    D.A. 83
    Lucinda(Morris) 83
Routt, Henry L. 167
    Phoebe(Blanton) 167
    Rodham 167
Rowe, William 27
Rowland, Nancy 47
    William 47
    Zachariah W. 47
Rowlett, Simeon P. 155
Royalty, Margaret(Robertson)
    161
    Robertson M. 161
    Thomas 166
Royce, Nancy[Coates] 10
Rubey, Samuel C. 163
    Thomas 163
Ruddell, Sarah[Davis] 23
Ruddle, Abraham 79
Ruke, Nettie[Ewell] 95
Rusk, William D. 167
Russell, Elizabeth[Allen] 11
    Elizabeth(Penn) 28
    Elizabeth(Williams)31
    Jeremiah 158
    John T. 28
    Joseph 28
    Richard 31
    Robert S. 28
    Robert T. 28

Russell(cont.)
  Sallie C(Ware) 28
  Samuel 31
  William H. 58
Rutherford, Catherine[Cloud]
  101
  Hannah(Roman) 91
  Shelton 91
  William T. 91
Rutter, Edmund 161
  Elizabeth(Phillips) 161
Ryan, David 123
  Henry O. 47
  James 47
  Martha J[Snow] 50
  Wealthy(Rockwell) 47
Ryle, Lucy N[Bruce] 19
  P.S. 20
Ryley, D.P. 167

Sacry, George 58
  John 58
Sale, Eliza[Allen] 88
  Willis B. 66
Sallee, Abraham 33
  John 73
  Lucy(Haden) 33
  William 33, 73
Sals, Eliza[Allen] 88
Samples, Charles 73
  John L. 73
Sampson, John H. 31, 111
  Mary(Watkins) 111
  Richard 111
  Thomas W. 111
Sams, Lurana[Held] 14
  Mary[Stephens] 68
Samuel, Edward M. 83
  George W. 83
  Reuben 83, 145
  Robert L. 145
Samuels, Martha[Medford]
  144
Sanders, Culvin 149
  Edie[Robbins] 83
  H.P. 163
  James 118
  Joel 58
  John B. 149
  John J. 58
  Mary[Million] 110
  Mary M(Fore) 149
  Nancy[Jones] 122
Sandidge, Aaron 73
  Micajah 81
  Polly(Thompson) 73
  Robert S. 73
  Tifny 99
Sands, Martha[Bratcher] 71
Sandusky, John 161
  Martha(Huntley) 161
  Samuel D. 161
Sanford, Elizabeth(Rans-
    dell) 123
  Frances[Usher] 133
  John 123
  John R. 123
  Thomas S. 123
Sanfords, Mary[Kirtley] 20
Satterwhite, Jane 135
  Lizzie 135
  Mortimer 135
Saunders, Fannie[Baker]
  105

J.H. 112
John 112
Nancy 112
Richard 112
Savage, John D. 38
  Mary(McCrosky) 38
  Mary E[Locke] 117
  Nicholas 38
Scates, Nancy[Chick] 40
Scearce, Jane(Ashurst) 167
  Laban 167
  William 167
Scholl, Joseph 47
  Lavinia(Boone) 47
  Nelson 47
  Sallie 47
  Septimus 47
Schooler, Benjamin 58
  Henry 58
  Martha(Foster) 58
  Narcissa[Hukel] 45
Schooling, Susan A[Walker]
  124
Schrest, J.R. 58
  John 58
  Lydia(Vaughn) 58
Scimmones, Andrew J. 70
  Mary A(Mackvoy) 70
  Thomas 70
Scott, Abraham C. 94
  Adeline(Johnson) 145
  Annie[Campbell] 82
  Dorothy(Hawkins) 145
  Elijah T. 132
  Emiline[Shelton] 154
  Enokiel 145
  George S. 114
  George W. 114
  Granville 76
  Hannah(Denney) 94
  James F. 94
  James T. 83
  Joel 145
  John 58, 120
  John C. 145
  John W. 120
  Leah[Gullion] 38
  Margaret[Hersman] 56
  Minerva(Ewing) 120
  R.M. 114
  Rachel(Miller) 114
  Robert 58
  Robert J. 145
  S.M. 114
  Sallie(McDaniel) 58
  Sarah(Thurman) 114
  Sarah H(Tate) 132
  William 132
Scriggs, Matilda[Gray] 41
Scrivner, D.M. 53
  Hulda(Tudor) 53
  John 53
  Martin D. 53
  Pamelia(Clements) 53
  V.H. 53
Scrogin, America(Curry) 65
  Frank E. 65
  Thomas D. 65
Scruggs, J.V. 145
Scudder, Charles 118
  John A. 118
  Mary H. 118
Seamans, Isaac 62
  William E. 62
Searcy, Polly[Perry] 13

Sears, Frances[Bush] 54
  Mildred[Crim] 44
  James 158
Seaton, Mary[Tyler] 88
Sebastian, Alexander H. 34
  Clinton B. 34
  Nancy[Stamper] 136
  Tabitha A(Jacobs) 34
Secrest, Luannah[Brown] 60
Sechrist, Theodophilus 70
Sedore, Mary[Preston] 31
Selby, Joshua 133
  Margaret(Riggens) 133
  William M. 133
Sergeant, G.B. 155
Servner, Nancy[Warford] 53
Settles, Jane[Hancock] 136
Sevier, John W. 123
  Mary(Richardson) 123
  Thomas R. 123
  William 123
Sexton, Joseph E. 118
  Lafayette 58
Shackett, B.W. 77
  Barbara[Willett] 120
  Benjamin 77
  Elizabeth(Ashcraft) 77
Shackleford, Adaline[Studi-
    vant] 52
  Elizabeth[Norfleet] 163
Shanklin, Elizabeth[Park] 61
  Sallie P[Pogue] 118
Shanks, Elizabeth[Brannock]78
  Lucy(Harris) 58
  Reuben N. 58
  John 99
  Richard L. 99
  Sarah(Gaines) 99
  William B. 58
Shannon, E. 145
  E.D. 83
  Eliza A[Sharp] 133
  Elizabeth(Ellison) 65
  Jane(McClanahan) 88
  Jeremiah 88
  John 88
  Lewis S. 65
  Nancy 145
  Patsey[Hinton] 144
  Polly[McCune] 26
  William H. 65
Sharp, Absalom M. 42
  C.L. 149
  Eliza A(Shannon) 133
  Fedilio C. 42
  G.B. 58
  James 58
  Jane(Calahan) 58
  Joseph W. 133
  William 133
Shaw, (Burdett) 42
  Fieldin L. 132
  Milton A. 42
  Thomas 42
  Turner R.H. 42
Shawhan, Charles R. 28
  David 28
  John T. 28
  Minerva 28
Sheeks, Rosa 163
  William H. 163
Sheely, Eliza[Stapleton] 59
Shelby, Elizabeth[Kirtley] 20
  Nancy(Edmondson) 114
  Thomas 114; William 114

Shelman, Adam 34
  Martin 34
  Mary(Hays) 34
Shelton, Ann[Woods] 119
  A.H. 154
  Charles G. 154
  Elizabeth(Mason) 49
  Elizabeth(Rhodes) 70
  Emiline(Scott) 154
  Ezekiah H. 49
  Louisa H[Moseley] 41
  W.R. 70
  William A. 49
  William H. 70
Shelly, George M. 36
  James M. 36
  Louisa(Stubblefield) 36
Shepard, David B. 62
  Lydia 62
  Robert 62
Shepherd, Elizabeth 47
  Mary[Wilson] 77
  Phoebe 58
  Thomas 47
  William 47, 58
Sheridan, Margaret 118
Sherl, Jane[Ketcham] 81
Sherman, Annie[Callaway]
    78
  Charles R. 88
  Julia A(Porter) 88
  William 88
Sherrow, L.D. 68
  Reuben 68
Shields, E.O. 163
  Egbert O. 158
  Ellen(Brent) 158, 163
  George H. 132
  George W. 132
  Henry C. 158, 163
  Martha(Howell) 132
  Mary[Leveridge] 109
Shindler, George 149
  Lafayette 149
  Susan 149
Shipley, R.W. 58
Shipp, U.T. 167
Shircligg, Mary L[Pike]
    131
Shirley, L.P. 123
Shirrod, John 154
  Julianna 154
Shobe, Absalom 158
  Jane(Dunn) 158
  John 158
Shock, David H. 58
Shocklee, James M. 114
  James R. 114
  Nancy A(Lee) 114
Shofner, Chloe[Daniel] 72
Shomaker, Catherine(Met-
    calf) 137
  L.C. 137
  Landers 137
Shoot, Frederick 102
  James H. 102
  Rebecca(Taylor) 102
Short, J.M. 52
  Mary I(Rivers) 153
Shotwell, Jabez 119
  John 119
  John W. 119
  Nathaniel 119
  Sarah(Burris) 119
Shouse, Abraham 128

B.F. 167
B.P. 167
Benjamin F. 167
Frances(Prichett) 128
Hamilton 128
John 65
John W. 65
Lewis 167
Margaret(Farra) 167
Sarah(Slaughter) 65
William O. 167
Shrader, Caroline[Force] 82
  James P. 135
  Julia[Smith] 83
  Mary(Blevins) 135
  Philip 135
Shrewsbury, Anna 68
  Drew 68
  Elijah W. 68
Shropshire, Agnes(Pemberton)
    79
  George W. 79
  M.P. 79
  Nancy[Parrish] 27
Shryock, Daniel 58
  Samuel 58
Shuck, Sarah J. 161
Shumate, George W. 163
  James 163
  Jane 163
Shuttleworth, Allen 115
  Anna(Washburn) 115
  James A. 115
Sidener, [Smith] 28
Sigler, Meashek 112
Siler, Salata J. 164
Silvey, J.W. 135
Simmons, Alfred 34
  Amanda(Williams) 155
  David M. 103
  John W. 103
  Joseph A. 155
  Samuel 155
  Sarah(Gallaway) 103
  Sarah[Ragar] 102
  Susanna 53
  Susanna[Davenport] 44
Simpson, A.E. 35
  Benjamin 68
  Catherine[Hagan] 71
  Catherine[Kerr] 162
  E.A. 68
  George 151
  Isaac 35
  J.W. 68
  Louisa[Grady] 10
  Martha[Mays] 90
  Mary[Hull] 156
  Monroe I. 158
  Nancy[Morgan] 158
  Nancy M(Cutcheon) 151
  Pauline(Arnold) 68
  Rachel B.C(Tygart) 35
  Samuel 151
Simrall, Cynthia(Fritzlen)
    149
  Horatio F. 149
  James 149
Sims, Abram 112
  Alfred 112
  Elizabeth(Morris) 83
  Gracie(Robards) 112
  Thomas A. 83
  Thomas G. 83
  William 94

Shroyer, Catherine[Hall] 144
Sinclair, Charity[Herndon]
    144
Singleton, Anna M[Johnson]51
  Elizabeth[Allega] 66
  Louis 91
  Milton R. 91
  Rebecca(Robards) 91
Sipple, John 79
  William H. 79
Sites, John 28
  William 28
Skidmore, Dahl 99
  Elizabeth(Carman) 99
  Jesse D. 99
  James C. 99
  Joseph 99
  Nancy(Adams) 99
Skinner, Rebecca[Hawkins]
    108
  Susan[Garnett] 20
Slack, William V. 119
Slaton, Mary[Randolph] 81
Slaughter, Lucinda S[Major]
    64
  Nancy A[Strother] 132
  Sarah[Shouse] 65
Sleeper, Elizabeth[Friend]
    86
Sloan, Artie(Cooper) 163
  James R. 58
  Marie R. 58
  Mathew D. 163
  William 163
Small, Cynthia A[Clarkson]
    51
  Thomas M. 119
Smarr, John H. 33
  R.C. 33
Smart, Amanda C. 128
  Mary[Ratekin] 128
  Robert G. 128
  Thomas A. 128
Smith, A.B. 37
  Alice[Yager] 88
  Ballard S. 83
  Benjamin M. 83
  Catherine[Noe] 57
  Charlotte(Havins) 163
  Clark 36
  Cynthia A[Dishman] 151
  D.A. 52
  David 77, 158, 163
  E.B. 37
  Edith 49
  Elizabeth 31
  Elizabeth[Garland] 72
  Elizabeth(Pope) 31
  Emily(Bunnell) 123
  Enoch 128
  Ephraim 31
  Flavius J. 68
  George S. 91
  George W. 123, 136
  H.H. 123
  Harriet[Tolbart] 130
  Henry 68
  Henry C. 84, 167
  Hercules 77
  J.D. 123
  J.L. 38
  James 158
  James W. 38
  Jane[Perrin] 99
  Jeremiah B.P. 31

Smith (cont.)
John A. 68
John R. 163
John S. 91
Julia[Shrader] 83
Julian D. 95
June[Cox] 63
Lawson 133
(Lockett) 91
Lucinda[Belise] 36
Lucy(Gordon) 36
Lucy[Moseley] 91
Martha[Haden] 24
Martin 79
Mary[Carter] 72
Mary[Clarkson] 22
Mary A(Gray) 77
Mary E(Davis) 38
Matilda[Fogle] 75
Milton 79
Milton C. 119
Nicholas J. 84
Permelia(Long) 68
R.H. 149
Rebecca[Cleaver] 71
Rebecca(Linseg) 37
Rebecca[Mayhew] 61
Reuben 151
Robert 36
Robert J. 36
Sarah(Julian) 95
Sarah(Riley) 133
Sarah(Spears) 79
Sarah[Titterington] 42
Sarah[Wills] 42
Sarah E[Spencer] 119
Solomon S. 94
Spencer R. 36
Susan B[Terrill] 69
T.L. 123
Thomas A. 123
Thomas F. 91
Thomas S. 91
William 95, 123
William C. 150
William L. 133
Smithson, H.D. 28
Smock, Catherine[Costin] 86
Smoot, Sarah A[Price] 27
Sneed, Achilles P. 65
Elizabeth(Gibson) 65
John M. 32
Landon C. 65
Robert C. 32
Snell, Annie[Pence] 145
Fannie[Keene] 144
John 145
Loudon 145
Mary[Adkins] 142
Nancy(Hamilton) 145
Snider, Elizabeth(Gray) 149
Henry G. 149
Richard 149
Snodderly, John H. 58
Snoddy, Anna[Wallace] 113
Elizabeth[Campbell] 106
Snodgrass, Mary[Hammett] 157
Snow, A.F. 50
Frank G. 50
Martha J(Ryan) 50
Snyder, Christopher C. 88

Diana 164
E.W. 88
James M. 164
John 164
Malinda[Haley] 55
Mattie(Guill) 88
Sarah[Creekmore] 164
Sodowsky, Fannie S(Gatewood) 91
James 91
T.J. 91
Sommer, Anna M(Bahlman) 93
J.J. 93
Soper, Eleanor H[Chrisman] 55
Souders, Avan(Amos) 52
Isaac 52
John 52
South, Margaret[Drake] 147
Sower, Alfred 119
Sparks, James P. 84
Mary[Hannah] 24
Robert T. 84
Sallie(Threlkeld)84
William 93
Spears, Adam 79
George C. 58
H.C. 58
John M. 79
Leah(Baxter) 79
Nancy[Apperson] 125
O.P. 79
Sarah[Smith] 79
(Weatherford) 79
William F. 80
Speed, Dorinda 40
James 40
John J. 51
Marris S[Warren] 32
Mathias W. 40
Spellman, Rachel[Carlton] 75
Spence, Andrew 145
Rebecca(Lemon) 145
Samuel B. 145
Spencer, Ephraim 119
James 140
Jesse 48
John W. 119
Jonathan 140
L.J. 140
Louisa J(Cooper) 140
Mary[Lillard] 122
May(Gadberry) 140
Sarah E(Smith) 119
Sperry, James L. 96
Sphar, J.M. 47
Mary E. 47
Willis F. 47
Spickert, John M. 88
Mary A. 88
Willis F. 47
Spillman, Charles W. 84
Thomas N. 84
Spilman, Louisa A[Metcalfe] 155
Spratt, Amos D. 128
Robert 128
Sena(Wilkerson) 128
Springate, (Gritten) 123
William 123
William P. 123
Sproul, Joseph E. 100
Spurgeon, John 28
Spurlock, Elijah 48
Elizabeth[Oxford] 48

Sally(Hurd) 48
William 48
Stacy, Elizabeth(Hull) 140
Fountain 140
James 140
P.M. 140
Simon 140
Stafford, J.B. 96
Stagg, W.C. 123
Stagner, David 112
Charlotte(Elledge) 112
J.N. 112
James C. 112
John T. 112
L.R. 112
Nancy(Poppine) 112
Thomas 112
Stallard, Rebecca[Langsford] 131
Stallsworth, Mary[Crawley] 14
Stamper, Daniel J. 136
Hiram 136
Jesse 136
Nancy(Sebantin) 136
Sallie(Cobb) 136
Stanbury, George W. 100
Malinda(Stansberry) 95
Melinda(Stansberry) 95
Samuel 95
William 95, 100
Standley, Henrietta[Thornton] 112
Stansberry, Malinda[Stanbury] 95
Melinda[Stanbury] 95
Stanton, Nancy[Belk] 141
Staples, Martha J[Griggs] 120
Mary(Hughes) 149
Samuel 149
William 149
Stapleton, Eliza(Sheely) 59
Thomas H. 59
William H. 59
Stark, Adam 152
Eleanor(Stillwell) 152
John 152
Mary(McLoed) 26
Starkey, John R. 119
Starns, Elizabeth[Stringer] 140
Hannah[Stringer] 140
Steele, Brice 59
Dudley M. 91
Elizabeth(Mitchum) 91
Elizabeth(Thornsbury) 59
Elizabeth M(Wilson) 71
J.W. 59
Leonidas L. 21
O.C. 59
Richard B. 71
Samuel C. 91
William T. 112
Steen, Enoch 123
Hanretta[Cox] 85
William 123
Steerman, Nancy[Orr] 133
Steers, Rollins 80
Sarah E. 80
W.H. 80
Stemmons, Rhoda[Crow] 51
Stenimons, Felix B. 103
Harriet 103
J.M. 103

Wood (cont.)
 Helen(Julian) 65
 J.J. 140
 J.T. 119
 James 124
 James L. 94
 John 94
 John M. 65
 John S. 140
 John T. 119
 Joseph M. 124
 Lucretia 129
 Margaret(Mane) 94
 Mary(Boyce) 124
 Rachel(Webb) 119
 Richard J. 65
 Sallie(Thomas) 124
 Sarah[Jones] 136
 William 33, 65, 124, 129
 William T. 124
 Winnie(Lawny) 159
Wolff, Abraham B. 88
 Alfred 36
 John J. 36
 Marcus A. 88
 Susan(Franklin) 88
Wolfskill, George 163
 Joseph 163
 Mary(Ross) 163
Wolrath, Ann L. 129
Woolfolk, Nancy[Burton] 147
Woodford, W.W. 36
Woodress, James A. 95
Woodrow, John T. 74
 Mary(Cain) 74
Woods, Ann(Shelton) 119
 Elijah 100
 Elizabeth[Reid] 68
 Henrietta(Dunn) 100
 John 100
 Mary[Frost] 89
 Patrick 113
 Sarah[Boothe] 54
 Susanna[Mullins] 110
 William 119
Woodsmall, Charlotte[Mount]
  135
 W.G. 132
Woodson, A.M. 49
 Betsey(Haines) 52
 C.R. 97
 David H. 159
 Drury L. 52
 Hylda A(Young) 81
 I.B. 92
 Martha(Haynes) 159
 Robert S. 81
 Shadrack 52, 159
 Silas 94
 Thomas D. 81
 Wade N. 94
Woodward, Edward 36
 Jacob 36
Wooldridge, Drewery M. 42
 Edward 42
 H.H. 77
 Jesse 77
 Madison B. 42
 Margaret(Brasher) 42
 Susan(Hays) 77
Woolery, Nancy[Todd] 112
Wooley, Mary 69
 Mary(Sulton) 69
 William 69
Woolsey, Zerilda[Boucher]11

Word, Margaret(Burch) 94
 Nelson 94
 William 94
Wornall, John B. 47
 Richard 47, 150
Wortham, Charles G. 77
 Isaac J. 77
 John 77
 Mary(Grundy) 77
Wright, Allen 163
 Angeline E(Moore) 161
 Ann(Poague) 92
 C. 163
 C.W. 161
 Charles W. 161
 Cornelius P. 50
 Editha[Orr] 155
 Elizabeth[Haines] 108
 Elizabeth(Hickerson) 161
 Elizabeth[Maston] 144
 Elizabeth[Middleton] 34
 Elizabeth(Parker) 161
 George W. 161
 J.B. 159
 James G. 92
 James P. 161
 John 65
 John H. 65
 John W. 161
 L.B. 136
 Martin 163
 Mary G(Wallace) 159
 Matilda(Moore) 161
 Morgan 161
 Nathaniel 161
 Nathaniel P. 161
 Rebecca(Vestal) 163
 Richard W. 161
 Theresa(Anderson) 92
 William M. 159
Wyatt, Anthony 47
 Crittenden 152
 Frank 47
 James D. 62
 Mary[Bland] 130
 Mary(Denman) 62
 Micajah 62
Wythe, Samuel 129
Wymore, Eliza(Downing) 59
 George W. 53
 Samuel 59
 Sarah[Featherston] 56, 89

Yager, Alice(Smith) 88
 F.J. 88
 Fountain C. 88
 Julia[Houston] 144
Yales, Haston 115
 John 115
 Laura T(Butler) 115
Yancy, Sophia[Fant] 135
Yantis, Aaron 150
 J.C. 150
 John L. 69
 Martha 150
Yarnall, Samuel 80
Yater, Mason 69
Yates, Benjamin 150
 Hiram 146
 James T. 150
 Jeptha 150
 Mary[Montgomery] 160
Yeager, Amand[Basket] 146
 Elijah 135

 Elizabeth(Graham) 135
 Elizabeth(Redd) 135
 John R. 135
 Nancy[Doke] 30
 R.L. 135
Yeaman, Lucretia(Helm) 77
 Stephen M. 77
 William P. 77
Yelton, America[Gosney] 37
Yocum, Harvey 129
 Jonathan 129
 Rachel(Williams) 129
Yontsey, Adam 37
 Archibald S. 37
Yost, Elizabeth(Ritter) 92
 G.J. 92
 George 92
 Thomas F. 92
 William E. 92
Youd, Archibald 137
 Mary(Newton) 137
 Samuel 137
Young, Andrew 49
 Ann F(Booker) 150
 Anna[Samples] 73
 Archibald L. 92
 Charles A. 159
 D.G. 152
 Edith(Smith) 49
 George W. 150
 Hylda A[Woodson] 81
 James 150
 James E. 47
 Jessamine 92
 John 159
 John A. 35
 John T. 59
 Julia 104
 Mary[Field] 86
 Mollie 104
 Paulina[Porter] 85
 Sarah E(Hudnell) 159
 Thomas 104
 William 150
 William S. 49
Younger, James 103
 William C. 103

Zachary, B.J. 140
 H.L. 140
 Nancy I[Higgerson] 109
 Nancy(Paschal) 140
Zook, Mary[Miller] 64